Translation and Multilingual Natural Language Processing

Editors: Oliver Czulo (Universität Leipzig), Silvia Hansen-Schirra (Johannes Gutenberg-Universität Mainz), Reinhard Rapp (Johannes Gutenberg-Universität Mainz, Hochschule Magdeburg-Stendal)

In this series:

1. Fantinuoli, Claudio & Federico Zanettin (eds.). New directions in corpus-based translation studies.

2. Hansen-Schirra, Silvia & Sambor Grucza (eds.). Eyetracking and Applied Linguistics.

3. Neumann, Stella, Oliver Čulo & Silvia Hansen-Schirra (eds.). Annotation, exploitation and evaluation of parallel corpora: TC3 I.

4. Czulo, Oliver & Silvia Hansen-Schirra (eds.). Crossroads between Contrastive Linguistics, Translation Studies and Machine Translation: TC3 II.

5. Rehm, Georg, Felix Sasaki, Daniel Stein & Andreas Witt (eds.). Language technologies for a multilingual Europe: TC3 III.

6. Menzel, Katrin, Ekaterina Lapshinova-Koltunski & Kerstin Anna Kunz (eds.). New perspectives on cohesion and coherence: Implications for translation.

7. Hansen-Schirra, Silvia, Oliver Czulo & Sascha Hofmann (eds). Empirical modelling of translation and interpreting.

8. Svoboda, Tomáš, Łucja Biel & Krzysztof Łoboda (eds.). Quality aspects in institutional translation.

9. Fox, Wendy. Can integrated titles improve the viewing experience? Investigating the impact of subtitling on the reception and enjoyment of film using eye tracking and questionnaire data.

10. Moran, Steven & Michael Cysouw. The Unicode cookbook for linguists: Managing writing systems using orthography profiles.

11. Fantinuoli, Claudio (ed.). Interpreting and technology.

12. Nitzke, Jean. Problem solving activities in post-editing and translation from scratch: A multi-method study.

ISSN: 2364-8899

Problem solving activities in post-editing and translation from scratch

A multi-method study

Jean Nitzke

language
science
press

Nitzke, Jean. 2019. *Problem solving activities in post-editing and translation from scratch: A multi-method study* (Translation and Multilingual Natural Language Processing 12). Berlin: Language Science Press.

This title can be downloaded at:
http://langsci-press.org/catalog/book/196
© 2019, Jean Nitzke
Published under the Creative Commons Attribution 4.0 Licence (CC BY 4.0):
http://creativecommons.org/licenses/by/4.0/
ISBN: 978-3-96110-131-3 (Digital)
       978-3-96110-132-0 (Hardcover)

ISSN: 2364-8899
DOI:10.5281/zenodo.2546446
Source code available from www.github.com/langsci/196
Collaborative reading: paperhive.org/documents/remote?type=langsci&id=196

Cover and concept of design: Ulrike Harbort
Typesetting: Sebastian Nordhoff, Felix Kopecky, Jean Nitzke
Proofreading: Andreas Hölzl, Aniefon Daniel, Carla Parra, Caroline Rossi,
Jeroen van de Weijer, Joseph T. Farquharson, Rosetta Berger, Umesh Patil,
Yvonne Treis
Fonts: Linux Libertine, Libertinus Math, Arimo, DejaVu Sans Mono
Typesetting software: XꟻLATEX

Language Science Press
Unter den Linden 6
10099 Berlin, Germany
langsci-press.org

Storage and cataloguing done by FU Berlin

Freie Universität Berlin

Contents

Contents

Contents

Acknowledgments

Hold your breath and count to ten,
And fall apart and start again,
Hold your breath and count to ten,
Start again, start again...
Placebo – English Summer Rain

Sag nicht alles so kompliziert
Weil ich versteh das garantiert nicht
Denk nicht alles so kompliziert
Weil ich versteh, dass das nix wird
Wanda – Wenn ich Zwanzig Bin

Two songs and eight lines that came to my mind again and again while preparing this book, although (often) quoted out of context. I regularly remembered the Placebo song during statistical analyses – a completely new field for me at the beginning of this whole project. Although I always enjoyed learning this new, advanced method of data analysis (like presumably most translation students in Germany, I had no clue about statistics, never took a course on data analysis during my B.A. or M.A. programmes and had to rely on what I had learnt in school, which almost ended with calculating means and medians), it was often incredibly frustrating and time-consuming. Back in the early days I learnt what correlations are and how to perform them in R – my best friend and my worst enemy – but I did not realise that you have to check for normal distribution first to decide on suitable correlations. So I started to correlate data, and correlated more data, and correlated even more data, until somebody finally told me: You need to check for normal distribution first. Hold your breath and count to ten; Fall apart, start again.

The second song by the Austrian band Wanda often accompanied me when I was reading literature that was written in an incredibly complicated way and where the main points were masked (or even hidden) by unusual words and very long sentences (this was usually literature written in German). As a result, I often tempered myself during my own writing process and tried to keep it simple and understandable.

Much more essential than music, however, were the people around me, who supported me in so many different ways. First of all, I would like to thank my flatmates and friends who stood by my side although my mood sometimes became unbearable and who still want to be my friends although I have not had much time for them recently: Maike Dankwardt, Sylvana Teifel, Christiana Rohner, Helene Schächtele, Marcella Apple, Lisa Schewe, Sebastian Kriegler, and Simon Bode. Many thanks to my friends who also happen to be professional translators and interpreters (now) – you were always willing to give opinions on matters that concerned me from a practical and not a scientific perspective: Lisa Rüth, Julia Dolderer, Rosa Schröder, Lara Eusemann, and Tina Puetsch. For me, it is very important to keep the reality of the profession in mind when conducting research on translation and translators' behaviour. Many, many thanks to my parents, Heiko and Jutta Nitzke, who always believed in me, always supported me, and always seem to be proud of what I am doing. I could not have done it without you.

By now, I consider most of my colleagues friends, sometimes even close friends. Discussing issues and questions with you helped me a lot in developing my thoughts and approaches. Without your help, some parts of this project would never have been possible for me – both in terms of theoretical approaches and statistical analyses, but also moral support and helping me with my teaching duties: Silke Gutermuth, Katharina Oster, Moritz Schaeffer, Wendy Fox, Sarah Signer (sorry you had to proof-read all of this!), Marcus Wiedmann, Sascha Hofmann, Katja Abels, Don Kiraly, and Tomasz Rozmyslowicz.

Finally, of course, my utmost thanks goes to my supervisors Silvia Hansen-Schirra and Oliver Czulo. Thank you for all your patience, your time, and your willingness to supervise me in the first place. Your guidance through all parts of academia truly helped me to find my way in navigating the entire landscape – from teaching to attending conferences. Thank you for all your essential remarks, hints, and comments that shaped my thinking and, in the end, this book. Last but not least, many thanks to Michael Schreiber who is the third person who jumped into this project and took the time to assess my work.

There are so many more people who helped and/or supported me over the years – I cannot name every single one of you, but thanks, thanks, thanks!

Abbreviations

CAT	computer assisted translation
Dur	production time of translation unit
FAHQMT	full-automatic high-quality machine translation
FixS	fixation count on the source text unit
FixT	fixation count on the target text unit
GazeS	total fixation duration on the source text unit
GazeT	total fixation duration on the target text unit
HCross	word order entropy value
HTra	word entropy value
InEff	inefficiency value
MPE	monolingual post-editing
Munit	number of micro units necessary for target unit production
MT	machine translation
MTS	machine translation system
PA	problem area
PE	post editing
TFix	fixation count on both source and target text
TfS	translation from scratch
TGaze	total fixation duration on both source and target text
TM	translation memory
TMS	translation memory system

1 Introduction

The working environment of translators has changed tremendously in recent decades. Typesetters have been replaced by computers, printed sources of information have been replaced by electronic and online sources of information. Instead of translating every single word from scratch, translation memory systems store translations and recall them when certain similarities exist between new source text segments and a source text segment that has been translated before. Instead of word lists and printed glossaries, translators use terminology management systems to assure consistency. Machine translation (MT) systems have been developed for over 70 years now – nonetheless, they only recently started to affect the working environment of most translators. To improve efficiency and cost-effectiveness, organisations increasingly use MT and edit the MT output to create a fluent text that adheres to the relevant text conventions. This procedure is known as post-editing (PE). Although PE has also been around since the 1980s, it remained a rather niche market for decades. This, however, has changed with PE being established on the translation market in recent years – causing mixed feelings among professional translators. The working conditions are changing and some translators are comfortable with this change, while some are not. But what changes for the professional translator who disregards external circumstances? What influence does the integration of MT have on the cognitive load of professional translators?

The aim of this study is to investigate different problem solving behaviours in translation from scratch[1] (TfS) and post-editing (PE). I assume that some problems might already be solved by MT output, while, on the other hand, the MT system might also create new translation problems. Hence, participants will exhibit at least some different problem solving behaviour in the two tasks. This will be analysed according to research behaviour as well as the syntactic quality of MT output. These analyses will not only include screen-recording data and final translation products, but also keylogging and eyetracking data. Finally,

---

[1] The term "translation from scratch" was used – instead of „human translation" for example – because it implies that no further CAT tools were used for the translation, like translation memory or terminology management systems.

this study will focus on problem identifiers in translation process data. While early translation process research (e.g. Krings 1986b) attempted to identify and classify problems via think-aloud protocols, I will focus on unconscious process data, namely keylogging and eyetracking data, to initially determine which parameters might be interesting for predicting translation problems and to then model an approach to find translation problems in translation process data with the help of mere keylogging data.

Another key aspect of this study will be the theoretical concept of *translation problems*. While (theoretical) translation studies have already addressed this issue, the resulting assumptions do not necessarily coincide with assumptions, concepts, and models developed in psychology. Therefore, this study will also introduce the insights on *problem solving* generated in both fields, what they have in common and how the differences can be resolved.

This study is structured as follows: §2 provides a brief overview of MT, while §3 introduces PE. The next chapter (§4) explores how MT and PE are perceived in different areas of translation. The concept of *problem solving* is explored from different angles in §5. Next, the research question is implemented (§6), the data set and the experiment are specified (§7), and the questionnaires used in the experiment are assessed (§8). The next three chapters examine the translation process data. First, an analysis is conducted on the research behaviour of the participants (§9), then eyetracking and keylogging data are compared in regard to the different syntactic quality of the MT output (§10), and finally keylogging parameters are analysed to define the extent to which they help in predicting problematic translation units (§11). §12 introduces an approach to identify translation problems according to keylogging data. A summary of the findings is presented in §13 and the final chapter (§14) deals with aspects that could be examined in the future.

2 Machine translation

This chapter will introduce the main concepts of machine translation. The term *machine translation* (MT) can simply be defined as "[a]utomatic translation from one human language to another using computers" (Al-Onaizan et al. 1999: 1). The idea behind MT goes back to cryptography as discussed by Weaver (1955). The basic idea is that information is encrypted in one language and therefore cannot be understood if the encryption is unknown. However, if the code used to encrypt language A is known and it can be transferred into language B, the information will be available in language B, too.

> All languages – at least all the ones under consideration here – were invented and developed by men; and all men [...] have essentially the same equipment to bring to bear on this problem. They have vocal organs capable of producing about the same set of sound [...]. Their brains are of the same general order of potential complexity. (ibid.: 16)

Even then, Weaver was aware that it would not be that simple to automatically translate human language. In a letter to Norbert Wiener, he suggested that one could take scientific texts into consideration for MT as they are semantically not as complex and that the result may then not be perfect but intelligible (cf. ibid.:18).

In addition, MT has always been one of the main focuses and challenges of research in artificial intelligence (cf. Mylonakis 2012). However, many problems and challenges of MT have not yet been solved, or as Warwick (2012) puts it:

> Machine translation is a field that includes the research areas of translation science, computational linguistics and artificial intelligence. Although there are some real-world applications of machine translation, the development is not as great as in 'the finance, manufacturing and military sectors' where applications 'are performing in ways with which the human brain simply cannot compete'.

This chapter will introduce the development of MT, the different approaches to MT, as well as the application and the state of the art of MT. It is not meant to be an exhaustive description of the whole field, but instead to provide a short overview.

2.1 Machine translation development

Research on MT started more or less simultaneously with the invention of the electronic computer in the 1940s. However, the idea for MT goes back even further: Some origins can be traced back to 17th century philosophical thought on universal and logical languages as well as mechanical dictionaries. Early technological development did not facilitate working mechanical systems. In 1933, two patents were granted for MT-resembling ideas in France and Russia, which are considered the first real precursors of MT systems (Hutchins 2004 – who also provides a detailed description of the two forerunner systems). These ideas, however, did not receive much attention and only Warren Weaver's memorandum "brought the idea of MT to general notice" (Hutchins & Somers 1992) and research on MT was launched during the next years.

Initially, the idea was received with great enthusiasm: In 1954, the Georgetown Experiment was presented – the first public presentation of an MT system, developed by Georgetown University in cooperation with IBM. It raised many expectations of MT development, although the presented text was well-selected and vocabulary entries and grammar rules were very restricted. This led to more funding in the US and to new MT projects all over the world, especially in Russia. Although research at this time had a significant influence not only on MT research but also on computational linguistics, artificial intelligence, and theoretical linguistics, a proficient system was not developed and the high expectations were not met (cf. ibid.: 6). Therefore, the US government assigned the Automatic Language Processing Advisory Committee (ALPAC), which was formed in 1964, to determine how well MT was actually working in 1966. The resulting report was devastating and stopped funding for MT almost entirely for the next decades in the United States. According to the ALPAC report, MT was not worth funding, because post-editing of MT was as expensive as human translation. The committee recommended funding other research areas such as computational linguistics and investing in the development of methods to improve human translation.

Despite this regress, MT was not fully abandoned and the first commercial systems were launched on the market after 1966 – mostly outside the US. Two examples are *Météo* (1976) – a system developed at the university of Montreal to translate weather forecasts – and *Systran* – a company founded in 1968, which is still one of the most famous MT companies on the market; Systran's system was installed by the US Air Force in 1970 for Russian-English and by the European Union in 1976 (cf. Hutchins 1995: 139-142).

In the meantime, the development of MT had reached Europe as well. Some bigger projects were the *Ariane* system developed by the GETA-group (CETA in earlier days) in Grenoble, France, and the *SUSY* system of the Saarland University in Saarbrücken, Germany. Both research facilities prevailed in the huge *EUROTRA* project of the European Union. The European Union naturally has a huge demand for translations. Therefore, they became very interested in MT at a very early stage. The EUROTRA project spanned 150 scientists from 18 institutes and ten member states at the end of 1989. It was intended to cover all 72 language pairs that were required in that the respective state of the Union (today even more language pairs need to be covered). Although the project never produced a working system, the research had a major influence on computational and linguistic research (cf. Hutchins & Somers 1992: 239-241).[1]

It was only in the 1990s that the first tools were developed for computer assisted translation (CAT tools) which are intended to support the human translation process (cf. Garcia 2009: 199). The most beneficial tools are translation memory systems (TMSs) which essentially save completed translations and provide translation suggestions of former translations to the translator when a similar (*fuzzy matches*) or identical (*100% matches*) segment occurs. The source text is usually segmented on a sentence basis and matches are presented accordingly, but the translator can also search the translation memory to find single words or phrases (*concordance search*). TMSs simply store translations and recall what they have stored when matches occur, but they do not produce translations automatically. Most TMS also incorporate a *terminology management* system. TMS have become indispensable in translation practice, especially for translators who have to deal with domain-specific texts like texts related to technology, law, medicine, etc.

With the spread of the Internet, it was only a matter of time until MT went online. Systran provided the first online MT for users of *Minitel* in France in 1988. The users could send Minitel the texts requiring translation. The service was provided for English and French (both directions) as well as from German into English and the systems were capable of translating 22 pages per minute. In 1992, *CompuServe* introduced MT for their users. In addition to the MT service itself, CompuServe offered PE services for an extra fee. Most customers requested MT rather than PE services, though: In 1997, 85% of all requests were for MT only. However, the PE tasks were generally conducted for longer texts – therefore, the percentage was 60% MT and 40% PE on a word-basis (cf. Gaspari & Hutchins 2007: 199-200).

---

[1]More details on MT systems in the EU, especially in the European Commission, are provided in §4.3.2

Bable Fish was developed by Systran and AltaVista and went online on 9 December 1997. It was the first live MT service that was available for all Internet users and was free of charge. This launched a new era of free online MT services. In 2007, over 30 similar services were online (cf. ibid.: 200). One of the most famous online MT systems nowadays is *Google Translate*, which covers 103 languages and also recently integrated neural MT.[2] Google Translate can be used on a desktop, mobile device, offline, and even in connection with other apps. The user can contribute to the MT development by rating or providing translations.[3] Further tools like the *Translator Toolkit*[4] – an environment resembling a translation memory, where the source text is segmented and automatically translated and that can be used to improve the MT suggestions within this tool or to assign the job to a language service – are also provided by Google. Although MT systems – especially popular online MT systems like *Google Translate* – are often not taken seriously by some Internet users, because the mistakes amuse native speakers of the target languages[5], *Gisting* (raw MT for information retrieval, see §2.3 for more details) has become a common phenomenon on many websites. Furthermore, many websites work in cooperation with online MT services and offer an automatic translation of their contents by a simple mouse-click (see examples in §2.3).

In the meantime, the projects *EuroMatrix* and its successor *EuroMatrixPlus* had also been generating ground-breaking results in the field of statistical and hybrid MT[6] in Europe. They impacted the development of the open source MT system *Moses*, which enables users to train a statistical system with their own corpus data or other freely available corpus data. *Moses* is one of the most frequently used MT systems in academia and the translation industry. The projects aimed at generating an exemplary MT system for every EU language, providing the necessary corpora to build an MT system (the "Euromatrix" with monolingual resources, parallel corpora and MT systems, can be accessed freely via the Internet[7]), and bringing MT systems closer to the end user (cf. Busemann et al.

---

[2]More information is provided in §2.2.

[3]cf. http://translate.google.de/about/intl/en_ALL/index.html, last accessed 15 March 2017.

[4]cf. https://translate.google.com/toolkit/list?hl=de#translations/active, last accessed 15 March 2017.

[5]e. g. http://ackuna.com/badtranslator (last accessed 4 April 2016) – a website that translates back and forth from English into different languages to show that the mistakes of MT add up after many translations to a misleading/funny text – or http://www.boredpanda.com/funny-chinese-translation-fails/?afterlogin=savevote&post=73070&score=-1 (last accessed 4 April 2016) – a website showing funny Chinese to English translations.

[6]More information on the different approaches of MT is provided in the subsequent chapter.

[7]http://www.euromatrixplus.net/matrix/, last accessed 16 March 2017.

2012). The Europarl Corpus (cf. Koehn 2005), for instance, gathers data of parallel corpora in 21 European languages taken from the proceedings of the European parliament.[8] The latter is not only important for developing MT systems, but it also enables professional translators to access valuable reference material for free.

Although full high-quality MT is still not possible and probably will not be any time soon – although hope and expectations are rising again with the newly developed neural MT systems[9] – MT is a thriving research area. This persistence was already explained in detail by Kaiser-Cooke (1993):

> Despite the many set-backs it has experienced, MT has proved extremely re-silient. This can be explained partly by the external fascination of language in general and translation in particular, and the ambitions of the AI com-munity to prove the practical applicability of their theories, as well as the unshakeable conviction of many that MT has enormous commercial poten-tial.

2.2 Machine translation approaches

In general, MT was historically divided into two different types: *rule-based* and *data-based. Hybrid systems* combine both approaches and have only been devel-oped in recent years. The latest approach is called *neural MT*, which is also based on data, but is based on neural networks. In the following, the different systems will be briefly introduced and their advantages and disadvantages will be high-lighted. The following sources were used to create this overview – if not speci-fied otherwise – and can be used to find more detailed descriptions: Goutte et al. (2009), Hutchins & Somers (1992), Koehn (2010), and Wilks (2008).

Rule-based approaches launched the development of MT. Generally, these sys-tems attempt to define the single characteristics of the source language and how these need to be converted into the target languages. Different rule-based ap-proaches to realise MT have been developed over the years: *direct MT, transfer-based MT*, and *interlingual MT*. Chesterman (2016: 28–29) mentions that he sees this early form of MT as "the Linguistic meme of translation theory" (ibid.: 29), because it assumes that languages can solely be expressed through rules, which, accordingly, must also be representable in algorithms.

---

[8] http://www.statmt.org/europarl/, last accessed 16 March 2017.
[9] See next chapter.

Direct translation is the oldest approach. This type of MT is constructed specifically for one language pair and usually one translation direction. Essentially, the words of the source text are morphologically analysed and then looked up in a dictionary, which means that ideally all morphology rules are defined, so that the dictionary only has to contain the stems of the words. In the next steps, the words of the source language are replaced by the words in the source language and all morphological changes required by the target language are applied. The main disadvantage of this approach is that it takes a lot of effort to develop such a system, because the better the intended system, the more rules have to be defined. If morphology, grammar, and syntax are only defined superficially, the source text might be interpreted incorrectly which may lead to (severe) mistakes in the target language. Further, the rules have to be defined from scratch for every language and every language direction.

The *transfer-based approach* constructs a syntactic representation of the source text (often in a tree structure) that is free of ambiguities, etc. Next, this representation is generated for the target language with the help of a grammar that contains the bilingual transfer rules. Now, the target text can be produced. Theoretically, it is possible to use these systems in both language directions, but this is rarely done in practice, because the transfer rules often do not apply in both directions.

The last rule-based approach that should be introduced is *interlingual MT*, which experienced its peak in the 1980s and 1990s. For this approach, an Interlingua needs to be created that represents meaning in an abstract form, which can theoretically be achieved by either a natural or an artificial language or a language-independent representation. The basic principle of this approach is that the source text is translated into the Interlingua and then the Interlingua into the target language. Due to the abstract Interlingua, it would be easier to add a new language. However, the task of presenting content and meaning in a formal and neutral manner so that it can be applied to various languages is one of the biggest challenges in the field of Artificial Intelligence and is still an unsolved issue.

At the end of the 20th century, a new concept of MT became popular in MT research: *data-based translation*. The explosion of the world wide web made many mono- and bilingual corpora available that enabled MT researchers to construct systems that are independent of linguistic rules: *example-based MT* and *statistical MT*.

The *example-based approach* was mainly developed in Japan starting in the mid-1980s. Essentially, the systems search in bilingual corpora for the sentence that is closest to the source sentence and combine it with (an)other sentence(s) from the corpus. These fragments then generate the new sentence in the target language. The basic functionality is similar to a translation memory system. However, a TM system only searches for similar sentences that have been translated before, but it does not automatically combine these with other sentences to present a full target sentence. In their study, Carl & Hansen (1999) compare example-based MT with two different TMS approaches. Both TM systems translate the reference sentences better with 90.7% and 89.4% for entirely correct sentences, respectively, than the example-based MT system (85.5%). However, when the translation score was decreased, the example-based MT system outperformed the TM systems, i.e. 96.6% of the sentences from MT output were translated correctly at least 66% of the time, while the TM systems only delivered 93.7% and 95.0%, respectively. This means that the TM systems generate good translations if the training corpus contains (almost) identical sentences, while the MT system can treat sentences that are not literally contained in the training data.

The most extensive research was conducted in *statistical MT* in the last decades. Statistical MT emerged in the late 1980s as a result of IBM's first successes in speech recognition. The basic idea is to generate a translation from a parallel training corpus by calculating the most likely equivalent of a source word/phrase/sentence in the target language. Statistical translation models are generated and trained on the corpus/the corpora with the help of machine learning. Both mono- and bilingual corpora are used to capture the typical linguistic structure of the languages – the monolingual corpora generate the language model, the bilingual parallel corpora generate the translation model. These models are constructed during the training phase. Further, additional information can be extracted during the training phase from all corpora, e.g. models of relative sentence length or information about word order. All these models and information receive a value in the tuning phases. These values represent the weight of the models and information, when the most probable translation of the source text is translated. During the decoding phase the target text is produced. Statistical MT uses word-aligned n-grams – sequences of words (usually $n \leq 7$) – that are assigned probabilities representing how probable the word (or the sequence) is in the training corpus and combined those with the additional information, for example information from the monolingual corpus (see Hearne & Way (2011) for detailed information).

Recent developments have attempted to unite different approaches (usually rule-based and statistical) in]hybrid systems so that the advantages of the respective approach can be combined. While systems with deep integration construct a whole new system that combines the advantages of two approaches, shallow integration systems unite two or more existing systems in one new system (cf. e.g. Eisele 2007).

The latest approach to MT is the use of neural networks, which is also a data-driven approach and uses parallel training corpora. However, neural MT systems try to build one large neural network for translation, while statistical MT systems are composed of many small sub-components. This MT approach usually uses an encoder-decoder system, with one encoder and one decoder for each language. The sentence is read and encoded by the encoder for a vector with a fixed length. This vector is then processed by the decoder which is also responsible for constructing the target sentence. In these systems, the decoder is the hidden layer between input and output. It is called hidden layer, because it can only assess what is put into the system and what comes out of the system, but not what happens in between. The whole encoder-decoder system is trained simultaneously for one language pair to increase the probability of a correct translation. Pressing all the necessary information of a source language into a vector with a fixed length becomes problematic when long sentences need to be translated. This issue can be addressed when the translation is aligned and translated simultaneously. The source sentence is not necessarily encoded into one vector, but into a sequence of vectors, or an alignment model is added. Further, NMT systems can consider the context through a word embedding layer, which appears between the input layer and hidden layer. It represents words that occur in similar contexts and hence helps predicting the next word. Although the MT approach with neural networks is very new, the results are already promising and the combination with existing MT systems has already superseded the previous state-of-the-art of MT performance (cf. Bahdanau et al. 2014: 1-2 and Koehn 2017).

2.3 Machine translation applications

MT is used in many professional and private contexts (cf. Koehn 2010: 20). There are roughly three different areas of application for MT that can be realised: *assimilation* – the (final) target text is used for information gathering – *dissemination* – the (final) target text is used for publication – and *communication* – the (final) target text is used for communication purposes.

The most desirable application for MT is *Full-Automatic High-Quality Machine Translation* (FAHQMT), which means that the MT output does not need any editing by a human. This is the highest goal of MT research. However, this aim has only been achieved for very restricted domains and text types so far like weather forecasts, summaries of sport news, train and plane information, due to the general complexity of language and unresolved problems in MT development, (cf. ibid.: 20-21).

One of the most wide-spread uses of MT is *gisting*. Gisting describes the concept of using MT solely for information gathering. Therefore, the output does not need to be perfect in terms of language. Many websites use online MT systems to make their content accessible to a wide range of users/customers. One popular example is *Facebook*[10] which offers online MT to its users so that posts by other users in foreign languages can be translated automatically. The MT is powered by Microsoft Bing; the platform's interface, however, is localised into many languages by humans. *TripAdvisor*[11] uses MT to translate recommendations/reports on holiday destinations, hotels, restaurants, sights, etc. into the user's mother tongue (MT provided by Google). Therefore, the users can write their reports in their native language and can still be certain that their recommendations will be read all over the world. On the other hand, users can read reports (or at least get an idea about the reports depending on the MT quality) they might otherwise not have understood at all. The homepage of the English town of *Lincolnshire*[12] provides a Google Translate implementation that can translate the page's content. These examples present a vital aspect of gisting: It would not be economical to translate all the information of the aforementioned websites into several languages. For town communities, for example, translations of their homepages are relevant in order to support tourism. However, the costs may be too high for small communities especially considering the running expenses of translating news, etc. Moreover, gisting is of great interest for home security departments in order to observe local news and the communication of other countries, because there is no need (and time) to get perfect translations. Finally, gisting is very helpful to judge information and to estimate whether the document should be translated or post-edited by a human (cf. ibid.: 121).

In a broader sense, MT is further used in combination with speech recognition to facilitate real time translations of spoken conversations, audio data or telephone calls. This special form of MT is particularly difficult, because it includes two extra steps. First, speech must be recognised and transcribed so that an MT system can translate the text and finally, the translated text must be rendered as speech (although written output is possible, too). Further, all components must work in both participating languages or language directions, respectively. Two main areas of use can be categorised: consecutive interpretation of dialogue for mobile appliances as well as static simultaneous interpreting of longer monologues or speeches. Consecutive mobile translation applications were ini-

---

[10] https://www.facebook.com/; last accessed 2 February 2016.
[11] http://www.tripadvisor.de/; last accessed 2 April 2016.
[12] www.lincolnshire.gov.uk; last accessed 2 April 2016.

tially extremely restricted and could be used only in specific situations, such as medical emergencies or for police operations. In 2009, the first speech-to-speech system was published that was not restricted to any domain and could also be used offline, called JIBBIGO[13]. Simultaneous automatic interpreting is advancing tremendously, too, although many problems are still unsolved. The Karlsruhe Institute of Technology (KIT), Germany, for example uses an automatic interpretation system that translates lectures from German into English for those students who are not able to understand German perfectly. The quality of the automatic interpretation is not perfect, but it is a help for the students, nonetheless. Further, the students can access the German transcription – which can also be useful for hearing impaired students – and the English translation via a website (cf. Waibel 2015).

The development of MT for offline applications is also of great interest. Early experimental systems were used by aid workers in developing countries or soldiers in the line of duty (more information on projects of DARPA is provided in §4.3.4). Last but not least, the use of MT for PE is becoming increasingly frequent (cf. Koehn 2010: 121f-123). As PE is one of the main topics of this thesis, it will be explained in detail in the following chapters.

---

[13] http://jibbigo-translator-2-0.soft112.com/, last accessed 28th October 2016.

3 Post-editing

Post-editing (PE) "is the correction of raw machine translated output by a human translator according to specific guidelines and quality criteria" O'Brien (2011: 197–198). Due to an increasing need for translations, more and more companies machine translate texts and send them for editing to (professional) translators afterwards in order to supposedly increase productivity. As Allen (2003) points out, PE introduced a new perspective to translation science, because translators never really had to deal with half finished texts before. One of the most important research questions in PE is hence "to what extent MT output texts are acceptable, and how much human effort is necessary to improve such imperfect texts" (ibid.: 298). From a scientific point of view, PE "is a field in which the human translator and the machine meet – as well as the two disciplines MT and TS [= translation studies, J. N.]" (Čulo 2014: 35).

In PE, the target text does not need to be produced from scratch. The translators already have an outline for the final product. Hence, PE and human translation can be considered different tasks. Further, machine translated texts have different characteristics than human translations. Therefore, PE cannot be seen as another form of proof-reading either. While some mistakes, like spelling and typing errors, hardly ever occur in MT output, some mistakes, e.g. syntactical or lexical ones, would almost never occur in human translation (cf. Nitzke 2016a).

> The differences lie in the frequency, repetitiveness, and types of errors. Where a human translator may slip and mistranslate a word once [...], the machine translation system will plow ahead, consistently mistranslating the same word or phrase over and over again.[1] (Koby 2001: 7)

Depending on the purpose of the final post-edited text, PE is divided mainly into *full* and *light* PE[2]. *Full PE* is usually required when the final text is intended for publication. The text must be comprehensible and accurate; grammar and syntax must be flawless. The style of the text is acceptable but does not need

---

[1]However, this does not entirely apply to statistical and neural MT systems.

[2]To my knowledge, this is the most common differentiation. Allen (2003), for instance, refers to them as "maximum" and "minimal" PE. The latter is sometimes also referred to as "rapid PE".

to be as good as a human translation. Where low quality is good enough for the final product, *light PE* aims to make MT output understandable. According to the TAUS[3] guidelines, a light post-edited text also needs to convey the same meaning as the source text, but style is not important. Further, the text might also contain imperfect grammar or syntax and the reader might realise that the text was generated by a machine. The main aspect is that it delivers the same information as the source text (cf. Massardo et al. 2016: 16-18) In the end, the chosen approach in every PE job is dependent on the purpose and function of the final text and the client – just like translations from scratch.

In the next section, we will take a look at this new field in translation science, which is not all that new in translation practice. Some thoughts on PE development as well as controlled languages and pre-editing will be discussed: Chapter 4 will then concentrate on teaching PE, PE in practice, and PE in research (theoretical and empirical approaches).

3.1 The development of post-editing

PE has been a feature of the translation industry for some decades now. Basically, the development of usable MT systems and PE have always gone hand-in-hand (see a more detailed description in Garcia 2009). For example, the US Air Force employed 43 people in their MT project (including post-editors) in 1964 with the aim of translating about 100,000 words from Russian into English per day (cf. ibid.: 295). In the early days (starting around the mid 1950s), the MT process was included a pre-editor who is an expert in the source language, and a post-editor who is an expert in the domain and the target language, who did not necessarily have much knowledge of the source language (cf. ibid.: 299-300). As mentioned above, the ALPAC report resulted in a big cut in MT financing and also reduced PE activities. The report stated that PE was not cost-effective and that the money should rather be invested in other language studies and tools. Similarly, the first empirical studies on PE can be traced back to the mid 1960, around the time of the ALPAC report. These studies dealt with PE time and rating MT output. After the ALPAC report, almost no empirical, academic research was conducted for a number of decades (cf. ibid.: 300-302). However, research on PE was initiated by non-academics in the 1980s and the introduction of Aslib's annual conference on Translating and the Computer in 1978 also launched many conferences on the topic. (cf. ibid: 302-303) Nonetheless, PE did not vanish entirely but continued to

---

[3]Translation Automation User Society

be performed in a less prestigious environment in institutions and companies. (cf. ibid.: 295-296) The MT system SYSTRAN, for example, was implemented in the Commission of the European Communities in the late 1970s to assist translators handling the amount of translation work needed in the organisation. During that time, the European Union had to deal with "a mere" seven official languages. In the EU context, Laurian (1984: 236–238) suggested in 1984 that dfferent types of PE needed to be developed for different text types and translation purposes. Further, it was pointed out that post-editors still needed to be very well-trained and proficient, even if they only post-edited rapidly and changed just the major errors. (cf. Garcia 2009: 304) With the development of PCs, PE could be performed on screens rather than on paper or a typewriter, which greatly influenced the task as new skills were required from the post-editor such as proficiency in using the keyboard and positioning the cursor. Further, word processing functionalities like using macros, and search and replace functions helped accelerate the PE process. (cf. ibid.: 297) The advancing functionalities of PCs and the ongoing research into MT continued to decrease the PE effort, e.g. PE services at the European Commission increased from 30,000 pages in 1990 to 180,000 pages in 1995. (cf. ibid.: 298) While PE remained a relatively unobserved field for many years in translation science, it has been implemented in some organisations for decades now, of which some examples will be introduced in §4.3. The application of PE was organised by the companies and organisations themselves. Guidelines were developed individually and depended on the MT system as well as the needs of the respective company or organisation. However, PE has become a recognised field in translation studies, especially in translation process research, in the last few decades and is studied academically again. Furthermore, prototypes of PE guidelines were developed, e.g. by TAUS[4], in recent years. Research began to focus on PE with the increasing use of MT in professional translation situations. Furthermore, CAT tools, like CASMACAT[5] and MateCat[6], were developed with the purpose of supporting PE and not only translation from scratch. Last but not least, the possibility of integrating MT systems into translation memory systems has become a standard feature in most systems, which is highly relevant for professional translators. Combining MT and TM can be the most effective way to approach professional translations, because the advantages of both can be used. The most common way both systems are combined is when no match is found

---

[4]https://www.taus.net/academy/best-practices/postedit-best-practices/machine-translation-post-editing-guidelines, last accessed 14 October 2016 and Massardo et al. (2016).
[5]http://www.casmacat.eu/, last accessed 13 November 2016.
[6]https://www.matecat.com/, last accessed 13 November 2016.

in the TM: The segment is then machine translated, i.e. 100%-Matches and Fuzzy Matches up to ~70% are taken from the TM system and the remaining segments are machine translated.

The study presented by Gaspari et al. (2015) provides a current and independent overview of the translation market situation with special regard to translation technologies and MT. In total, 438 individuals from around the world responded to an online survey (with the main focus on Europe, though) in November 2012. The study included professional translators, people working in the industry, academia, and governments or institutions. Of the participants, 36% stated that they did not use MT, 22% that they did not use MT but instead use TMS, 21% stated that they use MT, and the last 21% use both. Of the participants who were not already using MT (30%)[7], 32% claim that they would (probably) not use MT in the future, 22% claim they (probably) would, and 16% were undecided. The follow-up question asked when the participants were planning to adopt MT in the work environment: 228 participants (which equals 82% of those who were not using MT (yet)) did not plan to use it in the near future, while 60 participants (18%) would implement MT (very) soon. Interestingly, most of the participants who used MT use free online MT systems (190 participants) and/or uncustomised MT systems (187 participants)[8]. This shows that most participants who used MT did not use it to its full potential. Concerning the 285 participants who answered the question whether or not they were post-editing, 38% reported that they post-edited all MT output, but 30% also answered that they never post-edit MT output. The others post-edited MT output, but not always. These results raise the question for which purpose the participants used MT output, especially those 30% who never post-edit. The quality of MT output was rated quite negatively: 24% of the 289 participants who answered this question rated the quality as poor, 28% as low, 37% as medium, 10% as high, and only 1% as excellent. Most participants assessed MT output through human evaluation, while only few used automatic evaluation systems. The final MT related question was concerned with the assessment of which PE scenario might be especially interesting for the participants and their work environment. Most opted for improving medium MT output for high quality translations, then improving low MT output for high quality translations, and improving low MT output for medium quality translations was chosen

---

[7]It is not explained why the numbers do not agree with the numbers in the former question. Probably, participants answered the question, even though they chose the answer that they use MT or MT and TM in the first question.

[8]Here again, the numbers are not quite self-explanatory. I assume that some participants who used free online MT systems did not answer the question whether or not their MT system is customised, because it is obviously not, while others did answer it.

the least often (cf. ibid.: 346-350). In summary, the findings of this study support "other reports of the growing prevalence of MT in the translation industry." (ibid.: 350)

3.2 The influence of pre-editing and controlled language

The effort that a translator needs to make in order to post-edit MT output is strongly related to the quality of the MT output. To improve the quality of the MT output, pre-editing techniques and controlled languages are sometimes used. This chapter will briefly introduce the key aspects of pre-editing and controlled languages and how they influence MT output.

In contrast to PE, pre-editing is applied to the source text before the text is machine translated. The aim is to create a source text that can be translated more easily by the machine because predictable, problematic units are changed. The pre-editing rules can be applied manually by a human or automatically by a machine. The pre-editing rules used in the ACCEPT project are an illustrative example. The ACCEPT (Automated Community Content Editing PorTal) project was created to enable better MT output for community contents (both in commercial and non-profit environments) for EU citizens. Therefore, pre-editing rules were defined for English and French, which the system applies (semi)automatically – either the text is analysed automatically, suggestions are made to the user and the user has to choose whether to apply the rules, or the rules are applied automatically without the user's intervention. The source texts are produced in the Acrolinx software that already provides its own rules that highlight problematic text segments for the user. "It is then up to the user to improve the text by reading the help text, choosing a replacement suggestion, manually changing the text or ignoring the marking." (ACCEPT 2012: 3) The suggestions should improve spelling, grammar, terminology, readability, and style. However, it turned out that different rules are necessary to improve statistical MT than for standard Acrolinx procedures. Correcting spelling mistakes is a rule that improves both the source text as well as the MT because the statistical MT system usually only recognises words that are in the training data. For the same reason, one rule was specified to exchange lexical items that are unknown to the system with synonyms. However, that does not necessarily improve the source text. Another rule was to rearrange syntactic structures so that they are closer to the target language, but might become ungrammatical in the source language. Accordingly, changes were either suggested to the user when the suggestions would improve the source text, or applied automatically when the suggestion would impair the source text as users would probably not accept suggestions that would impair the source text (cf. ibid.: 3-5). Another form of pre-editing was made possible in the SUSY system. The user was able to mark units in the text, e.g. when a user marked a headline as a headline, the system would know that it could not analyse the segment as a full sentence but as a phrase. Similarly, the user could mark subordinate clauses or proper names. The user had to set these marks manually, without the help of an automatic instance (Hutchins & Somers 1992: 151-152).

The main aim of controlled languages is to improve the readability, translatability, and reusability of texts through consistent and clear writing. Controlled languages are restricted natural languages, not artificial languages such as Esperanto. They are usually applied in very restricted areas of communication including technical documentation or other domain specific texts, e.g. for manuals, instructions, or safety notes. The first controlled language for a technical environment was Caterpillar-Fundamental English (today: Caterpillar Technical-English), developed by the Caterpillar Tractor Company in the late 1960s. The advantages of controlled languages are that laypersons better understand technical documentation, because readability is improved and misunderstandings and misinterpretations are reduced. Further, localisation of the texts is simplified, costs are reduced, and quality is improved. The texts are more understandable to native and non-native speakers, which is helpful when exporting the product. On the other hand, the text authors are very restrained in the writing process and it takes long for the authors to become acquainted with the new rules (cf. Ferlein & Hartge 2008: 39-45, Lehrndorfer 1996).

Some rules can repeatedly be found for controlled languages, e.g.,

- Use a restricted vocabulary (700-5000 entries).

- Every word has only one meaning, e.g. "fall" means "move downwards due to gravity" not "decrease".

- Use only one word per meaning, e.g. only use "start" not "initiate" or "begin".

- Use short words like "make" instead of "manufacture".

- Use only defined tenses.

- Use simple sentences instead of passives or participial constructions.

- Make sentences and paragraphs short.

- Every sentence contains only one statement.

- Avoid noun compounds. (cf. ibid.)

To sum up, the purpose of pre-editing is to improve MT output, while controlled languages are supposed to make the source text easier and more well-structured. Pre-editing might improve the source text and controlled languages might improve the MT output, but these are not the objectives of the respective language rules. Accordingly, controlled languages are not necessarily used in the MT context, even if they improve MT output, but to generally simplify the texts.

4 Dealing with post-editing and machine translation – five perspectives

PE and MT have influenced the field of (human) translation in many aspects. However, research and practice do not always go hand in hand. The present chapter will introduce five fields of translation – theoretical translation studies, empirical translation process research, translation practice, the professional translation community, and didactics – and analyse their work with and on MT and PE to give a comprehensive overview of the opinions and approaches in translation research and practice. The early years of MT and PE will not be considered as the processes (also concerning translation from scratch) were too different from today's standards, e.g. using a typewriter instead of a computer. However, the PAHO, for example, established MT and PE in the late 1970s, early 1980s and still uses both today. Hence, this organisation is the example with the longest history in PE and sets the historical starting point of the portrait.

4.1 Post-editing and machine translation in (theoretical) translation studies

Although hardly anyone who professionally deals with MT systems (including users, computer linguists, and translators/translation scientists) maintains that these systems are capable of fully replacing human translators at the moment or any time soon, translators are still very suspicious towards MT. This section will present (in excerpts) how MT is received in (theoretical) translation studies and how the arising new changes and challenges are assessed.

In her unpublished dissertation, Kaiser-Cooke (1993) wanted to analyse the interplay of the different types of knowledge that are important in the translation process – "what translators do and how they do it or, in other words, what they know and how they know it" – to finally provide MT researchers with information on what to take into account and what is important for the translation process. She argues that translation is more than a mere transferral of words from a source language into a target language and more than just a transferral of meaning. A translator needs knowledge of the target language and culture and must know what is to be reproduced and in which manner in the target language. Further, a translator needs to have domain knowledge and problem solving skills. All these characteristics cannot be replicated by a machine. Translation is a constant decision making process in which problems may occur. For each decision that a human or a machine has to make while translating, there might be a few correct choices, but there are many more incorrect choices, which is why MT is so difficult to implement. A human translator usually knows from (translation) experience as well as linguistic and cultural knowledge, how to make the correct decision or which choices are acceptable. The machine does not (ibid.: 172-188). One important question MT and human translation have in common, but from very different angles, is how much the machine/the translator needs to know in order to translate properly. Especially in domain-specific translation, not every translator can be as competent as a domain expert, but (s)he has to know enough to ensure a complete and correct target text and delivery of the same message to experts in both cultures. (cf. ibid.: 161-162) Kaiser-Cooke concludes that translators need comparative language knowledge and cultural knowledge as well as translation expertise, which MT cannot offer, because "as a 'hard' discipline, [MT] necessarily sees itself constrained to work on the basis of an objective, concrete world and is thus forced to operate with concrete, quantifiable data." (ibid.: 219) Furthermore, Kaiser-Cooke argues that fully-automatic MT might become possible, if computers learnt how to deal with the individuality of each translation situation, how to present a situation from two different angles, and how to simulate human processing skills such as abstraction and extrapolation. If this was given, the only thing missing to enable MT would be comparative and cultural knowledge for the respective languages. She concludes that MT has a future if computer scientists start to become more acquainted with the human translation process and translation scholars are willing to deliver a theoretical basis for the translation process. These theories need to be rooted in translation practice and require validation from experiments that include knowledge of other disciplines like artificial intelligence, linguistics, psychology, cultural studies etc.[1] (cf. ibid.: 220-225)

> Machine translation and translation studies could both benefit from mutual recognition of the other's problems and achievements and by furthering

---

[1] During that time, translation process research was a very new field and the explorative first think-aloud studies had just been published. Today, the field is thriving and we are getting more and more insights on what is going on in the translator's mind.

the interdisciplinary cooperation necessary to unravel all the complexities of translating as a highly skilled specialist activity. (ibid.: 230)

Cronin (2003: 111–119) exemplifies the arbitrary world in which MT exists: while some translators refuse the use of MT and summon the extinction of translation professionals, the need for translation increases exponentially. Every day, multilingual websites of large companies change their web-content, which has to be localised accordingly. Similarly, multinational companies, e.g. Caterpillar, may produce hundreds of pages of written content every day that need to be distributed to all plants all over the world. There are not enough human translators available to cope with these amounts of text. Hence, technology and automation are necessary to handle this demand. Nonetheless, many translators speak ill of CAT-tools and MT:

> Although an understandable reaction to cyberhype, the endlessly recycled translation howlers from failed MT projects and the derisive dismissal of 'pocket translation' and free MT services on the Web are unhelpful both because they misinterpret the history or achievements of CAT and MT […] and, more seriously, perhaps, because they blind translators and many of those who write about translation to the close connection between translation and the new economy in the global age. […] Translation, like every other sector of human activity, is affected by economic and technical developments and so the move towards automation […] cannot simply be rejected as a malevolent action of technocratic Philistines intent on the dumbing-down of culture. (ibid: 113)

Cronin states that the translation profession not only enables a digitalising and technologising world through the texts they translate, but that the profession is also shaped by these technologies, turning translators into *"translational cyborgs"* (ibid.: 112). There should be no expectation for MT to automatically translate e.g. literary classics, but it should rather be seen as a tool that can help accelerate the translation process; or MT can be considered a tool that undertakes simple gisting tasks. This also means that MT systems cannot simply replace the human translators (and interpreters) overnight.

Similarly, Heller (2012: 280–281) points out that translations and human translation processes have not yet been replaced by other acts or processes in this globalised world, and are therefore socially and (inter-)culturally highly relevant. However, she concedes that MT might replace human translation at least to a certain extent in the future. To her, the fact that MT has attracted so much attention in recent years only proves that the need for (fast) translations is currently even higher than it used to be and that this demand can hardly be handled exclusively by human translators.

Pym (2013) also acknowledges the influence of technology and MT on the field of translation. He suspects that the combination of MT and translation memory systems will at some point replace full human translation in many aspects of translation and consequently the translator will be required to have different skills. Furthermore, the spread of online MT systems might also change the social aspect of translation. When using MT/TM, the translator must be able to evaluate what output can be trusted. After assessing different aspects of translation – language, area, and intercultural knowledge - Pym (2013: 491) concludes that "[t]he active and intelligent use of TM/ MT should eventually bring significant changes to the nature and balance of all other components, and thus to the professional profile of the person we are still calling a translator" and therefore, he adds, some doubts about traditional terminology like *translator* or *source text* and traditional translation models. While translators used to have to apply their skills to identifying and generating possible solutions for problems in translation from scratch, he assumes a shift towards selecting between available solutions when technologies are involved. Accordingly, new strategies for translation didactics have to be developed (see further discussions in §4.5).

While Kaiser-Cooke and others in the last decades were rather open-minded towards MT as early as in the early 1990s, this is not always a commonly shared state of mind. Even in the second edition of his book "Übersetzung und Linguistik"[2] that was published in 2013, Albrecht (2013: 76) speaks disparagingly about MT systems:

> My experiences with these so called 'translation systems' give me no reason to go into detail. [...] With regard to all the useful goals that need to be tackled by computer linguists and computer scientists in the field of computer-assisted translation, the development of full-automatic translation systems seems to be intellectual dalliance, at least for the practising translator[3] (ibid. [translated by J.N.])

One problem with the contemptuous opinions of MT is that this attitude is communicated to student translators who read these types of textbooks or attend

---

[2] "Translation and Linguistics"

[3] „Meine Erfahrungen mit sogenannten 'Übersetzungssystemen' lassen mich davon absehen, auf diese Hilfsmittel einzugehen. [...] Angesichts der vielen sinnvollen Aufgaben, die im Bereich der computergestützten Übersetzung auf Computerlinguisten und Informatiker warten, erscheinen die ehrgeizigen Versuche, vollautomatische Übersetzungssysteme zu entwickeln, zumindest dem Praktiker als intellektuelle Spielerei."

lectures in which MT systems are criticised instead of dealing with the topic reasonably. Instead of looking down on automated systems, students should, in my opinion, learn what these systems are capable and (especially) what they are not capable of, so that they can reason with clients. The spread of MT and PE seems threatening to some (professional) translators who fear for their job instead of recognising the opportunity. This fear often results from unfamiliarity with the technology and its advantages and disadvantages. Hence, it cannot be helpful to either endorse these fears or spread unjustified or uneducated personal opinions.

Similarly as Kaiser-Cooke (1993) reported in her unpublished dissertation, Čulo (2014) points out that both MT developers as well as translation scientists need to learn from each other. MT could integrate insights yielded by translation studies to improve MT systems e.g. in regard to the linguistic behaviour of text types, domain convention, or register, while translation studies could acknowledge MT as a form of documentary translation, which would probably enhance the acceptance of MT in the field in the long run.

Rozmyslowicz (2014) analyses the need for translation theory to deal with MT. He argues that the basic assumptions underlying *translation* have to be revised in order to include MT in translation theory. MT has become part of everyday translation and communication – not only for professional translators, but especially in the everyday life of laypersons. In recent translation theories, the term *culture* has become indispensable to define *translation,* to disengage *translation* from its purely linguistic history, while *culture* is often used in a vague manner. It is, however, often not acknowledged that defective communication still initialises communication. Rozmyslowicz hence suggests to assume *understanding* as the initial point of *communication.*

> [T]he degree of technological perfection or imperfection in computers is theoretically irrelevant. What *is* relevant is that communication is initiated and maintained without necessarily presupposing another conscious being as the direct source of an utterance, and the same holds true, by extension, for translation – at least since the advent of machine translation. Whether and to what extent the 'defects' of machine-generated translations become a communicative problem is an empirical question and cannot be decided by theoreticians, [...] for as long as no one "protests", we have no reason to assume that translation has failed (Vermeer 1978: 101). (ibid.: 158, emphasis in original text)

In conclusion, Rozmyslowicz argues, similar to Pym (2013), that concepts such as *agency*, *translation*, *culture*, or *communication* have to be revised to theoretically embed MT into translation studies.

In his book on training translators and interpreters, Orlando (2016) acknowledges that technology, MT, and PE have become part of the industry and that translators and interpreters are expected to deal with these technologies. However, the book does not indicate how to integrate these technologies in training. Some publications have already devoted ideas on integrating MT into translation didactics, which will be introduced in §4.5.

In summary, most translation scholars introduced in this chapter agree that MT technology has arrived in the translators' work environment, but also in the everyday life of laypersons. Some recognise that MT (in combination with other translation tools) will partly replace full human translations, which is also necessary, because the need for translations is growing continuously.

4.2 Post-editing and machine translation in translation process research

A rather different approach to PE (and consequently MT) can be found in (empirical) translation process research. This research area has already identified the practical need for PE and has included the task in numerous studies. The following overview of such studies is not intended to be exhaustive, but to highlight some ideas on research interests in the field.

The first translation process study on PE was published by Krings (2001: this summary refers to the English version, the first edition in German, however, was published in 1997). This think-aloud study dealt with technical texts that described simple every-day appliances in English, French, and German. The texts were automatically translated by the SYSTRAN system used by the European Community (English and French into German), and the METAL system at the Institute of Applied Linguistics in Hildesheim (German into English). Three types of data were collected: for PE with and without the source text and for translation from scratch. As think-aloud is a quite intrusive method, three control data sets were recorded: two sets with other verbal data, i.e. retrospective commentary and dialogue protocols, and one without verbal data. The study was conducted with pen and paper, except for one control set. (cf. ibid.: 186-195) Taking all languages, translation modes, methods, tools, and participants into account (the participants in one experiment were professionals), 13 experiments were prepared (for an exact list see Table 5.4 in ibid.: 194). Altogether, 52 subjects took part in 48 sessions.

The participants were enrolled in the technical translation studies programme in Hildesheim and were picked from a pool of volunteers. The experimental session took about 2.5 hours and the participants received monetary compensation. Further, they had to fill out a questionnaire that gathered basic information on their course of studies before the experiment. Some dictionaries (mono- and bilingual) as well as one encyclopedia on sciences and technology were provided for the participants. (cf. ibid.: 195-204) To put the analysis of the TAPs into perspective, MT output was ranked on the sentence level – on a scale from 1 to 5, one meaning that the quality is poor, five meaning the quality is good. These results were then compared with the monolingually post-edited texts, which were given 0.81 to 1.57 points more than the MT output. (cf. ibid.: 253-258) Then, attention was shifted to parameters concerning time, verbalisation, and final product. Time-related parameters were processing time, processing speed, and relative PE effort. The processing speed was a little higher for PE without source text and higher for PE without thinking aloud. In addition, experienced post-editors were a bit slower and the quality of the MT output seemed to show a negative correlation with processing speed (the better the output the less time was needed). Relative PE effort as the relation of translation speed to PE speed[4] showed that PE was 7-20% faster. (cf. ibid.: 276-286) Further, verbalisation effort and relative PE effort in relation to verbalisation effort were measured as well as the similarity of the MT output and the post-edited text. For the latter, Krings (cf. ibid.: 300-301) found that the final texts were 36.9% similar to the MT output, ranging from 24.2% to 44.6% between the texts. In the next step, the recorded processes were categorised, which demonstrated that all tasks showed a comparable basic structure, involving seven distinct processes and various sub-processes. Most of these processes were target text related (about two thirds) and the most time was spent on the process of text production. Research in the reference books was chosen more often in TfS than in PE and in PE high quality MT output requires much less research than low and medium quality output. Interestingly, PE (with the source text) demanded more source text related processes than TfS, and PE effort was higher on medium quality MT than on low level MT. Finally, text production and text evaluation processes were independent of MT quality. Krings (cf. ibid.: 318-320) further summarises that – considering changes in attention focus – less cognitive effort is necessary for PE than for TfS, but in general "post-editing, seen as a process, led not to less, but rather tended towards more cognitive effort" (ibid: 534).

---

[4]A quotient of one would mean that PE was as fast as translation from scratch, a quotient under one would mean that PE was faster and over one that PE was slower than translation from scratch.

In her dissertation, O'Brien (2006) analysed the impact of negative translatability indicators (NTIs) on PE effort. She used controlled language checkers to locate the NTI instances. Her participants were twelve professional translators who worked at IBM and had to fill out a questionnaire in advance to check whether they were suitable for the study. Nine of them had to post-edit the MT output, while three translated the texts from scratch as a baseline. The text was from the IT domain and contained 1777 words. Additionally, different kinds of passages were chosen that contained typical characteristics of IT texts such as descriptive and instructive passages, lists, abbreviations, menu names, etc. O'Brien used keylogging software (Translog) and Choice Network Analysis for her analysis. First, she analysed the temporal effort during PE. In general, PE was faster than human translation. Her results show that NTIs significantly extend the PE duration of each segment. Most segments caused a lower Relative Post Editing Effort (RPE) than translation effort. However, not all NTIs have the same effect. Some seem to be more demanding than others. The analysis of technical effort showed that segments with few NTIs needed significantly fewer insertions and deletions than those with many. Finally, the Choice Network Analysis showed again that some NTIs influence PE effort more than others.

The study by Arenas (2008) compares the productivity and final quality of fuzzy matches and post-edited segments. Nine participants, all of them professional translators, had to translate segments from scratch, edit fuzzy matches (different degrees of agreement), and post-edit MT output without knowing the origin of the pre-translation. The job was performed in a special web-based PE tool that records the editing/translation time and was fed with a trained MT system, TM entries, and a terminology list. Further, the participants had to fill out a questionnaire dealing with their experience concerning localisation, tools, domains, and PE. Three hypotheses were investigated: First, Arenas assumed that post-editing MT output would take as long as editing a fuzzy match segment with 80–90% agreement. Further, it was hypothesised that the quality of an edited fuzzy match and post-edited MT output is equal. Finally, it was assumed that participants with greater technical knowledge would be more productive as the texts were taken from the localisation industry. The analysis showed that, on average, the participants were faster when they post-edited MT output (25% faster than from scratch), and when they edited fuzzy matches (11% faster than from scratch). They were slowest when they translated from scratch. (cf. ibid.: 14) Interestingly, most mistakes were found in the final text segments when they originated from TM output. The fewest mistakes were made in translations from scratch, except for two participants who made fewer mistakes when post-editing MT, and one who made the same number of mistakes in both segment types. We have to keep in mind, though, that the translators could not go back once they marked the segment as done and could not review their translations. The total number of errors in segments translated from scratch and post-edited segments was quite similar (27 and 34, respectively), while the distance to the TM segments was much higher (64 mistakes in total). The error type that occurred most often is "accuracy". (cf. ibid.: 15-16) Arenas (ibid.) argues that TM segments contain more errors because they are more fluent, as they originate from other manual translations and which makes it harder to detect mistakes. In the next step, a penalty according to the number of mistakes the participant made in the segment type was added to the processing speed. The new productivity gain calculations, including the penalty, showed that six out of eight participants were still faster when they post-edited MT output instead of translating the segments from scratch. However, only three were faster when editing fuzzy matches (cf. ibid: 17). In general, editing MT output was still 25% faster, while editing fuzzy matches was 3% slower. Finally, experience seemed to have a positive influence on the processing speed, but not on error rates. (cf. ibid.: 18-19)

In a pilot study, Carl et al. (2011) compared the PE behaviour of seven post-editors to the behaviour of 24 translators who translated from scratch and the quality of the output of these sessions. For the latter, four evaluators were presented with one source sentence and four final versions – two post-edited sentences and two human translated sentences. The evaluators had to rank the four final versions from best to worst – ties were allowed – without knowing whether the sentences were post-edited or translated from scratch. Interestingly, the post-edited sentences achieved an altogether better rating than the human translations. However, some sentences were presented to the evaluators twice and did not necessarily get the same ranking, which indicates that the assessment may not be completely reliable. (cf. ibid: 133-136) The editing distance did not correlate with the score of the post-edited sentence, which shows that more editing does not necessarily improve the quality. The PE sessions took on average only slightly less time (7 min 35 s for PE per text vs. 7 min 52 s for TfS per text), which is quite surprising, but the post-editors were not experienced in PE and CAT tools, while the translators were experienced. The eyetracking analysis showed that more gaze time was spent on the screen for PE than for TfS. There might be two reasons for this: First, the translators might have spent more time looking at the keyboard as they initially had to produce text and second, they might have had to spend more time thinking about a translation solution and they did not have to look at the screen while they think. The eyetracking data further showed that in PE, more time was spent processing the target text (total gaze time and fixation count were significantly higher on the target text), while source and target text were looked at equally long in translation from scratch. Moreover, the fixations on the source text are significantly longer than on the target text in the translation from scratch task. (cf. ibid.: 138-140) Carl et al. (ibid.: 140) explain that

> [m]anual translation seems to imply a deeper understanding of the ST, requiring more effort and thus longer fixations, whereas in post-editing, the ST is consulted frequently but briefly in order to check that the SMT output is an accurate and/or adequate reproduction of the ST.

De Almeida investigates two main questions in her dissertation from 2003. First, whether translation experience influences the PE performance and second, whether similar languages evoke similar PE behaviour. The study further explores typical difficulties in PE and introduces strategies to cope with these difficulties. Finally, the insights of the study can be used to improve MT systems and develop new MT-related translation tools. A total of 20 translators participated in the study – 10 translating into Brazilian Portuguese and 10 into French (all of them native speakers of the respective language). The participants were either professionals or students. Some had PE experience, some did not. In the recruiting phase, participants had to complete a short survey that was concerned with translation and PE experience, as well as academic education. An additional questionnaire had to be filled out right before the experiments and dealt with the participants' attitude towards MT and PE. Further, the PE sessions were recorded with a screen recording and keylogging software. All data were combined with the final PE products to analyse the process. The texts were from the field of IT and contained 1008 words (74 segments). The participants could use the Internet for research if they wanted. The time for the sessions was limited to two hours and the participants were paid for their work (cf. ibid.: 73-77). In addition, the workbench in which the participants had to post-edit was similar to SDL Trados and PE instructions were provided that explained the task, defined PE, outlined the expected quality and listed which changes needed to be carried out (cf. ibid.: 108-116). The PE products were classified according to the following schema (cf. ibid.: 95):

- master categories:
  essential changes, preferential changes, essential changes not implemented, introduced errors

- subclasses of master categories:
  accuracy, consistency, country, format, language, mistranslation, style, lexical choice (with further subcategories for accuracy, country, and language)

- to examine how former translation and PE experience as well as attitude towards MT influence the PE performance, the following items were analysed:

- number of corrections

- type of corrections (according to schema introduced above)

- total time

- switches between keyboard and mouse (and time spent per input method)

- amount of conducted online research

- items researched

- existence of final revision

Further, the data of the two languages were compared to test whether similar strategies were used in both languages. The analysis part of the study presents correlations between former experience with and attitude toward the categories introduced above, but unfortunately does not report the p-value of the correlations, so the reader does not know whether these results are statistically significant. She concludes, however, that previous translation and PE experience do not influence the PE performance. Translation and PE experience does not seem to influence PE time. Further, translation experience does not influence the decision whether or not to revise the text. Inexperienced translators seem to have researched more online than experienced translators. The participants who performed best overall had translation and PE experience and conducted little to no research. Similar changes were made in both languages indicating similar PE behaviour in related languages. (cf. ibid.: 199-201)

The cognitive demand and cognitive effort in PE are topics of major interest in PE research, because they are, aside from PE productivity, the most important indicators of whether or not PE is more effective than TfS. Lacruz et al. (2014) wanted to find an expressive measure for cognitive demand in their study, i.e. the demand established by the MT output rather than the cognitive effort that is actually required by the individual post-editor. They also wanted to investigate which pause ratio is usable for cognitive effort by correlating the pause to word ratio (PWR[5]) with the different pause thresholds; how the MT quality (measured in HTER[6]) influence PWR; and how MT quality ratings correlate with PWR. Finally, they hypothesise that the type of error in the MT output influences cognitive demand. (cf. ibid.: 75-79) Five participants with English as their first language and Spanish as their second took part in the study. They were enrolled in a Master's Programme in Spanish translation and had all passed a course on PE and TM systems. The four Spanish source texts could be considered texts written in general language – excerpts of TED talks[7]. Each text was automatically translated by two adaptive MT systems, i.e. the PE changes of one segment influenced the automatic translation of the next segment. Each participant translated each text once, i.e. two texts per MT system. The training sessions contained ten segments, while the remaining three experimental texts contained 30 segments each. They used an online PE tool that simultaneously logged key strokes. The participants could work from home. They were also requested to rate the MT quality on a scale from one ("gibberish") to five ("very good"). The final texts were independently rated by two experienced translators (cf. ibid.: 79-80). The results of the study show that a pause threshold of 300ms seems to be very reasonable; that an increasing HTER score (decreasing MT quality) has a strong positive and significant correlation with PWR; that a low human rating of the MT output increases PWR accordingly (strong negative correlation); and that transfer errors – errors where the translator has to consult the source text – generate more cognitive demand than mechanical errors – errors that can be fixed without consulting the source text. (cf. ibid.: 80-82)

In their study, Moorkens et al. (2015) tested how perceived PE effort actually correlates with real PE effort, including temporal, technical, and cognitive aspects (the latter was measured with eyetracking data). Three stages and two groups were necessary for this study. Group 1 involved six professional translators who first had to rate two texts on how much effort it would take to post-edit the single segments (Stage 1). A few weeks later, the same participants had to post-edit the same texts (Stage 2); only four participants completed this task entirely so that the estimated and the actual PE effort could only be compared for these four participants. Finally, students with little PE experience post-edited the

---

[5]PWR = number of pauses / number of words

[6]HTER = number of required edits / number of reference word refers to the least number of necessary changes for PE; most post-editors, however, do not chose the easiest way; low HTER equals high MT quality

[7]"Source texts were extracts of Spanish language transcripts of TED talks on matters of general interest with little technical language." (ibid.: 79)

texts and their temporal and technical effort was also recorded (Stage 3). Additionally, they received an indicator for half the segments showing how high the PE effort had been estimated for the segment in Stage 1 (green – low effort, yellow – medium effort, red – high effort) to measure whether this has an influence on PE performance. The texts were Wikipedia excerpts written in general language and were post-edited from English into Brazilian Portuguese in an online PE tool. (cf. ibid.: 267–273) The correlation of the individual ratings of the segments' estimated PE effort and the average group ratings were significant but not very strong (r = .373), which already indicates that perceived PE effort is not really reliable. Similarly, the rating of the estimated PE effort correlated significantly but not strongly (r = .492) with the time the participants needed to post-edit the segments (cf. ibid.: 274–276). When measuring cognitive effort through eyetracking, it could be observed that the eyetracking data (total numbers of fixation and mean fixation duration) increased when the segments were rated badly; however, there was only a significant difference between green and yellow segments and green and red segments, but not between yellow and red segments. Furthermore, manual ratings and technical effort correlated significantly and strongly (r = .652), while temporal and technical effort correlated significantly and moderately (r = .524). (cf. ibid.: 276–278). The significant correlations between eyetracking data and time propose "that some segments presented time-consuming PE problems that required a related measure of cognitive effort without requiring a related amount of edits to the text." (ibid.: 278) Time spent on PE was very similar for the professional and the student groups, but students edited more than professionals. Further, the indication of the segments' ratings did not noticeably influence PE time or technical effort. (cf. ibid.: 278-281) In summary, the study showed on the one hand that the ratings of perceived effort predict the actual effort, but not as strongly and confidently as might be expected and on the other hand that confidence scores might not be beneficial at all. (cf. ibid.: 281–282)

To conclude, the main task in empirical PE research seems to be – as predicted by Allen (2003: 298), see Chapter 3 – to prove that PE is more efficient than translation from scratch with or without the help of TM systems in regard to temporal, technical, and cognitive effort. More studies on PE will be presented in §7.4 in regard to the data set and in §9.1 with regard to research efforts in PE.

4.3 Post-editing and machine translation applications in practice

Krings (2001: 558, emphasis in original text) concludes his extensive think-aloud study on PE with the following statement on the practical use of MT: "As long as *fully automated high-quality translation* remains an unreached future prospect [...] how the machine can support the translator will in practice remain the true measure, and not the machine itself." Accordingly, some organisations and companies will be introduced in this chapter that apply MT and/or PE in their everyday business or conduct research in (one of) the respective fields. The aim is to show that PE is not a job that might emerge for translators some day, but has already been established in some companies/organisations for years. This is intended as an excerpt of PE practice and not a complete elaboration, because on the one hand some examples suffice to paint the picture and on the other hand many companies and organisations do not publish much information about their processes and best practices (as also mentioned in Allen 2003).

4.3.1 Pan American Health Organization (PAHO)

The Pan American Health Organization is a regional sub-organisation of the World Health Organization for the American continents and therefore part of the United Nations Organization. It was founded in 1902 after a yellow fever epidemic spread in parts of South America in 1870, which even reached the United States eight years later. The expansion of sea transportation enabled the international spread of diseases and a control instance between different countries became necessary. Altogether, PAHO has 35 member states and four associated members. The main goal of PAHO is to improve and maintain people's health. Further objectives are to ensure technical cooperation between the member states to fight diseases and their causes, improve the health systems, and act in emergency situations. Everyone in the member states should be able to access the medical care that (s)he needs. (www.paho.org[8])

The PE service at PAHO might be the oldest and one of the best examples of PE in practice (Aymerich 2004, Aymerich 2005). The success of PE is based on the organisation's own rule-based MT system (named PAHOMTS) that was established in 1980. At that time, the first language combination that was established was from Spanish into English. Nowadays, PAHOMTS includes engines for

---

[8]http://www.paho.org/hq/index.php?option=com_content&view=article&id=91&Itemid=220&lang=en

all language combinations between English, Spanish and Portuguese. A special characteristic of PAHOMTS is that the engine was not only developed solely by computational linguists, but is also improved by translators who give feedback on the MT output so that dictionaries and algorithms can be adapted accordingly. PAHOMTS runs on Windows (Windows Vista – Windows 10), has a trilingual user interface as well as trilingual online support, and each MT dictionary contains over 150,000 words, phrases and rules. The latest version (4.12) was released in December 2015. (cf. www.paho.org[9])

The PE activities began with the establishment of PAHOMTS, which has been trained with PAHO documents for decades now. Therefore, the MT output is of very good quality in the PAHO contexts and is only post-edited if the document is intended for publication and not only for gisting purposes. Furthermore, the long-lasting use and the well-tried functionality of PAHOMTS explains why PAHO still uses a rule-based MT system, because it has been customised so well that newer approaches would not improve the MT output. All in all, MT is used to prepare 90 percent of the documents. The translators rarely use the MT in combination with translation memory systems (only for five percent of all translation jobs) and when they do, it is only for financial reports as well as governing body documents due to the repetitiveness of these text types. When a translator has to post-edit a text, (s)he gets the source document, background texts if available, the unedited translation file, a side-by-side file, and the list with the words that had no dictionary entry. The MT systems are not only specialised on medical texts but can also be used for manuals, reports, scientific articles, etc. Finally, the source texts neither undergo pre-editing processes nor are they written in controlled language, although an assistant revises the source text according to the general guidelines, e.g. spell check or formatting (cf. Aymerich 2004).

PAHOMTS has processed over 88 million words since 1980. Thanks to post-editing, the increase in productivity is estimated at 30–50%. In addition, licenses for PAHOMTS can be bought by educational institutions, international and inter-governmental organisations, government agencies and NGOs, but not by private persons or businesses (cf. www.paho.org[10]).

4.3.2 European Commission (EC)

As was already mentioned in §2.1 and §3.1, the European Commission also started to approach MT relatively early. With 24 official languages today, and policies

---

[9]www1.paho.org/english/am/gsp/tr/machine_trans.htm last accessed 28 July 2018.
[10]www1.paho.org/english/am/gsp/tr/machine_trans.htm last accessed 28 July 2018.

that specify that every official document needs to be available for every citizen in the official language(s) of the country (s)he lives in, the need for MT in the European Union is obvious. SYSTRAN was already established in the European Commission (EC) in 1976. However, it only became widely used when e-mails became a reliable source of communication for the different departments in the early 1990s and after the EUROTRA project (see §3.1) did not deliver a working system. The use of MT increased to 260,000 pages per year in 1998 (cf. Senez 1998: 1).

In 1994, the PER-Service (PER = post-édition rapide/rapid post-editing) was established at the EC. At the beginning, a small group of freelancers volunteered to handle the PE tasks. They were not trained in the task, but gained experience in this new area through practice. MT and the PER-Service were only used when necessary, e.g. when deadlines did not allow for human translation, because there was only enough time available to make a few changes in the MT output. The customers of the PER-Service had to complete questionnaires concerning general satisfaction with the service as well as feedback on the terminology so that new terminology could be fed into SYSTRAN and changes could be communicated to the translators. The use of the service increased by 20–50% per year between 1994 and 1998 and one post-edited page was about half the price of a human translated page (cf. ibid.: 2-3).

The first job vacancy for PE was advertised in 1998 when the EC was looking for a post-editor for the languages German, English, and French. In general, the EC distinguished between *correcting* MT output, which meant that the MT output was used as the first draft of the translation and was then edited into a full translation, and *post-editing* MT output, for which the final output did not need to be perfect and that was only the chosen approach if there was not enough time and the target text was not intended for publication. The main goal of post-edited documents was to reliably deliver the information and content; style was not important. The final product was shaped by the urgency of the task and therefore perfection was not the main objective (cf. ibid.: 3-6).

Different environments were developed in the context of MT. The *Machine Translation Help Desk* was introduced to enable communication between developers and users of SYSTRAN. Further, the POETRY interface was created and allowed the customer to choose what was supposed to happen with the document: it could either be translated by humans, summarised in writing or orally, proof-read, or post-edited (cf. ibid.: 2-5).

While the early MT system was able to translate German, English, and French, things were about to change for MT when it was decided to add the rest of the official languages as well. The goal of incorporating all languages combinations in an MT system finally seemed impossible after the latest EU expansions in 2004 and 2007. The MTS was ruled-based and it would have taken far too long to develop new MT engines for all languages, language pairs, and language directions. At that time, translation memory systems were considered to be much more effective than MT because less money needed to be invested to make the systems efficient and they worked equally well for all language pairs. Hence, financing for the development of MT ended. However, translation memory systems were neither the perfect nor the final answer because they could only repeat what had been translated before (cf. Bonet 2013: 4-5).

A superior solution for the EC's requirements was found in statistic MT and resulted in the launching of a new MT project in 2010. The aims of this project were the following: The rule-based MTS was replaced with a statistical one; the MTS was to be used by every member of the EC; communication was to become faster; the judgement of whether or not a text required translation was to become easier; and experts were to be able to communicate their knowledge no matter how well they knew the language. (ec.europa.eu[11])

The MT system called *MT@EC* is available free of charge to the staff working for an EU body or agency as well as for all public administrations of any EU country, Norway, and Iceland. Furthermore, interested individuals can download translation memory entries for free. Documents in eleven different formats and text snippets can be automatically translated within seconds or a few minutes – depending on the length of the documents – in all language combinations of the 24 official EU languages. The output retains the original format and indicates the expected quality. The website specifically states that the MT output is raw translation data and that a "skilled professional translator" must revise the text if a high-quality translation is required (www.ec.europa.eu[12]).

4.3.3 Ford

The Ford Motor Company was founded by Henry Ford in 1903. The current headquarters are in Darborn, Michigan, USA. In 2015, the company employed about 199,000 people in 67 plants worldwide. FORD (2016: 1) Years before Ford started to use MT systems in 1998, they had already established a controlled language.

---

[11]http://ec.europa.eu/isa/actions/02-interoperability-architecture/2-8action_en.htm, last accessed on 7th November 2016

[12]http://ec.europa.eu/dgs/translation/translationresources/machine_translation/index_en.htm, last accessed 7th November 2016

In 1990, Ford established the *Standard Language* at *Ford Body & Assembly Operations* in the USA. Standard Language is a Ford-specific, restricted version of English that focuses on vehicle assembly processes. It is only used in unpublished documents, but is used by the staff in Ford plants around the world. Further, an AI-system uses process sheets that are composed in Standard Language to generate work assembly instructions. First introduced in the USA, Standard Language has spread into Ford plants in Europe, South America, and Asia, too. (cf. Rychtyckyj 2006: 1)

SYSTRAN was introduced for MT in 1998. Many challenges arose because the MT system needed to be adapted to the controlled language, called Standard Language. Standard Language uses, e.g., unconventional or non-existing grammar rules to specify information on time and motion. These rules not only need equivalents in the target languages but are also unknown to the MT system. However, the controlled language was also adapted to the MT system in some aspects, e.g., the system now adds articles (which are optional in Standard Language and are often left out to save time) to words/phrases when parsing. This improves the quality of the MT output. (cf. ibid: 6-8). The MT system is capable of translating English into German, Dutch, Spanish, and Portuguese. In addition to the texts in Standard Language, the MT system also has to translate comments that the authors added to the instructions, which are in natural language and hence more difficult to translate for the MT system that was adapted to Standard Language. Therefore, an additional component was added to the system that converts the natural language into a more MT-friendly language before the translation is performed. In general, the translation of the process sheets does not require human intervention, but the employees at the assembly plants can correct the translation manually in the online system if they think it is necessary. When the glossary is updated, the process sheets are re-translated so that users can benefit from the changes (cf. Rychtyckyj 2007).

4.3.4 DARPA

The first wave of MT financing and development can be traced to the early years of the Cold War. And even today, MT is still important in the military sector. DARPA (*Defence Advanced Research Projects Agency*) is a US agency that was established in 1957 with the launch of Sputnik and is part of the US Defence Department. The mission of DARPA is to finance new technologies for national security. It employs 220 people who oversee about 250 research and development programs.[13] Some of these projects focus on MT application because, on the one hand, information from news or blogs in other languages needs to be accessed very quickly and, on the other, soldiers need technology to help them communicating with civilians. (cf. DARPA 2008: 98) In the following, some projects will be introduced briefly. Although they do not include PE tasks, these projects present important examples of how raw MT output can be used.

The first project presented is the GALE (*Global Autonomous Language Exploitation*) programme. This programme concentrates on developing MT systems for Chinese (Mandarin) and Arabic (Modern Arabic Standard Language) into English to monitor news, web pages, and TV reports in real time. The system is also supposed to convert audio data into written text first if necessary. The ultimate goal was envisioned as automatically produced, live subtitles for news broadcasts and other TV shows. The previous system, *eTAP*, was only 35–55% accurate but still significantly reduced manual labour because it helped make decisions about whether a document needed to be translated. The result was that only 5% of the documents were considered important enough for translation. The main GALE objective, however, was to raise accuracy up to 95% for formal texts (slightly lower for informal texts) and to 90% for (controlled) speech.[14] The MT component is hybrid and consists of rule-based and statistical components. (cf. ibid.: 98-100)

Another noteworthy project is the TRANSTAC (*Spoken Language Communication and Translation System for Tactical Use*) programme. This project focused on developing a bidirectional translator for spoken language to enable communication between soldiers and locals outside the USA. The main difference to GALE was its aim to capture spoken language, which is not as controlled as language on TV or in other media. Civilians speak in dialects and may have different pronunciation habits, which makes speech recognition and MT much more complicated. Further, the device should be mobile and hence has to be wearable. In 2001, a forerunner device was developed that could translate several hundred pre-defined spoken phrases into Arabic, Pashto, and other languages. Ideally, TRANSTAC, should be able to use a lexicon with tens of thousands of entries as well as specialise "tactically relevant questions and answers" (ibid.: 101). After interviewing soldiers and marines about necessary phrases, native speakers of all languages involved (initially, English and Iraqi Arabic) were asked to record different interactions in a studio. The recordings and transcripts were used to train and build

---

[13]http://www.darpa.mil/about-us/about-darpa, last accessed 8 November 2016.

[14]Reports on the final accuracy could not be found, which might suggest that the goals were not met.

the machine. The system could handle 25 questions and answers in ten minutes in 2007 (cf. ibid.: 100-101). In the end, the system reached an accuracy of 80% but did not gain much acceptance from the potential users. (cf. www.slate.com[15])

The task of the MADCAT (*Multilingual Automatic Document Classification, Analysis and Translation*) programme is to translate foreign language text images into English. The technologies are able to analyse, classify, and segment the image, determine the script and the text, produce transcripts in the source language, and finally produce an accurate translation into English.[16])

The last project that will be presented here is the LORELEI (*Low Resource Languages for Emergent Incidents*) project, which targets languages with low resources. The aim is to develop "partial or fully automated speech recognition and/or machine translation" within 24 hours after a new language is needed, e.g. in emergency situations. The goal is not to develop a full working system, but to identify parts of the information in the respective language like names, places, topics, events, etc. (cf. http://www.darpa.mil[17])

4.4 Post-editing and machine translation in the professional translation community

In this chapter, we will focus on MT in professional translation communities. The BDÜ[18] is one of the leading German professional associations for interpreters and translators with more than 7500 members, and will be used as an example for the professional communities. The BDÜ has recognised the need to talk about MT and PE in recent years and published a number of articles, co-hosted a conference, and offered training in and on the topics. These will be briefly presented in the following.

First of all, the respective publications will be discussed. The internal magazine of the BDÜ is called MDÜ[19] and is published once every quarter. Two issues have

---

[15] http://www.slate.com/articles/technology/future_tense/2012/05/darpa_s_transtac_bolt_and_other_machine_translation_programs_search_for_meaning_.html, last accessed 8 November 2016.

[16] http://www.darpa.mil/program/multilingual-automatic-document-classification-analysis-and-translation, last accessed 8 November 2016

[17] http://www.darpa.mil/program/low-resource-languages-for-emergent-incidents, last accessed 8 November 2016

[18] Bundesverband für Dolmetscher und Übersetzer – Federal Association for Interpreters and Translators

[19] Fachzeitschrift für Dolmetscher und Übersetzer – Professional Journal for Interpreters and Translators

been (partially) concerned with the topics of MT and PE in recent years. First, the final issue of 2012 called "The Future of Translation and Interpretation" devoted two articles to the topics. The first one by Reinke & Seewald-Heeg (2012) evaluates whether MT will be able to replace human translators. In the first part of the article, Reinke argues that context is important for comprehension and that natural language is very vague and hence is very problematic for machine processing. After very briefly introducing rule-based, statistical and hybrid MT approaches, he discusses useful applications of MT. They assess that use for professional translation is very restricted and that most texts would require PE, which, he muses, would be much more time consuming for many texts than human translation[20]. However, he acknowledges that the combined use of MT and TMS can increase productivity by up to 40% and sees the main use of MT in private translation for information gathering. He summarises that full automatic translation will not become a reality in the near future. Seewald-Heeg elaborates on the potential of combining MT and TM technologies. The second article by Elsen (2012) deals with PE. He first generally defines what PE is and how it can be cost effective. Next, he explains how PE works in the TM environment and what differentiates PE from human translation. A sensible use of MT is only possible if the output is post-edited and the quality of the MT output is reasonable. He concludes that PE needs to be learned and that good post-editors will develop their skills with training, experiences, and good self-assessments. Finally, he adds that a sceptical opinion towards MT systems may even be good for post-editors – a contrary opinion to many academic writers and studies. These two articles are written for a target audience that knows a great deal about translation but only little about MT. While both cases only provide a rudimentary presentation of the different approaches to MT, the knowledge about TM systems is taken as a given. Further, the titles[21] of the articles already suggest that the target audience is sceptical towards MT, but that MT is nothing to be afraid of.

The second issue is a special issue on MT and contains five articles on the topic. The first article collection by Keller et al. (2016) deals with technical aspects of the integration of MT in the TM systems *Across v6.3*, *SDL Trados Studio 2015*, and *STAR*. The next article by Rüth et al. (2016) presents two reports with practical experiences of MT in real life professional translation. Rüth reports on the positive experiences she and her colleagues have had with the use of MT

---

[20] An opinion which is not shared by me nor by most empirical studies on post-editing.

[21] "Den Tiger reiten" which translates literally as "ride the tiger" and figuratively roughly as "tame the beast", and "Postediting – Schreckgespenst oder Perspektive?" which means "Postediting – Ghoul or Perspective?".

suggestions in the TM tool on a word/phrase basis rather than on a segment basis. If the automatically suggested word/phrase is reasonable, the translator can approve the suggested translation and continue with the rest of the segment; if it is not, the translator can ignore the suggestion and translates the word/phrase from scratch. Hunger and Altmann, on the other hand, present one good and one bad example of client behaviour. One client insisted on the use of the MT output and only wanted to pay the price of a fuzzy segment for the MT segments (with partly poor quality); an unreasonable amount for MT segments that needed major changes. Another client judged the MT output as suggestions and paid as much for MT segments as if they were translated from scratch – the translators were free to choose whether or not they wanted to use the MT output. Muegge (2016) explains in his article how well-trained MT systems can become available for small- and medium-sized companies. After explaining statistical MT, traditional approaches to MT training, and the functionality of cloud-based MT, he advises the reader to maintain the TM data before feeding it to the MT system, to invest into (human) training courses, and to keep expectations realistic. Nitzke (2016a) explores the differences between PE and proof-reading, special characteristics of the PE task regarding the main occurring error types those that hardly occur in MT output, different PE requirements (light vs. full PE). She concludes that PE is not comparable to traditional proof-reading, but rather a special form of translation and that the translator/post-editor might have to advise the clients if they cannot entirely judge what post-editing MT output means. The last article on PE and MT in this issue by Ebling (2016) deals with the automatic processing of natural language into sign language and vice versa. The technology could be useful in everyday situations when a sign language interpreter is not available.

According to the content and the details of the articles, we can observe a change in the reception of MT and PE. While the articles in the 2012 issue provide more of an overview and suggest that the target audience might be uninformed and insecure about the topics, the articles in the 2016 issue are much more specialised and show that PE and MT have arrived in the everyday work environment of professional translators. This attitude was maintained by the BDÜ, which published a Best Practice guide (Ottmann 2017) for professional translators and interpreters covering all topics relevant for the market, including a whole chapter on PE.

The insecurity of the translation sector, which was already expressed in the earlier publications of the BDÜ, might explain the following publication (also available online[22] since 2012); a rather bad example of information about MT

---

[22] http://www.bdue.de/uploads/media/2796_BDUe__Pressedossier_MenschMaschine_10.2012. pdf last accessed 6 July 2017

published by the BDÜ (2012). The article evaluated the use of Google Translate, back then a statistical MT system. The study deemed the programme a great online source for private communication, e.g., for holiday preparation or as an aid while on holiday but insinuated that the free programme was not suitable and reached its limits very quickly in business communication. The BDÜ article concludes that it can be embarrassing and bad for business to send error-laden e-mails or, even worse, run badly translated websites. (cf. ibid.: 9) Although the latter points are very true, the study itself and the way it was conducted have to be treated very critically. Professional translators were asked to evaluate MT output for common language texts (newspaper articles about politics and menus/recipes), a part of a manual for a technical gadget, general terms and conditions of an online shop, and a business e-mail. Although different domains were covered, only one translator evaluated each text per language combination (German into English, Spanish, Polish, and Chinese) and each domain was represented by only one text. Further, the texts created by the MT system were evaluated using a pointing system that is equal to the German grading system (1 to 6, with 1 being the best grade and 6 the worst) in the following categories: correct content, grammar, spelling, idiomacy, and overall satisfaction with the text. The grades for the MT output texts were very bad for most text types – except in the category spelling. However, this way of grading the texts is very subjective and does not represent what is actually important for MT output. From a research point of view, the question of interest should rather be: When the MT output is used in a professional environment, how much effort does it take to turn it into a reasonable target? In the BDÜ study, PE was also acknowledged as a necessary step to achieving a meaning target text (cf. ibid.), but was not explained or referred to in detail. The advantage of the study is that it shows translators and potential translation vendors that Google Translate is not almighty and that it cannot work without the help of a human translator. However, automatic translation is a rapidly developing branch and it has to be acknowledged how far the field has developed and that the systems can work quite adequately. Further, it should have been made more explicit that free online MT systems do not represent the best MT systems have to offer. Systems that are trained for one text domain and for one company will achieve much better results – assuming that they are used for the texts they were trained for: A system that was trained for manuals of household appliances will probably not produce good translations for medical package inserts.

Finally, the BDÜ has hosted three conferences so far that dealt with the professional fields of translation and interpreting. The first two were called "Übersetzen in die Zukunft" ("translating into the future") and covered current developments in the field. The first conference, in 2009, included one presentation about PE and two presentation on MT (Baur et al. 2009).[23] At the second conference in 2012, two posters and four presentations dealt with MT, while no presentation directly focused on PE[24]. The third conference was held in 2014, in cooperation with the *International Federation of Translators (FIT) World Congress*, and was subsumed under the heading "Man vs. Machine? The Future of Translators, Interpreters, and Terminologists". As the main topic of the conference was MT, over 20 presentations dealt with the topic, six presentations focused on PE, and another four posters were presented on the topics. Further, the panel discussion's topic was "Machine Translation – Blessing, Curse, or Something In Between?". Conclusively, the topical focus of the conference also reflects that the topics MT and PE have become more important in recent years and are now taken seriously by the community.[25]

Taking the work of the BDÜ as a mirror of the German translation and interpreting market, the publications and conferences presented in this chapter show that MT and PE reached the German job market once and for all during the last five years. The technology is no longer ignored and it is not only international organisations and businesses that employ a few post-editors or freelancers for PE; it is now a feature of the entire profession. Although many professional translators still seem anxious about or unmotivated by MT technology, many seem to be accepting that it is part of the professional field now, which is reflected in the aforementioned best practice guidelines and a publication that deals exclusively with MT and PE (Porsiel 2017).

Of course, other translation associations also consider and discuss the topics of MT and PE, either in articles in their magazines or in articles, white-papers, etc. on their websites. The American Translation Association (ATA), for example, published two articles about PE in the last volume of their Chronicle in 2015. The first article by Cassemiro (2015) describes how a self-trained, rule-based MT system can be used as a tool for translations from scratch. Further, he emphasises that translators should not be afraid of PE and MT and should not fight it. Instead, they should embrace the new technology and use it to their advantage in order to meet the current needs of the market. In the second article, Green (2015) argues

---

[23]Unfortunately, the conference programme is not available online anymore. Hence, the information about the programme was taken from the conference proceedings.

[24]BDÜ. „Übersetzen in die Zukunft". Online programme. http://uebersetzen-in-die-zukunft.de/util/download.php?art=konf12_dl&dokument=2754. last accessed 10 October 2016 (11:09).

[25]This is only one of many examples. The IATIS conference, for example, hosted a conference on 'Innovation Paths in Translation and Intercultural Studies' that hosted 12 presentations on PE as opposed to one presentation three years earlier.

that PE might be such an ill-received task, because the MT systems do not learn from their mistakes and translators have to correct the same errors over and over again. After presenting a brief overview of the history of PE, he, therefore, introduces three interactive PE systems that learn from the changes made by a post-editor. Both articles allude to the translators' resistance to cope with PE and MT. While Cassemiro, on the one hand, encourages the translators to be open towards the new technologies, Green rather acknowledges the negative attitudes of the translators. At the end of his article, however, Green encourages translators to give those more interactive solutions another chance.

4.5 Post-editing training

Although the field is thriving, little has been published solely on PE training yet. While many empirical studies conclude with implications on what needs to be integrated in PE training or that PE training is necessary to educate professional post-editors, only few publications focused on how to design PE training. The available publications on the topic will be introduced in the following chapter.

Probably the first publication to focus on PE training was written by O'Brien (2002). First, she explains why PE training would be necessary as an addition to regular translation training. There is still a growing demand for translations, PE skills are probably acquired gradually and are different from translation skills, and translators who are familiar with MT and PE will probably be less hostile towards the topics, which in turn is necessary for successful PE. O'Brien (2002) further argues that although some characteristics of PE and MT are contrary to human translation, translators should be the ones trained for PE. However, this training should be optional for students seeking a translation degree. Next, she argues that there are certain skills that well-trained post-editors need in addition to the skills well-trained translators have, like the ability to use macros and code dictionaries for the MT system, knowledge of MT and a positive attitude towards MT, the ability to use terminology management systems (a skill many translators already acquire when they learn how to use TM systems) and solid text linguistic skills, knowledge about pre-editing and controlled languages, and at least some basic programming skills. Finally, she proposes a PE module that could be integrated into translator training, which would best be offered in a late undergraduate stadium (B.A. degree) or even only in postgraduate training (M.A. degree). One half (approximately) of this module would focus on theoretical issues, including an introduction to PE, MT, and controlled languages, basic programming skills, and higher terminology management as well as text linguistic skills. The other half of the module would include practical exercises for prefer-ably all language combinations the individual student studies and with different MT systems, as well as combining MT output with TM tools, using different PE guidelines, and using terminology management tools. O'Brien additionally in-troduces some ideas on how practical experiences in controlled authoring tools, corpus analysis tools, and programming could be integrated.

Belam (2003) introduces a workshop on PE guidelines that was held in the scope of a machine-assisted translation course. The students were in the last year of their undergraduate programme in Modern Languages. One lecture of this course was on basic PE knowledge and required the students to submit one practical assignment, in which they post-edited a text and commented on their procedure. In the scope of this assignment, students started to demand more precise PE guidelines, which was the starting point of the discussion workshop, where the focus was also on different PE types (rapid, minimal and full as sug-gested by Allen (2003)). In the workshop, the students were given a text to post-edit in groups and then asked to develop PE guidelines. The most obvious rules were defined immediately and without much discussion, such as "Correct any word which had not been translated." Guidelines for less obvious errors in the MT output, however, were much harder to define and error categories had to be summarised in one guideline. Similarly, it became more difficult to decide which rule needed to be applied to which PE type (cf. ibid.: 2-3). Belam (cf. ibid.: 3-4) reports that students were much better at formulating the guidelines and match-ing these to the PE type as soon as they started to construct a scenario for the PE job. In the end, two guidelines – one for rapid PE and one for minimal PE (full PE was abandoned at the beginning of the workshop, because this would require the same quality standards as human translation) – were developed with three to four dos and don'ts (cf. ibid.: 7).

Depraetere (2010) analyses a corpus of ten post-edited texts in her study. She asked ten students to post-edit a text from English into French consisting of 2230 words (110 segments) of which half were pre-translated by a customised rule-based MT system and the other half by a customised statistical MT system[26]. The participants, who were all French native speakers and were receiving train-ing to become translators, post-edited in a web-based online tool. The aim of this study was to determine what problems occur in texts post-edited by translation students who are not trained in PE, to assess what students should be taught in PE classes and what they intuitively deem necessary for correction. Hence,

---

[26]Unfortunately, the author makes no comments of the quality or the differences of those to MT systems.

they only received few PE instructions and a few examples of necessary and un-necessary PE corrections. Unfortunately, the results of this study are not quanti-fied and only observations are reported. MT translations are usually very literal translations; nonetheless, Depraetere observes that students did not change the phrasing of the texts as long as it was not incorrect, which means that the stu-dents did not change anything just to improve the flow of the translation, even though there may have been a more idiomatic solution. Hence, she concludes that it is not necessary to over-emphasise in classes that style should not be con-sidered in PE. The same applies to terminology – the MT output is accepted as long as it is not wrong, even if a better solution exists. The students were slightly careless when it came to formatting issues and capitalisation. Depraetere claims that the most striking observation was that students were often too careless to-wards improving the MT output, as they missed numerous mistakes made by the MT system. Some students did not even realise that some source text units were untranslated. No clear strategy could be detected concerning grammatically in-correct verbs, which would therefore need to be addressed in a PE class. In her conclusions, Depraetere summarises that trainees need to be confronted with typical MT errors so that they do not blindly rely on the MT output. Further, the need for consistency and formal accuracy needs to be highlighted.[27] She further states that PE trainers have to keep in mind that students might not produce per-fect translations, because they have less experience than professionals. Therefore, it might be easier for students to accept imperfections. All in all, this study gave valuable insights into what might be necessary to prioritise in PE training. How-ever, the participant number was low and there might be other issues in other language combinations. Hence, more data need to be collected in order to paint a clearer picture.

As discussed in a previous chapter, Pym (2013: 494–497) also discusses teach-ing technology (including MT) to translators. First he points out that it is most important to learn how to learn to use new tools, because most will be outdated within a few years. Further, it seems important that (future) translators learn to assess which data can be trusted and which cannot be trusted. It is dangerous to blindly trust MT output, while disregarding and overanalysing all MT output does not contribute to the original purpose of MT, namely increasing produc-

---

[27]This is something we also observed and reported in our studies. In the data set at hand, e.g., some participants did not change the translation of nurse as *Krankenschwester* (female nurse, as suggested by the MT system) into *Krankenpfleger* (male nurse) in the PE task (cf. Čulo et al. (2014)). Further, we observed inconsistencies in terminology in the PE task in a study with domain-specific texts. These inconsistencies were introduced by the MT output and were often not eliminated by the participants (cf. Čulo & Nitzke 2016).

tivity. Additionally, the overall text as the greatest macro-unit has to be kept in mind and special revision strategies should be developed. Pym (cf. ibid.: 497–499) further advises that the technologies should be used as often as possible during training, that the classrooms need to be sufficiently equipped, that it might be helpful to work in pairs or groups (to assess and reflect on their own translation processes) and that working with field experts would be very valuable.

Another study on PE guidelines is presented by Flanagan & Christensen (2014). They asked three MA students to retrospectively interpret the PE guidelines for publishable quality developed by TAUS and CNGL[28], which the students had to use for their final assessment. The aim of the study was to see whether the guidelines were straightforward as well as easy to understand and apply. The module, in which this final assessment was included, was a Case Module, which the students could choose in the third semester of their Master's degree instead of a work placement. This module consisted of two workshops: The first introduced MT and PE, the second was a hands-on session, in which the students learnt to use the technology. Further, they had to complete two assessments. The first was for training purposes - students had to post-edit according to guidelines that aimed at an output that was good enough to understand the content. The second assessment, which this study focuses on, was the final exam that was graded. They had to post-edit a medical text for publishable quality and write a ten-page reflective report. Three weeks later, the students were asked to come for a retrospective interview on the guidelines. This interview and the post-edited texts were taken into consideration in this study. (cf. ibid.: 261-262) The findings showed that the students had problems interpreting the guidelines which was on the one hand due to little PE experience in general, but also caused by the wording in the guidelines themselves. A guideline was considered problematic, when a) at least two students did not adhere to the guideline or ignored it, b) at least two students misinterpreted the guideline, or c) one of both (cf. ibid.: 263-264). After the analysis of the interview and the PE products, the introductory part and all guidelines except two were classified as problematic. Hence, Flanagan and Christensen adjusted the order and the wording of the guidelines accordingly so that these became easier to understand and apply.

Kenny & Doherty (2014) describe in their article how statistical MT should be integrated in translation training. Translation technology has changed the translation profession and professional translators need to decide which translation technology they want/need to apply. Accordingly, translation trainees need to learn to handle these technologies to make educated decisions, when and

---

[28]Translation Automation User Society (TAUS) and Centre for Global Intelligent Content (CNGL)

whether to use which translation tool. Surveys on the translation market do not agree on the importance of MT and PE (and most studies do not take freelance translators into consideration). Hence, Kenny and Doherty (ibid: 286) conclude in regard to translation training that "there is a growing demand for post-editing services, but that it may not be wise for those who are about to graduate to focus on post-editing at the expense of other 'traditional' translation skills." Further, they discourage post-editors from using free and online-based MT systems, because they have many disadvantages especially concerning data protection and security. On the other hand, Do-It-Yourself statistical MT systems like Moses are very hard to implement for people with little experience in computer science, which applies to many translators and translation students. Therefore, they suggest the use of cloud-based statistical MT. The user can use his/her own monolingual and bilingual data (sometimes as an addition to the data of the service provider) to train the MT system and the software does not have to be installed locally. Further, the user can go through all stages of the MT cycle, which is especially interesting for student training purposes: he/she has to upload the data, train and test the engine, intervene to improve the MT quality, retrain and deploy the system in the end. The user interface is usually easy to handle, developers can interact with reviewers and testers, and the systems can be kept private, shared with others, or can be published for everyone to use. (cf. ibid.: 287-290)

In the accompanying paper, Doherty & Kenny (2014) provide more information on the syllabus they integrated in the curriculum at Dublin City University. Half of the module on translation technologies focuses on training how to implement and use statistical MT. The content was delivered partly as lectures and partly as hands-on sessions in labs and included the following topics (ibid.: 299-300):

- brief history of MT

- rule-based MT (basic architectures, linguistic problems, etc.)

- statistic MT (basic architecture, alignment, n-gram processing, models)

- MT evaluation (human and automatic)

- pre- and post-processing (controlled languages, post-editing)

- professional issues with MT like ethics, payment, etc.

The knowledge of the students was tested in an assignment that was worth 60% of the module grade. The students had to create and evaluate a statistical MT system by themselves with the skills and knowledge they acquired in the lectures and lab sessions. They had to find training data, train an engine on a cloud-based platform, test the engine with texts from the same domain as the training data and with another domain, evaluate the output, consider ways of improving the output (e.g. more training data or the use of controlled language), use those potential improvements, retest the engine, and evaluate the output. The students had to describe how they proceeded and critically assessed their processes (cf. ibid.: 300-301). To evaluate the course outline, Doherty and Kenny (cf. ibid.: 305-307) used a ten-item self-efficacy questionnaire that the students had to complete at the beginning and at the end of the course. In total, 29 students participated and the questionnaire proved that self-efficacy of the students increased significantly during the course. In their written assessment, many students reported on technical problems and evaluation issues. However, the students completed the task successfully. (cf. ibid.: 307-310)

All in all, little research has been published on PE training. O'Brien's (2002) early study presents a reasonable outline on how to design a PE module, but detailed course contents are not provided. While some theoretical thoughts and some results from final exams in PE courses were mentioned, the Doherty & Kenny (2014) course outline on integrating statistical MT is very detailed, seems very reasonable and could be adapted easily at other universities. However, none of the above mentioned publications describes to a full extent how PE as a translation task should be taught. As we have seen in §4.2, numerous process research studies focus on PE. These findings need to be included in PE training. Hence, PE training is a topic that still needs to be addressed more thoroughly in the future so that process research results can be used in training and trained post-editors can be used in process studies.

In summary, both MT and PE are rapidly developing fields. While fully-automatic MT has been an unfulfilled dream for many decades now, PE has only recently found its way into professional translation practice (although, some counterexamples show that it has been around longer than generally appreciated) and translation science. The developments and the attention given to MT and PE in translation in the last five to ten years indicate that MT and PE has come to stay.

5 Problem solving in psychology and translation studies

This study will not only focus on the PE task itself, but in particular on problem solving behaviour during the PE task compared to the TfS task. The aim of this chapter is to define the terms *problem* and *problem solving* in regard to TfS and PE. To this end, the literature on problem solving in translation was analysed. However, it quickly became obvious that, depending on the instance, the term *problem* is used in different ways and maybe sometimes too carelessly in translation studies. Therefore, the terms *problem* and *problem solving* will first be approached from the perspective of psychology, in which problem solving is a thriving field. Then, the approaches in translation studies will be introduced and the insights from both fields will subsequently be combined to define problem solving in TfS and PE. First, however, a general introduction will be provided and the chapter will be clearly outlined.

During our life, we are forced to deal with problems on a daily basis. Although, over time, we familiarise ourselves with the problem solving strategies that we need for everyday problems, new problems regularly arise. We might not consciously realise that we are dealing with a problem each time we encounter one: e.g. "How do I get to work?", which includes decisions on questions like "What means of transportation do I take? Which is the right way? When do I have to leave so that I do not arrive too late?". Once we find a solution to the problem, we can use this solution again and the situation no longer poses a problem for us every morning – as long as the basic situation does not change: if we have to take a bus, because our bicycle is broken, a new problematic situation arises. Additionally, problems may occur although we have been in the same situation before ("I'm hungry on my lunch break, but I forgot my lunch at home. Where can I get something to eat now?"); and some problems may seem insurmountable ("I lost my job after fifteen years and all my applications for a new one are failing. Will I ever find work again?").

Due to its ubiquitous nature, problem solving is not only an issue in our everyday life, but also in many social and political settings, as well as almost every scientific discipline. Problem solving methods and strategies need to be shared so that science can evolve and not every individual has to overcome the same problems over and over again. But the processes underlying problem solving itself are of central interest in many fields: In mathematics, statistics, and physics, it is a basic feature of the discipline with which to learn the required strategies to manually, or with the help of software, calculate arising numeric problems (e. g. Engel 1998 "Problem solving strategies", Kamal 2010 "1000 solved problems in modern physics" and Quirk et al. 2013 "Excel 2010 for physical sciences statistics; a guide to solving practical problems"[1]). Computer science frequently deals with problem solving and much literature has been published in special areas like artificial intelligence (e.g. Zhang & Zhang 2004 "Agent-based hybrid intelligent systems: An agent-based framework for complex problem solving") and on how to solve problems in or with the help of programming languages (e.g. Hanly et al. 2013 "Problem solving and program design in C" or Savitch & Carrano 2012 "Java: An introduction to problem solving & programming"). Specific models and methods have been developed to help solve problems in engineering (e.g. Gómez-Pérez 2010 "TRIZ for engineers; Enabling inventive problem solving") and economics (e.g. Gómez-Pérez 2010"Acquisition and understanding of process knowledge using problem solving methods"). Medicine deals with strategies to diagnose illnesses accurately and rapidly (e.g. Aghamohammadi & Rezaei 2012 "Clinical cases in primary immunodeficiency diseases: A problem-solving approach") and pharmacy tries to use nature to find cures to illnesses (e.g. Mehlhorn 2011 "Nature helps - How plants and other organisms contribute to solve health problems").

In the following, two fields will be analysed to determine a theoretical framework: problem solving in psychology (§5.2) and in translation studies (§5.3). Psychology was selected for analysis because it, just like translation, does not belong to the hard sciences but deals with the concept of problems and problem solving also on a theoretical basis. Finally, psychology does not only apply the concepts, but also deals with their very nature. Problem solving is a much discussed topic in psychology. Hence, it is not the scope of this chapter to describe every detail and approach in the field, but only a selection will be introduced. This selection concentrates in particular on notions that can be related to translation studies. The psychological theories and findings will be used to evaluate and extend the work on problem solving in translation studies (§5.4). But first, we will attempt to define the term *problem* and differentiate between *problem solving* and *decision making* – two terms that are often used synonymously.

---

[1]At this point, the titles of the books are specified in the running text to emphasise their problem solving content, although this differs from the standard citation method.

5.1 Defining the term *problem* and differentiating between *problem solving* and *decision making*

Dörner (1987: 10) describes a *problem* as a state which is not desirable for the individual, but that the individual does not have the means to change at that moment. Three basic components characterise a problem: First, there is an undesired initial state. Then, there is a desired final state. And finally, there is a hurdle between these two states that prevents the transformation from the initial state to the desired final state for the time being. Further, Dörner (ibid.: 10-11) differentiates between *problems* and *tasks*. *Tasks* are mental challenges which the individual knows how to solve. This means that a task lacks the third property of a problem, namely the hurdle, to overcome the initial state. While it might be a problem for a third grader or for someone who has never actively learned to calculate to divide 625 by 25, it becomes a simple task only for people who are experienced in division (this might not even be a task for people who had to learn square numbers by heart at some point in their life, but something they can recall from memory).

Jonassen (2000: 65) also argues that problems consist of more characteristics than initial and desired state. While he agrees that there needs to be a gap between the current state and the desired (unknown) target state, he adds that a social, intellectual or cultural motivation is required to bridge the gap. "Finding the unknown is the process of problem solving" (ibid.). If nobody has the desire to bridge the gap, problem solving is not necessary.

The concepts *problem solving* and *decision making* are often closely related and are regularly mentioned in the same breath. Strohschneider (2006: 577) states that problem solving and decision making are often regarded as synonyms, but that in his opinion, decisions are only one (often central) measure (or a collection of measures) in the problem solving process. The difference between the two terms does not seem to be immediately obvious. Therefore, the focus will be on defining *problem solving* and *decision making* and deciding which term is more appropriate for further discussion of the translation process.

In *The Dictionary of Psychology*, the term *decision making* is defined as the "[a]bility to make independent and intelligent choices, a process which counsellors seek to enhance" (Corsini 2002: 253), while *problem solving* is described as "[p]rocedures, overt or covert, in the solutions of problems" (ibid.: 762) with different references to other problem solving categories. These short definitions highlight that decision making is one activity in the human mind, whereas problem solving is a more complex pattern.

The Oxford *Dictionary of Psychology* provides more detailed definitions for the two terms with an increased focus on the field of psychology. *Decision making* is defined as

> [t]he act or process of choosing a preferred option or course of action from a set of alternatives. It precedes and underpins almost all deliberate or voluntary behaviour. Three major classes of theories have guided research into decision making: normative, descriptive (or positive), and prescriptive theories (Colman 2009: 217).

while *problem solving* is described as

> [c]ognitive processing directed at finding solutions to well-defined problems, such as the Tower of Hanoi, Wason selection task, or a water-jar problem, by performing a sequence of operations. Problem solving by means of logic or logical analysis is usually called reasoning.[2] (ibid.: 693).

The latter definition signalises that logical problem solving is called *reasoning*. *Reasoning*, in turn, is defined as the "[c]ognitive processing directed at finding solutions to problems by applying formal rules of logics or some other rational procedure" (ibid.: 620). If one attends translation classes at an undergraduate level, one often hears that a translation solution was selected, because "it sounds fitting" or sometimes, that something was disregarded, because the person "sensed it was not correct due to a feeling for the language". However, these seemingly intuitive arguments decline with growing experience and knowledge about translation and language, because professional translators know the rules of language and translation. They know about grammar, registers, text type and domain conventions, etc. They can, hence, tackle a problem through reasoning.

Returning to the difference between decision making and problem solving: The main difference that becomes clear in these definitions is that decision making is often a one-step operation while problem solving embodies more than one operation. This point is also featured in Koppenjan & Klijn (2004), who begin their book on problem solving and decision making (both terms are used in the subtitle of the book) for the management of uncertainties in networks with a short "[e]xample of wicked problems: the greenhouse effect" (ibid.: 2). Although the example does not aim to explain the difference between problem solving

---

[2]In the following chapters, it will become obvious that problem solving does not only apply to well-defined but also to ill-defined problems (both terms will be described in more detail in §5.3). However, the definition fits its purposes for these initial considerations

and decision making, it indirectly points out an interesting fact: In such complex problems, it is possible and necessary to make a lot of decisions to improve the situation. However, it takes a while (if it is possible at all) to solve the problem of the "greenhouse effect" – it does not matter on which political level which decision is made; solving the problem (a) takes time and (b) requires thousands of people to participate, accept and adhere to the decision. Conclusively, a decision does not necessarily solve a problem, but is one part of the problem solving process. The world is filled with complex problems that force the decision makers to form networks. Similarly, complex translation jobs are seldom handled by a single person, but include project manager(s), numerous translators, proof-readers and, potentially, even more people.

Similarly, Jonassen (2000) integrates decision making problems into his scale for the degree of complexity of problems. This scale starts with very well-defined problems and ends with very ill-defined complex problems (e. g. "Should I move in order to take another job" (ibid.: 76) – see further information in the next subchapter) – and simple decision making problems are more complex than logical problems or algorithms problems and often include more factors to be considered. Furthermore, what appear to be simple cases of decision making with only one answer ("Should abortion be banned?" – the answer to the decision is either yes or no), are sometimes categorised as dilemmas and are the most difficult problems to solve. If a decision is made, it does not solve the personal dilemma of whether abortion is legal or not and to what degree. Further, parts of the population to whom the law applies will not be satisfied with the decision.

However, there are theories in decision making that deal with complex decision making situations. As an example, one of these deals with *phased decision strategies* that suggest that, in complex decision making situations, not only one decision making rule is used but rather different rules are applied successively or even randomly (Jungermann et al. 2010). Therefore, decision making is also considered a multiple-phase activity.

Wilss (1994) is one of a few in translation who discusses the difference between problem solving and decision making, which to him are "not identical", but "occasionally equated with each other since the boundary between the two cannot always be clearly drawn" (ibid.: 132). He argues that problem solving is the wider concept, that decision making is part of problem solving, and that decision making processes only start when all factors and criteria for the decision have been defined. However, both activities are essential in the translation process.

The terms *problem solving* and *decision making* are not used consistently. However, a tendency seems to be that decision making is used for one step operations, where one out of two or many options needs to be chosen, while problem solving often includes more steps. Further, problem solving involves a hurdle between initial and desired state to make the situation problematic, which is not necessary in the case of decision making. Hence, the term *problem solving* is more suited to translation processes than the term *decision making*, because we have an initial state (the source text) and a desired final state (the target text) and do not immediately know how to get there (hurdle) – an extensive discussion will follow in §5.3 and §5.4. Decisions have to be made for single translation items, as many possible translation equivalents exist in the target language. The translator can make these decisions consciously or subconsciously. However, the choice is not always obvious to the translator. Hence, a hurdle exists between source and target text, and the translator then has to solve a translation problem. How can we decide when and why a translation unit is a decision or a problem? And is translation generally rather a decision making or a problem solving activity? Can a clear line be drawn in a construct as complex as translation? The following analysis will attempt to shed some light on these questions.

5.2 Problem solving in psychology

Problem solving is an important sub-field in psychology. As Funke (2006a: XXI) describes, problem solving is viewed as a part of the thinking process. Thinking is considered a higher cognitive function that takes advantage of simpler cognitive functions like perception, learning, and memory. Further, thinking has different appearances: In logical deductions, the human mind makes deductive judgements; conclusions for future events are drawn when judging probabilities; thinking with problem solving in mind helps to fill gaps for planned actions; and creative thinking creates new and helpful connections between what is already known.

Before we turn to problem solving, the general connection of thinking and language will be briefly described according to Dörner (2006). While some philosophers like Plato, Aristotle, and Wilhelm von Humboldt have stated that thinking and language are clearly the same – thoughts are expressions of inner speech – others such as the scientists Faraday and Einstein strongly disagree with this assumption. In their opinion, speech is only a means to transmit information and even interferes with the thinking process (which can be demonstrated, e.g., when using think-aloud protocols[3] in psychological studies: some participants think in

---

[3] Find more information on think-aloud protocols in §7.1.1

a more structured way when they have to express their thoughts aloud, while others are delayed in their thinking process). These positions could not be further apart. However, a combination of both seemingly contradictory positions may hold the truth: Thinking is not possible without language, and thinking has nothing to do with language (cf. ibid.: 619-621). Complicated thinking processes are probably not possible without language, but even simple, non-language phases of thinking, e.g. during sleep, have their origin in memories of language-based thinking phases (cf. ibid.: 640). When we go to the bus stop closest to our home, perform other routine operations, or operations that are similar to what we have done before, we do not have to verbalise those thoughts in our head and still make it to the bus stop safely (cf. ibid.: 635-636), which is an argument for thinking without language.[4]

Thinking can sometimes be categorised as a problem solving activity, considering that one has to find a path between a starting point and a final point. However, if the path has been created once before, it is not problem solving, it is solely remembering. Memories, however, are part of the thinking process as well. Further, thinking also creates opinions and ideologies which, on the other hand, influence our problem solving behaviour Dörner (2006: 621–623). So, we can conclude that not all thinking is problem solving, but all problem solving is thinking. If we remember the solution to a problem, because we encountered the problem before, there is no hurdle between the present state and the desired state. We need to think to get to the desired state, but we do not have to solve a problem (again).

If we assume that thinking is most often connected with language, problem solving has to be connected with language, too. Language is not fixed. Many words have numerous lexical meanings which we can apply accordingly in everyday language. Depending on education, profession and interests, our lexicon is specialised in different fields and every person has an individual lexicon. A gardener may be able to differentiate between various apple trees; this does not make him a different thinker, but rather a more informed person from whom we can learn. Misunderstandings are part of our everyday life and we learn through experience that we have to adapt our speech (and texts) according to who we are talking to, e. g. other experts or laypersons. Hence, our way of thinking is not solely determined by the language we grow up with and which we develop over time – a gardener might not solve a mathematical problem much differently than

---

[4]However, in my opinion, this cannot be categorised as thinking, because it is an automated action during which we can verbalise other thoughts in our head. I would argue that if anything really new happens to us – nothing similar has ever happened before – we would verbally think about it first (setting aside reflexes that might intervene in the situation).

a dog breeder – but there are tendencies (Dörner 2006: 627–628). Accordingly, problems are perceived differently depending on our life experiences, which will be discussed in more detail later in this chapter, but also depending on the vocabulary we developed during our lives and the semantic connections we have with these words.

Coming back to the theory of problem solving, problems are basically categorised as well-structured (or well-defined) and ill-structured (or ill-defined) problems. Well-structured problems "require a finite number of concepts, rules, and principles being studied to a constrained problem situation" (Jonassen 2000: 67). These problems are also known as transformation problems and are often encountered, for example, in school and university environments to check whether students have studied the subject and have familiarised themselves with the subject's contents and strategies. All elements of the problem are presented to the problem solver in the initial state. The operators required to arrive at the solution are known (or should be known) to the problem solver, so (s)he "only" has to apply rules and principles which (s)he has previously learned in advance[5]. Finally, the desired target state is sometimes even known as well (e. g. in mathematical text problems).

Unfortunately, well-structured problems are hardly encountered in real-life situations. Problems do not usually possess a predictable or concurrent solution in private or work situations. The steps to solve the problems were not specifically learned in advance; experience from different domains is required – more experience in (one of) the crucial domains the problem is situated in will probably help to solve ill-defined problems more easily – and personal opinions and judgements are often necessary. Furthermore, different solutions, approaches or even no solution at all are possible outcomes when trying to solve an ill-structured problem. Accordingly, the solution of the problem cannot be assessed as simply correct or incorrect (cf. ibid.: 67). While "[w]ell-structured problems focus on correct, efficient solutions, [...] ill-structured problems focus more on decision articulation and argumentation" (ibid.: 73). However, this is only a preliminary division and further categorisations are necessary to embrace the variety and complexity of problem categorisation (cf. ibid.: 64).

While much research focused on well-defined problems in the early days of problem solving research, studies on complex problem solving have their origins in the late 1960s, early 1970s and deal with ill-defined problems (Funke 2006b:

---

[5] Many pupils, who are not very strong in mathematics, will probably agree that it is not as easy as it might seem to apply mathematical rules and principles to algorithmic problems.

376). According to Funke (cf. ibid.: 379-380), a problem becomes a complex problem when it fulfils the following five characteristics:

- *complexity* – numerous variables are involved

- *interconnectedness* – the variables are connected

- *dynamism* – the problem changes over time

- *non-transparency* – not all the information necessary to solve the problem is available to the problem solver

- *multiple aims* – more than one criterion needs to be optimised

Not all of these characteristics are unique for complex problems – some apply to simple problems as well. It is self-evident that problems can be differentiated with regard to the difficulty of the problem. However, it is less evident to decide what makes a problem difficult. A term which is often referred to in the context is *complexity*.[6] The more variables need to be accounted for in a problem, the more difficult it becomes. However, another aspect that needs to be taken into account is how these variables are *connected*. Fifty interconnected variables might form a more difficult problem than 100 unconnected variables, because interconnected variables influence each other. *Dynamic* problems change while they are being solved. They are not static tasks, but processes that need to be steered into the right directions so that the initial situation improves. In the problem solving scenario called "fire fighting", the participants are asked to extinguish a burning wall in a computer game. However, it might be possible for the wall to start to burn in another area. Hence, the fire cannot be fought sequentially and the problem changes over time. Further, a problem becomes more difficult when it is *not transparent*, which means that not all information necessary to solve the problem is available to the problem solver. Therefore, decisions are made with uncertainty in these situations. Complex problems often pursue not only one purpose, but many (*multiple aims*). Consequently, the evaluation process is also more complex – the solution cannot be judged as correct or incorrect (cf. Funke 2006b: 399–410).

In another attempt to categorise problem types, Jonassen (2000) describes eleven different types of problems, which were created based on 100 problem scenarios, starting with very well-structured problems that result in correct or incorrect

---

[6]The terminology in this discourse has room for improvement, e.g. it is difficult to claim that one characteristic of a complex problem is its complexity. However, it would go beyond the scope of this dissertation to make adjustments.

solutions (which can be evaluated easily) and ending with the most ill-structured problem types, which have no single, exact solution and the solutions are difficult to evaluate:

logical problems: abstract tests of reasoning, like matchstick puzzles, the Tower of Hanoi puzzle or a Rubic's cube®; they are usually not embedded in any authentic context and are therefore abstract and hardly transferable

algorithmic problems (like multiplying or statistical testing)

story problems: algorithmic problems presented in a story; the variables and the mathematical operator have to be selected by the problem solver, e. g. how long does it take Lorry A to overtake Lorry B

rule-using problems: problems with correct answers but different possible approaches to solutions; can be of different complexity, such as expanding a recipe for more people, finding information with a search engine, or card and board games

decision making problems: select one option from many alternatives with different consequences; can vary a lot in terms of complexity and may include risk and uncertainty

troubleshooting problems: among the most common everyday problems, e. g. mechanics who fix broken cars; require the problem solver to have different skills and knowledge

diagnosis-solution problems: any kind of medical diagnosis and treatment proposal

strategic performance: "involves real-time, complex and integrated activity structures, where the performers use a number of tactics to meet a more complex and ill-structured strategy while maintaining situational awareness" (ibid.: 79); e. g. flying an aeroplane, arguing in front of a judge, playing professional sports

situated case-policy problems: real-life, job-related problems where analysing situated, complex case problems is essential for the work; the goals cannot be strictly defined, little is known about how to approach the problem, there is no overall agreement on what a good solution needs to include; e. g. international relations problems or business problems

design problems: creating a product or system; there are only vague requirements on the output, no predefined approach to the solution, and general
and domain-specific knowledge needs to be included; usually do not have
clear standards on evaluation; e. g. writing a poem, designing a bird table
/ bridge / vehicle that flies, developing a curriculum for a university

dilemmas: personal, social, and ethical dilemmas; often appear as decision making, but are the most ill-structured, because there are no solutions that sat-
isfies everybody, compromises are necessary, often involves a large group
of people; e. g. should healthcare be regulated privately or by the government, resolving the Middle East conflict

The ranking is not related to how difficult it is for the individual to solve problems of the different groups. Some logical problems like matchstick puzzles might
be unsolvable to one person, while (s)he has no difficulty in design problems such
as writing a poem on a specific topic. In addition to the type of problem and its
complexity, domain specificity and problem representation influence the problem solving activity. Further, individual differences of the problem solvers also
affect the problem solving activity. This includes, amongst others, the individual's familiarity with the problem type, his/her domain-specific knowledge, the
cognitive ways (s)he processes information (cognitive controls), his/her reflection on information and the problem (metacognition), his/her epistemological
beliefs, and his/her attitude on and motivation for the problem (cf. Jonassen 2000:
67-72).

How can problems be solved? The simplest way to solve problems is via trial-
and-error, which might be sufficient to solve simple problems but is not very efficient. For more complicated problems, it is necessary to plan internally/mentally.
Different operators might be necessary to find the solution of the problem. Sometimes these operators are known, but it is not evident how to combine them,
and sometimes these operators are unknown. If both the operators and the combination of the operators are familiar, it is not a problem solving activity, the
individual simply has to solve a task (cf. Dörner 2006: 623-624).

Pretz et al. (2003: 3–4) suggest that problem solving activities can be considered a cycle with the following seven steps:

1. Recognize or identify the problem.

2. Define and represent the problem mentally.

3. Develop a solution strategy.

4. Organize the knowledge about the problem.

5. Allocate mental and physical resources for solving the problem.

6. Monitor the progress toward the goal.

7. Evaluate the solution for accuracy.

These steps do not have to be executed in the given order and not all steps are always necessary – a successful problem solver is flexible and can adjust the cycle to his/her needs. These steps are considered a cycle, because in complex problem solving situations, the solution to a problem might lead to a new problem. Hence, the solving process has to restart for the new problem and the single steps have to be executed again. It also seems plausible that complex problems can be divided into smaller problem units that will be solved individually in this cycle or parts of the cycle. For example, "defining the problem mentally" in step two could also include "define subordinate problem units". The following steps would then be implemented first for the individual subordinate units and in the end for the whole problem. The last step may be expanded to "evaluate the solution for accuracy for the problem unit and the whole unit".

We have already connected problem solving with individual traits, amongst others the problem solver's familiarity with the problem type and his/her domain knowledge. Ericsson (2003) links problem solving with expert performances and considers problem solving a major contribution to acquiring expert knowledge. Even the most talented individuals have to learn the tasks they seek to become experts in and have to enhance their knowledge. "Different levels of mastery present the learner with different kinds of problems that must be solved for the skill to develop further" (ibid.: 31). At the beginning of the learning process, every individual can only successfully conduct the simplest tasks, activities, and challenges. The knowledge base is developed with the help of instructions and training, and reinforced by experience and exercises. If a person wants to solve a task that is too difficult for him/her, because his/her selection of methods and skills is not sufficient, (s)he cannot solve the task. On the other hand, if the person only encounters the same problems/exercises over and over again, (s)he does not become more skilled in the field. Only new problems and tasks challenge the person and help expand the knowledge of the individual. The problems that were initially impossible to handle, become easier and less problematic with increasing expertise. Problems have to be solved to increase the level of expertise as they broaden "cognitive mechanisms, representations, and knowledge" (ibid.: 32). Expertise is not only characterised by acquired knowledge, but also by different reactions to problem situations. Novices might not even be able to create one solution to the problem, while experts come up with different approaches and choose the most efficient. But it is not only speed and capacity, it is also "complex, highly specialised mechanisms" that make experts superior "in representative domain-specific tasks [...] such as planning, anticipation, and reasoning" (ibid.: 62-63).

Everyday problem solving is often text and comprehension related (cf. Whitten & Graesser 2003) – as soon as kitchen appliances, software, electronic items or even our means of transportation do not work properly and we do not know how to fix them, we consult a manual, the Internet or any other source of information (if we do not have a human instructor who can teach us). We have to understand the instructions and learn how to fix the problem. If the learning process is unsuccessful, we have to consult an expert for help, which often means additional costs and waiting for a certain length of time until we can use the item again. Hence, the learn-and-fix solution should be more desirable. Whether a text can be understood and transferred to the problem is related to the text's cognitive representation, which is basically dependent on two property classes: human factors (e. g. reader's domain knowledge and reading skills) and text factors (e. g. organisation of the text). Whitten & Graesser (2003: 215) also remark that most discourse psychologists agree that the reader's general knowledge has a huge influence on text comprehension. The more familiar the individual is with the problem or the domain the problem is located in, the easier it is for him/her to understand and apply the instructions in the written text. Further, it might be possible for the individual to recognise mistakes in the text and overcome them, which is impossible for individuals who have no prior knowledge of the problem/domain. Nonetheless, understanding the written text is still part of the problem solving activity: If no instructions were needed, the text would not be consulted at all. On the other hand, if the potential problem solver does not even understand the original problem, the best instructions will probably not help in solving the problem.

Another final aspect of problem solving that will be introduced is *full insight problem solving*. Although the term is used differently within the field, it usually describes the phenomenon where a solution to a problem seems to be found by accident rather than by consciously applying strategies. The problem solving process does not deliver any solutions; the solution only comes to mind all of a sudden when the problem is not thought about actively (cf. Knoblich & Öllinger 2006). Different anecdotes about scientific puzzles are known that were supposed to be solved by insight problem solving. Although it is thought to be a myth, the story of Archimedes is the most famous: The local tyrant hired Archimedes to figure out whether the goldsmith betrayed him and replaced some parts of the golden crown with silver. After struggling to find a way to prove whether the crown was pure gold or not, Archimedes found the solution to the puzzle by accident in the public bath. He observed that the more of his body was immersed in the water, the more water was displaced and that the amount of replaced water exactly equalled his body volume. Hence, the volume of the crown could be measured by putting it into water, and then the weight of the crown could be compared with the weight of an equal amount of gold. If the crown weighed less, the goldsmith did not make the crown from solid gold exclusively. Jubilant about his discovery, Archimedes exclaimed "Eureka! Eureka!" ("I've found it! I've found it!") and ran home naked. Therefore, this so called "Aha!"-effect is also referred to as the "Eureka effect". Other scientific breakthroughs are said to have originated in similar out-of-context situations like Einstein's theory of relativity and Newton's discovery of gravity – an apple fell on his head when he was sitting beneath an apple tree (cf. Biello 2006).

However, insight problem solving is more the exception than the rule. Problems are more often solved step by step (*partial insight problem solving*), according to rules and strategies, as mentioned before. When the problem seems to be unsolvable, it needs to be placed in another problem space, which means that the problem needs to be represented in another way. In this new space, the approach to solve the problem can be very easy, because part of the thinking process has been previously performed. This can lead to a very fast, full insight problem solving situation, or the approach can still be difficult and numerous steps may still be necessary to solve the problem (cf. Knoblich & Öllinger 2006).

In the decision making context, Jungermann et al. (2010) discuss the selection of rules in decision making tasks. First, they point out that the literature does not use the terms *rule* and *strategy* consistently. However, they define a *rule* as the way information is processed and the decision maker chooses between different options, while a *strategy* describes the way a decision maker chooses between these rules. They further specify two characteristics that affect the decision making[7] task: the *complexity of the problem* and the *types of information supply*. *Complexity* can be defined in different manners (as discussed above), but Jungermann et al. consider the following the most important in their context: amount of options, amount of features of the single options, and similarity of the options and time pressure. *Information supply* refers to the way in which the

---

[7]In my perspective, this would rather apply to problem solving tasks than decision making tasks.

information necessary for making a decision is present or presented (e.g. in an experiment), which naturally influences the problem solving activity.

In this section, approaches of psychology regarding problem solving were presented. First, we learned that problem solving is connected with thinking and discussed how thinking is related to language. Further, problems can be categorised as well- and ill-defined or as less or more complex. Jonassen (2000) introduced eleven more fine-grained categories for problems sorted by the structure of the problem, starting with well-defined problems and ending with the most ill-defined category. Moreover, problem solving can be performed in a cycle that starts with identifying the problem and ends with assessing the problem. They cycle may have to be repeated, for example when a new problem results from the old, or when individual subordinate problems are processed one after the other. Another aspect is the level of expertise the problem solver has in the respective domain. Finally, we learned about the text representation aspect of problem solving and the phenomenon of insight problem solving. In the next chapter, we will address problem solving in translation and more specifically how it has been discussed in translation studies so far.

5.3 Problem solving in translation studies

Some thoughts and ideas on problem solving have been posited in translation studies as well and will be discussed in the following chapter. In contrast to psychology, there are no published overviews on translation and problem solving that merely focus on theoretical aspects, but single studies exist that address the topic empirically or in which problem solving was part of a broader theoretical framework. This chapter aims to introduce the most important of these studies, but no claim to completeness is raised. The methodology of the selected empirical and process-related studies will be described briefly for reasons of completeness and for later analogies to the own methodology. As a side note, some of the translation scientists consider and cite thoughts and ideas from psychology literature as well, which will be mentioned if relevant. Nonetheless, this chapter will only introduce the work in translation studies on problem solving, while §5.4 will discuss whether these considerations were sufficient from the psychology perspective and will expand or adapt them if necessary. Accordingly, I do not agree with all statements that are presented in this chapter – it shall merely describe the state of the art of problem solving in translation studies.

Levỳ (1968) was the first to describe translation as a decision making process.[8] The translator may have different equivalents of a source item for the target text, but (s)he has to decide on one of them. Hence, as soon as one decision is made, the rest of the text has to be interpreted in favour of this decision. Translators' decisions can be motivated or unmotivated, necessary or unnecessary. The methods of defining decision making problems introduced in the paper should be seen as a starting point to develop a generative model of translation. Reiss (1981) and Kußmaul (1986) referred to translation as a decision making process as well – the former in regard to decisions regarding text types in literary translations, the latter in regard to translation mistakes analyses and translation didactics.

As I argue that translation is not only a decision making task, but occasionally also a problem solving activity, the studies on problem solving in translation will be discussed more extensively in the following. First of all, I will discuss terminology issues concerning the difference between translation *difficulties* and translation *problems*. First raised by Nord (1987), she categorises translation difficulties as learner-dependent and translation problems as learner-independent. Translation difficulties are components in the text that the translator struggles with because (s)he does not know a lexical, syntactic, or grammatical element in the source language, does not yet know how to solve the particular translation problem, lacks domain-specific competences, etc. Translation problems on the other hand may result from the source text, the translation skopos, differences between source and target culture or gaps in the involved languages. Translation as a teachable and learnable task should not be taught only by doing, but

> the attention of the translator should be directed on the one hand to the (cognitive graspable and solvable) translation problems. On the other hand, he has to learn to recognise his subjective translation difficulties and to apply suitable methods to overcome these[9] (ibid.: 5, translated J.N.).

Krings (1986b) published an extensive study on the processes during translation based on think-aloud protocols of eight language learners who translated from their foreign language into their native language (four participants) and vice versa. The analysis of the think-aloud protocols was based on the identification of translation problems. As professionals can hardly constitute a homogeneous group because of their different experiences and as it is assumed that

---

[8] §5.1 discusse the differences between problem solving and decision making.

[9] Original phrasing: "daß die Aufmerksamkeit des Übersetzers zum einen auf die (kognitiv erfaßbaren und lösbaren) Übersetzungsprobleme gelenkt wird und daß er zweitens lernt, seine subjektiven Übersetzungsschwierigkeiten zu erkennen und geeignete Methoden zu ihrer Überwindung einzusetzen"

with increasing experience certain processes become automatised and hence will not be verbalised in the think-aloud protocols, professional translators were not taken into consideration for this study (cf. ibid.: 51-52).[10] Krings' motivation was to explore the translation process in a structured, psychological manner with empirical data to develop a theoretical model of the translation process, as translation studies relied mostly on theoretical assumptions and product data (cf. ibid. 10-11). Altogether, Krings (1986b: 484–499) identified 117 features of the translation process, of which most could not have been found with a simple analysis of the translation product. He specified a model with primary and secondary problem indicators that can be specified in the translation process, when the translators are asked to think aloud[11] (cf. ibid.: 120-143):

- primary indicators

  - explicit or implicit problem identification by the translator
  - use of aids (dictionaries and alike)
  - gaps in the target text

- secondary indicators

  - many equivalent translation choices
  - changes in the translated text
  - underlining of source text items
  - negative judgement of the translation by the translator (the translator is unsatisfied with the translation)
  - not enough attention to the function of the target text
  - unfilled pauses
  - paralingual indicators, like sighing, groaning, or laughter
  - primary equivalent associations

It is assumed that either one primary or two (or more) secondary indicators imply a problem. Events in the think-aloud protocols like reading the source/target text out loud or comments during the production of the translation were not considered problem indicators, because they have other functions like attention

---

[10] Automation of translation processes was also considered the reason why about 90% of all verbalisations were related to translation problems (Krings (1986a: 118)).

[11] The translations were produced manually without any electronic aids in this study.

control or justification of translation choice. Translation problems are further categorised as comprehension (the source item is problematic), reproduction (the transfer into the target language is problematic) or comprehension-reproduction (both are problematic) problems, depending on the level in the translation process at which the problem arises. These problems arise either from language deficits or from translation problems, which depend on whether the problem results from problems in the mother tongue[12] or second language, or whether they result from a transfer problem, i. e. the problem is not merely linguistic (cf. ibid.: 144-171). Krings (ibid.: 175, translated J.N.) defines translation strategies as "potentially conscious plans of a translator to solve a specific translation problem in the scope of a specific translation task"[13] at two strategic levels: the macro- and the micro-strategic level. The study concludes with two extensive models. Both start with the question of whether a translation problem occurs or not. If a translation problem occured, different problem solving strategies were found for the translation from the foreign language on the one hand – including equivalent finding strategies, evaluation strategies, retrieval strategies, and reduction strategies – and into the foreign language on the other – including equivalent finding strategies, evaluation strategies, and decision making strategies (cf. ibid. 480-482). These models are summarised in one translation process model in another publication (Krings 1986b; cf. Figure 5.1), which also has its starting point in the question whether a translation problem occurred.

In her article, Kaiser-Cooke (1994) combines expertise, knowledge and problem solving. Due to differences in available knowledge, knowledge processing and other ways of recognising problem representations, novices and experts behave differently in problem solving in general, which can also be transferred to problem solving in translation. Further, she states that experts do not have to reflect on problems over and over again, but the path to the solved problem is shortened with increasing expertise until it is routinised. Hence, the procedure is automatised and the cognitive load decreases. As translation fits all criteria, it can be considered an expert task and hence a problem solving task, which can be seen in the inability of novices and laypersons to translate and judge a source text in terms of its difficulty. She concludes that "not only [...] all translations are problem solving activities but all are difficult [...], although some are, of course, more difficult than others" (ibid.: 137).

---

[12] Problems in the mother tongue might not occur due to deficits in the participant's language knowledge, but due to deficits in the source text.

[13] Original phrasing: "potentiell bewußte Pläne eines Übersetzers zur Lösung konkreter Übersetzungsprobleme im Rahmen einer konkreten Übersetzungsaufgabe."

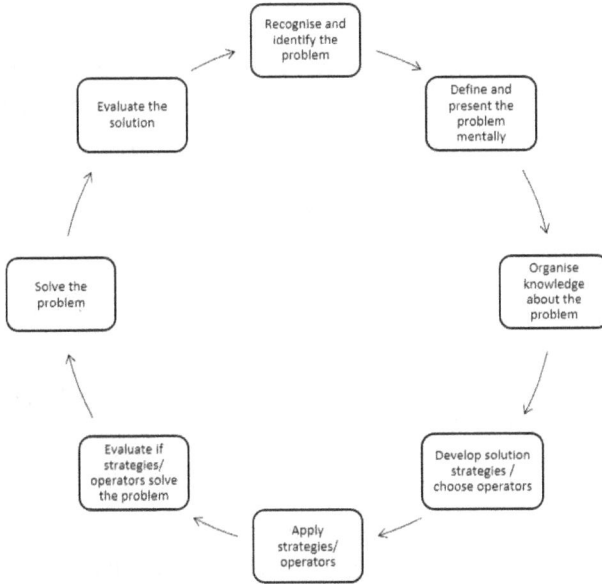

Figure 5.1: Krings (1986b: 269) tentative model of the translation process

Wilss (1996) argues that, as translation items usually have more than one possible target language representation, the translator has to decide which to choose; this choice is determined by various characteristics of the individual translator as well as environmental influences. The translator needs declarative and procedural knowledge, which (s)he has to apply to macrocontextual problems – that apply to the whole text, including factors like overall content, communicative purpose and intended readership – as well as microcontextual problems – "includ[ing], amongst others, singular (episodic) phenomena of the text-to-be-translated" (ibid.: 135). General problem solving strategies can hardly be applied in the translation process, as translation problems can seldom be generalised and it is further possible for the translator to "schematically reduce translation problems to a sequence of standardly operative moves guaranteeing translational success" (ibid.: 136). Instead, the translator needs to learn problem solving strategies according to different domains and text types to create informed, professional translations. Further, Wilss points out that the problem solving strategies might differ a lot between novices and expert translators, as they are learnt and evolve with increasing professionalisation. Finally, he divides the problem solving activity into six stages (ibid.: 145): problem identification, problem clarification (description), information collection, considerations on how to proceed, the choice of a solution, and the evaluation of translation result. Wilss (1996: 47–48) later agrees with Kaiser-Cooke (1994: 136) that "all translations are problem-solving activities" (and Risku 1998 agrees with this opinion, too), but reduces the range of problem solving activities to translation problems and therefore also implies that not every translation activity is problem solving. This idea is continued later in his argumentation:

> Whereas translation method always requires problem-solving activities, the essential feature of translation techniques […] is the subconscious, so to speak "self-monitoring" reproduction of specific, interlingually standardized text segments on the basis of functional one-to-one correspondence (with or without formal one-to-one correspondence). (Wilss 1996: 155–156)

Further, he argues that translation science has not described problem solving systematically yet, but is aware of it and "has had, and still does have, great trouble in defining a suitable and reliable conceptual framework for problem-solving" (ibid.: 47). Additionally, he suggests that the field should explore problem solving in longitudinal studies on translation students, because there might not be "a straight-line, continuous growth from less to more competence in problem-solving" (ibid.: 48). Such investigations would provide insights into problem solving development and how this could be integrated into translation teaching.

A rather extensive theoretical approach on problem solving is offered by Risku (1998) in her discussion on translation expertise, in which she also considers literature from psychology. She, like Dörner (1987), considers the hurdle as a characteristic of problems, but in a different way: In her understanding, every act of thinking in general is a problem, because building a representation in the mind already requires overcoming a hurdle – only reflexes occur automatically and do not create something new (cf. Risku 1998: 50). Hence, translation is always a problem, never a task for Risku:

> Translation, however, can never be a task in this sense.[14] The translator would need to be privy to source and target situation, the intentions of the client, the own role in the framework of action, would need to have already developed an individual production strategy suitable for the target communication, and would have finished the decision making process in

---

[14] Referring to Dörner's differentiation between problem and task.

order to posses all knowledge for the translation job right at the beginning. The translation would already need to be completed.[15] (ibid.: 226-227)

Conclusively, according to Risku there is no difference between thinking and problem solving.[16] However, problem solving shall remain a concept in research as it emphasises the connection between internal and external activity and helps create models that represent cognitive activity in action situations (cf. ibid.: 50-51). Funke's (2006a) concept of *complex problem solving* is considered especially appropriate by Risku for translation studies as it defines problem making situations with many dependencies and components; complex problems require plans for whole chains of courses of action. Hence, the ability to solve complex problems and the way these are solved are indicators of the level of expertise Risku (1998: 89). Experts can combine learned methods with their own experience, which makes these methods more appropriate for certain (translation-related) communication and problem types, and enables the experts to cooperate with all involved people (cf. ibid: 105) – the more connected knowledge exists, the more usable it is in problem solving situations (cf. ibid: 110). While novices tend to approach each single problem with formerly learned micro rules, experts let themselves be guided by communicative macro strategies and approach single problems more slowly, because not as many single problems evolve when the focus is on the macro level (cf. ibid.: 220). Risku's (cf. ibid.: 117) cognitive procedural approach assumes that the cognitive reality of the problem solver is characterised by four elements which all influence each other:

- the problem solver him/herself with his/her cognitive characteristics

- the situation as the socio-cultural position and role of the expert

- the aim of the translation from the translator's perspective (macro strategy)

---

[15] Original phrasing: "Übersetzen kann aber nie eine Aufgabe in diesem Sinne sein. Um bei der Auftragssituation das gesamte zum Übersetzen nötige Wissen 'bereit' zu haben, müßte der Übersetzende die Ausgangs- und Zielsituation, die Intentionen des Auftraggebers und die eigene Rolle in diesem Handlungsrahmen kennen, eine eigene, zielkommunikationsadäquate Produktionsstrategie entwickelt und den Entscheidungsprozess durchlaufen haben. Die Übersetzung müsste also bereits buchstäblich 'in der Tasche' sein."

[16] As we have seen at the beginning of §5.2, approaches in psychology and philosophy do not necessarily agree and neither do I. Find the discussion of the different thoughts and opinions in §5.4.

- the system that needs to be recognised and controlled (i.e. the translation purpose and the target communication with its references to the source communication)

An underestimated part of problem solving is the recognition of problems contained in a source text, which requires a great deal of expertise. As soon as the problem is identified, four problem solving strategies that influence each other can be determined for the translation process (based on Dörner's solution requirements for complex problems): integrating information, composing a macro strategy, planning actions, and planning action schemes & making decisions. The translation situation offers the guiding principles that tell the translator what to do and suggest the macro strategy for the individual translation job. Only the action plans and decisions tell the translator how to act (cf. ibid.: 136-139).

O'Brien (2006) presents an interesting approach to problem identification in PE – one of the few studies that deal with problem solving in PE – in her dissertation (find more details on and findings of the study in §4.2). In the study, the source texts were examined by two controlled language checker systems that highlighted the parts of the source segments that did not abide the rules of the controlled language, so-called negative translatability indicators (NTIs). Controlled languages are natural languages that are restrained in certain aspects to make texts easier to read for a broader audience. Consequently, it is assumed that texts written in a controlled language are easier to translate for both human translators and MT systems (for more information on controlled languages see §3.2). The NTIs include source text characteristics such as ungrammatical constructions, misspellings, or disrupted syntactic structures which are obviously source text defects but also regular parts of speech, which might be harder to process e.g., abbreviations, gerunds, slang, ellipses, etc. This is one of very few empirical studies that bases translation/PE problem identification not on the translator's behaviour during the experiments, but first identifies potential problems and then tests whether or not these then influence the PE effort.

Kubiak (2009) presents in his PhD thesis a study using think-aloud protocols on problem solving in semi-professional translators. Eight participants were asked to translate a newspaper text from German into Polish and vocalise every thought and emotion that came to their mind without any omissions. The participants were grouped according to translation direction. Kubiak does not differentiate his participants into natives and non-natives, because the non-natives had a very heterogeneous Polish-speaking family background, but he differentiated participants who were educated in Polish (four participants) or in German (four participants).[17] He analysed the problem solving behaviour of his participants and compared both groups to identify the differences in both groups and the preferred strategies. Another research goal was to uncover which deficits can be observed in the translation processes and where low-quality translations and mistranslations originate. In his theoretical framework on problem solving, Kubiak bases his considerations mainly on Risku's (1998) as well as Krings's (1986b) observations from the translation perspective and Dörner's (1987) work from the psychological perspective. Hence, he agrees that translation can be categorised as complex problem solving. Factors that influence the composition of the problem space – the mental representation of the problems – are (Kubiak 2009: 46-85):

- individual factors: translation knowledge/competence (linguistic, cultural, domain, and tool knowledge), memory, creativity, and further factors (e. g. emotions, motivation, etc.)

- translation skopos

- environmental factors

Kubiak (2009: 96) defines translation problems as subjective difficulties[18] that a translator with certain knowledge in a certain translation situation has to overcome to produce a target text that fulfils the translation skopos. In contrast, problem solving strategies are "potentially conscious behavioural patterns of a translator to solve emerging translation problems which have to be seen as a transcultural translation task within the scope of a certain translation task"[19] (ibid.: 99, translated J.N.; The similarity to Krings' (1986a) definition of translation strategies, mentioned above, cannot be denied). The think-aloud protocols were transcribed and analysed qualitatively according to Krings' (1986b) primary and secondary indicators for problems. Kubiak replicates the study of Krings with other participant groups and combines the thoughts on problem solving of Krings and Risku. However, the study does not really contribute anything new to the field and, hence, is only described for the sake of completeness here.

Prassl (2010) focuses on different decision making processes that could be identified in the think-aloud protocols in her study. She bases her categorisation on

---

[17]The studies were conducted at the Adam-Mickiewicz University in Poznań (Polish group) and the University of Vienna (German group).

[18]As opposed to Nord (1987).

[19]Original phrasing: "Unter Problemlösungsstrategien sind potenziell bewusste Verhaltensmuster eines Übersetzers zur Lösung emergierender Übersetzungsprobleme im Rahmen einer bestimmten Translationsaufgabe als transkultureller Kommunikationsaufgabe zu verstehen."

Jungermann et al. (2005) classification and adapts it to the translation process, resulting in four decision making types: routinised, stereotype, reflected, and constructed decisions. *Routinised* decisions happen unconsciously and the options are evaluated automatically; similar patterns have been handled before, the choice for the option is routinised, the cognitive effort is very small. In *sterotype* decisions, options are perceived unconsciously as well, but a minor uncontrolled evaluation takes place. A translator might, for example, first decide on one option, but change the translation immediately in favour of another option. The cognitive effort is still very low. Part of the option occurs automatically in *reflected decisions* as well, but these options are not satisfying for the goal, which usually has to be defined first, and new options have to be generated. Experts show different patterns and behaviour in dealing with reflected decisions than novices. Experts rather look for satisficing (satisfying and sufficient) than optimising strategies, because optimising strategies might lead to a never-ending process (a phenomenon well known to translators). The decision is not made right away, but might be postponed until enough evidence for the right decision has been gathered. A high degree of cognitive effort is necessary. *Constructed decisions* have to be made when the translation goal is not clear and the translator might not understand the translation unit due to lacking linguistic or world knowledge. Internal and external knowledge has to be consulted to generate options, because newly acquired knowledge is necessary for the decision. The decider cannot rely on previous experience and habits. The cognitive load is very high. If not enough information can be gathered due to lacking time and/or external resources, the translator might end up having to guess a solution (cf. Prassl 2010: 61-65). The data that were analysed in Prassl's (ibid.) study were part of the TransComp research project.[20] The decision making processes of 12 BA students at the beginning of their studies were compared to those of ten professional translators by looking at the translation process data (screen recording, keylogging and think aloud protocols) of five difficult source text phrases that occurred in the texts. Her analysis shows that professional translators made correct decisions more often than novices, although only slightly more than half of the decisions (13 of 25) of the professionals could be considered correct – and only two of 25 decisions of the novices were correct. Further, professionals used routinised decisions more often than novices, which was expected, and the success rate of reflected decisions was much higher for professionals than for novices.

In another think aloud study, Angelone (2010) combined uncertainty manage-

---

[20] A longitudinal translation process study; for an overview and detailed information see e.g. Göpferich et al. 2008.

ment and problem solving. As a basic definition, translation is seen as a "higher order cognitive task, like reading and writing, but with a very significant problem solving component concerned with mediation between languages" which makes the translation task a "chain of decision making activities relying on multiple, interconnected sequences of problem solving behaviour" (ibid.: 17). Uncertainty is specified "as a cognitive state of indecision" and can be recognised by "an observable interruption in the natural flow of translation" (ibid.: 18), which helps to identify the problem. The problem solving activity is divided into three elements which are also the three elements that constitute the optimal problem solving bundle: problem recognition, solution proposal, and solution evaluation (cf. ibid.: 20). It is assumed that problem solving bundles are used to manage uncertainty. One professional and three student translators were asked to translate a 50-word excerpt from a travel guide in this study to identify when, where, and how problem solving bundles are used, how the metacognitive activity varies between professionals and semi-professionals and when the metacognitive activities are associated with uncertainty management. Screen recording and think-aloud protocols were applied, analysed, and triangulated. The results suggest that professional translators have a greater capacity to recognise problems than novices.

As we have seen, translation studies uses the terms *decision making* and *problem solving* for the analysis of the translation process. However, there seems to be no consensus on how these terms are used and whether translation can be described as one and/or the other. These desiderata will be tackled in the following section.

5.4 Modeling the concept of problem solving in translation studies by adding psychological approaches

In this section, the views and ideas of psychology on problem solving will be applied to the translation process and there will be an examination of what has been discussed about problem solving in translation studies in recent approaches. Let us first discuss the terminology. Truly, a translator has the choice of many different expressions, structures, styles, etc. and translation can accordingly be a decision making activity. However, often it is more than the simple selection of one of a variety of expressions, because (a variety of) target text expressions or units are not always immediately available for every source text unit in the mind of a translator. Dörner's (1987) basic definition of problems suggests that translation processes include both problems and tasks. When we apply Dörner's

definitions to the very foundation of translation, it becomes obvious that translation in its basic form is the task. The source text is the (undesired) initial state that
has to be transformed into the target text – the desired final state. As soon as the
translator has to deal with a hurdle that prevents him/her from transferring the
source text into the target text, the translator faces a problem and needs a plan to
solve this problem. Hence, the definitions and differentiations in psychology and
some publications in translation studies make it obvious that translation will be
considered a problem solving activity in the following if it exceeds the conditions
of a simple task – because it is a more complex activity than the simple selection
between different choices, although translation was also referred to as a decision
making process, especially in earlier considerations. A problem further requires
social, intellectual, or cultural motivation to arrive at the unknown target state,
as mentioned in Jonassen (2000). This clearly applies to translation situations.
If nobody wanted a translation of the source text in the target language, there
would be no translation job. However, the characteristics of a problem do not apply to every translation instance. Although Kaiser-Cooke (1994) and Risku (1998)
express as their basic assumptions that all translation activities are problem solving instances, which could be argued even from psychology's perspective on
problem solving, their considerations on problem solving contradict the definitions of Dörner (1987). A problem needs to have a hurdle between initial state
and solution to qualify as problem and not merely a task. If the problem can be
solved and the problem solver does not have to overcome a hurdle, it is not a
problem, it is a task. Hence, with a growing level of expertise, the translation
activity converts from a problem solving activity to a task solving activity (although some problems might still arise, no matter how experienced a translator
is), especially when the translator works in his/her standardised working environment (well-known text domain, text type, terminology, tool, client, etc.). It is
well documented that translators need to specialise to become good and efficient
translators[21] (e.g. Schmitt 2003a,b, Hommerich & Reiß 2011) and as I do not assume the existence of a general problem solver,[22] I do not assume the existence of

---

[21]If the job market allows the translator to specialise. This is possible for language combinations
with large translation volumes like English-German. However, combinations of very small
languages might require all-round translators instead.

[22]The notion of a general problem solver goes back to Newell & Simon (1972) and was very
influential in the field of artificial intelligence. Their computer system was capable of solving
a variety of well-defined problems, although not all of them in the same manner as a human
would have performed it. They computed their simulation according to think-aloud protocols
of humans who had to solve well-defined problems (for a brief introduction see e.g. Eysenck
2004: 341-342).

a general translation solver (neither human nor machine-made) or general prob-lem solving strategies as mentioned by Wilss (1994). Krings (1986b) does not view every translation action as a problem solving activity either. Rather, he defines different problem indicators from the think-aloud protocols, which indicate that only certain instances cause problems.

In line with these assumptions, both translation difficulties and problems as defined by Nord (1987) will be analysed and summarised as translation problems in the study at hand. The distinction by Nord (cf. ibid.: 7) is reasonable and in-sightful, but she also claims that only the "ideal" translator does not have to cope with translation difficulties, while the "real" translator always has to strug-gle with difficulties, even with a lot of experience (although they are supposed to decrease with growing translation experience). Therefore, she argues that it is part of the translator's competence to know how to deal with these difficul-ties. As the study comprises professional and semi-professional translators, I am not only interested in Nord's translation problems alone but also in what she defines as difficulties and how translators deal with both groups. Additionally, all participants have a certain amount of experience (even the semi-professional translators; see §8.1) which rules out beginner's mistakes. As the difference be-tween a translation difficulty and a translation problem according to Nord (1987) is that the first is an individual phenomenon (one translator has a difficulty with a source text unit, while the next translator does not have any difficulty with the source text unit), while the second applies to a text unit that is problematic in itself, independent of the individual, it is almost impossible to differentiate between difficulty and problem in mere process data. Further, the definition of *problems* in psychology would include translation problems as well as transla-tion difficulties, too, because there is a hurdle between the source text and the target text for the individual, which (s)he has to overcome.

We have to keep in mind that translation problems sometimes apply to small text units (micro structure) and sometimes to larger chunks or the whole text (macro structure). Still, the problems that are focused on in psychology are of-ten more broad and time-consuming than single problems in translation. Even well-structured problems might take longer to solve than most problems in trans-lations; well-structured problems do not need to be easy for a person who has never encountered the problem before. And some very ill-structured, complex problems such as ending the Middle-East conflict or stopping global warming might takes years to solve, if possible at all. Hence, we apply rules and assump-tions that were defined for broader contexts and situations to smaller units in the translation context. In general, however, translation problems can seldom be categorised as well-defined, but most often as ill-defined. One argument is that the desired final state of the problem is never known to the translator (however, sometimes the final state is already known in well-defined problems) and another is that the means that help the translators to arrive at a solution are sometimes also unknown to the translator. If a translator, e.g., simply does not know a lexical unit, (s)he knows that (s)he has to consult a dictionary or glossary. However, if a source text unit applies to a cultural or linguistic feature that does not exist in the target language/culture, the procedure of finding a solution is not that obvious. Accordingly, what might be ill-defined problems for novice translators, can be well-defined problems for professional translators because the translator familiarises himself/herself with more and more operators and develops more and more strategies to overcome hurdles with advancing training and experience.

To extend this context, experience and growing expertise change the translation process, and that which is considered a problem can become a simple task, as discussed by Ericsson (2003) for problem solving in general. While some difficult grammatical structures are problematic at first, because the inexperienced translator does not have any plans or strategies to solve this problem yet, an experienced translator might have encountered this structure various times and therefore only has to solve a task, not a problem, as there is no hurdle between source text and target text. Translation students might encounter numerous problems at the beginning of their studies as they still can be considered laypersons. However, solutions are found and strategies are learned for some problems with growing experience that can be reused in future translations. Therefore, there is no hurdle between the source and the target text (any more), which would classify the translation as a task rather then a problem solving activity. I suggest that many source texts contain translation problems, that problems can be encountered in addressing the target audience, fulfilling the translation skopos/ brief, or that problems can be caused by time pressure, missing information, cultural or linguistic differences, or (non-)usage of translation technologies – even for the most well-trained and most experienced translator. Nonetheless, the majority of translation activities become routinised (and automatised) over time and are therefore not problematic (any longer). This is also verified in translation studies as it is assumed that laypersons and translation beginners consider different aspects of the translation as problematic and use different problem solving strategies than experts. Beginners may rely more on the source text and on micro structural strategies, while experts are more influenced by their communicative macro strategies with smaller problems fading from the spotlight (cf. Risku 1998: 220 – an assumption that was confirmed for semi-professionals in

Kubiak's 2009 analysis of his data). This acknowledged change in problem solving strategies also implies that an expert translator has to deal with different (and presumably fewer) problems than beginners. The assumption by Jääskeläinen & Tirkkonen-Condit (1991) that certain activities in the translation process become automatised with increasing translation experience strengthens the premise that translators' problem perception changes with growing expertise (an assumption also posited by Wilss 1981, Krings 1986b – who excluded professional translators from his study, because the group would have been too heterogeneous and automatised translation processes cannot be verbalised in think-aloud protocols – and in later studies). The purpose of their study was to show that these automatised processes exist for experts and cannot be verbalised during think-aloud and hence the protocols differ naturally between novice and expert translators. The second goal was to examine whether automation also takes place during the translation task itself, which turned out to be true. When processes become automatised with growing experience, it cannot be assumed that all translation processes are problem-driven and that problem solving is ubiquitous in translation processes. Only translation units that are not automatised require a high cognitive load and hence can be considered problematic in the translation process. Jääskeläinen & Tirkkonen-Condit (1991: 106) conclude that "[w]hile some decisions become non-conscious, or 'automatic', the translator becomes sensitised to new aspects of the task which require conscious decision-making." Further, as Kaiser-Cooke (1993: 187) (emphasis in original text) puts it in her dissertation: "Decisions which seem trivial because they are taken 'automatically' by humans are still decisions." The statements confirm the assumption that translation is a constant decision making process, while problems only occur, when a hurdle between source and target text exists.[23] On the other hand, she argues (ibid: 217-218) that with growing experience, translators formulate problem prototypes which can be applied to new problems, but each problem is at least slightly different from another problem and hence "new problem-solving strategies, i.e. decisions which have not been taken before" (218) are required. Here again, it becomes obvious that the differentiation between problem solving and decision making is often difficult and not applied strictly.

Prassl's (2010) categorisation of decision making processes in translation supports the assumption of the automation of translation choices. While routinised and stereotype decisions are made unconsciously, and hence cannot be seen as problem solving processes, because there is no hurdle between source and target text for the translator, reflected and constructed decisions require a high amount

---

[23]This contradicts Kaiser-Cooke's (1994) statement that all translations are problem solving activities (as mentioned above).

of conscious thinking and cognitive effort. Therefore, these decision making processes can be categorised as problem solving activities. However, as Prassl mentions "guessing" as a possible solution strategy for constructed decisions, this would not qualify as a problem solving activity, because the hurdle between source and target text might still exist. Here again it becomes clear that a strict differentiation between problem solving and decision making is not available, neither in psychology nor in translation literature.

To extend on the points mentioned above, translation problems can often be categorised as ill-defined problems rather than well-defined, because the finale state is, as mentioned above, unknown and the operators to arrive at the final state are often unknown. Further, the assessment of translations is especially difficult because only few characteristics can be judged as strictly correct or incorrect (e. g. spelling or grammar) and personal opinions or judgements (preference of one translation option over another) are often necessary. Most of the problem solving studies in psychology (as mentioned in Funke 2006a and Pretz et al. 2003) focused on well-defined problem solving, because they are much easier to control and evaluate. Accordingly, it is also complicated to study problem solving activities in translation because translation problems can usually not be characterised as well-defined (which will be discussed in detail in the following paragraphs). Individual differences influence the perception of what is problematic and solutions to problems can – as mentioned above – hardly be evaluated as either correct or incorrect. Pretz et al. (2003: 26) conclude for problem solving in general that which also applies to problem solving in translation: Problem solving activities are influenced by the knowledge the problem solver gained in earlier experiences. Individual cognitive abilities, personality, and social background may explain why some people are better at solving problems than others.

Risku (1998: 129) argues that all five criteria that Funke (2006a) states for complex problem solving apply to the translation process as well. Her arguments for those criteria, which I do not consider suitable for translation (dynamism and non-transparency), are, however, not very convincing to me:

> [...] the dynamism of the communication situations requires fast or "multi-compatible" decisions; the non-transparency of texts and situations requires further information gathering; conflicts between multiple aims have to be considered like domain expertise vs. comprehensibility [...][24]

---

[24] original phrasing: "[...] die Eigendynamik der Kommunikationssituationen verlangt rasche bzw. 'mehrfach kompatible' Entscheidungen; die Intransparenz (Unbestimmtheit) der Texte und Situationen erfordert weitere Informationsbeschaffung; Konflikte zwischen verschiedenen Zielen wie Fachlichkeit und Verständlichkeit müssen abgewogen werden [...]"

In my opinion, Funke's (2006a) suggested five criteria for complex problem solving (complexity, interconnectedness, dynamism, non-transparency, multiple aims) are not all met by translation as a problem solving activity, which is why I do not agree with Risku's (1998) assumption, shared by Kubiak (2009), that translation processes are complex problem solving situations. While many interconnected variables influence the translation process (e. g. experience, time-pressure, text domain, translation skopos, etc. – hence the translation process is complex), translations are usually not very dynamic (translation jobs usually stay the same for the duration of the job, even if the source text might be changed by the client when the translation is already in progress) and quite transparent (if the skopos of the translation is defined and the whole source text is available). The last characteristic of complex problem solving (multiple aims) is hard to judge: On the one hand, a translation job often has only one aim/purpose, while the evaluation of a translation is usually still versatile and subjective, with no correct answer.

Further, Wenke & Frensch (2003) differentiate between ill-defined (or "ill-stated") problems and complex problem solving. Complex problems are ill-defined. However, they have additional features in Dörner's, Funke's, and Frensch's understanding of complex problem solving, like a dynamically changing problem situation or unknown exact properties of given state, final state, and hurdles. This leads to the conclusion that problems in translation situations are ill-defined, but not entirely complex (as categorised by Funke 2006a), because usually neither the problem situation changes during the solving process, nor are the exact properties of the given state unknown.

According to Jonassen's (2000) sorted list on well- and ill-structured problems, translations might be characterised as either strategic performance problems – as it is applied to expert tasks in which a certain degree of professionalism and know-how is required to cope with the problem – or design problems – which would put the focus more on the creation of creative text with a vague solution outline and an unknown approach to the solution. Considering that translation entails characteristics of both groups, it can surely be classified as an ill-structured problem, because both problem groups are more often categorised as ill-structured than well-structured.[25] However, as Jonassen only assessed and categorised a selection of possible problems, these categories might not be well suited for translation problems in general and another category might be appropriate.

As Dörner (2006) already pointed out, the trial-and-error strategy to solve a problem is for humans neither very efficient in everyday situations nor for trans-

---

[25] Problems that occur in PE might even be categorised as troubleshooting problems, because the dysfunctional MT output needs to be fixed by a professional, i.e. the translator.

lation in particular. If a translator is confronted with a hurdle between source and target text, (s)he has to plan how to solve the problem rather than trying to find a solution by accident. The seven-step-cycle on problem solving by Pretz et al. (2003) can be easily transferred to problem solving processes in translation. For the translation purpose, it would be reasonable to swap step three (develop solution strategy) and step four (organise knowledge about problem), as is done in the following. Further, I will include "The problem gets solved" as the second-to-last step. Several similarities to Krings (1986a) model (cf. Figure 5.1) can be found, which will be briefly highlighted in italics[26]:

- A translator has to realise that (s)he has a problem with a translation unit (recognise and identify problem); *problem? → yes*

- Then, (s)he has to figure out where exactly the problem in this translation unit is, e. g. lexical, syntactic, macro structural, etc. (define and represent problem mentally); *identification of problem*

- Have similar problems occurred in earlier translations? (organise knowledge about problem); not mentioned in Krings' model

- Next, the translator has to decide what strategy can be applied to solve the problem, e. g. look up words in a dictionary, read parallel texts, restructure the sentence/phrase (develop solution strategy); *what type of problem? →* either *comprehension problem* followed by *comprehension strategies* or *problem of rendering* followed by *retrieval strategies*

- The translator applies the strategy (allocate mental and physical resources); *potential equivalent found?*

- Now, (s)he has to evaluate whether the strategy will solve the problem (monitor progress); *monitoring strategies → one adequate equivalent* or *competing equivalents* or *no adequate equivalent*

- The translator solves the problem (not mentioned by Pretz et. al.); *target language text*

- Finally, the translator has to evaluate whether the translation is suitable for the translation purpose, text type and domain as well as the style guide

---

[26]Wilss' (1994) six steps for problem solving, namely problem identification, problem clarification (description), information collection, considerations on how to proceed, the choice of a solution, and the evaluation of translation result, can be recognised in this list, too.

references – and further influences (evaluate solution); not mentioned in Krings' model

These steps do not necessarily occur consciously or might be skipped automatically. For example, if the translator does not know one single term in a domain-specific list, the translator may not have to define the problem (step 2) as it is obvious and s(he) knows the exact strategy to solve the problem (step 3), and may continue with step 4 – looking up the word in a dictionary, a job-related terminology list, or via the concordance search in a translation memory system, etc. Further, in this simple translation problem, step 5 and 7 fuse, because while (s)he is consulting a dictionary, (s)he has to evaluate whether the suggestions in the dictionary fit the purpose etc. of the text. Meanwhile, the translator can evaluate whether the translation strategy actually solves the problem: If the dictionary does not contain an acceptable translation, another strategy might be useful, like consulting parallel texts or another dictionary. As Pretz et al. (2003) have also pointed out, the solution of one translation problem might lead to another problem, e.g. the solution of a lexical problem might lead to a collocation problem in the already existing translation. The cycle property is not represented in Krings' model. Angelone's (2010) optimal problem solving bundle, containing problem recognition, solution proposal, and solution evaluation, can be found in the cycle as well. In Figure 5.2, we can see the combined models (Pretz et al. 2003 & Krings 1986a) for problem solving in one cycle.

The problem solving cycle in Figure 5.2 applies both for TfS as well as for PE. However, recognising and identifying the problem are supposedly different in both tasks, because the problems that occur supposedly vary to a high degree (see 6).

In Whitten & Graesser (2003) observations on the interconnectedness of language or reading comprehension and problem solving, the translator is not only a problem solver during translation, but also enables problem solving for the recipient of his/her translation. Depending on the text type, the translator has to translate and the need to solve a problem might be a big motivation for the target text reader (most obviously in manuals, but contracts or advertisements might also be read to solve a problem). The translator has to ensure that the target text is understandable in the target culture, that the approaches to problem solution are represented in a way the target audience can understand it (see in this regard the observations of Baker 1996 on explicitation and simplification). When troubleshooting a broken electrical appliance, a British manual might suggest to check whether or not the wall socket is turned on. However, German wall sockets cannot be turned on and off. Hence, this troubleshooting suggestion would

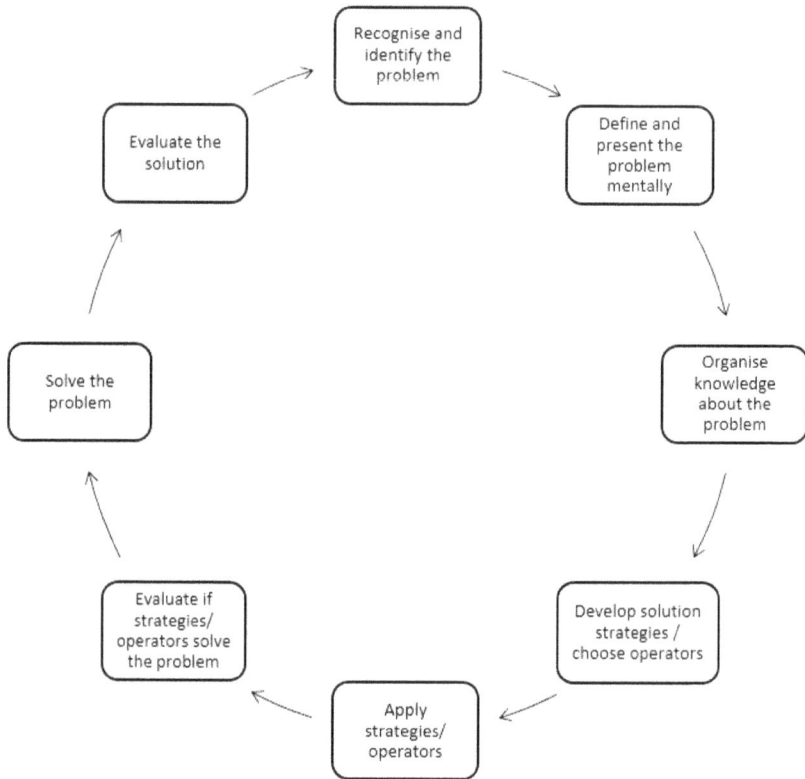

Figure 5.2: Problem solving cycle for translation

be unnecessary or even confusing in a German manual. In an even more general consideration, the translator solves the language hurdle that exists between the reader/recipient and the source text by delivering an understandable target text so that reading the text is only a task for the recipient, not a problem.

A few studies have been conducted in psychology that place cultural differences in the focus of problem solving behaviour (an overview can be found in Strohschneider 2006). It is likely that cultural differences have an influence on problem solving behaviour in translation, as well. This might be highly effected by the teaching methods at universities in the different regions. As the study at hand only includes German natives (find details in §7.2) who translated from English into German and were most likely all educated in Germany (at least mainly), this factor on problem solving behaviour is not taken into consideration in this study. However, cultural differences in problem solving behaviour could be a promising research area for future studies in translation process studies.

Usually, solving a translation problem is a one- or multi-step operation (partial insight). However, full insight into a problem is not uncommon. Every translator has probably experienced dissatisfaction with a target text representation of part of the source text, but could not come up with something more suitable. However, a great solution for this problem came to mind much later in the translation, during a break or when even not translating at all (see also Risku 1998: 204-205).

Translation processes consist of tasks and problems. How can these problems be identified? Studies have mainly used think aloud protocols to identify problem units in the translation from scratch task. This method, however, is very subjective and dependent on the participants' willingness to verbalise their thoughts.[27] However, is there a more neutral way or a more objective method to identifying translation problems? And do the same problems exist when the translators have to post-edit texts? The following chapter will formulate the research questions. Afterwards, I will focus on an empirical analysis of translation process data to tackle the research questions.

---

[27] The different methods will be introduced in §7.

6 Research hypotheses

Problem solving is an active field in psychology and was also considered in translation studies, where experiments with think-aloud protocols have been conducted. In the following chapters, I want to explore how the problem solving activities of (professional and student) translators change in PE – human editing of machine translated output with available source text – compared to the translation from scratch task. Further, there will be references to monolingual PE tasks – a task where no source text is available – which were part of the experimental settings; however, I assume that MPE is neither comparable with PE nor TfS. Therefore, the main focus will be on the differences between PE and TfS.

   In an article on the technologization of the translation process and the growing importance of MT and translation memory (TM) systems, Pym (2013: 493) suggests that the influence of TM/MT systems on translation can be defined easily:

> [W]hereas much of the translator's skill-set and effort was previously invested in *identifying* possible solutions to translation problems [...], the vast majority of those skills and efforts are now invested in *selecting* between available solutions, and then adapting the selected solution to target-side purposes [...]. The emphasis has shifted from generation to selection. (emphasis in original text)

   Taking this assumption out of the technology context, it refers to a difference between problem solving and decision making. While problem solving actively requires the translator to identify or generate solutions, (different) solution(s) are available to the translator (in his/her mental lexicon) in decision making and (s)he (simply) has to choose one of the existing solutions in his/her mental lexicon. Following this argumentation, PE would be considered a decision making task, and TfS problem solving. However, as we have seen in the last chapters, not all translation units can be considered problem solving in TfS. On the other side, the translator has to choose in PE whether or not the MT is acceptable. When (s)he decides that the MT is not acceptable, (s)he has to start from scratch. Hence, if a translation problem occurs, the MT might suggest a solution. If it does not present a solution, the translator still has to cope with the problem by him/herself.

Therefore, I assume that the MT output in the PE task sometimes already solves what might have previously been considered problematic, because the MT output suggests a final state (cf. Krings 2001: 472). However, MT might also introduce new hurdles between source text and target text due to unacceptable MT output. Hence, the translator has to overcome the hurdle. In other words, the defective MT realisation can be considered a hurdle between source text and acceptable target text solution.

Moreover, the participants of the experiment were separated into two groups, namely professional and semi-professional translators. The assumption that translating activity changes with increasing professionalism has been raised before, as mentioned in §5 and by Kiraly (1995: 41) "[...] translation processing is probably a mix of conscious and subconscious processes – a mix that may change as translators proceed through their training and become more professional". Further, it was already discussed by Pavlović & Jensen (2009) that students invest more cognitive effort into their translations than professionals – evidence was found in this study in regard to gaze time, task length, and pupil dilation, but not in average fixation duration – which might indicate that students have to handle many more translation problems than professionals.

As was mentioned above, MT output can either deconstruct hurdles, have no impact on the hurdles, or create new hurdles between source and target text. The same problems obviously exist in the source text for both human translation and post-editing. Therefore, my main hypothesis is that some problems are already solved by the machine translation (MT) output, while some new problems (can) arise from the MT output. Therefore, the patterns of the applied problem solving strategies change or new strategies – that may not be familiar for TfS – are necessary depending on the task. Further, different patterns develop in relation to the level of expertise of the participant.

Earlier quantitative research on problem solving in translation used think-aloud protocols, e.g. Krings (1986b), Lörscher (1986), Kubiak (2009), and Angelone (2010), as think-aloud protocols were considered useful for the task (cf. Wilss 1994: 143). This study, however, attempts to show how to explore problem solving with other methods of translation process research, namely eyetracking and keylogging. Questionnaires were used in the study as well, but not to analyse problem solving, but for meta-data and to analyse subjective attitudes towards MT and PE. I assume that not every translation act is simultaneously a problem solving act, but that most translation activities can be characterised as tasks (according to Dörner 1987) for both professional and semi-professional translators. Only in single instances do translators stumble across problematic parts that can be considered a problem and therefore need special attention. Problem identification can either be conscious or subconscious. Therefore, the eyetracking and keylogging data shall reveal subconscious as well as conscious problem solving activity. The first part of the analysis (§9) will deal with conscious problem solving, namely *lexical problem solving*, where information is retrieved via research – the screen recording software included in Tobii studio allows us to track the Internet research behaviour of the participants and no offline research options were available. The second part of the analysis (§10) will focus on *syntactic structures*, as those seem to be especially difficult for SMT systems for translations from English into German. The third part of the analysis (§11) is an attempt to characterise *keylogging* and *eyetracking parameters* that indicate (conscious and subconscious) problems or help to identify problem solving activity in TfS and PE/MPE in general without the help of obvious problem indicators like research or the quality of the MT output. In line with O'Brien (2006), I will present an attempt to identify problem solving activity in process data with the help of mere keylogging data (as identified in the preceding chapter) in translation process data in the final part (§12). Although translation is not in itself seen purely as a problem solving activity in this study, there is a common point of agreement that problem solving might be an indicator for expertise. Hence, the experience of the participants will be taken into consideration in the analysis.

§7 introduces the data set starting with an overview of translation process research methods. Then, I will present general information on the data set, the placement of the research hypotheses and previous research conducted with the data set, as well as a first overall analysis (session duration, complexity levels of the source texts, general keystroke effort and general error analysis of the final target texts, and critics of the methodology), before the empirical analysis is presented (starting in §8 with the assessment of the questionnaires).

7 The data set

This chapter will introduce the data set which will be used to contrast problem solving in PE and TfS. In the first part of this chapter, the methods of translation process research will be outlined with a special focus on those used in the study. Further, the focus will be on the importance of data triangulation and selecting participants. In the next section, the particular characteristics of the data set will be presented including the tools used to record the data, followed by a brief overview of other studies that previously used the data set to examine their research questions. Afterwards, the first general analyses will be presented, which will be useful to understand the study on a large scale. These analyses include the session's durations (§7.5), complexity levels of the texts (§7.6), general keystroke effort in the different tasks (§7.7), and an error analysis (§7.8). As the data were collected in a major attempt to gather comparable data in different languages, the process has some flaws which will be addressed in the final section (§7.9).

7.1 A short introduction to methods in translation process research

Different methods have been established to analyse translation processes in the field (for an overview see Göpferich 2008). Naturally, the analysis of the source text and the translation product is still very important for investigating the translation process. They are necessary to outline what might be happening in the translator's mind – without the source text, we do not know what structures we want to focus on when analysing the translation process; without the translation product, we cannot assess whether or not the translation was successful. To analyse the translation process, however, the following methods have been used most often: think-aloud protocols, questionnaires, keylogging, eyetracking, and neuroscientific methods like EEG or fMRI (find more methods and a categorisation of online and offline methods in Krings 2005). Three of these methods were selected for the study at hand, namely questionnaires, keylogging, and eyetracking methods, which will be explained in detail in the following. Think-aloud protocols and the neuroscientific methods EEG and fMRI will be outlined only briefly for the sake of completeness and because they are powerful tools, too. To reconstruct translation processes, it is necessary to combine different methods to benefit from the advantages of each method. This data triangulation can help provide interested parties with a better idea of what is happening in the translator's black box.[1]

7.1.1 Think-aloud protocols

Think-aloud protocols (TAPs) are used to record and analyse thoughts during the translation process. The translators are asked to verbalise their thoughts while translating. This can be done either directly during the translation or retrospectively; the first variant, however, is more common and has been conducted more often. The transcription of these verbalisations are called think-aloud protocols. Using TAPs has different advantages and disadvantages. Amongst others, one major disadvantage of immediate verbalisation is that studies have shown that verbalisation changes the thought process (cf. Jakobsen 2003) and therefore may also change the translation process. TAPs that are produced retrospectively do not change the translation process, because the translator is asked about specific translation units only after the whole translation was produced. The problem is, however, that a lot of valuable thoughts might get lost between translation production and verbalisation. Here, it is helpful to use a screen-recording of the session – maybe with eyetracking data – to help the participant remember the passages of interest. Further, only thoughts can be uttered that are conscious, and a high cognitive load during the task might prevent the participants from verbalising their thoughts. However, it is one of the few methods that can actually reproduce what is happening inside the heads of the participants, even if not completely (Jääskeläinen 2010). TAPs have their origins in cognitive psychology and are, despite criticism, still a standard research method in research on problem solving in psychology (cf. Knoblich & Öllinger 2006: 5). J. B. Watson was the first to use think-aloud protocols in psychology as early as 1920 (cf. Ericsson 2003: 37). Nonetheless, the first TAP studies in translation science were reported only in the 1980s (e.g. Krings 1986b).

The disadvantages outweighed the advantages for the analysis in this dissertation. Although think-aloud data might have been very helpful to analyse problem solving in translation, the experiment was not designed to focus on one research

---

[1]This term refers to an electronic device, whose internal mechanisms and functionality is unknown to the user. In a broader, non-literal sense, it is applied to all systems, objects, or concepts, the inner working processes of which are unknown to the user (cf. http://www.merriam-webster.com/dictionary/blackbox, last accessed 21 November 2016).

question only, but was supposed to collect a basis for various research questions.[2] As the experiment setting was also replicated for other language combinations, retrospective think-aloud data were not gathered either. Further, the aim of the study is to uncover not only conscious but also unconscious translation problems. Therefore, the data collected should be as close to the natural translation process as possible. Another aspect is that TAPs for six texts would have been cognitively very demanding for the participants and would have produced a huge amount of data that would need transcription. Finally, TAPs have been neglected more and more in recent years in translation studies in general because they affect the translation flow too much.

7.1.2 Questionnaires

Questionnaires are usually distributed in a written form – either on paper or electronically – and contain a set of questions. These questions can be open – the participant decides what to answer and in which detail – or closed – the participant can choose from a set of answers. Mixed questions contain a number of possible answers. The participant, however, has the possibility to add his/her own answers. Closed questions are much easier to assess which saves time and money. Open questions, however, deliver more extensive and more differentiated data. (Klöckner & Friedrichs 2014) Compared to interviews, questionnaires are easier to distribute and participants might be more willing to fill out a questionnaire whenever they have time than to schedule a date with the interviewer. Further, questionnaires are more discrete and more anonymous. On the other hand, the participants must be able to read and write, which excludes a few potential target groups (but this should usually not be a problem in translation process studies). Written answers will probably be shorter and less detailed than answers in an interview. Finally, a questionnaire does not allow for personal contact so that participants are not able to ask questions and the examiner cannot get an impression of the person.[3] (cf. Döring & Bortz 2014: 398–399)

According to the required information, five types of questions are differentiated in social sciences (cf. Reinecke 2014: 604–608), namely questions that ask for

- opinions – usually the participant has to agree or disagree with a statement according to a Likert scale, buttons, or a visual analogue scale, which usu-

---

[2]Details on the experiments that have been conducted with the data set can be found in §7.2.

[3]This is not necessarily a problem. Like in the study at hand, short questionnaires might be handed out and completed in the presence of the examiner, because they are only a part of the study and not the study itself.

ally has either five or seven response options between "I strongly agree" and "I strongly disagree".

- facts and knowledge – multiple choice questions with (usually) one correct answer, e.g. when asking for the participant's knowledge of history.

- incidents, attentions, and behaviour – relate to behaviour of the participant in the past; often with yes-/no-questions, open questions or bipolar scales ("very unlikely" vs. "very likely").

- social-statistical characteristics – questions about age, gender, education, marital status, income, etc.

- and network questions – concerning the social behaviour of the partici-pant.

The requirements for a high quality questionnaire include that the participant is able to answer the questions, and that it is objective, valid, and reliable. How-ever, even a very sophisticated questionnaire can cause non-responses and dif-ferent response qualities due to the individual characteristics of the participants. Furthermore, participants tend to follow certain response strategies, e.g. they prefer extreme categories or medium categories, they prefer the first or the last response choice (also called primacy or recency effect), or they answer according to social conventions (cf. ibid.: 612-613).

In general, a question might be hard to understand for the participant on a semantic and pragmatic level. Semantic difficulties might arise if the questions contain unknown terms, terms that are ambiguous, terms that can be interpreted differently by individuals or by groups, or if the questions are worded vaguely or are too difficult. Pragmatic problems arise when the question does not reveal what the researcher actually wants to know. Hence, terms should be used in the questions that are simple, distinct, and can only be interpreted in one way. If some of the used terms might be unknown to some participants, they have to be explained. Further, long and complex, or hypothetical questions as well as two stimuli or double negatives should be avoided. Researchers should avoid using imputing or suggestive questions. In general, the participant should be able to identify the required information. If necessary, it should be clear to which time period the questions refer. If the participants can choose from responses, these need to be disjointed and exhaustive. Finally, it is necessary that the context of the question does not influence the answer to the question. (cf. Porst 2014: 688-697) Similarly, the possible responses need to be sophisticated as well, if the questions are not open. For easy numeric questions, it might be reasonable to choose open answers rather than categories, because they are easy to assess even as open questions and the participants are not biased and have to think harder about their answer. The number of possible answers – especially on scales – can differ, too. More response categories give the participant more options and allow more nuances. However, they also increase the cognitive effort required to answer the question. Recent studies confirmed the rule of thumb that a choice of between five and nine responses is legitimate. Fewer response options are paradoxically less reliable and more often do not bring any advantages. Additionally, researchers have to consider the educational background of the participant group and the mode in which the questions are presented. Another aspect is whether to present an even or uneven number of responses. The advantage (and disadvantage) of even numbers is that the participant has to decide on a tendency. Generally, uneven scales are recommended. Sometimes it might be sensible to include the category "I don't know". It might not be necessary to label all possibilities of the scale, e.g. on a seven-item scale the only labels could be "I strongly disagree", "I do not agree nor disagree", and "I strongly agree". However, it is better to formulate all possibilities. Finally, the responses might start with the positive answers first and change to starting with the negative answers after a couple of questions to avoid response patterns. (cf. Franzen 2014: 703-709)

Depending on length and topic of the questionnaire, the order of the questions can be of utmost importance. The questionnaire should start with easy questions to motivate the participants and end with easy questions so they do not give up at the end. The questionnaire should not start with social-statistical questions, which are essential to most studies, because they might bore the participant and make him/her quit before any relevant questions have been answered. The most important questions should be placed in the middle of the questionnaire so that they are answered even if the participants do not make it to the end of the questionnaire. Very sensitive and awkward questions should be asked towards the end, because in an early stage they might cause the participant to quit the questionnaire and might influence the response behaviour for the following questions. Finally, questions should be ordered in content blocks to avoid confusing the participants. (cf. Klöckner & Friedrichs 2014)

For the study at hand, two short questionnaires were designed. One was distributed before the actual tasks, retrieving meta data from the participants and asking questions about experiences and first opinions, while the retrospective questionnaire dealt mainly with assessing personal performance and assessing the MT output. A detailed analysis of the questionnaires can be found in Chapter 8.

7.1.3 Keylogging

Keylogging software allows the researcher to analyse the text production process and the associated mental processes. All key (and mouse) activities are recorded during text production, including typing processes, special key combinations and deleting activities. Further, pauses are recorded, which indicate reading processes and the segmentation of the text, which is done subconsciously by the participant and might highlight text passages that require high cognitive effort. However, one has to keep in mind that the data only allows us to speculate on mental processes of participants engaged in text production. Other methods, especially eyetracking, can help to interpret the participants' behaviour, e.g. during pauses (cf. Jakobsen 2011: 37-38). Recording keylogging data with a keylogger is unobtrusive, because the programme runs in the background and, hence, the recording process is not noticeable (cf. Carl 2012: 4108). The keylogging recordings, however, only provide information about filled times, i.e. when a key was pressed, and about unfilled times, i.e. when no key was pressed. Therefore, the experimenter has to interpret what this filled and unfilled times mean in terms of the cognitive writing process (cf. Baaijen et al. (2012: 246–247)).

Keystroke logging is not only used to record translation processes but all kinds of writing processes, such as observing cognitive processes while writing in general, writing strategies in professional and creative writing, writing progress in children, first and second language acquisition, studies of writing difficulties or professionalism, as well as in educational environments. The main focus is often on pauses and revisions in these studies, because they are considered a clear indicator of cognitive effort and of discrepancies respectively, which also indicate problems in the writing process. (cf. Leijten & Van Waes 2013: 360–361) Writing process observations can further be divided into direct and indirect as well as synchronous and asynchronous methods. Keystroke logging can be characterised as indirect and synchronous, while think-aloud protocols would be considered indirect and synchronous and retrospective protocols indirect and asynchronous. An example for indirect and asynchronous methods would be the analysis of the produced text. (cf. ibid.: 361)

While the participants usually are informed about the recording process in scientific studies, keylogging software is also used to record keystrokes of computer and Internet users secretly, e.g. employers might use keylogging software to supervise whether the employees only use the computer/the Internet for job-related task, or keylogging software might be used by attackers in malware to steal passwords for e-mail or e-commerce accounts, etc. Although security software can usually cope with hidden keyloggers, it is very hard to detect this kind of malware, because it sends information via software which is very similar to the software of e-mail services and, hence, becomes almost undetectable. (cf. Davarpanah Jazi et al. 2014)

Different keylogging parameters will be used to assess the cognitive effort and to predict problem solving activity in the study at hand. The individual parameters will be introduced when they first become relevant in Chapters 9 to 12

7.1.4 Eyetracking

The term *eyetracking* refers to the methodology with which human eye movement can be recorded and assessed. The light enters the eye through the *pupil* in human vision, which is smaller when it is bright and bigger when there is only little light.[4] The images are turned upside down and projected onto the *retina* – the back of the eyeball. The retina consists of light-sensitive cells, called *cones* and *rods*. Cones are responsible for colour vision, while rods are very sensitive to light and enable vision even in dim environments. The *fovea* is a very small spot – about two percent of our visual field – at the back of our eyeball where cones are excessively over-presented. Hence, this is the spot where we can see the most clearly. Accordingly, we have to move our eyes so that the information we want to concentrate on is projected onto the fovea. The information gathered via the fovea is prioritised during processing due to a magnification factor. When recording eye movements, the pupil and the *cornea* are very important. The cornea covers most of the eye and reflects light. Light is reflected by the cornea and the lens as well, but the reflection of the cornea is the brightest reflection. Three pairs of *muscles* regulate human eye movement, which conduct the three-dimensional coordination of the eyeballs in the human head. The most important measurement in eyetracking does not report eye movement, but rather at which point the eye lingers and focuses. This point is called *fixation* and can last from a few milliseconds to a couple of seconds (Holmqvist et al. 2011: 21-23). The basic assumption is that the human pays attention to the point (s)he fixates on (a concept also known as the eye-mind assumption introduced in a reading study by Just & Carpenter (1980)), although this is not always the case. The eye, however, is not completely still when it fixates a point. There are also *tremors*, whose exact role is unknown, *drifts*, which move the eye away form the fixated points, and *microsaccades*, which bring the eyes back to the fixated point. The eye's movement from one fixation to the next fixation is called *saccade*. Saccades are the

---

[4]The pupil itself, however, does not get larger or smaller as it is a hole in the Iris that lets light pass through to the retina. The muscles *sphincter pupillae* and *dilator pupillae* are responsible for the dilation and the diminution of the pupil. (cf. Snell & Lemp 2013: n. p.)

fastest movements the body can make and they last only 30 to 80 milliseconds. Further, it is assumed that the human is blind during this movement. The eye does not always take the shortest way to the next fixation and does not always hit the correct position and hence has to reposition itself before fixating. This small repositioning movement is often called *glissade*. If our eyes follow a moving object, it makes a completely different movement, which is also controlled by a different part of the brain, the so-called *smooth pursuit*. "Smooth pursuit requires something to follow, while saccades can be made on a white wall or even in the dark, with no stimuli at all." (Holmqvist et al. 2011: 23) Eye movements are typically measured in *visual degrees* or *minutes* instead of mm on the screen. While the eyes often move in relation to each other, some eye movements also work in the opposite direction (*vergence* eye movement). Furthermore, most people have two equally weighted eyes, but there are also many people who have a dominant and a more passive eye. (cf. ibid.: 21-24)

Eyetracking is a very promising method for studying translation processes, because it records where and how long the eyes are fixating and accordingly what the participant is concentrating on – valuable insights into the process that cannot be recorded by other methods. The eye movement data give us promising and important hints about what is going on in the translators mind, although we can only interpret the data and cannot be entirely sure what is happening in the translators' black box. This research method, however, brings not only advantages, but also challenges to translation process research. The kind of eyetracking system, for example, has to be considered. A remote eyetracker is considered ecologically more valid, because the participant can move comparably freely in front of the computer screen, while head-mounted eyetrackers and eyetrackers with chin or head rests produce more accurate data. Eyetracking glasses, on the other hand, liberate the participants from the screen. In contrast to questionnaires, think-aloud protocols, and keylogging technology, which cause only very low costs if the experimenter has a PC or laptop, a recording device and/or Internet available (if necessary at all), eyetracking requires expensive hard- and software. Further, the eyetracking experiments must be conducted in a comparable environment, e.g. similar lighting conditions (cf. O'Brien 2009: 251–254; on detailed information on requirements for a suitable eyetracking lab see Rösener (2016: 251–254)). The texts should be no longer than about 300 words in eyetracking studies so that scrolling does not become necessary, because this makes the data harder to assess. Similarly, the texts should be in a font size of 16 or 18 and at least 1.5 line spacing so that the eyetracking data can be mapped correctly. (cf. O'Brien 2009: 261–262)

Eyetracking is not only relevant for translation process studies – indeed it is a rather small research area that uses eyetracking – but also in reading and writing research, psycholinguistics, neuropsychology, cognitive psychology, usability testing, research in sports, advertising, marketing, product placements, medical appliances, human-machine interactions, computer science, etc. (for more information on eyetracking applications see e.g. Duchowski 2003: 131-226) The analysis in the upcoming chapters will focus on fixation durations and fixation counts, however the concrete parameters will be introduced, when they appear first in §9 to §12.

7.1.5 Neuroscientific methods

Translation studies have only in recent years slowly begun to use neuroscientific methods to ultimately tackle the problem of what is going on in the black box while translating. In this chapter, I will briefly present the functionalities of *EEG* and *fMRI* methods. As these methods are used in very controlled experiments and cannot (yet) be used in authentic translation tasks, none of these methods were used in the study at hand.

Electroencephalography (EEG) is used to record electrical activity in the brain. To measure these activities, high conductance electrodes are put on certain locations of the human skull. Depending on what needs to be measured and how precise the recordings need to be, 16 to 256 electrodes are distributed on the head. The electrodes are usually placed on the participant's head with the help of a cap, and a special gel or another liquid is used to increase the conductivity between the electrodes and the skull. The EEG is either recorded in reference to one common passive electrode – monopolar (referential) recordings – or between different pairs of electrodes – bipolar recordings. EEG signals are recorded with a sampling rate of at least 100Hz, but 500Hz or higher are standard today. The electrodes are named according to the brain area they are located on (letters) and on which brain sites (odd numbers are on the left, even on the right), e.g. electrode F3 is on the frontal lobe on the left-hand side. The electrical activity in the brain produces oscillations which have been assigned to functions, and the pathology of the brain. However, not only oscillations but also typical patterns can be studied with the help of the EEG signals. Artefacts in the EEG signals can be produced by external influences like head movement, blinking, or other muscular activities. These artefacts can hardly be avoided and have to be eliminated from the recordings, if possible, before the signals are analysed and interpreted (cf. Freeman & Quiroga 2012: 5–6). One event-related brain potential (ERP) that can be measured with the EEG is the N400. This amplitude peaks negatively after about 400ms after a stimuli was presented. The N400 is widely acknowledged as a measure for semantic processing. If, for example, a sentence is presented including one stimuli that is semantically nonsensical, the negative amplitude will be greatly visible 400ms after the nonsensical stimuli was presented. (cf. Kutas & Federmeier 2011) Translation studies has used EEG, for example to investigate priming, monitoring and exhibiton[5]; conceptualisation (e.g. Grabner et al. 2007); or expectancy violations (e.g. Elmer et al. 2010). Details on the studies can be found in the overview article on EEG and translation published by Hansen-Schirra (2017).

Although the field of *functional magnetic resonance imaging* (fMRI) is still very young, the discoveries made so far are tremendous. The applications of fMRI include all areas of brain imaging and have become a very important tool for neuroscience research, both in clinical as well as cognitive research. (cf. Faro & Mohamed 2006: v-vi) The basic idea in brain imaging techniques goes back to first experiments in 1980 that assumed that the regional cerebral blood flow could mirror the activities of neurons. In 1990, it was documented "that functional brain mapping is possible by using the venous blood oxygen level-dependent (BOLD) magnetic resonance imaging (MRI) contrast" (Kim & Bandettini 2006: 3). The BOLD method depends on the level of deoxyhemoglobin, which can be seen in the signal intensity of magnetic resonance images when the level changes, and can hence be used for human brain imaging. fMRI can be used to study diverse brain functions like vision, language, motor abilities, and cognition (cf. ibid.). Language was one of the first functions that was ascribed to a particular area in the brain and has been the subject of research for over 100 years now. Compared to other brain imaging methods, fMRI is especially useful to show language areas in the brain, because it is non-invasive and produces images of good quality and with good localisation (amongst other benefits). It is rather difficult to assign brain regions to single language processes like phonetic, semantic, or syntactic processes, because they often work together. Carefully selected research designs with contrasting conditions can, however, help in tackling these problems (cf. Binder 2006: 245-248).

These methods for analysing the brain functions open doors to find out what is happening in the human mind. Although these methods are mainly used in a medical and diagnostic context, they also help us to understand the human black box. Especially concerning translation research, most of the work is still ahead of us, as these methods have hardly been used, yet, and it appears difficult to

---

[5]Which are being examined by Katharina Oster in her PhD thesis in Germersheim, Uni Mainz (work in progress)

test translation concepts with these methods. However, some work has already been done, e.g. the above mentioned studies using EEG, or Ahrens et al. (2010) or Franceschini et al. (2003) using fMRI. A great deal of exciting research can be expected in the next years, which might show if and in which aspects the translators' brains work differently to other bilinguals.

7.1.6 Data triangulation and choice of participants

Triangulation in research means linking two or more sources of data, researchers, methodological approaches, theoretical ideas or analytical designs so that the different advantages of each methods can be exploited (cf. Thurmond 2001: 253-257). As a result, data triangulation has become more and more important in translation studies, too (e.g. Alves 2003). Triangulation has the advantages that the research data become more reliable, inventive approaches are developed to comprehend and interpret research hypotheses, existing theories might be challenged or confirmed, and a phenomenon can be better understood. Every triangulation approach on its own has individual advantages ad disadvantages, whether it is data, researcher, methodological, theory, or analysis triangulation. In general, these include

> [an] increased amount of time needed in comparison to single strategies, [...] difficult[ies] of dealing with the vast amount of data, [...] potential disharmony based on investigator biases, [...] conflicts because of theoretical frameworks, and [...] lack of understanding about why triangulation strategies were used. (ibid.: 256)

Conclusively, triangulation is valuable to gather findings from different perspectives that are complete and confirm each other, and to strengthen the findings. The researchers, however, must be able to explain why they used the triangulation method and why it was necessary. (cf. ibid.: 257) Many studies have adopted this approach in translation process research in recent years, especially concerning data triangulation. The danger, however, is that, amongst other possible problems, the amount of data becomes overwhelming. Some solutions on how to deal with large data sets might be to work in research teams so that either the same research topic is analysed together or that different researchers analyse various hypotheses on the same data (O'Brien 2009: 260-261, 264).

No matter which methodologies are chosen for the individual study, they all have in common that the participants for the study must be chosen carefully. Although professional translators are often considered more valuable as they have practical experience, they are harder to acquire for a study and often expect financial compensation as they miss (part of) their work day. Students on the other hand are easier to acquire as eyetracking studies in translation process research are usually conducted at a university and the study might even be credited in classes. Further, the participants may complete some studies, like questionnaire studies, at home, while other studies, especially those that require special equipment like most eyetracking-, EEG-, or fMRI-studies can only be realised in special labs. In addition, one question is whether the participants will commit to the task with equal enthusiasm when they invest their free time in participating in studies as opposed to when they are paid or rewarded in a different manner for the task. Additionally, limited funding might restrict the number of participants that can be recruited for the study. However, it is doubtful whether small participant numbers, e.g. twelve participants or even less, can actually return generalisable results. Nonetheless, these studies are valuable to build hypotheses for larger studies. Finally, the professionalism of the participants has to be addressed. Not every translator with a degree in translation is equally capable of all tasks, e.g. domain and text types might play a role or experience with CAT-tools depending on the kind of study. Some issues may also occur which disqualify the participant for the study, e.g. his/her typing skills, the language competence, the ability to follow instructions, or if the participant feels intimidated, judged, or pressured during the session (cf. O'Brien 2009: 254-259, 262).

7.2 General information on the data set, post-editing guidelines, and setup of the experiment

The study was conducted at the University of Mainz, Faculty of Translation Studies, Linguistics and Cultural Studies in Germersheim by a team of the English Linguistics and Translation Studies in 2012 on behalf of the Center for Research and Innovation in Translation and Translation Technology (CRITT), Copenhagen Business School, Denmark. The experiments became part of the CRITT TPR database that collects translation process data for different tasks and in different languages (find more information on the database later in this chapter). In total, 24 participants took part in the study, twelve of them professional translators (university degree and at least some professional work experience), and twelve semi-professional translators (students of the university with only little professional work experience) – see detailed information in §8.1.

Four newspaper articles and two sociology-related texts with different complexity levels had to be processed – all English to German. The length of the texts varies between 100 and 148 words. Text 1 (148 words) deals with a former hospital nurse who killed four of his patients. Text 2 (139 words) covers the increasing prices in Great Britain that are not in balance to salary increases. Steven Spielberg's refusal to be part of the Olympics in China to protest against Chinese politics is the topic of Text 3 (132 words). These first three texts of this study were also part of Hvelplund's (2011) PhD thesis and three texts were added for this study. Text 4 (100 words) reports on the necessity that developing countries need to be supported in environmental issues. Text 5 (121 words) informs about the origins of the field of sociology. And finally, Text 6 (112 words) describes hunter-gatherer societies.

The participants were asked to translate two text from scratch (TfS), bilingually post-edit (PE) two machine translated texts and monolingually post-edit (MPE) two machine translated texts. There were no time restrictions and the participants could use the Internet freely as a research tool. Before and after the processing task, they had to complete questionnaires that dealt with general informations about the participant, his/her attitude towards MT, and a self-estimation (see Chapter 8). The texts were distributed in a manner that every text was translated eight times from scratch, bilingually post-edited eight times, and monolingually post-edited eight times, but no participant worked with the same text sequence (cf. Table 7.1).

Table 7.1: Distribution of the texts exemplified on the first eight participants

Participant	TfS		PE		MPE	
P01	Text 1	Text 2	Text 3	Text 4	Text 5	Text 6
P02	Text 3	Text 4	Text 5	Text 6	Text 1	Text 2
P03	Text 5	Text 6	Text 1	Text 2	Text 3	Text 4
P04	Text 2	Text 1	Text 4	Text 3	Text 6	Text 5
P05	Text 4	Text 3	Text 6	Text 5	Text 2	Text 1
P06	Text 6	Text 5	Text 2	Text 1	Text 4	Text 3
P07	Text 1	Text 3	Text 2	Text 4	Text 5	Text 6
P08	Text 3	Text 5	Text 4	Text 6	Text 1	Text 2
			etc.			

There were no time restrictions for the tasks and the participants were given the following guidelines for the PE task (see also Carl et al. 2014: 153):

- Retain as much raw translation as possible.

- Don't hesitate too long over a problem.

- Don't worry if style is repetitive.

- Don't embark on time-consuming research.

- Make changes only where absolutely necessary: correct words or phrases that are nonsensical, wrong, and if there's enough time left, ambiguous.

The tasks were conducted in *Translog II*, a program used to record keystrokes, mouse activities and gaze data with the help of the *Tobii TX300* eyetracker, which also recorded the sessions, keystrokes, mouse activities and gaze data in Tobii Studio. The eyetracking and keylogging data were combined in Translog II via word alignment. The aligned keylogging and eyetracking data are available in the CRITT TPR database. The data of Version 1.6 of the database were used for the analysis in the thesis at hand, if not stated differently. The keylogging software, the eyetracking system, and the database will be described in detail in the following.

Translog was first developed in 1995 with the primary goal of adding "hard information" to think-aloud protocol studies that were conducted frequently in the early days. The software is designed to log translation processes rather than mere writing processes. Further, the recordings of the sessions could be presented to the participants after the experiments for retrospective think-aloud interviews. The programme had three main functions: it could display the source text, it could record all key activities, and the recorded data could be displayed dynamically as well as linearly. The first Translog version for Windows was released towards the end of 1999 and called Translog2000 (cf. Jakobsen 2011: 38-39). Within the scope of the Eye-to-IT project, Translog was rewritten to supplement eyetracking with the keylogging data. This combination of methods was first available in Translog2006. However, an external eyetracking device is still essential to record the eyetracking data. The data are combined via a gaze-to-word mapping (GWM) application which was developed in Tampere. Further, the data were no longer stored as binary code, but as open XML code (cf. ibid.: 42-43). However, the transmission between the eyetracker and the GWM programme was not flexible enough, so a new version of Translog, *Translog II*, was developed, which directly communicates with the eyetracking hardware. The eyetracking and keylogging data can be mapped automatically via external software. If noise is in the data, the mappings can be improved manually (cf. Carl 2012: 4108-4109). In Translog II, projects with various properties can be created, run, and recorded. Further, the log files can be replayed in real time, analysed according to event statistics, and presented as linear presentations of the user activities as well as plots of the pauses. Two programmes are contained in the software. First, the experimenter can create, replay and analyse the projects in *Translog Supervisor*, while the experiments are conducted in *Translog User* (cf. ibid.: 4109). Translog II and other auxiliary tools as well as publications and instructions can be downloaded for free on the CRITT's website.[6]

The *Tobii TX300* is a remote eyetracker that records gaze data with a sampling rate of 300Hz. These raw gaze data include a time stamp, the eye position, the gaze point, the pupil diameter, and a validity code (indicating the confidence of correctly identifying which is the left and the right eye) for each eye. Due to the large head movement box, the participants can move their heads relatively freely in front of the screen (in an operating distance of 50-80 cm) and no chin rest or alike is necessary. All hardware is integrated in one eyetracking unit that looks like an ordinary screen so the participants can work in an almost natural environment. The single components are a screen unit including a web cam, an eyetracking unit, and a digital angle gauge (cf. tobii 2016). The software *Tobii Studio* can be used to set up and conduct the experiments (including an automatic calibrating system). Further, the experimenter can replay the screen recordings, track the key and mouse activities and assess the eyetracking data, which can either be downloaded as raw data or be automatically pre-interpreted by the software. However, Tobii Studio will not be presented in detail, because the experiment was conducted mainly via *Translog II* and most of the evaluation was done with the data of the CRITT TPR database (except for the analysis of the screen recording data).

As mentioned above, the data which are used for the study at hand is part of the CRITT TPR database (cf. https://sites.google.com[7]). The database contains process data of various studies conducted to explore the translation process. The data set at hand is part of a larger multilingual collection in which students and professionals worked with the same six texts, but translated and post-edited them in Translog II into different languages: Spanish, Japanese, Danish, Chinese, Hindi, and German. Sometimes only a subset of the tasks or texts was recorded. Additionally, one study dealt with copying the texts. The database further contains

---

[6]https://sites.google.com/site/centretranslationinnovation/translog-ii, last accessed 18 November 2016

[7]https://sites.google.com/site/centretranslationinnovation/tpr-db, last accessed 20th November 2016

eleven studies that were conducted in CASMACAT, a CAT tool especially designed for PE.[8] Finally, the database also includes 13 individual, unrelated studies that were all conducted with Translog, too. So, the database consists of 1562 sessions with seven source languages and nine target languages, 15 different tasks, 620,210 source text tokens and 657,948 target text tokens. The tables that are provided for each data set in the database already present a great deal of information on keylogging and eyetracking data, most of which are already aligned on a word and sentence level, which simplifies the evaluation. While some data are "pure" eyetracking and keylogging data, like *Del* that presents the number of deleted tokens or *FixS* that informs on the number of fixations on the source text unit, other parameters are provided which present processed data, like *Nunit* that reports on the number of micro units or *Nedit* that informs about the number of times the segment has been edited. Finally, there is also additional information on the source and target text units like *PoS*, which presents the part of speech of the token (cf. Carl & Schaeffer 2013 or Carl, Schaeffer & Bangalore 2016, the papers also provides a detailed description of the parameter contained in the database).

7.3 Placing the research hypotheses and methods into the field of translation process research

The exploration of the translation process seems like a bottomless pit because so many aspects of the process can be considered with various methods. Krings published an article in 2005, in which he attempts to model the countless aspects and methods of translation process research. These models will be used in the following to place the research hypotheses and methods into the field. In his factor model, Krings (2005: 344–347) summarises the single factors that influence the translation process in three main bundles: task-related factors, translator-related factors, and work environment-related factors. The individual factors that belong to these bundles are judged by Krings to be the most influential factors on the translation process, however he does not claim completeness.

The first bundle refers to the factors that influence the process due to the differences in the translation tasks and include factors like different source and target languages, different translation assignments, different text types and text domains, the language direction of the translation (from or into the native language or between two foreign languages), and differences and similarities to neighbour-

---

[8]http://www.casmacat.eu/, last accessed 20 November 2016

ing tasks like interpreting and PE. These factors are controlled by the experiment settings. Every translator works with the same texts, has to do the same tasks, and works with the same language combination.

The second bundle approaches the individual differences of translators like experience, language proficiency, domain knowledge, or individual strategical preferences. These factors are, on the one hand, retrieved in the questionnaires, and on the other hand, statistical methods are used in the analysis to figure out whether the findings in the sample of 24 individual translators could indicate assumptions for the total population.

Finally, the third bundle of factors includes the influence of technical aids or MT, the availability of research aids, and general factors like available time or possible contact to colleagues, etc. These factors are also predefined and controlled by the experiment settings. All participants had to work on the same computer, in the same editor, with the same MT output. They could use the Internet for research and could take as much time as they needed. Although this constricted setup prevents an all natural work environment, it still has the major advantage that all participants have to work under the same conditions.

7.4 Previous research with the data set

The data set used in this dissertation is highly relevant for the designated research purposes. In the following, different studies will be introduced that were published on the same data set but with different research hypotheses. This is not intended to be exhaustive, but rather to provide some insights on the diverse use of the data. First, studies are presented that dealt only with the English-German data set, then three studies are introduced that investigated multilingual relationships using the CRITT TPR database, including the English-German data set.

In a pilot study by Čulo et al. (2014), the authors concentrated not only on processes but mainly on the TfS and PE products. Therefore, different linguistic properties and their realisation in the TfS and (monolingual) PE tasks were analysed. The main focus was on the changes of translation strategies in the different tasks. PE should not only accelerate the translation process, but should produce an intelligible text, though questions of style and idiomacy may be secondary.

In addition to inconsistent translations and atypical syntax, unidiomatic translations were one issue for discussion. In Text 3, the translators had to deal with the phrase *In a gesture [...]*. While the translators naturally chose an idiomatic translation in the TfS task, e.g. *Mit einer Geste* or *Als Zeichen*, the MT system translated the phrase literally with *In einer Geste* which is unidiomatic in German. Five out of seven post-editors kept this translation and did not change it into an idiomatic expression in the bilingual PE task. This cannot be counted as an error given that the task was for post-editors to retain as much of the unedited machine translation as long as the final target sentence was understandable to a German native speaker. However, in the MPE task, more participants were inclined to change the unidiomatic version into an idiomatic one. This indicates that the PE process shifts priorities, maybe due to the fact that the translators are working with two texts in parallel instead of just one text.

The last analysed example in the paper highlights that MPE can be very problematic due to the missing source, as content mistakes might remain unnoticed. Although the other examples might suggest that the quality of the monolingually post-edited texts is better than in the post-edited texts, severe content mistakes only occurred in MPE (further information on content mistakes in MPE can be found in Nitzke (2016b) – the study will also be described briefly further below.)

In the final analysis, fixation counts were compared between TfS and PE in Text 3 for finite and non-finite clauses. While the fixation counts were equal for both clause types in TfS, fewer fixations were counted in the PE task and the results were not balanced: there were more fixation counts on finite clauses than on infinite. Therefore, the hypothesis that non-finite clauses cause errors in the MT output and interference effects was not confirmed nor that they cause longer processing times in PE.

The study by Carl et al. (2014) first discusses the motivation for PE in the translation business. Afterwards, different research areas for PE are introduced: different PE types that appeal to different target text functions, text types and their suitability for MT/PE, users' needs, PE effort, PE as a MT quality evaluation method, technical aspects, training of post-editors, and the changing role of translators. Further, they point out key aspects of CASMACAT, MateCat and Translog II, and provide a detailed description of the English-German data set.

In addition to some analyses of the questionnaires (see full discussion in Chapter 8), one chapter of the study is dedicated to the evaluation of the unconscious reading and writing data of the participants. The average time a participant needed to translate a word reveals that most participants needed more time for translation from scratch; only one participant required more time for the PE task and three for the MPE task. No translator was the fastest in TfS (see more details on session durations in). Further, different PE styles are discussed and visualised: In both PE and TfS, different production phases can be separated – "an (optional) orientation phase, a drafting (or post-editing) phase in which the actual translation is produced (or post-edited) and an optional final revision." (ibid:

159). Accordingly, different PE patterns can be identified, e. g. during drafting, some post-editors first read the source text (ST) and then check whether the MT reproduces the information from the ST, while other post-editors read the MT output and only refer to the ST when they come across words/passages that seem unlikely or problematic. In the subchapter on PE strategies, a relation between text complexity and eyetracking data is indicated: "Fixation duration as well as fixation counts clearly show that the values increase in dependence of the complexity during translation while source text complexity does not seem to have such a strong impact on the post-editing task." (ibid: 164) The keylogging data are also investigated for the PE task of Text 3. The eight participants who post-edited this text differ a lot in their editing activity. Therefore, a more sensitive value for inefficiency is introduced (*InEff*) which evaluates the amount of editing activity – a high InEff score indicates a lot of activity, which is less efficient, and vice versa. Despite individual PE behaviour, some phrases reach a higher inefficiency score than others, which indicates that either the ST phrases are very complex and difficult to translate or the MT output is hard to adjust.

In her study, Nitzke (2016b) explores research behaviour and target text quality of monolingual post-edited texts through product analysis as well as screen recording, keylogging and eyetracking data. Text quality aspects were divided into superficial mistakes and content mistakes. The data show that superficial mistakes are made almost as often in TfS, PE, and MPE with no significant correlation to the experience of the participants. Content mistakes (mean per session and participant: 2.23, sd: 1.18), however, occur much more often in MPE than in PE (mean: 0.30, sd: 0.51) and TfS (mean: 0.61, sd: 0.83). The screen-recordings revealed that fewer words and phrases are researched in MPE than in the other two tasks, but when a word/phrase is researched, it usually requires more steps to find a solution than in the other tasks. Further, no significant correlation between research behaviour and experience of the participants was found and sources were used slightly differently. The keylogging data indicate longer production times when the word/phrase was researched, but shorter production times for monolingual PE than in the other tasks. The eyetracking data (total gaze duration on the target text), however, do not suggest differences in the tasks (see also Chapter 9 on research behaviour). Unfortunately, the data set is not big enough for MPE to conduct statistical tests on these primary results.

So far, the three discussed studies have dealt exclusively with the English-German data set. However, the data set was also used for multilingual studies, which made use of the different subsets in the CRITT TPR database. Some of these will be summarised in the following.

Winther Balling & Carl (2014) examine which parameters have an effect on the time that is needed to translate from scratch or post-edit a target text equivalent of the corresponding source text unit. For their analysis, they used keylogging and eyetracking data of 65 translators translating and post-editing the same English ST into Chinese, German, Hindi, and Spanish (all data sets are taken from the CRITT TPR database).

After a brief overview of the field of translation process research and its methods, the software Translog II, and the CRITT TPR database, they introduce the concepts Alignment Unit (AU), Fixation Unit (FU), and Production Unit (PU), because the main aim of the study is to explain differences in AUs. An AU represents (a) word(s) in the ST and the corresponding word(s) in the TT. The tokens in this unit do not need to be coherent, i. e. the AU might be separated by parts of another unit. Therefore, AUs can be grouped into continuous and discontinuous units.

In the next chapter, a detailed analysis of the considered variables is presented as well as the multiple regression model. Variables that were not significant were removed. Finally, the chapter discusses the results, which include amongst others that TfS takes longer than PE in all languages; that ST words with a low frequency take longer to be produced in the TT, especially by students; that a high number of translation possibilities has slowing effects in PE but not in TfS; that parallel processing (shifting the attention between ST, TT, and the keyboard) is time-consuming; and that the overall translation time is different for the different target languages (translations into Hindi take the most time, while Spanish translators were the quickest).

It is assumed in numerous theories that one-to-one translations are less difficult to produce than differently phrased translations. The literal translation hypothesis assumes that translators translate a source text unit literally first and then develop a looser version for the target text (cf. Chesterman 2011). In a paper by Schaeffer & Carl (2014), a metric is introduced that measures how literal translations are. Further, they evaluate the effort that is necessary for non-literal translation. To investigate the issue, they use the gaze behaviour of translators for different language pairs from the CRITT TPR. Different lexical realisations of source words were counted and for some words a higher variation was detected than for others. Therefore, some words require more effort to realise in the target language than others. Next, on a syntactic basis, alignment crossing is introduced: The metric computes the *Cross* values for single words, based on their position in the source and the target language. Depending on the point of view, the *Cross* value can be realised from the source text as a reference and the target text as output (*CrossS*) or the other way around (*CrossT*). The smaller the

Cross value, the more similar the texts are in terms of structure; when the *Cross* value is high, syntax varies significantly.

In chapter three of the article, where translator behaviour is analysed for various aspects, different parts of the database were used. To map the alignment crossing, 313 translation sessions (source languages: Danish and English; target languages: Chinese, Danish, English, German, Hindi, and Spanish) were used for analysis. The analysis showed that higher *Cross* values strongly correlate with total reading time on source and target words and, therefore, prove that high syntactic variation takes more effort to produce. In the next subchapter, alignment crossing in the PE tasks is analysed (96 sessions of nine English target texts that were post-edited for German, Hindi, and Spanish). Strong correlations were found between negative *CrossT* values and total reading time on the source text as well as between *CrossS* and total reading time on the target text. Finally, 24 TfS sessions from English into Danish and 65 PE sessions from English into Spanish and German were considered for the translation choices analysis. Different realisations of source text items were counted and, for the analysis, only items were taken into consideration that were realised at least in nine different ways. A strong correlation was found between production time of target text word and number of alternative translations. Further, "[w]ith few choices posteditors are quicker than translators, but this distance decreases as the number of translation choices increase." (ibid.: 34). Additionally, a strong correlation was detected between total reading time on target text word and number of alternative translations. For translation from scratch, a correlation was found between total reading time on source text and translation variations. However, no correlation was detected for PE.

The role of co-activation of languages in translation and its influence on the translator's behaviour is investigated in Bangalore et al. (2016). Four subsets of the database were used for evaluation: the translations and post-edits of the English source text into Danish, German, and Spanish as well as the English-English copying study, which was used as baseline. The syntactic variations in those data sets were measured with the help of manually created annotations that include three features – valency of the verb, voice, and clause type. On the basis of this annotation, entropy values were calculated for the target sentences, which were then used to correlate them with measures of cognitive effort, in this case total reading time on source and target text as well as coherent typing activity. The findings were compared across languages.

In TfS, syntactic variation could be positively correlated with total reading time per source word and production time. However, no effect of syntactic variation on the total reading time was found for PE, which indicates that the MT output primes the participants in the PE tasks. A highly significant positive correlation between syntactic entropy and lexical translation entropy confirms that lexical and semantic aspects cannot be examined completely autonomously. In addition, the study supports the hypothesis that source and target texts are co-activated and that different levels of co-activation can be detected during translation.

This overview shows the potential of the multilingual CRITT TPR database. Many different research questions can be addressed concerning translation products, translation processes, and cognitive effort during translation. The study at hand will expand on the existing studies and explore problem solving behaviour in the English-German data set.

7.5 Session durations

The first analysis of this study will be on the time the participants spent on each text and task. This was similarly assessed by Carl et al. (2014: 157–158) for the data set and will be considered here, too. They showed that for most participants TfS took the longest. Only one participant (P18) needed more time on average for PE than for TfS, and three participants (P13, P14, P20) needed longer for MPE. However, due to illustration purposes, the data will be re-composed. Figure 7.1 shows the times for the single sessions per participant. Four MPE, four PE, and three TfS sessions were missing, so 44 MPE and PE sessions, and 45 TfS sessions were available for the evaluation. Considering all complete session, P05 and P22 needed most time to finish all tasks and texts.

As can be seen in Figure 7.2, most of the time was spent in the TfS task and the least in MPE. The differences between PE and MPE are not very noticeable. The mean time spent was highest for TFS (mean: 989.4 s, sd: 258.8 s), then PE (mean: 748.1, sd: 206 s), and the least time was spent on MPE (mean: 668.9 s, sd: 200.1 s). As the visualisation already suggests, the difference between PE and MPE is not significant ($t = -1.32, p = 0.1931$). However, the differences between PE and TfS ($t = 3.544, p < 0.001$) as well as between MPE and TfS ($t = 4.76, p < 0.0001$) are significant, proving that TfS takes significantly longer than both PE tasks.

The differences between the the total required time per session is not very different for students and professionals (see Table 7.2) and do not show significance for the whole task set ($t = -0.3, p = 0.7705$) or for the single tasks (TfS – $t = -0.04, p = 0.9634$; PE – $t = -0.61, p = 0.5504$; MPE – $t = -0.17, p = 0.8682$).

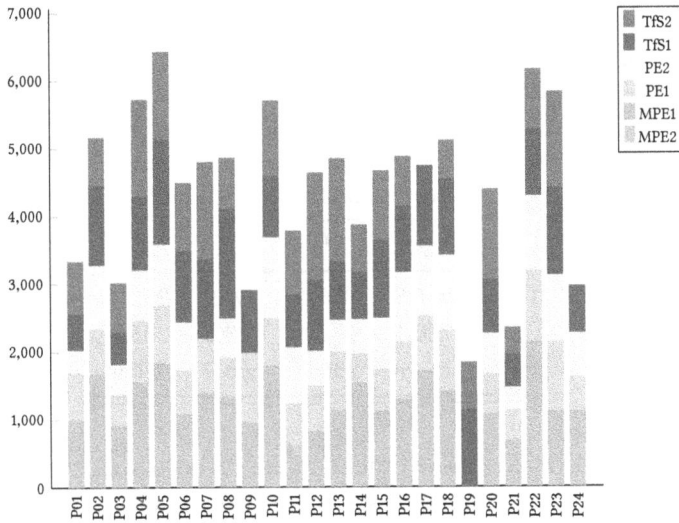

Figure 7.1: Length of sessions per participant in seconds

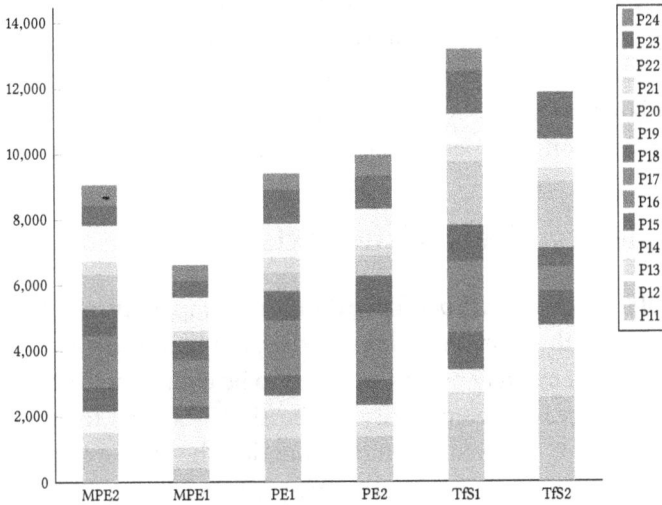

Figure 7.2: Added length of sessions per task in seconds

113

There is also no correlation between experience[9] and time neither for the complete data set ($r = -0.117$, $p = 0.334$) nor the single tasks (TfS – $r = -0.068$, $p = 0.7506$; PE – $r = -0.162$, $p = 0.4596$, MPE – $r = -0.312$, $p = 0.1464$).

Table 7.2: Mean and standard deviation for the duration of the sessions according to task and status

	Professionals		Students	
	Mean	SD	Mean	SD
TfS	986.9	276.4	991.9	252.3
PE	720.4	212.4	773.5	205.9
MPE	661.3	236.6	675.9	170.5

The result that TfS takes more time than the PE tasks was to be expected. Saving time is supposed to be one of the main benefits of PE, which was indeed achieved in this experiment. Interestingly, MPE saves a significant amount of time, which may have been expected as the participants do not have to process the source text. Further, it is quite surprising that there is no significant time difference between students and professionals in all tasks. A hypothesis could have been that professionals are significantly faster at least for the TfS task, because they are more experienced in this task. One reason why there is no significant difference might be that professionals are unfamiliar with the text type, because they do not have to deal with general language texts in their professional life. Another explanation might be that the professional translators are more careful with their translations/post-edits and hence spent more time on revising.

7.6 Complexity levels of the texts

Texts, even of the same text types, have different complexity levels. Therefore, the assumption is that the more complex a text is, the harder the text is to translate and the more problems may occur that need to be overcome. The following table (Table 7.3) introduces the complexity of the six texts used for the experiments. The higher the score of a text the more complex the text, except for the Flesch reading ease score, where it is the other way around.

---

[9] Find further information on the experience vector in §8.1.

Table 7.3: Complexity levels according to different test scores

	Text #					
	1	2	3	4	5	6
Flesch reading ease score	79.2	57.9	38.1	42.7	48.6	29.7
Automated readability index	7.6	13.7	20.5	14.9	14.1	13.8
Flesch-Kincaid grade level	5.6	10.9	16.1	12.3	11.5	13.1
Coleman-Liau index	9.2	12.3	15.1	15.6	14.6	16.4
Gunning fog index	8.9	14.7	20.2	16.4	15.3	16.8
SMOG index	8.7	12.7	16.1	14.2	13.5	14.1
Mean value[a]	8	12.9	17.6	14.7	13.8	14.8

[a]Excluding Flesch reading ease score

The scores from Table 7.3[10] show that the complexity level rises from Text 1 to Text 3, which was also stated in Hvelplund (2011: 88–93), who did not only take reading scores into consideration, but also word frequencies, and the amount of non-literal expressions. Starting with Text 4, the picture is not that clear. According to the Flesh reading ease score, Text 4 and 5 would be less complex than Text 3, but more complex than Text 2; and Text 6 would be the most complex. Some of the other scores contradict the picture. The Colman-Liau index indicates that Text 4 and 6 are more complex than Text 3, while other scores state that Text 3 is the most complex. Therefore, the mean value of the scores was calculated to summarise the results of the single scores, excluding the Flesch reading ease score, because it represents complexity with low numbers and in general the numbers are much higher than for the other scores. The mean of the scores rank the texts in the following order (least complex to most complex): Text 1, Text 2, Text 5, Text 4, Text 6, Text 3 – see Table 7.3. Note that the difference between Text 4 and Text 6 is very low.

7.7 General keystroke effort for modifications

This chapter presents the number of tokens that were inserted and deleted in the different tasks, first for all participants, then for professionals and semi-profes-

---

[10]Calculated on http://www.editcentral.com/gwt1/EditCentral.html (last accessed on 18 November 2014).

sionals separately. The data were automatically generated in Translog II. See also Carl et al. (2011: 132–133) on keylogging data evaluation for the first three texts.

Table 7.4 displays the total token count (*Token*) for all participants, the percentage of the insertions/deletions in relation to the total modification count for the single tasks (*Percent*), the mean (*Mean*), the standard deviation *(SD)* and median (*Median*) values for all participants, and finally the highest (*Max Token*) and lowest (*Min Token*) number of tokens that occurred in all the data. The corresponding participant is listed in the last two rows indicating the maximum and minimum token.

Table 7.4: Total token count

	MPE (42)		PE (41)		TfS (45)	
	Insertions	Deletions	Insertions	Deletions	Insertions	Deletions
Token	13450	12401	14913	13888	52509	9468
Percent	52	48	51.8	48.2	84.7	15.3
Mean	305.7	281.8	346.8	323	1117.2	201.4
SD	188.9	176.1	170.7	168.9	200.6	121.8
Median	273	258	286	265	1097	175
Max Token	1159 (P22)	1057 (P22)	956 (P22)	972 (P22)	1695 (P12)	598 (P22)
Min Token	92 (P1)	61 (P1)	138 (P13)	121 (P23)	750 (P12)	32 (P18)

MT produces a full target text, although it is often very error prone. Accordingly, it seems obvious that the number of inserted tokens is quite similar to the number of deleted tokens for MPE and PE. The defective target text segments are replaced by (expectedly) improved target text segments. However, it is interesting that in both tasks a few more tokens were inserted than deleted. In total, 68.2% of the participants inserted more tokens than they deleted in MPE, similarly 67.4% added tokens in PE. On average, the texts were 23.4 tokens longer after MPE and 23.8 tokens longer after PE. One reason might be that German translations are in general longer than the corresponding English source texts. The MT output, however, is often very literal. Therefore, it might be necessary to expand some text segments. Further, more insertions and deletions were made on average in the PE task compared to the MPE task, which might already indicate that the participants could recognise flaws in the MT output more easily and effectively when they were able to refer to the source text.

The nature of TfS explains that the number of insertions is much higher than the number of deletions. In contrast to the PE tasks, a target text has to be produced first. However, the number of deleted tokens is quite high, especially when we take into consideration that the number of inserted tokens includes the tokens that were deleted again at some point later in the session. This proves that human translators do not produce fully intact translations right away, but they may correct spelling mistakes as well as reconsider their initial decision. Of course the roots of the mistakes are very different, but a perfect translation does not come naturally, neither for the human nor for the machine. Finally, changes to the initial version and the final version are not only visible in the deletions but are also hidden in the insertions. Rephrasing does not necessarily mean deleting tokens and typing new tokens, but texts can be improved by insertions. One case could be that content was forgotten in the first text creation (unlikely with MT).

However, another very important characteristic of fluent texts, especially in German, is the use of particles. One example can be found in P18_T6 (participant 18 is the one with the lowest deletion number): The participant turned the sentence "Diese Gesellschaften sind folgerichtig oft nicht reich bevölkert", which is a correct sentence grammatically and in terms of content, into "Diese Gesellschaften sind folgerichtig oft**mals auch** nicht reich bevölkert",[11] which is an equally grammatically correct sentence with the same content. *Oft* and *oftmals* can be used synonymously, while *auch* emphasises the relation between this sentence and the previous sentence. This participant apparently thought that the text would be more fluent, if these particles were included, although the PE guidelines implied that stylistic improvements should not be made (see §7.3).

The amount of changes in the MPE and PE tasks are impressive: While some participants only needed a few tokens to adjust the MT (92 insertions and 61 deletions in MPE and 138 insertions and 141 deletions in PE), the participant who changed the most in one MPE task (1159 inserted tokens and 1057 deleted tokens) has a higher modification rate than required for the average translation (1117.2 inserted tokens and 201.4 deleted tokens) and almost as high a number for PE (956 inserted tokens and 972 deleted tokens).[12]

Table 7.5 and Table 7.6 divide the presented numbers into insertions and deletions for professional and semi-professional translators. The differences between both groups are not very great. As can be seen in Table 7.7, there is no significant differences between students and professionals, and no significant correlation between experience and keylogging behaviour. What catches the eye are the differences between max. token and min. token, which are not as major for the semi-professionals as those of the professionals. However, most of the max. token in the professional group were produced by one participant, which might suggest extensive editing behaviour of this participant.

---

[11]Highlighted by the author.

[12]According to the numbers, one of the MPE sessions and the PE session of participant 22 would qualify as outliers. However, as no technical reasons could explain the data, the sessions are not excluded from the data.

Table 7.5: Total token count of professional translators

	MPE (21)		PE (19)		TfS (23)	
	Insertions	Deletions	Insertions	Deletions	Insertions	Deletions
Token	6942	6543	7326	6907	26935	5233
Per cent	51.5	48.5	51.5	48.5	83.7	16.3
Mean	330.6	311.6	385.6	363.5	1171.1	227.5
Median	259	266	329	284	1141	184
SD	252.4	233.3	200.8	202.4	175	134
Max Token	1159 (P22)	1057 (P22)	956 (P22)	972 (P22)	1632 (P07)	598 (P22)
Min Token	92 (P01)	61 (P01)	138 (P13)	121 (P23)	882 (P21)	69 (P19)

Table 7.6: Total token count of semi-professional translators

	MPE (23)		PE (24)		TfS (24)	
	Insertions	Deletions	Insertions	Deletions	Insertions	Deletions
Token	6508	5858	7587	6981	25574	4235
Per cent	52.6	47.4	52.1	47.9	85.8	14.2
Mean	283	254.7	316.1	290.9	1065.6	176.5
Median	276	249	268	254	1044	142
SD	103.7	97.5	139.5	132.5	213.3	105.7
Max Token	564 (P18)	537 (P18)	723 (P09)	598 (P09)	1695 (P12)	546 (P12)
Min Token	104 (P4)	101 (P20)	138 (P14)	123 (P14)	750 (P12)	32 (P18)

Table 7.7: Significance tests for keylogging data

	Mann-Whitney-U-test			
	Insertions		Deletions	
	W	p	W	p
Total	2643.5	0.3302	2560	0.5341
MPE	250.5	0.775	258	0.9037
PE	327	0.1693	277.5	0.7749
HT	365	0.05964	342.5	0.1601

	Correlation with Experience			
	Insertions		Deletions	
	r	p	r	p
Total	0.067	0.2527	0.086	0.1493
MPE	0.126	0.2304	0.138	0.189
PE	0.125	0.2341	0.015	0.8864
HT	0.085	0.412	0.155	0.1353

7.8   General analysis of errors in the final texts

Before analysing the problem solving strategies, the translation product will be examined for errors in this chapter to assess the quality of the TfS and PE tasks. Quality assessments of translations have been widely discussed in translation studies, e.g. House (1997), Hönig (1997), Mertin (2006) or Reiss (2014), and some studies were published on the quality of MT, too, e.g. Fiederer & O'Brien (2009) or Lacruz et al. (2014).[13] However, too complex models and typical error categories cannot be applied in this study, because the PE guidelines (see §7.3) stated clearly that not all linguistic aspects are important for the final target text; i.e. stylistic characteristics cannot be considered while analysing the target texts when the PE guidelines dictate that style is to be neglected.

To explain the nature of errors, Rasmussen's skill-rule-knowledge framework differentiates three levels (cf. Reason 1990: 42-44, Jungermann et al. 2010: 38-40): skill-based, rule-based, and knowledge-based errors. The skill-based level describes errors that happen in every day situations by accident. Usually, the person knows what (s)he is doing and intends to do it correctly, but accidentally makes a mistake. In translation, a typical example would be typing errors. A set of rules for the situation is known to the person on the rule-based level, but (s)he applies those rules incorrectly. A translation-related example of rule-based errors would be the wrong application of grammar rules. Finally, errors on a knowledge-based level occur, when the situation is new to the person and (s)he does not have a predetermined set of rules to cope with the situation. This might happen in translation, when the translator chooses a wrong term in the context, because (s)he does not know better. As the examples showed, all error levels can be detected in translation situations. Therefore, they will be applied to the error categories later on.

In Schäfer (2003), error categories are introduced that were established at SAP AG to develop a standard PE guide. At the time the paper was published, four different MT systems were used at SAP AG for different languages. The guide is intended to help the translators with the new task of PE as well as to encourage the translators to keep an open-mind towards MT and should be applicable for the output and workflow of all four MT systems. The four error categories introduced are: *lexical errors, syntactic errors, grammatical mistakes,* and *mistakes due to defective source texts.* The latter did not occur in the six source texts in this

---

[13]Furthermore, there are numerous publications on automatic MT output evaluation. Two of the most famous automatic matrices are BLEU (Papineni et al. 2002) and METEOR (Lavie & Denkowski 2009). The MQM framework has been developed to evaluate both human translation and MT (Lommel et al. 2014)

study, which is to be expected in an experimental setting. However, this is an important aspect when technical texts are translated in practice (cf. Horn-Helf 1999; 2007) . Another aspect is that MT output was analysed in Schäfer's study, while the study at hand will focus on mistakes in the final target texts. Therefore, syntactic mistakes were not included, because they appear less often in the post-edited text than in MT output and some syntactic structures could instead be categorised as bad style, which is not included in this analysis.

Further, Mertin (2006: 232–258) error categories were consulted, as well. Due to the inclusion of the PE and MPE task as well as the experiment setting, most translation relevant criteria, all reference relevant, formal, and job specific criteria had to be excluded. However, all criteria concerning language rules were included: Spelling mistakes and typos were condensed into one category (spelling), punctuation was extended for the category "spaces", and grammar was considered. Only two categories could be included from the translation relevant criteria, namely content mistakes and word mistakes, which were summarised in the category "lexical mistakes".

To put it in a nutshell, this chapter will only focus on superficial error categories to make the analysis more objective and adaptable for both tasks.[14] This also means that the error analysis is incomplete. The following error categories were established: spelling, grammar, punctuation, spaces, and lexical mistakes. Other common categories like style and collocations were not included, because they are usually, at least to some degree, subjective. Further, in the PE instructions the participants were asked to correct only the most important mistakes, keep as much of the MT output as possible, and disregard style and personal preferences. Finally, those mistakes can be detected without consulting the source text which makes the counting process faster. Unfortunately, this procedure had the side effect that content mistakes could not be included.[15] However, an elab-

---

[14]The MPE task will be excluded from this analysis, because the nature of the tasks requires assessments on a content level, where most or the more severe mistakes are expected. However, more details can be found in Nitzke (2016b).

[15]While assessing the texts, hardly any content-based mistakes became obvious. If content had appeared to be a serious problem in these two tasks, the source text and the error category would have been included. Despite the familiarity with the texts, some content mistakes could be found nonetheless, e.g.: In Text 3, the source texts says "which includes one minister charged with crimes against humanity", which was realised by one participant as "zu der auch ein Minister [...] mit der Einhaltung der Menschenrechte beauftragt wurde". Next to the misuse of "zu" or the missing verb (could be both and was counted as one lexical mistake) the content is not correct ("to which one minister [...] was mandated to adhere to the human rights").

oration on content mistakes in the English-German data set can be found in Nitzke (2016b), where there is also more information on the mistakes in the MPE texts. The latter produced many more content mistakes than the other two tasks, while the non-content related mistakes presented in this chapter occurred almost equally often in MPE as in the other two tasks.

Spelling mistakes refer to typos in most cases. Translog II does not provide an automatic spell-checker as it is a component of most document and word processing tools as well as translation memory systems. Therefore, most spelling mistakes may not have occurred if another software had been used. However, the repeated occurrence of spelling mistakes reflects on the fact that translators (and probably all other computer users, too) have become used to this kind of assistance and how challenging it is to find typos in self-produced texts. Most spelling mistakes should be skill-based errors, but might occasionally be knowledge-based as well (e.g. the correct writing of a new term is unknown).

The same applies to *grammar* mistakes. Most of these probably have their source in either typos or the reorganisation of the sentence structure. When not enough attention is paid during the latter, suffixes of grammatical cases or articles might survive the reorganisation that are wrong in the new syntactic structure. These mistakes occur more often in German texts than in English texts because of the more diverse grammatical inflection in German. Grammar mistakes may either be on a skill-based or rule-based level. The knowledge-based level can be ruled out as all participants are German native speakers and trained translators.

Most *punctuation* mistakes can be traced back to missing or too many commas, or missing hyphens etc. Mistakes concerning *spaces* include two or more spaces where there should only have been one and missing spaces behind hyphens. For the same reason as mentioned above for grammar mistakes, punctuation and space mistakes should occur on a skill-based or rule-based level as well.

Lexical mistakes only concern errors that can be detected without consulting the source text in this analysis. This means that the translator may have chosen the wrong lexical realisation and this mistake is not included in this category. Only mistakes that could be detected without the source texts were counted. That may include words that do not exist in German or their meaning does not suit the context, e. g. compromise was translated as "kompromittieren" which means expose/denounce/put someone in a bad light etc. rather than impair or endanger. Other lexical mistakes were wrong realisations of the chosen words, e.g. the official abbreviation of "Jahrhundert" (century) is "Jh." and not "Jhdt" in German. Most lexical mistakes should either be skill-based or knowledge-based errors.

In all 92 sessions (45 PE and 47 TfS), 139 mistakes were counted (overall data set – mean: 1.51, sd: 1.32; TfS – mean: 1.47, sd: 1.28; PE – mean: 1.56, sd: 1.36), which were distributed as follows:

Table 7.8: Mistake count

mistake	spelling	grammar	punctuation	spaces	lexical
count	51	29	23	14	22
%	36.7%	20.9%	16.5%	10.1%	15.8%

Of those mistakes, 70 were made in the PE, 69 in TfS; 81 by semi-professionals, 58 by professionals. However, professionals (44) completed fewer sessions than students (48). Therefore, the following table shows the mean values:

Table 7.9: Mistakes (mean and SD) per text related to task and status

	TfS – mean	TfS – SD	PE – mean	PE – SD
professionals	1.217	1.204	1.429	1.287
students	1.708	1.334	1.667	1.434

The standard deviation is quite high, which indicates that the results for the individual participants are very different and cannot be back-tracked to task or status of the participant. However, a correlation test shows that there is a statistically significant correlation between the experience factor[16] and the number of mistakes when the whole data set is taken into consideration. The correlation is negative and very weak ($r_\pi = -0.175$, $p = 0.0294$), which means that the more experienced the translator is, the (slightly) fewer mistakes (s)he makes. However, there is no significant correlation when the data are separated by tasks (TfS[17] – $r_\pi = -0.212$, $p = 0.0612$, PE – $r_\pi = -0.108$, $p = 0.3504$). A Mann-Whitney-U-test showed that there is no significant connection when the data set is divided by groups ($W = 877$, $p = 0.1481$), nor between task and number of mistakes ($W = 1092.5$, $p = 0.78$), or between previous PE experience and the amount of mistakes ($W = 1053.5$, $p = 0.3573$).

---

[16]See further information on the experience vector in §8.1

[17]It seems plausible that the data for TfS might have reached significance if more participants had taken part in the experiment.

7.9 Criticism of the data set

When we want to find out what happens in the translators mind, we want to keep the experiment situation as natural as possible to mirror translation behaviour that is as close to real-life behaviour as possible. On the other hand, experiments on cognitive processes need to be as controlled as possible to achieve generalisable results. These conflicting interests can hardly be united in translation process studies. Though the study at hand aimed to be as controlled and natural as possible, at the same time, some points in setup and conduction of the experiments can be criticised, which will be done in the scope of this chapter.

To create natural translation environments, the keylogging system runs in the background so that the participant is not aware that his/her keystrokes are recorded. Furthermore, a desktop eyetracker is used in the experiments. Compared to a head-mounted eyetracker or an eyetracker with a chinrest, a desktop eyetracker does not physically influence the participant and allows him/her to move relatively freely.[18] However, there are still a lot of factors that change the work environment, like O'Brien (2009) already pointed out: the monitor is most likely different to the one translators use at home, the computer might be equipped with an unfamiliar operating system or different software (or different versions), and the non-identical keyboard might result in typing errors and the translation processes might be slowed down (at least until the participant has adjusted to the keyboard). These factors probably influence professional translators more than student translators, because the latter most likely do not have a working environment as fixed as the professional translators. Students may, e.g., be required to use computers at the university for particular courses. A completely natural work environment could only be possible if the participants participated in the experiments with their hard- and software at home or in their offices. This, however, is not possible with the eyetracking system, which needs to be installed and adjusted. On the other hand, it would be difficult to guarantee that all participants finished all texts in a row and under the same conditions.

Another very critical point in this experiments is the choice of the text type. Professional translators hardly deal with newspaper articles – it is almost insignificant for the field. Most professionals specialise in a certain domain at the beginning or during their career (cf. Schmitt et al. 2016), which might be technical, IT, economic, law, medical translations etc. and may have not translated newspaper articles for years or decades, if at all. In an online survey published

---

[18]The area in which the participant can move is of course restricted, but translators tend to sit quite still when they work (see §7.1.4).

by Hommerich and Reiß (cf. 2011: 71), which was conducted on behalf of the BDÜ (see §4.4), the authors reported that 49% of the members that participated in the study (in total 1570) specialised in the field "Industry and Technology (general)", 45% in "Law and Administration", 41% in "Economics, Trade, and Finances", 25% in "Medicine and Pharmacy", and 23% in "Information Technology". Only few translators specialised in fields that might require the use of general language like "Culture and Education" (13%), "Sports, Recreation, and Tourism" (10%), or "Media and Art" (9%), although most of these fields might require domain-specific language and terminology as well.[19] However, student translators often have/had to translate newspaper articles in courses to gain general translation competence in Germersheim.[20] Therefore, some of the statements about translation competence that will follow may not be meaningful to a full extent, because we cannot judge the balance between familiarity with the text source and translation competence (cf. O'Brien 2009).

If we consider real life translation situations, a MT system other than Google Translate should have been chosen to prepare the source text for PE. A much higher quality could be achieved with MT systems that were trained with company-specific corpora, so the PE task would be much more efficient. However, the resources are very limited at a university. Therefore, it is not plausible to train a system for only one experiment. On the other hand, as was already discussed, newspaper articles are not a typical text type in professional translation and it is highly unlikely that a company would train a MT system to translate these text types. Google Translate might, therefore, be a quite sophisticated MT system for our purposes, because it is trained with all kinds of text from the world wide web.

Last but not least, the data were collected to gather comparable translation process data for different language combinations that can be accessed for free via an online platform to tackle various research questions. Therefore, the data existed before the research question and the hypotheses were formulated. Methodologically, this could be judged as quite critically because the tasks were not precisely tailored to assess the research question and the conditions cannot be controlled. On the other hand, relatively natural texts were used; and due to the large scope of the experiments, the study at hand can be expanded to other languages in the future. Further, as was already presented in §7.4, many other studies have been conducted with the data set. Another aspect is that all participants started with the TfS task, followed by the PE task and finished with the MPE, which

---

[19] The follow-up study from 2016 presents very similar numbers.
[20] This approach is controversial from a didactics point of view, as well.

might have influenced the task behaviour, because the participants became tired towards the end of the experiment or first had to get used to the text type at the beginning of the experiment. Further, this might have influenced the answering behaviour in the retrospective questionnaires, which will be discussed in §8.3 on flaws in the questionnaire.

8 The questionnaires

As part of the experiment, the participants were asked to complete two questionnaires, one before the experiment and another immediately afterwards. The results of these questionnaires are presented in this chapter. A general introduction to the methodology can be found in §7.1.2. The questionnaires focused on social-statistical characteristics of the participants, and ask for facts, behaviour, and opinions. They contained open questions, yes-/no-questions, and Likert scale questions. The latter is a psychometric scale and the scale is used predominantly in social sciences. The responses are usually at least five-ary and every item measures a different intensity of the measured feature/phenomenon (cf. Döring & Bortz 2014: 268–269). In the following section, values will be calculated for most questions to better illustrate the general opinion of the participants and in which direction it points. The explanation for the single values is presented with the associated question. Some of the questions from these two questionnaires were already briefly discussed in Carl et al. (2014). The questionnaires and the data recordings were part of an extensive multilingual translation process research project initiated by the Copenhagen Business School. The data are comparable for different languages and is publicly available (for more information see §7.2). Hence, the questionnaires were not adjusted to the research questions at hand, although that might have been necessary to some degree.

All analyses in this and the following chapters were conducted in either Microsoft Excel (mainly for simple calculations and diagrams) or R (R Core Team 2013; mainly for statistical tests).

8.1 The questionnaire prior to the experiment

The aim of this questionnaire was to elicit general information about the participants (degree of experience, languages) as well as rough opinions on MT and its relevance in translation practice.

The first point of interest was the gender of the participants: 17 women and 7 men participated in the experiments. Taking into account that the majority of translators are female this is quite a balanced ratio (cf. Hommerich & Reiß

(2011: 60) reported that 81% of the participants were female in a members' survey of the BDÜ – one of the biggest associations for translators and interpreters in Germany). Additioally, the focus of this study will not take gender or any socio-cultural aspects into account.

The next question was whether the participants wore glasses or contact lenses, because glasses and contact lenses can influence the quality of the eyetracking data (Poole & Ball 2005: 216). While the use of optical aids is not important to evaluate the performance of the translator themselves, it could rather be used to explain irregularities in the gaze data. Seven participants wore glasses, five contact lenses and twelve neither. The gaze precision for the single recordings are indicated in percentage in the Tobii Studio software. For example, if eye movement was recorded for 12 minutes in a 15 minute long session, the gaze precision would be 80%. Reasons for no recorded eye movement could either be technical difficulties or situations where the participant was not looking at the screen (and instead was looking at the keyboard while typing, etc.). The mean gaze precision for the single sessions shows differences according to the optical aid: When the participants wore no optical aid 82.9% of the eye movement were recorded (sd: 13.9). This is a little more than what was recorded for the group of participants who wore contact lenses (mean: 75.8%; sd: 9.4). Finally, only for 58.9% (sd: 30.8) of the eye movement was recorded in the sessions where the participants wore glasses. The differences between the three groups is statistically significant ($p < 0.0001$)[1]. The high standard deviation observed for the participants who wore glasses might indicate that not all participants with glasses are difficult to record, but maybe some characteristics of the glasses complicate the recording (e.g. the size or the thickness of the lenses, or the frames of the glasses). Further, it was expected that less eye movement is recorded for the translation from scratch task, because more text production is necessary and hence it may be plausible that the participants spent more time looking at the keyboard than for the other two tasks. However, when ordered according to task, only minor differences can be recognised (MPE – mean: 74.2, sd: 23.7; PE – mean: 78.2, sd: 19.0; and TfS – mean: 73.5, sd: 21.3), which are not statistically significant ($p = .2941$) and hence will not be discussed further.

The subsequent three questions dealt with the background of the translators: All participants were German native speakers and considered English their first

---

[1]The tests for significance were conducted with a Kruskal-Wallis test because the data were divided into three groups and were not distributed normally. The exact data were Kruskal-Wallis $\chi^2 = 24.4967$, df = 2, $p = 4.793 \times 10^{-6}$ for the test between the percentage of recorded eye movement and the type of optical aid, and Kruskal-Wallis $\chi^2 = 2.4475$, df = 2, $p = 0.2941$ for the test between the percentage of recorded eye movement and the task.

(83%) or second foreign language (17%). The formal translation education of the professionals was on average 5.04 years (sd: 0.92), whereas the students had on average 3.46 years (sd: 1.66) through their studies (see Table 8.1 – together 4.25 years on average – sd: 1.54).

Table 8.1: Years of education

	Professional translators					Student translators						
years of education	3	4	4.5	5	6	1.5	2	2.5	4	4.5	5	6
no. of part.	1	1	1	5	4	1	4	1	2	1	1	2

According to Table 8.2, the participants had 4.71 years professional translation experience on average (sd: 6.14). Self-evidently, the group of professional translators had far more translation experience (mean: 9 years, sd: 6.19 years) than the students (mean: 0.42 years, sd: 0.67 years), and the professionals had a broad age range which also explains the high standard deviations.

Table 8.2: Years of experience

	Professional translators										Stud. transl.		
years of exp.	0	0.5	4	4.5	8	10	12	14	17	20	0	1	2
no. of part.	1	1	1	1	2	2	1	1	1	1	8	3	1

Most of the students are in the middle or the final stage of their studies; some of them even have professional experience. Therefore, they are not beginners and are rather classified as semi-professionals. The high standard deviation in the experience values – for the all participants-group as well as for the sub-groups – are the reason for the introduction of a new figure which will better represent the experience of the participants and will unify years at university and professional experience. This value will be called *experience coefficient* (see also Nitzke 2016b). The simple equation that is used to calculate the experience coefficient is the following:

(1) Experience = years of education $*$ 1 + years of professional experience $*$ 2

This new experience coefficient has a number of advantages: First, we have one figure combining experience at university and work experience instead of two. In two cases, the professional translators have less experience than a few students, because they only recently received their degree and did not gather any professional experience during their time at university. Further, the professional experience within both groups is very inhomogeneous (see Table 8.3). Although differentiating between students and professionals is appropriate in many scenarios, students who have studied for two years at university and students who have studied for five years and have had one year of professional experience outside university should not necessarily be clustered together. The same applies to professionals who have had two years of professional experience and professionals who have had more than ten years of experience. Finally, a single numeric figure for experience will simplify calculation of statistics, like correlations, between phenomena and experience and is more useful than calculating statistics only according to the two statuses *semi-professionals* and *professionals* (e.g. Martínez-Gómez et al. 2014 or discussion in Singla et al. 2013). Table 8.3 illustrates which participant has which status and how much experience according to the experience coefficient at the point when the experiments were conducted.

Table 8.3: Experience coefficient

Participant	1	2	3	4	5	6	7	8	9	10	11	12
Status	P	S	S	S	S	P	P	S	S	S	S	S
Experience	14	6.5	3	4	8	45	20.5	5	2.5	6	6	5.5
Participant	13	14	15	16	17	18	19	20	21	22	23	24
Status	P	S	P	S	P	S	P	P	P	P	P	P
Experience	6	2	30	2	19	2	40	4	34	13	25	26

It is assumed that professionals translate a lot more in their everyday life than students at the university, where they "only" attend a few translation courses per semester (if at all) and also concentrate their studies on other topics like translation theory, linguistics, cultural studies, etc. which might indirectly improve their translation behaviour, set the basis for responsible translation choices, and develop the problem solving ability. These activities, however, are not as substantial as full-time translating. Hence, professional experience was weighted stronger than years of study. Further, a learning curve was not implemented in the calculations, because there are no studies known to the author that describe how a learning curve for professionalism in translation would look, and, additionally, other studies used simple years of experience as well for calculating correlations between translation behaviour and experience (e.g.: De Almeida 2013).

Moorkens & O'Brien (2015) examine in their study with nine expert translators (on average 11.3 years translation experience and 4 years PE experience) and 35 undergraduate student translators the productivity/speed of the participants, the edit distance of their final product, and their attitude towards PE. The professional group was much faster than the students, while the students tended to edit less of the MT output and they had a more positive attitude towards PE – although almost half of the students had negative feelings about PE, too. Conclusively, this study shows that it might be reasonable to distinguish between professionals and novices because they displayed a different working behaviour and different attitudes towards PE. However, the study does not specify how heterogeneous or homogeneous the participants were. In the analysis chapters of the study at hand, the differentiation between the status of the participants will not be disregarded because visualising data in two groups is much more expressive than according to experience. Further, the status of a participant naturally gives a first impression of the experience. In general, students are less experienced than professionals. When it is tested whether the experience coefficient is significantly different between students and professionals, we get a highly significant result ($W = 134.5, p < 0.0004$[2]).

The last experience-related question of the pre-experiment questionnaire asked whether the participants had any experience with PE. In the professional group, half of the participants had post-edited prior to the experiments, while only 17% of the students had experience with PE. Unfortunately, this question does not provide any insights on how often the participants have post-edited before, whether they do it regularly and whether they gained the PE experience recently or years ago. In future research, this question needs to be more detailed to achieve a better understanding of the PE experience.

The experience of the translators is quite important for the analysis, because it influences the outcome of the translation and, from a problem solving perspective, it is assumed that "[t]he difference in performance between experts and less skilled individuals is not a simple difference in accumulated knowledge about past experience", but also "appear[s] to reflect differential ability to react to representative tasks and situations that have never been previously encountered" (Ericsson 2003: 57). Hence, one could expect that the more experienced translators with no PE experience are better post-editors than semi-professional translators with no PE experience. On the other hand, both tasks are quite different and it also seems plausible that more experienced translators stick to already

---

[2] The test was conducted with a Mann-Whitney-U-test, because the experience coefficient is not distributed normally.

established translation behaviours and strategies that might not be suitable for PE. Further, experienced translators might even be more reluctant to use MT output (see e.g. Silva 2014). The PE guidelines specified, for example, that style did not need to be addressed. However, it might be hard for an experienced translator who had to apply high quality standards to his/her translations for years and decades to discard this aspiration, which might hinder the PE task. Therefore, I assume that translation experience plays a vital role in problem solving behaviour (see §6).

   After collecting general information about the translation background of the participants, the next part of the pre-experiment questionnaire dealt with experience with and opinions on MT. The questions will be stated at the beginning of the paragraph in italics in the following.

   Q1: How frequently do you use machine translation? – The participants could choose between different answers – *every day, every 2 to 3 weeks, every month, once or twice a year, never* (see Figure 8.1). These answers are ranked with different values so that the total value for all participants reflects the answers. Therefore, *never* is given the value *zero*, adding one point to every answer that indicates an increased use of MT, ending with the value *four* for the answer *every day*. The resulting values show that the participants use MT quite rarely (mean: 0.71, sd: 1.08); the professionals using it even less (mean: 0.58, sd: 0.79) than the students (mean: 0.83, sd: 1.34). The distribution of the answers is shown in Figure 8.1. According to the numbers, the group uses MT systems less than once or twice a year. This self-assessment of the use of MT systems remains questionable. As explained in §2.1, MT is quite common in the world wide web nowadays. Therefore, it might be possible that participants are faced with MT much more often than they care to admit or even realise, because they might not be aware how often they are confronted with MT output when they visit websites. Or they consider the question in a solely professional way and do not consider encounters with MT in their everyday Internet use.

   Q2: From your previous experience with machine translation outputs, how would you rate your level of satisfaction in relation to machine translation? - The range for this questions is *very satisfied, somewhat satisfied, neutral, somewhat dissatisfied, highly dissatisfied.* The distributed values have the purpose of reflecting whether the attitude is rather negative (the value will be negative) or rather positive (the value will be positive). Therefore, the answer *neutral* gets the value *0* representing a neutral opinion, *somewhat satisfied* and *very satisfied* the values *1* and *2*, respectively, representing a positive opinion, and *somewhat dissatisfied* and *very dissatisfied* the values *−1* and *−2*.

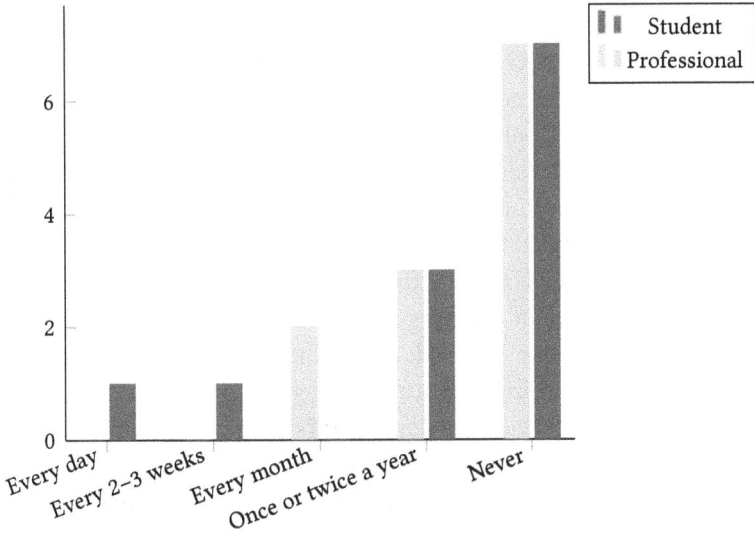

Figure 8.1: How frequently do you use machine translation?

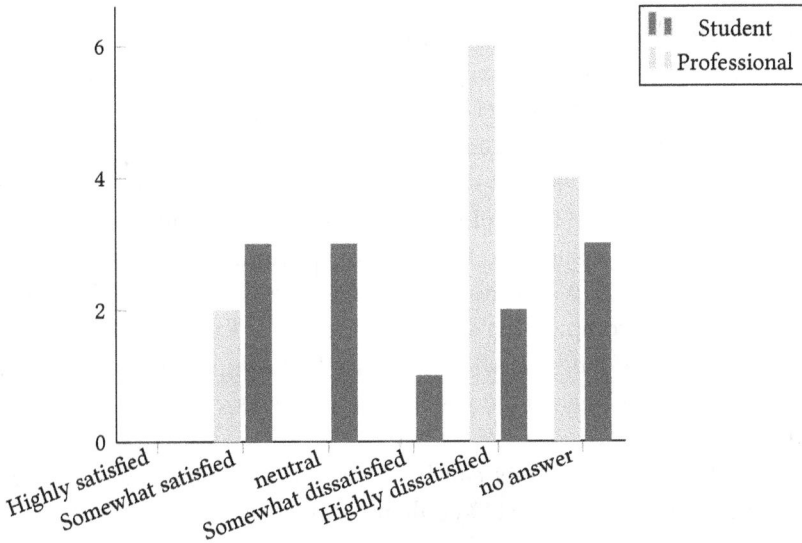

Figure 8.2: From your previous experience with machine translation outputs, how would you rate your level of satisfaction in relation to machine translation?

Some respondents chose not to answer to this question (see Figure 8.2). A simple explanation for this is that over half of the participants claimed to have never used MT. However, the number of respondents who have never used MT and the number of respondents who did not provide an answer to the question are not equal. More participants answered the question than claimed to have never used MT which shows that they nonetheless have a certain amount of experience and/or opinions on MT – a sign that they might have only considered the professional environment or that they have prejudices towards MT output. When non-responses occurred, they were not considered in the calculated value, i.e. the total number of answers decreased. Altogether, the general opinion on MT is very low (mean: −0.71; sd: 1.36), which is in line with Gaspari et al. (2015: 348–350), who found in their study, which tries to draw a picture of the translation market, that 52% of the participants who have used MT judge the quality as low or very low, 37% said the quality was medium, and only 11% perceived the quality as high or excellent. However, this is not in line with the findings by De Almeida (2013: 157) – most of her participants expressed a neutral or positive opinion of MT in the questionnaire which was filled out before her experiment. The value for the professional group is −1.25 (sd: 1.39). The value for the student group is not as negative but still in the negative area (mean: −0.16, sd: 1.2). It is rather hard to attach meaning to these opinions. From my subjective experience, translators tend to evaluate MT output from what they would expect from human translations. MT systems, however, cannot deliver fully automatic high quality translation (yet), except in very restricted domains (cf. Hutchins & Somers 1992: 147–149). Especially, unspecialised systems that are trained on all kinds of data, which most systems available online are, cannot meet these requirements. Further, the mistakes a MT system makes are more obvious and hence easier to deplore than it is to value what the systems are capable of. This negative attitude might even multiply, when the source language is known to the MT user and (s)he can directly compare the source text to the MT output.

Q3: Do you think that you will want to apply machine translation in your future translation tasks? - The simple yes-no question was extended with *not sure* (see results in Figure 8.3).

Generally, the participants can hardly see themselves using MT systems in their future translation jobs (17% could imagine using MT, 50% could not, and 33% were not sure). The professionals are not very convinced that they could use MT for their work (58% of the professional participants decline the suggestion and only one answered with yes), while the students are more open to integrating MT into their future translation tasks (25% of the student participants can imagine

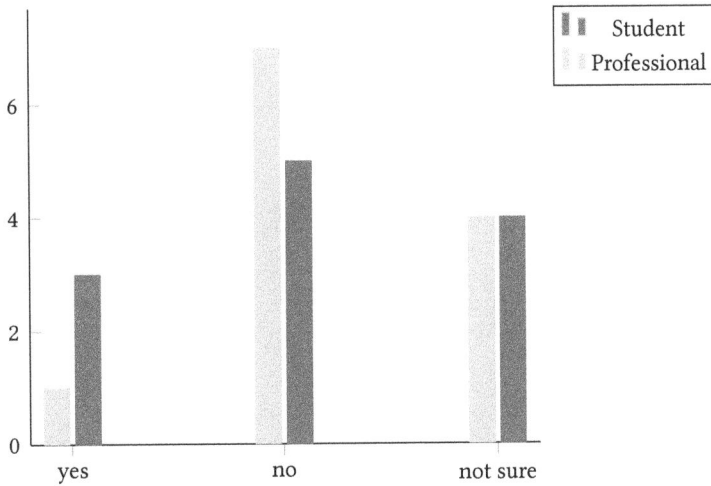

Figure 8.3: Do you think that you will want to apply machine translation in your future translation tasks?

using MT in the future; 42% cannot). As Figure 8.2 showed, the participants are not very convinced of MT output in general. Therefore, the tendencies shown in Figure 8.3 are in line with Figure 8.2.

Q4: In general, how feasible do you think it is to apply machine translation to professional translation services? – Similar to the question about the satisfaction in relation to MT, the answers were the following: *very likely, somewhat likely, neutral, somewhat unlikely, very unlikely*. Accordingly, the distribution of the values was similar: *0* points were given for *neutral, 2* points for *very likely, –2* points for *very unlikely*. The values are quite close to zero in general (mean: –0.08, sd: 1.10) and for both separate groups, but for the professionals the value is barely positive (mean: 0.08, sd: 1.08), while it is negative for the student group (mean: –0.25, sd: 1.14). The distributions of the answers can be seen in Figure 8.4.

Interestingly, the participants judge this question rather neutrally, which is contradictory to the answers from the last two questions. Professionals consider MT (slightly) feasible for translation services, although they hardly use MT, their general opinion on MT is very low, and they doubt that they will use MT in their own future translation tasks. This could have various reasons. One could be that they might have specialised in areas that are not targeted by MT (literature, advertising, marketing etc.), and can see the potential usability in other domains but not in their own. Further, they might include in their considerations future developments in MT, meaning that they can imagine that MT output might be useful

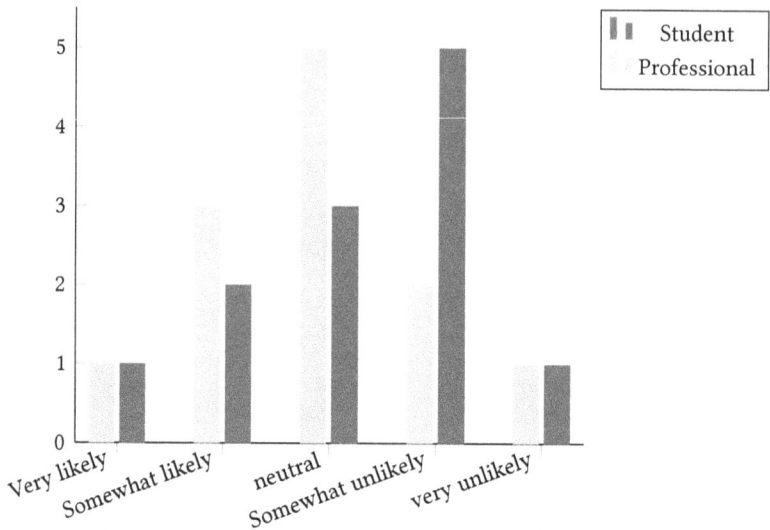

Figure 8.4: In general, how feasible do you think it is to apply machine translation to professional translation services?

at some point but not now. Another aspect is that professionals are less negative than students, although it was the other way round in the other questions. A reason could be that professional translators are more sensitive about judging the application of tools due to their more profound experience. Compared to the group of professionals, the student group is rather open to MT. They use it more often and have a better attitude towards MT. However, they are more negative about the possibility that MT should find its way into professional translation tasks. Again, we can only try to interpret the meaning. Maybe students are more often confronted with MT, but cannot see how it could be used in a professional environment (which most of them are not familiar with). There may be various other approaches to interpret these findings, but the number of participants is not very representative, so not too much importance should be attached to the different directions indicated by these questions.

Further, questions Q1, Q2, and Q4 were tested statistically for a difference between students and professionals and none of the tests proved significance (t-test or Mann-Whitney-U-test, depending on the distribution of the data): Q1 – $W = 70, p = 0.9222$; Q2 – $W = 21, p = 0.1342$; Q4 – $t = 0.7348, p = 0.4703$.

Unfortunately, the metadata collected in this questionnaires did not cover the fields in which the translators specialise or have specialised and whether they deal with general language texts in their professional work at all. The semi-professional participants might even be more familiar with this text domain, because general language translation is part of the curriculum of the B.A. programme (and can be chosen in the M.A. programme). The translation process might be influenced by the translators' specialisation. As Lubart & Mouchiroud (2003: 130) summarise, "high levels of domain knowledge can sometimes bias problem solving, limiting the search space to readily available ideas". They further argue that many problems can be solved with this "canned knowledge". Nonetheless, creative problems often require the problem solver to break away from what is already known. Different characteristics of individuals (character traits, domain knowledge, motivation etc.) create the individuals' creative problem solving ability, which explains why some people are able to work creatively in one domain, but are not creative in others – creativity is not only necessary for the arts and literature, but can also be found in engineering, physics, mathematics etc. (ibid.: 130-136)

8.2 The retrospective questionnaire

The retrospective questionnaire was filled out directly after the experiments and dealt mainly with a self-assessment of the performance during the experiment and the evaluation of the machine output. The proximity of time has the advantage that the participants are mentally still very involved in the TfS/PE/MPE tasks. Moreover, the participants did not have to come to the lab a second time for further questions. However, the participants probably were exhausted after this quite extensive study. Hence, it is possible that they did not give much thought to the questions (for more details on advantages and disadvantages of retrospective surveys, especially in connection with think aloud methods see Göpferich 2008). Unfortunately, one of the candidates – a professional translator - was not able to conduct the whole experiment and therefore did not fill out the second questionnaire. All in all, 23 questionnaires are available for assessment, eleven from professional translators, twelve from semi-professional translators. We will mostly continue to work with the original division of the participants in semi-professionals and professionals for illustration reasons at this point of the study.

The first question dealt with the post-editing task: *Q5: How satisfied are you with the translation you have produced through post-editing?* The participants could choose from five answers – *highly satisfied, somewhat satisfied, neutral, somewhat dissatisfied* and *highly dissatisfied.* The self-assessment was rather positive (mean: 0.43, sd: 1.08), especially for the student candidates. The values were calculated in the following manner: *highly satisfied* gained *2* points, *neutral 0* points and *highly dissatisfied –2* points. The professionals reached a general value of 0.18 (sd: 1.25), which can be interpreted as neutral – keeping in mind that over half of them were somewhat or highly satisfied. The students were even more satisfied and assigned their output a general value of 0.67 (sd: 0.89). 75% of the student participants were somewhat or highly satisfied, which is a lot.

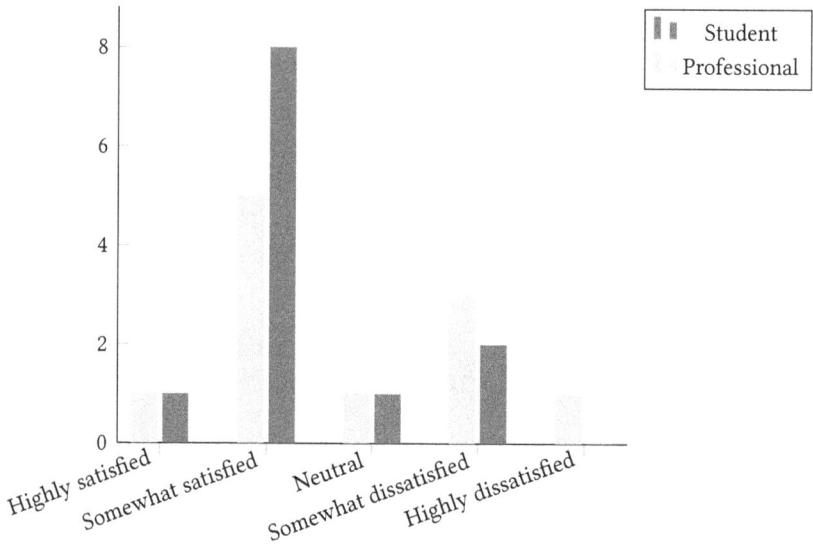

Figure 8.5: How satisfied are you with the translation you have produced through post-editing?

The next question was concerned with the personal assessment of the monolingual post-editing task: *Q6: How satisfied are you with the translation you have produced through editing?*[3] The answer range was the same as in the question above due to the similar nature of the question. Accordingly, the values were calculated as in the prior question. The evaluations were more negative than for the PE task (mean: –0.26 and sd: 1.29). The professionals were quite critical of their work and were not satisfied (mean: –0.68, sd: 1.43). The students were in general neither satisfied nor dissatisfied with their work (mean: 0.08, sd: 1.08), although half of them were somewhat satisfied. The difference between both groups is not significant for PE ($W = 52, p = 0.3557$) and MPE ($W = 44.5, p = 0.18$).

The next step was to find out whether the translators consider the MT output helpful or obstructive. *Q7: Would you have preferred to work on your transla-*

---

[3]Unfortunately, the questionnaire did not ask for the satisfaction with the human translation task, which would have been interesting to compare to the two PE tasks.

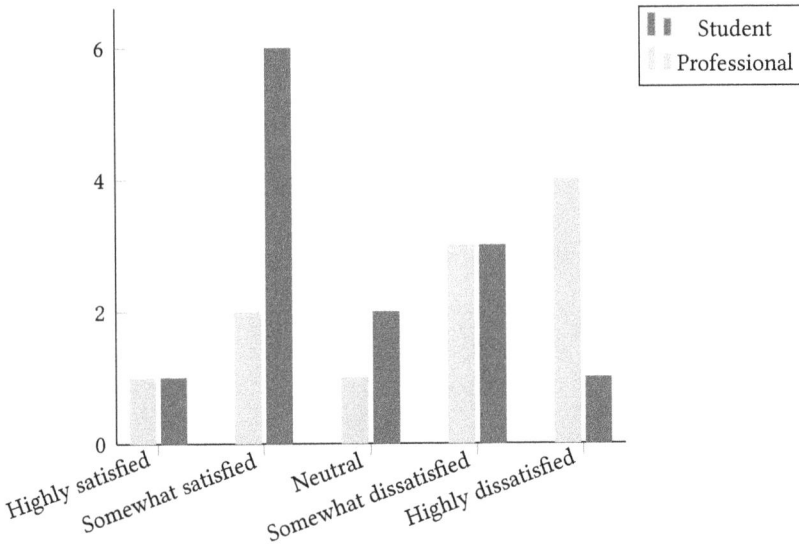

Figure 8.6: How satisfied are you with the translation you have produced through (monolingual post-)editing?

tion from scratch instead of post-editing machine translation? This was a simple yes/no question. The responses were very clear: 91% of the professional translators would rather have translated from scratch than post-edited the MT. The general opinion among the semi-professional translators is similar, but not as striking (75% of them would rather have translated from scratch). For the group that means 83% of the participants considered the MT output obstructive.

Similar to one question in the first questionnaire, the translators were asked whether they would integrate MT in their future translation tasks: *Q8: Do you think that you will want to apply machine translation in your future translation tasks?* As in the question in the prior questionnaire the simple yes-no question was extended by not sure (see Figure 8.7).

Although it is the same question, which had already been asked in the first questionnaire, the results are different (26% answered *yes, at some point*, 39% chose *no, never!*, 35% were not sure – professionals: 18% yes, 36% no, 45% not sure; students: 33% yes, 42% no, 25% not sure). Even more surprising is that the translators were more open to the idea of using MT in future translation tasks, although the participants would rather have translated the post-edited texts from scratch than post-edited the MT output and the general evaluation of the MT output was very bad (see next question). A contrast and a discussion of this question and the different results before and after the experiment will follow in §8.3.

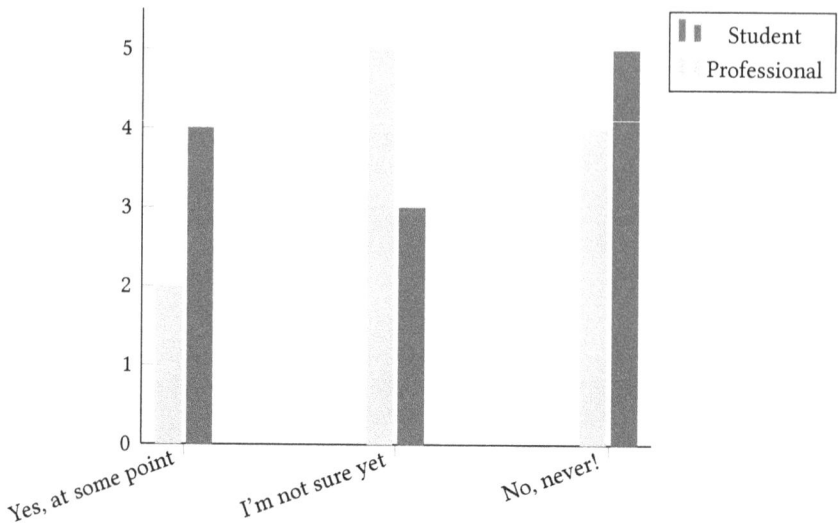

Figure 8.7: Do you think that you will want to apply machine translation in your future translation tasks?

The next question was concerned with the assessment of the MT output. The
focus of this question will not be on the differences between the students and
professionals, although they will be pointed out, but rather on the average evaluation, which resulted in a very negative judgement (see Figure 8.8). *Q8: Based
on the post-editing task you have performed, how much do you rate machine translation outputs on the following attributes - grammaticality, style, overall accuracy
and overall quality?*

The following answers were possible for all four categories (in the diagram in
Figure 8.8 from left to right): *well below average, below average, average, above
average, well above average.* None of the translators ranked any of the four criteria as *well above average.* For every criterion, a score was calculated in the
following manner: *well below average* was attributed –2 points, average got 0
points and well above average would have been 2 points. The scores given by
the translators for the individual criteria were on average all negative. *Grammaticality* was rated –1.26 (sd: 0.92; professionals – mean: –1.64, sd: 0.67; and
students – mean: –0.92, sd: 1.0); *style,* which is the least important in PE according to most guidelines, was considered the worst criterion with a value of –1.43
(sd: 0.9; professionals – mean: –1.55, sd: 1.07; and students – mean: –1.33, sd: 1.07);
overall accuracy received the "best" evaluation with a value of –1 (sd: 0.85; professionals – mean: –1.27, sd: 0.9; and students – mean: –0.75, sd: 0.75); and *over-*

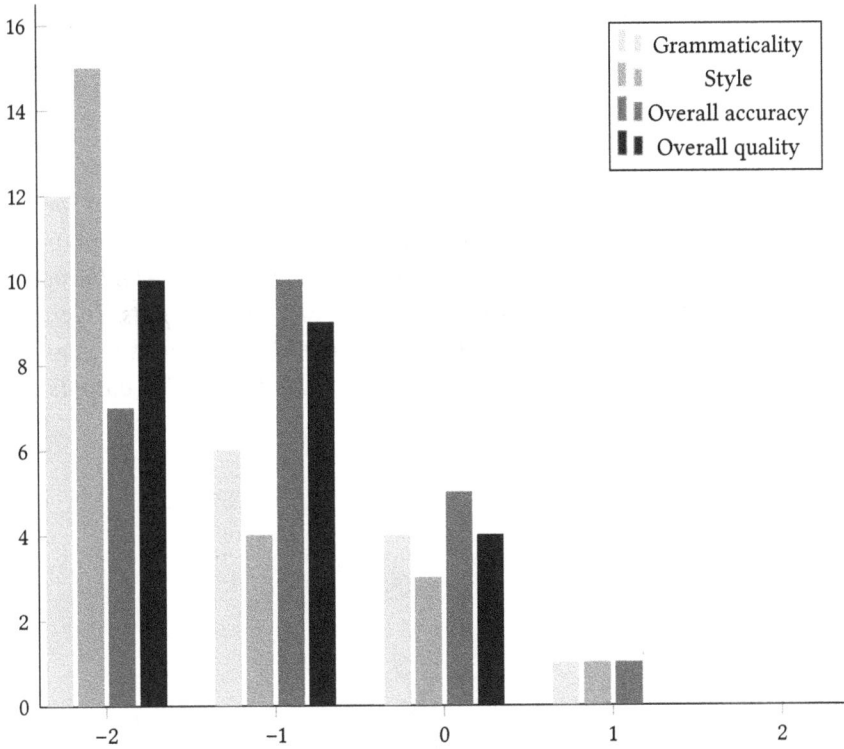

Figure 8.8: Based on the post-editing task you have performed, how much do you rate machine translation outputs on the following attributes - grammaticality, style, overall accuracy and overall quality?

all quality gained −1.26 points on average (sd: 0.75; professionals: mean: −1.36, sd: 0.81; and students: mean: −1.17, sd: 0.72). It was tested whether the ratings of both groups were significantly different, but no significant difference could be observed: *grammaticality* − $W = 37.5, p = 0.0595$; *style* − $W = 63.5, p = 0.8844$; *overall accuracy* − $W = 43, p = 0.1401$; *overall quality* − $W = 55, p = 0.4844$.

These results are in line with the answers from the first two questions and the question whether they would have preferred to translate from scratch as those assessments were quite negative, too. Apparently, the translators were really disappointed by the MT output. The results are a little surprising because other studies have shown that the MT output is not that bad, at least in what efficiency increases are concernded (Läubli et al. 2013). First, it is doubtful whether the participants can really judge what is above and below average when more than half of them claim that they have never used MT before. Second, the MT quality assessment is very subjective and the participants may have based it on what they would expect from human translators. Further, some questions in the pre-experiment questionnaire already proved a rather negative attitude towards MT or bad experience with MT output (see Figure 8.2 and Figure 8.3).

The last two questions focused again on the PE task. *Q9: Based on the post-editing task you have performed, which of these statements will you go for?* The aim of this question was to evaluate how much work was left after applying the MT. The participants could choose whether they *had to post-edit ALL the outputs, about 75% of the outputs, 25–50% outputs,* or *only VERY FEW outputs.* To create a figurative value, the first answer *I had to post-edit ALL the outputs* was given 0 points, whereas the last answer *I only had to post-edit VERY FEW outputs* got 3 points.

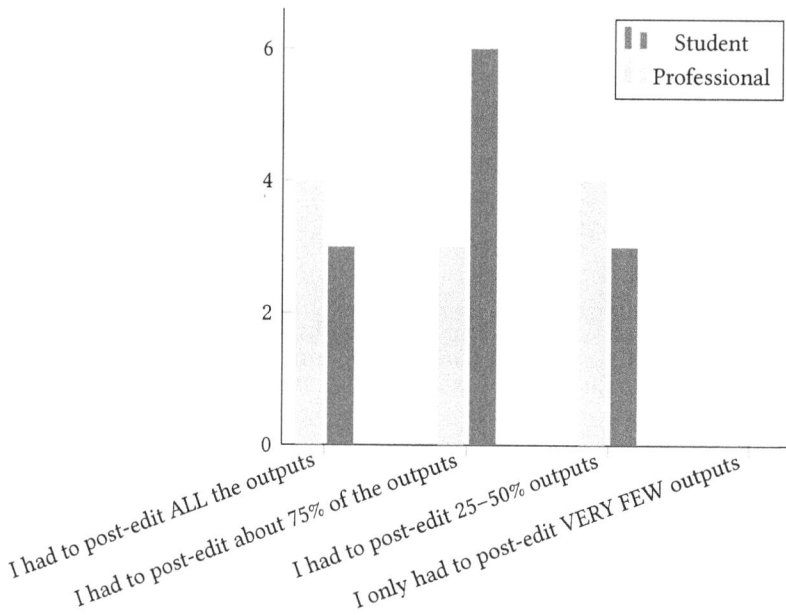

Figure 8.9: Based on the post-editing task you have performed, which of these statements will you go for?

Although the distribution is a little different, professionals as well as students agree on an average value of 1 (professionals sd: 0.89; students sd: 0.74), meaning that in general the groups felt that they had to post-edit about 75% of the outputs.

Similarly, the next question asked: *Q10: Based on the post-editing task you have performed, how often would you have preferred to translate from scratch rather than post-editing machine translation?* The acceptable answers were similar: *always; in most of the cases (75% of the outputs or more); in almost half of the cases (approx. 50%);* and *only in very few cases (less than 25%)* with *always* matching 0 points and *only a few cases* 3 points.

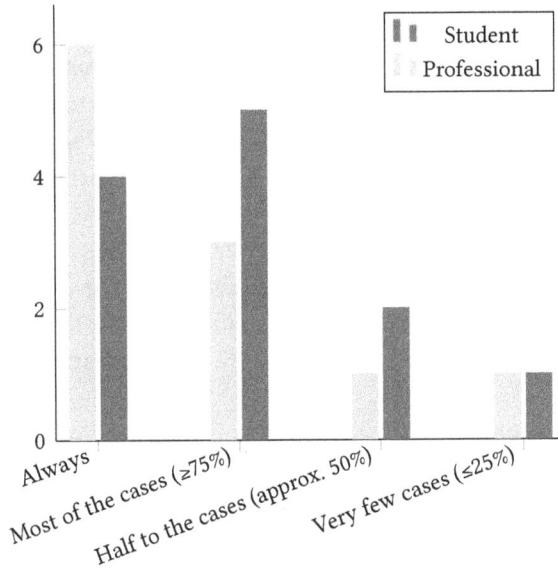

Figure 8.10: Based on the post-editing task you have performed, how often would you have preferred to translate from scratch rather than post-editing machine translation?

The value for the professionals is 0.73 (sd: 1.01) and for the students 1 (sd: 0.95). Hence, the first group would have preferred to translate more than 75% of the texts from scratch, while the students would have preferred to translate about 75% of the content from scratch. These last two questions showed (again) that the participants were not very satisfied with the MT output and judged that they hardly had any benefits from using the output. Questions Q9 and Q10 might be influenced by the personal opinion about MT and PE even more than Q8 and its sub-questions, because they may want to prefer TfS. As we saw in §7.3, PE (and MPE) was (were) more efficient at least regarding time. No significant difference between both groups was found again for the last two questions: Q9 – $W = 66$, $p = 1$; and Q10 – $W = 53$, $p = 0.4107$.

As a final note, the last two questions were not worded properly and would have to be adjusted if the study was replicated. The presentation of the single response option is very blurry. When one option is *I had to post-edit all the outputs,* which can be interpreted as 100% and another *I had to post-edit 25–50% of the outputs*, the option *I had to post-edit about 75% of the outputs* would imply everything between 50 and 99%. Accordingly, the options are not weighted equally. While one option only includes 1%, another includes 49%. This improper scaling, however, indirectly shows the emotional situation of the participant. Although the data show that they did not have to post-edit all the output, one third of the professionals and one fourth of the students chose that option. The same applies for the last question. While the question we just discussed left little room for interpretation (95% might have been considered as *all the output*), the last question directly says that *always* means 100%, because the next option *in most of the cases (75% of the outputs or more)* directly states that everything including and above 75% is included. The option *in almost half of the cases (approx. 50%)* applies to 25 to 74% and *only in very few cases (less than 25%)* for the remaining percentage. The weight of the single items is again unbalanced. The percentage for the participants who opted for *always* is even higher than in the other question: Over half of the professionals and one third of the students chose that option. This is a strong statement against PE. However, we have to bear in mind that the MPE task was the last task conducted in the experiments. Hence, the frustration might not have been that severe for PE, but the participants could have been biased by the MPE task.

8.3 Discussion

O'Brien (2002: 102) states that a positive attitude towards MT is one of the attributes required by a post-editor to successfully complete the task. When the translators were asked to give their opinion on their previous experiences with MT engines, they claimed to be rather unsatisfied with the MT output (cf. Figure 8.2). The questionnaire did not ask in detail which MT engines the individual participants had gathered experience with or when they had used them. So, it can be assumed that their attitude towards the PE and MPE tasks was rather negative right from the beginning, which might have a negative influence on the final post-edited target text. Further, only 50% of the professional and 17% of the semi-professional translators had previous experience with PE, which might indicate that some translators had difficulties with the task itself and do not have any coping strategies, yet. It was not part of the questionnaire, but it seems probable that the Translog II environment was new to most of the participants as the use of Translog II is not very widespread outside of translation process research. Further, the output was produced by an online MT system (*Google Translate*) that is not customized to certain text types or the translators' needs. When MT is used in professional translation environments, the MT engine is usually customized to the special needs of the company (cf. §4.3). Therefore, the output of an online MT system does not represent the quality that MT technology can provide. All (these) additional coefficients may have contributed to the negative evaluations of the MT output (cf. Figure 8.8)[4].

Another interesting point is that although the participants were unsatisfied with the MT output (cf. Figure 8.8), they claimed that they could hardly see any use in the MT during PE, and would rather have translated from scratch (cf. Figure 8.9 and Figure 8.10), they were rather satisfied with the final version of their post-edited texts (cf. Figure 8.5), and not that unsatisfied with their monolingual post-editing task (cf. Figure 8.6 – especially concerning the self-assessment of the students). One might have expected that the translators would be even less satisfied if the MT output was very poor and the translators could not even refer to the source text. These slightly contradictory assessments could be an indicator of emotional impact and subjectivity. Although the proximity of time has it advantages, the results of this questionnaire might be coloured by the emotions the participants experienced during the experiments. If a participant potentially had problems with a post-editing task, his/her feelings about the MT output might have been rather bad directly after the experiment, because (s)he may still have been annoyed etc. Therefore, the evaluation of the MT, for example, might be worse than it would have been after a couple of hours/days distance from the tasks.[5]

Further, it is striking that the participants were more satisfied with their PE outcome than with the final text of the MPE task. As the data were not distributed normally, a Mann-Whitney-U-test was conducted which did not show significant differences between the evaluation of PE and MPE task for both professionals and students combined ($W = 346.5$, $p = 0.0574$), but might have with a higher number of participants. The different results in the self-evaluation might be related to the fact that most participants were unfamiliar with the PE task and probably even less were familiar with MPE because they could not consult the source text (as they do in TfS, too) to confirm or reject the MT output. Furthermore, the available source text in the PE task can be characterised as a valuable aid that is missing in the MPE task, which makes the task naturally more difficult.

---

[4] As mentioned above for the questionnaires in general, the MT system was also not adjusted, because of the predetermined setup.

[5] As the setup of the experiment was predetermined by CRITT, who originally composed the study, these considerations and decisions were not made by myself.

In both questionnaires, the participants were asked whether they thought they would apply MT in their future translation tasks (Figure 8.3 and Figure 8.7). After examining the satisfaction with the MT output in the experiments, it is expected that fewer translators could imagine using MT for their translation tasks as they are highly dissatisfied with the PE tasks and the MT output. However, almost the opposite is the case: Before the experiment, 8.3% (one of twelve) of the professionals could imagine implementing MT for their future translation tasks, 58.3% could not, and 33.3% were not sure. After the experiment 18.2% (two of eleven) could imagine implementing MT for their future translation tasks, 36.4% could not, and 45.5% were not sure. The percentage of participants who could imagine using MT in their translation tasks (about 9.9% - two translators) and who were not sure (about 12.2% - three translators) increased, while the percentage of people who could not imagine using MT in the translation tasks decreased about 22.1%. The only explanation that comes to mind is that some translators could not imagine a way to use MT at all for their translation work before the experiment. However, the question about the feasibility of MT (cf. Figure 8.4) contradicts this assumption, because the professional translators were rather positive about it.

The tendency is the same for the semi-professional translators, but the picture is not as clear: Before the experiment, 25% (three out of twelve) of the students could imagine implementing MT into their translation tasks, 41.7% could not, and 33.3% were not sure. After the experiment, 33.3% were open to using MT in the future for translation, 41.7% could not imagine it and 25% were not sure. Therefore, the percentage of people who would use MT increased by about 8.3% and the number who were not sure about using MT decreased by about 8.3%. The simple explanation would be that one student who was initially not sure about MT in professional translation tasks would not use it. Hence, there was not much change in the evaluation of the feasibility of MT in the student group.

Table 8.4 illustrates the (potential) change of mind after the experiments. It is quite striking that nobody changed his/her opinion from *Yes* or *Not sure* to

Table 8.4: Changed answers in the two questionnaires

	From **Yes** to			From **Not sure** to			From **No** to		
	Yes	Not sure	No	Yes	Not sure	No	Yes	Not sure	No
professionals	0	1	0	1	3	0	1	1	4
students	2	1	0	2	2	0	0	0	5

No, which, as mentioned above, could have been expected according to the other evaluations. Only two people went from *Yes* to *Not sure*, while the rest of the participants retained or improved their opinion on MT as an aid for translation tasks. This is contradictory to the negative opinions on the MT output and the PE and MPE tasks from the other questions. One argument to explain this tendency may be that some of the translators may have never considered MT systems as a possible tool for their translation tasks and they changed their judgement accordingly after they had gained experience. It would have been interesting to know how many participants recalled the question and how this influenced the answer to the question, but this factor was not checked for.

To summarise the results, the participants – neither professionals nor semi-professionals - had a negative attitude towards MT before or after the experiments. They did not enjoy the PE task and they ejoyed the MPE task even less. In fact, they would have rather translated the texts from scratch. Nonetheless, the participants would consider MT output as an aid for their future translation tasks even more than before the experiments. In general, the students had a slightly more positive attitude than professional translators. Principally, the attitude towards MT/PE seems to have a major influence in the questionnaire data. Although the following analyses (§9 - §12) very often focus on subconscious behaviour, we cannot be certain whether and how much this attitude had a (negative) influence on the results of this study. This is not measurable in the scope of this study. However, it would be very interesting to investigate whether and to what extent this negative attitude had an influence on the participants' behaviour during the tasks.

9 Lexical problem solving: Internet research

The first problem solving strategy that will be analysed examines the instances in which the participants looked up words or phrases in the Internet. Hence, we will look at external resources[1]. This strategy is accordingly classified as a conscious problem solving strategy because the translators actively decide that they have difficulties with a certain text part and therefore consult an Internet-based resource to find help. The following sub-sections will first introduce the theme of lexical research, theoretical assumptions, and previous studies. Then, the focus will be on the evaluation of the translation process data of the experiments according to screen-recording, eyetracking and keylogging data.

9.1 Lexical problem solving: Introduction

The use of dictionaries and other translation aids is a topic that has already been studied to some degree in empirical translation studies. This graspable and expressive part of the translation process can provide valuable insights to translation behaviour in general as well as differences between professionals, semiprofessional, and laypersons.

In regard to general lexical research behaviour, Müller-Spitzer et al. (2015) examine the log files from 2013 of the German version of Wiktionary to observe the behaviour of the users. They find a relationship between corpus frequencies of the individual words and how often these words were looked up in the dictionary. Further, polysemantic words are looked up more often than monosemantic words. Social relevance additionally impacts the lookup rate.

Risku (1998: 160–175) points out that two sources of information integration exist in the translation process: first, the existing knowledge and the reference material provided by the client and, second, research. Research comprises much more than only dictionaries and terminology lists. Often, translation also requires using encyclopedias, domain-specific books/texts, or parallel texts as well as ask-

---

[1]Find details on internal vs. external resources in the next chapter

ing other translators, experts in the domain, or the client concrete questions on contents of the text. Further, the way in which translators conduct research supposedly differs significantly between beginner and expert translators. Risku assumes that research strategies of expert translators are not universal and distinct, but flexible and problem-oriented. However, three general tendencies might be identifiable: Experts use research, draw on abstract problem representation, and adapt their research according to needs and the available time.

In a study with professional translators and foreign language teachers, the PACTE (2005) group analyses the types of resources used in the translation process. They suggest two main sources: internal and external resources. Internal resources describe the knowledge the translator already has, while external resources consolidate all information gathering processes. However, it is not always one or the other type of resource that is used exclusively by the translator, but a combination of both resources is often used to generate a translation solution. These can be identified according to the actions the translators undertake during translation. While a total of 16 types of actions were identified in the exploratory test, five were selected to identify the resources: reading the source text, pauses longer than five seconds, provisional solutions, definitive solutions, and consultations. According to these actions, five sub-categories of resources used during translation were identified (cf. ibid.: 615-616):

- Simple internal support – the translator only uses his/her knowledge;

- Mainly internal support with additional external support – translation aids are consulted, but do not directly help to find the final translation choice;

- Balanced internal and external support – translation decisions are created with both resources taken into account;

- Mainly external support with additional internal support – complex consultation of external resources from which the solution is drawn;

- Simple external support – a bilingual dictionary is used to find the solution.

This schema was adapted in a few studies – as introduced in Alves & Liparini Campos (2009) – according to Jakobsen's (2005) notion that pauses indicate either orientation or revision processes. As resources can only be used for either orientation or revision – when a translation is drafted, a (first) translation decision has been made during orientation, which can be assessed afterwards, but is not done during the drafting process – the following sub-categories were developed:

- simple internal support for orientation (SISO) and for revision (SISR)

- simple external support for orientation (SESO) and for revision (SESR)

- dominant internal support for orientation (DISO) and for revision (DISR)

- dominant external support for orientation (DESO) and for revision (DESR)

This part of the study at hand will concentrate on external support, which may or may not be used combined with internal resources. I suggest that most external research is combined with internal knowledge, except if a problem is purely lexical. And even then, the translator has knowledge about how this word/phrase is syntactically and grammatically embedded in the text and knows the context. Hence, (s)he knows how to make a decision for one or the other lexical choice offered by a dictionary etc.

In his think-aloud study, Krings (1986b: 128) observes that the use of aids is directly linked to problem solving and can be easily determined in think-aloud protocols. The translators used aids in over 60% of all detected problems – when they translated from their mother tongue into the foreign language, the participants used bilingual dictionaries in 80% of the units identified as problems. Monolingual dictionaries were mainly used to find more information on a translation unit in the foreign language (cf. ibid.: 166). However, compared to bilingual dictionaries, monolingual dictionaries played a minor role – they were not used for the translation into the mother tongue – and other aids no role at all (cf. ibd.: 218)[2]. Furthermore, many comprehension problems – about 75% – were solved (or were tried to be solved) with the use of aids, and if they did not use aids, it was mostly because the participants were convinced that the dictionary would not contain the required entry. In only six out of 113 instances, the participants arrived at a solution to a problem via inferences according to the think-aloud protocols. This does not mean that participants do not use inferring as a strategy, but they hardly use it without any additional aids (cf. ibid.: 221-222). Although the participants in Krings' study are neither translation students nor professional translators, the study reveals that research is a very important indicator of problems in translation.

In her empirical study on translation aids, Nord (2002) analyses translation aids for research. She divides translation aids (or external aids) in general into

- physical aids for translation, like a desk or a chair;

---

[2]The participants were asked to bring their own printed aids, which were mainly dictionaries.

- administration aids, e.g. software to generate invoices, data bases;

- communication aids, like a telephone or an e-mail client;

- text production aids, like pencil and paper or computer hard- and software;

- and finally the aforementioned research aids that help with the translation itself and to expand the knowledge of the translator. (cf. ibid.: 6)

Special translation tools like translation memory systems combine both text production and research aids. Nord explores definitions of parallel texts and dictionary typologies and gives a detailed overview of the state of the art systematic and critical dictionary research in translation studies as well as research on dictionary use. Concerning critical dictionary research in translation studies, she concludes that translation scholars agree that bilingual dictionaries are not suitable translation aids as they do not incorporate text factors, the translation situation and the involved cultures. However, Nord criticises that, on the one hand, scholars do not define their understanding of translations and translators and hence consider different concepts. On the other hand she criticises[3] that they only explore the topic theoretically and not empirically (cf. ibid: 64-65). Next, she introduces some empirical studies on translation aids and finds little agreement in these studies. However, she highlights five fairly common results (cf. ibid.: 92):

- Less experienced translators tend to use bilingual dictionaries, while more experienced translators use monolingual dictionaries and other aids.

- Dictionaries are used to find or check equivalents or the meaning of lexical units, or to determine alternative translations.

- Translators use a translation aid 1.1 to 2.9 times per problem or source text unit. Experienced translators use translation aids more often than less experienced translators.

- Monolingual dictionaries contain 84% of the requested information, bilingual dictionaries only 54–73%.

- The use of dictionaries hardly improves the quality of the translation (which is measured very differently in the studies), some mistakes only emerge from the use of a dictionary.

---

[3]I fully agree with this point of criticism.

For her study, Nord (2002: 102–114) approached 16 professional translators (three for the pre-study, 13 for the main study) and observed them in their usual work environment. Every participant translated texts from his/her own everyday workload. The participants were asked to think aloud. However, the sessions were not recorded with a recording device but manually logged by the experimenter. Six parameters were evaluated: frequency of use, cause of use, reason for use, research request, choice of aid, and consequences of use. She concludes (cf. ibid.: 214-223) that translators need research aids and they need them very often (on average 17 times per hour). Different reasons for using dictionaries were found: either the translator does not understand the source text unit, (s)he does not know how to express the source unit in the target text, (s)he wants to recheck the own translation idea, or because the translator does not know how to integrate the target unit into the target text. The participants mainly used aids for lexical problems; missing domain and cultural knowledge is almost never the reason for research. Generally, they know how to handle research aids and know exactly which aid to use for which purpose.

The results of Nord's study (cf. ibid.: 227-247) culminated in a theoretical framework for a specific translation dictionary and implications for teaching the use of translation aids. Her dictionary framework should be realised as a database that includes information on text type conventions, meaning, equivalents, use, spelling, grammar, context, synonyms, and non-linguistic information.

In the last decades, the world wide web became very influential and changed the work environments in many jobs – translation is no exception. While translators conventionally used printed media like mono-, bi-, and multilingual dictionaries, encyclopedias, etc., these research media are being increasingly replaced by electronic aids, which can be used on the computer either on- or offline. It is argued though that electronic research tools, especially online tools, do not necessarily accelerate the translation process, because the sources of the information need to be validated and that the information you can access on the Internet may be more error prone (cf. e. g. Albrecht 2013: 60). Nonetheless, the experimental setup of the study at hand did not provide any printed research aids, because it is easier to record and follow the research process with electronic aids. It is impossible to provide all printed aids that might be helpful for the participants; if only a selection is presented, it cannot be assumed that these are the favourite dictionaries etc. of the participants, which creates an unfamiliar work environment; even if the participants had been contacted before the experiments and had been asked to name their favourite printed translation aids they used most often, it could not have been guaranteed that these would be enough to cope with all lexical translation problems in the texts. Another aspect is that certain kinds of research aids like encyclopedias are hard to provide in a printed version. Bringing their own dictionaries was ruled out as it would have been an extra burden for the participants, they might have forgotten to bring their dictionaries, the research behaviour would not have been comparable, and the participants were not supposed to know which domain to prepare. Furthermore, it is assumed that the participants are trained in and used to using electronic aids from their daily work routine – both students and professional translators. They know which sources and websites they can trust and know how to assess the presented information. They were free to use everything available on the Internet, offline tools were not provided. Further, the study at hand is part of the CRITT-TPR database and the same texts were translated/(monolingually) post-edited in many different languages (see §7.2). Hence, allowing all participants to use the online sources they prefer makes the study comparable.

In other translation process research studies, online tools were the only provided search aids, too. Daems et al. (2016) present a study in which they aim to compare participants' use of external resources during TfS and PE and to figure out how these external resources can be used for successful problem solving concerning quality and productivity. The texts were translated in CASMACAT, an online translation and PE environment, and the research instances were recorded with *Inputlog*, a keylogging tool. Ten participants who were all studying for their Master's degree in translation studies were asked to translate and post-edit four newspaper texts each. All participants had no experience in PE. In the analysis, Daems et al. grouped the used online resources into five main types, i.e. search engines, concordancers, dictionaries, encyclopedias, and others. Next, they analysed the time the participants spent in external resources and found that the participants spent significantly more time for research in TfS than in the PE task. However, there was no significant relation between the types of aid used for external research and the task (cf. ibid.: 120-121). In terms of productivity, the participants needed significantly more time for human translation and also spent more time on research in this task. Further, the more often external research aids were used, the longer the overall session became (cf. ibid.: 123). The final criterion they analysed was the influence of external research aids on the quality of the text. As quality is a trait that is hard to measure, they developed a schema that focuses on acceptability and adequacy. No significant difference for quality was found between TfS and PE. However, the more sources were used in PE, the worse the quality of the final target text became; while in contrast, the more sources were used in human translation, the better the quality became.

They explain this finding with the lack of experience in PE (as the participants have already developed successful research skills for human translation) and the priming effects of the MT output (cf. ibid.: 123-127). When adequacy and acceptability are considered individual quality criteria, no significant differences were found between TfS and PE. A longer or more frequent use of dictionaries seems to increase the quality of adequacy, while extensive research in encyclopedias seems to reduce acceptability of quality[4] (cf. ibid.: 127-131). They conclude their study with the statement that "whereas search strategies during the translation process are more effective than those used when PE, PE is still faster than human translation without negatively affecting the final quality of the product." (ibid.: 131). The following chapter will quantify the Internet search instances in a similar way. However, these will not be analysed with regard to the quality of the final texts, but will be regarded as a problem solving indicator. Hence, I will compare the lexical problem solving behaviour expressed by Internet research between TfS and PE/MPE as well as between professionals and semi-professionals.

To understand the nature of the problems in the texts, we will approach them lexically on a word or phrase level and will look at broader units in the next chapter (§10) on syntactic problems. In the context of the lexical analysis, I consider a *phrase* a word unit that contains more than one word; these words, however, share meaning and could be considered a semantic unit. The main focus of the analysis will be on the differences between PE and TfS. However, the MPE task will be analysed as well, because we can assume that most of the participants – students and professionals – have little experience in MPE[5] and therefore cannot draw on much task knowledge. Accordingly, the analysis will focus on the differences related to translation experience. The participants are separated into professional and semi-professional translators so that both groups can be compared. However, the groups are in themselves not uniform, which applies especially to the professional group – while one participant had only half a year of professional experience, another had 20 years experience. To get a more in-depth picture of the influence of experience, an *experience coefficient* will be used as well (see details in §8.1). It consists of the years of translation training plus two times the years of professional experience. Therefore, for example, a participant who spent five years studying translation and has 4.5 years of professional experience achieves a coefficient of 14.

Due to technical problems, some of the sessions could not be replayed in Tobii Studio and accordingly the Internet search instances could not be observed.

---

[4]Daems et al. (2016: 130) explicitly point out that this relationship might not be causal.
[5]We have to remember that only 1/3 (cf. §8.1) of the participants have PE experience.

Although at least one session could not be replayed for every task, the total number of all sessions per tasks is almost equal and there is not a lot variation in the number of sessions per tasks. In the following table, the number of experiments that could be observed is listed (24 sessions should have been recorded per task):

Table 9.1: Number of session recorded

Task	Professionals	Students	Total
MPE	20	23	43
PE	19	23	42
TfS	21	21	42

9.2 Lexical problem solving: screen recording data

This sub-chapter discuses the screen recording data with regard to the Internet research conducted by the participants. Screen recordings of the sessions are a useful method to protocol the use of research aids, which was traditionally done manually either by the experimenter or by the user him/herself, or via think-aloud protocols (cf. Nord 2002: 99). The automatised capturing of the screen is less error prone compared to manual recordings and certainly complete if no technical difficulties occur that might leave us with no recording at all. The purpose of this analysis is to characterise the research behaviour of the participants before the keylogging and eyetracking data are analysed. First, the hypotheses for the screen recording data will be introduced and will be tested in the following sections.

9.2.1 Introduction of hypotheses for lexical problem solving (screen recording data)

The overall hypothesis is that the different tasks show different search patterns. The MT output might suggest translations for difficult or low-frequency words/ phrases that are acceptable and the translator does not need to do any research on the word/phrase. On the other hand, the MT might be lexically unacceptable in the context, e.g., inappropriate or incorrect collocations or wrong lexical choices, and might cause insecurity which, in turn, might make the translators research words which they may have not researched without the unacceptable MT output. The Internet was used for context research, as well. Further, I assume that with a growing level of expertise, the translators show different patterns as well (find more details in §6), e.g., more research is done by less professional translators or less professional translators recheck their translation choices more often than more professional ones, because they are more insecure. Hence, the main hypothesis for external lexical research is:

- H: In the different tasks, the translators show different search patterns. The patterns also differ according to their expertise level.

  H_0: In the different tasks, the translators show the same search patterns. There is no difference between professionals and semi-professionals.

To disprove the null hypothesis, we will look at a number of subordinate hypotheses to cover different aspects of the topic, which are listed in the following. This is only done to give the reader an overview of covered topics. Detailed information on the object of investigation and the motivation for the individual hypotheses can be found in the respective section (indicated in brackets). These subordinate hypotheses are executed in the same order in the following chapters. Every hypothesis contains two sub-hypotheses – one concerning the different tasks, one concerning the difference between students and professionals – to keep the number manageable. This does not imply, however, that there is a compulsory relationship between task and professionalism.

- H_1: The Internet is consulted more often in TfS than in the PE task. The Internet is consulted more often by students than by professionals.[6] (§9.2.2)

  H_{01}: The Internet is consulted as often in TfS as in the PE task and students and professionals use it equally often.

- H_2: Fewer words/phrases are looked up in the PE tasks compared to TfS.[7] However, when a word/phrase is looked up, the same word/phrase is looked up more often in PE. (§9.2.3)

  H_{02}: The amount of words/phrases looked up is equal in PE and TfS. Further, they are looked up equally often in both tasks.

---

[6]We have to keep in mind that the PE instructions specifically stated that the participants should not "embark on time-consuming research" (see §7.2).

[7]H_1 and H_2 are similar, but H_1 measures all research instance, without considering whether the same word/phrase was looked up more then once. H_2 considers only single words/phrases and not how often a word/phrase was researched.

- H_3: The Internet is not consulted in some sessions at all. This happens more often in the PE session than in the TfS session; and experts do not consult the Internet more often in the entire session than students. (§9.2.4)

  H_{03}: The Internet is not consulted in some sessions at all. This happens as often in the PE session as in the TfS, and both students and experts do not consult the Internet in the entire session to the same extent.

- H_4: The more complex a text, the more research is necessary. (§9.2.5)

  H_{04}: There is no connection between complexity level of a text and research effort.

- H_5: In both PE and TfS, the bilingual dictionary is the source that is used most often. This being said, bilingual dictionaries and other sources are distributed differently in both tasks. Students use bilingual dictionaries more often than professionals. (§9.2.6)

  H_{05}: In both PE and TfS, the bilingual dictionary is not the source that is used most often and bilingual dictionaries and other sources are distributed equally in both tasks. Students and professionals use bilingual dictionaries equally often.

- $H_{6.1}$: Participants need more time for research per single word/phrase in PE than in TfS. Students need longer to find a translation than professionals if they research. (§9.2.7)

  $H_{06.1}$: Participants need as much time for research per single word/phrase in PE as in TfS. Students and professionals need equally long to find a translation if they research.

  $H_{6.2}$: Participants spend more time on research in TfS than in PE in the overall session. Students spend more time on research than professionals. (§9.2.7)

  $H_{06.2}$: Participants spend as much time on research in TfS as in PE in the overall session. Students and professionals spend the same time on research.

- H_7: Translators do most research in the drafting phase in TfS, while they do most research in the orientation and revision phase in PE. (§9.2.8)

  H_{07}: Translators do research equally often in the same phases in TfS and PE.

- H$_8$: Students re-check their translations more often than professionals. (§9.2.9)

  H$_{08}$: Students and professionals re-check their translations equally often.

Both the grouping of the participants into professionals and students as well as the experience coefficient introduced in §8.1 will be used to analyse the data. This is due to the simple reason that the experience coefficient is a new value that needs assessment for its general usability. Hence, both will be used throughout this book so that an assessment of the experience coefficient is possible at the end of this book.

9.2.2 Number of research instances

H$_1$: The Internet is consulted more often in TfS than in the PE task. The Internet is consulted more often by students than by professionals.

As I assume that the MT output already solves some lexical problems, it is reasonable to predict that the translator has to consult the Internet more often in the TfS task than in PE, which was also already observed by Krings (2001: 318–320). Throughout all experiments, the Internet was consulted 685 times - this quantification includes a) opening the browser, b) using a new research resource (in the same or a different tab), c) switching between tabs, d) searching for a new word in the same research resource. The distribution can be seen in Figure 9.1 according to task and status.

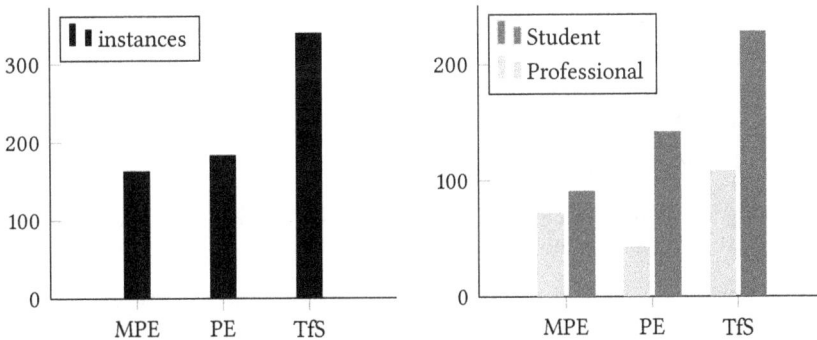

Figure 9.1: Total amount of websites used for research per task for all participants and for the single groups.

Participants looked up words/phrases 163 times in the Internet in MPE, 185 times in PE and 336 times in TfS. As was suggested, there is more research conducted for TfS compared to PE (and MPE) of the MT output. This is still true if the data is divided into professional and semi-professional translators: Although the numbers are different, the look up instances conducted between PE and TfS is equally significant: A Chi-Square-Test shows that the number of website use per task differs significantly between students and professionals, taking into account all three tasks ($\chi^2(2, N = 684) = 17.34, p < 0.0002$) as well as only PE and TfS ($\chi^2(1, N = 521) = 4.17, p = 0.0412$). When we compare MPE to PE ($\chi^2(1, N = 348) = 16.22, p < 0.0001$) and to TfS ($\chi^2(1, N = 499) = 6.38$, $p = 0.0116$), both differences become significant, too. Accordingly, as we can see in Figure 9.1, professionals research less in all three tasks compared to students. Interestingly, professionals research more in MPE than in PE, which is contrary to the student group and what was expected. This reason might not be that professionals experience more lexical problems, but that they look up one problematic item more often than they have to in the PE because of the missing source text. The first sub-hypothesis can be confirmed regarding both the difference between the tasks – more research is conducted in TfS than in PE/MPE – and regarding the two groups – students research more than professionals.

In the following, I will also take time into consideration. In Appendix A, Table A.1 presents an overview of how many words were processed on average between two research instances and how much time passed between two research instances. Let us first look at the average times that passed between two research instances by dividing time by research instance as was done by Nord (2002: 117). For the overall data, 298.2 seconds (sd: 240.5 s) lay between two research instances. However, as the high standard deviation already indicates, there is a high variation in the data. These differences become obvious, when the data are divided according to status of the participant (professionals – mean: 348.9 s, sd: 282.5 s; students – mean: 265.2 s, sd: 205.0 s) and according to task (TfS – mean: 223.3 s, sd: 224.2; PE – mean: 320.4 s, sd: 234.5 s; MPE – mean: 383.3 s, sd: 250.8 s) and for both parameters (see Table 9.2).

Table 9.2: Time in seconds between two research instances according to task and participant group

	TfS		PE		MPE	
	mean	sd	mean	sd	mean	sd
professionals	309.6	316.5	448.5	310.0	255.9	74.0
students	162.9	97.0	241.0	125.5	461.8	290.0

The problem with this method is that there were sessions in this study in which the participants did not use the Internet for research at all (see §9.2.4), which did not happen in Nord's study. As numbers cannot be divided by zero, these sessions were not included in the calculation (value=n.a.). Hence, to adjust the calculations, I divide time by research instance plus one ($\frac{t}{n+1}$) so that the sessions with no research are represented by the overall time of the session ($\frac{t}{0+1}$). If research was done once, it is assumed to be in the middle of the overall session ($\frac{t}{1+1}$) etc. The data change in the following manner: 320.5 s (sd: 248.9 s) passed on average between two research instances. Similarly, values differ for status (professionals – mean: 400.2 s, sd: 288.5 s; students – mean: 246.9 s, sd: 178.1 s) and task (TfS – mean: 290.4 s, sd: 319.9; PE – mean: 275.9, sd: 188.3 s; MPE – mean: 393.4 s, sd: 207.3 s) and both parameters (see Table 9.3[8])

Table 9.3: Adjusted time in seconds between two research instances according to task and participant group.

	TfS		PE		MPE	
	mean	sd	mean	sd	mean	sd
professionals	429.9	399.4	372.2	225.1	395.9	207.1
students	151.0	97.0	196.4	100.0	391.1	212.2

As we have seen in the analysis above, students research much more than professionals. The differences between students and professionals becomes much more obvious, when calculating on the basis of research instance plus one in the TfS task. Although the difference was clear from the beginning, the gap becomes greater when no-research instances are included in the comparison[9]. The data do not change much for PE, naturally the values become smaller, but the difference between the two groups is not considerably different. The values are very similar for both groups in MPE, which again might be explained by the lacking experience of both groups in the task and non-recognisable connections to regular translation tasks. When the time per research instance (plus one) is correlated with the experience coefficient to achieve a more fine grained impression of the relation between experience and time between research instances, there is

---

[8]When the mean numbers become smaller than in the former calculations, it indicates that the assessed sessions usually included a research instance. When the mean number becomes higher, it indicates that no research was done in a number of sessions.

[9]The data become significant for $n + 1$ in a Mann-Whitney-U-test ($W = 330.5$, $p = 0.006$), in contrast to the data for n ($W = 183$, $p = 0.1385$).

a positive small but significant correlation for the overall data ($r_\tau(4.11) = 0.256$, $p < 0.0001$), for TfS ($r_\tau(3.28) = 0.363, p = 0.001$) as well as PE ($r_\tau(2.37) = 0.261$, $p = 0.0179$). As was to be expected, no significant correlation can be found in the MPE task ($r_\tau(1.13) = 0.122, p = 0.2602$). When the data are divided by group, the tests are also significant considering all tasks ($W = 2707, p = 0.0008$), TfS ($W = 330.5, p = 0.0059$), and PE ($W = 320, p = 0.0096$), but not for MPE ($W = 237, p = 0.8948$).

While O'Brien's (2006 – find more details on the study in §4.2) participants were not allowed to research using the Internet or printed aids, she used the dictionary component of Translog[10] to provide some terminology for the participants. The participants used the internal dictionary remarkably seldom: two participant did not use the dictionary at all, seven participants used it once, and two participants used it five times. Although they received instructions on how to use the dictionary tool before the experiment, only one participant succeeded in looking up a term – one participant looked for words that were not included in the dictionary, while five did not remember how to use the dictionary properly. The students in her pre-study, however, used the dictionary much more often: One student did not use it at all, one used it twice, one 16 times, one 24 times, one 27 times, and one 42 times. Further, the ratio between successful and unsuccessful look ups was much more balanced. Nonetheless, the unsuccessful research trials were also caused by misusing the dictionary component (cf. ibid.: 160). Considering the text length of altogether 1777 words, the student use of dictionary behaviour is much closer to the findings of this study than the behaviour of the professionals (although missing knowledge of how to use the dictionary might have prevented more research in the main study).

The participants in Nord (2002: 117) are classified as professional translators and consulted an aid on average every 203 s. In the study at hand, professionals used online research aids only every 309.6 s (leaving out the sessions with no research – when they are included it is only every 429.9 s, although this value is calculated with one extra research instance per session). The students group in this study, however, does more research (every 162.9/151 s)[11] than the professional translators in Nord's study. Nord's participants might have researched more in a certain amount of time, because they had to deal in general with more domain-specific texts than our participants. Further, the texts/sessions were longer in Nord's study and were taken from the participants' everyday work. Therefore, these sessions might not include (prolonged) orientation and revision phases (on

---

[10] She used a now outdated Translog version and the component is not part of Translog II.
[11] $\left(\frac{n}{n+1}\right)$

orientation, drafting, and revision phases see Jakobsen 2002), but only or mostly translation drafting, which includes most of the research instances (see §9.2.8 for the analysis of phases in this study). Figure 9.2 visualises these and the upcoming results.

As became apparent in the later analysis, the results are more meaningful when they are calculated with research instances plus one. Therefore, the same method will be applied when calculating the number of source words translated/(monolingually) post-edited between two research instances. The average is 60.6 (sd: 49.0) source words processed per research instance for the overall group and for all tasks. Dividing the group by status, professionals processed 74.9 words (sd: 51.0) and students 47.4 words (sd: 43.4). A total of 84.2 words (sd: 46.7) were processed on average per research instance in MPE, 55.4 (sd: 45.3) in PE, and 41.5 (sd: 45.9) in TfS. The differences considering group and task are outlined in Table 9.4.

Table 9.4: Words translated/(monolingually) post-edited between two research instances according to task and participant group

	TfS		PE		MPE	
	mean	sd	mean	sd	mean	sd
professionals	61.0	54.4	75.2	48.0	88.3	48.8
students	22.0	23.7	39.1	36.3	80.3	45.3

When we look at the correlations between experience coefficient of the participants and the number of words processed between research instances, most tests proved significant – for the total group ($r_\tau(3.51) = 0.220, p < 0.0005$), for the TfS ($r_\tau(2.58) = 0.286, p < 0.01$), and for the PE task ($r_\tau(2.36) = 0.263, p = 0.0183$). Only the data for the MPE task ($r_\tau(1.25) = 0.14, p = 0.2129$) did not prove significant. Similar results can be seen when the results are tested according to the groups. The difference between professionals and students is significant for the total group ($W = 2690.5, p = 0.0011$), for TfS ($W = 323.5, p = 0.0099$), and for PE ($W = 332.5, p = 0.0041$). However, no significant difference can be found for MPE ($W = 248, p = 0.6877$) between the groups. These results are in line with the data of the time passed between research instances.

Interestingly, the data show more consistency for the parameter words processed per research instance compared to time passed per research instance (see Figure 9.2). While the downward trend is very linear for professionals from MPE

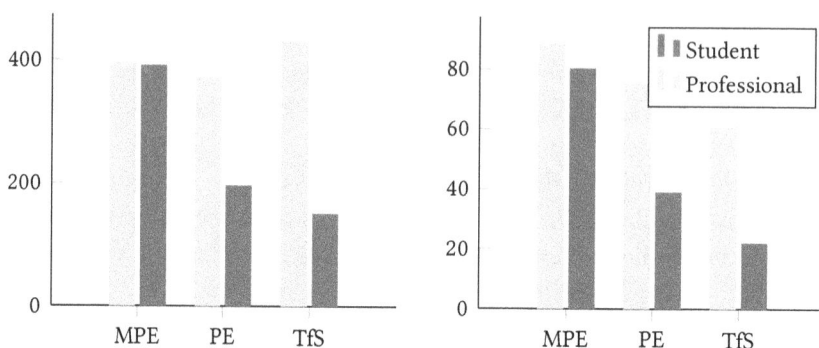

Figure 9.2: Time passed (left) and words processed (right) between research instance (plus one)

to PE to TfS in words translated/(monolingually) post-edited – a decreasing number of words processed per research instance – this tendency cannot be observed
for time passed between two research instances, even though the number of research instances is equal. Less time passed in PE compared to MPE, but the most
time passed in TfS. The research instances increase for TfS, but the time needed
for the whole translation increases even more (see §7.5 for the session times) –
a phenomenon which cannot be observed for student translators. When we take
the time between two research instances of professionals into account, the most
time passes between research instances in TfS, then in MPE and least in PE, but
the least words are processed between two research instances in human translation. This means that professionals refer to their internal resources (see categorisation of PACTE 2005 earlier in this chapter) much more in TfS than they might
do in the other two tasks and do it more often than student translators, because
their internal resources are not that extensive and they tend to refer to external
resources. Of course text production time needs to be taken into account, as well.
While in PE the participants can use the available MT output, the target text has
to be created from scratch in TfS, which is also the factor that prolongs the time
span between two research instances in professionals' TfS sessions.

The analysis of the time passed and the words processed between two research
instances also proved that hypotheses H_1 can be confirmed. The Internet is consulted more often in TfS than in PE, which is true for professional and student
translators. Further, it can also be confirmed that students use the Internet more
often than professionals. Only in MPE, so professionals and students use the Internet almost equally often.

9.2.3 Research effort

H_2: Fewer words/phrases are looked up in the PE tasks compared to TfS. However, when a word/phrase is looked up, the same word/phrase is looked up more often in PE.

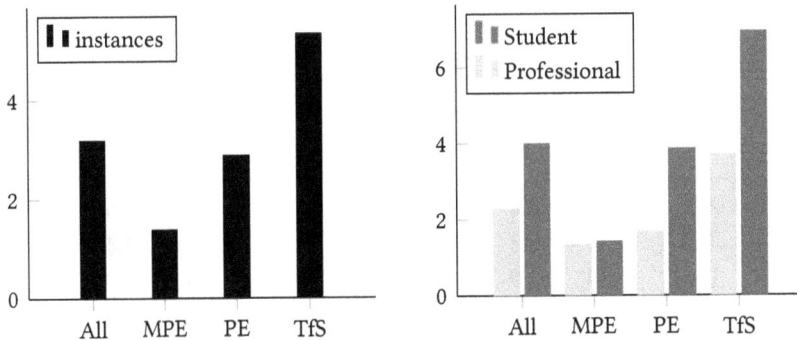

Figure 9.3: Average amount of words/phrases looked up per task and status.

The first part of the hypothesis, namely that fewer individual words are looked up in a PE session, is based on the observations of the previous chapter. However, I assume that the participants need more search attempts for an individual word in MPE/PE compared to TfS, because the MT system already produces a translation suggestion. If the participant is not satisfied with this suggestion and cannot provide a satisfying suggestion him/herself, the lexical item might be particularly difficult and hence need more research. In all tasks, an average of 3.2 words/phrases were looked up (see summary and SD values in Table 9.5). When separated into the different tasks, an increase of looked up words/phrases is obvious throughout the tasks (MPE – mean: 1.4 words/phrases; PE: 2.9; TfS: 5.3). When the expertise level is considered, the same pattern is observable: Although students generally tend to look up more words/phrases than professionals, the increase from MPE to PE to TfS remains consistent. The difference between MPE and PE is more eye-catching for students (light in Figure 9.3) than for experts (dark in Figure 9.3), though. Interestingly, the values for MPE are almost the same for professionals (mean: 1.35) and students (mean: 1.43). Editing MT output without the help of the source text might be as unusual and new to professional translators as to translation students. Therefore, it might be plausible that both groups show similar patterns. Further, the least research takes place in MPE in both groups. Therefore, the counts naturally become more balanced. While the research instances in this study suggest that much more dictionary research was needed in TfS than in PE, the total numbers seem to be much more balanced in Daems et al. (2016: 117) for both tasks. More research was conducted in their study, in general, but the difference between the tasks is less striking compared to the study at hand.

Table 9.5: Average mount of words/phrases looked up per task and status.

	Total	Mean			SD		
		All	Prof	Stud	All	Prof	Stud
All	685	3.2	2.28	4	3.37	2.91	3.58
TfS	339	5.3	3.71	6.95	3.95	3.78	3.49
PE	183	2.9	1.68	3.87	2.63	2.03	2.7
MPE	163	1.4	1.35	1.43	2.03	1.93	2.15

Some words and phrases were looked up not only on one but on several websites to confirm the results of one website or to continue research. A summary of the mean- and sd-values can be found in Table 9.6. The results, which are visualised in Figure 9.4, resemble the results of the looked up words/phrases. When we look at the correlation between both values, the similarity of the correlation with the experience factor can be explained easily ($r_\tau(125) = 0.872, p < 0.0001$).

Table 9.6: Amount of every look up instance according to task and status

	Total	Mean			SD		
		All	Prof	Stud	All	Prof	Stud
All	685	5.4	3.72	6.88	5.9	4.63	6.52
TfS	339	8	5.14	10.86	6.52	5.19	6.57
PE	183	4.4	2.26	6.17	4.29	2.62	4.62
MPE	163	3.8	3.6	3.96	5.88	5.22	6.51

When the experience coefficient is taken into consideration, the experience and the amount of look ups can be correlated. The correlation between research and experience is significant, when the tasks are not considered, and negative, but very low ($r_\tau(-3.41) = -0.222, p = 0.0007$), meaning that the more experi-

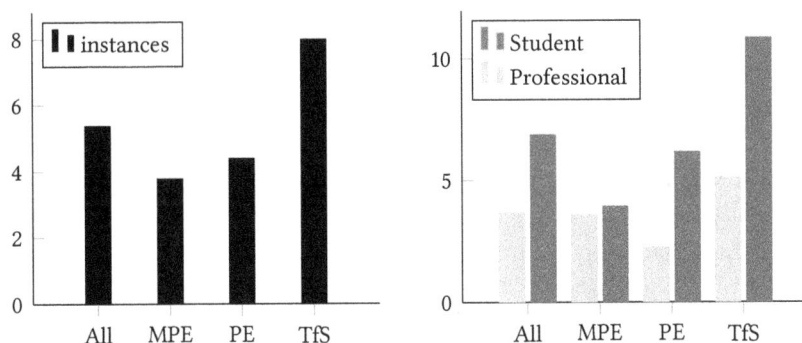

Figure 9.4: Total amount of look ups according to task and status

enced the translators are, the less words they look up. The correlation between the amount of search instances and experience shows the expected differences when separated by task: amount of search instances per individual word in TfS and experience correlate the strongest ($r_\tau(-2.98) = -0.34, p = 0.0028$), meaning that the more experience a participant has, the less (s)he researches. PE look ups and experience correlate a little less ($r_\tau(-1.86) = -0.214, p = 0.0629$), and MPE look ups and experience correlate the least ($r_\tau(-1.46) = -0.172, p = 0.1436$). The correlation for both PE and MPE, however, does not reach statistic significance. This means that, as opposed to TfS, experience has no statistically significant influence on the research behaviour of the participants in PE and MPE and that we cannot rule out that the weak negative correlation occurred by accident. All participants (probably) have the most experience in the TfS task, because they are trained in the task and most professional translators perform TfS[12] as their main work. Therefore, the more experience they have, the more confident they are in TfS and the less research they require. On the other hand, a bigger data set might prove significant at least for PE, as the overall data suggest a significant correlation between experience and look up rate. When the data are divided by group, the difference between professionals and students reach significance for all data ($W = 1332, p = 0.0009$), for TfS ($W = 104, p = 0.0033$), and for PE ($W = 97.5, p = 0.0022$), too. The difference between both groups is again not significant for MPE ($W = 200.5, p = 0.4333$).

The correlation between the amount of single words/phrases that were looked up and the experience factor is very similar (all tasks combined: $r_\tau(-3.71) =$

---

[12]Here, *translation from scratch* (*TfS*) does mean translation without any automatic pre-translations by a system. Hence, working with Translation Memory Systems is included in *translation from scratch.*

$-0.244, p = 0.0002$; TfS: $r_\tau(-2.94) = -0.335, p = 0.0033$; PE: $r_\tau(-2.42) = -0.281$, $p = 0.0155$; MPE: $r_\tau(-1.63) : -0.195, p = 0.1036$) to the correlation between total look up instances and experience, and can be explained in a similar way. The MPE task is again not significant, so it does not correlate with experience. However, the data for PE proved significance in this test, which supports the assumption that a larger data set might have turned significant for the test on the previous words/phrases looked up, as well. The tests for the single groups delivered the same results, the difference is significant for all three tasks ($W = 1340.5, p = 0.001$), for TfS ($W = 115, p = 0.0079$), and for PE ($W = 105, p = 0.0039$), but not for MPE ($W = 204.5, p = 0.4955$).

There can be different reasons why students look up words/phrases in more instances than professional translators. One might be that learning and improving the second language is a life-long process as long as the learner practises his/her second language. Therefore, professional translators might have more knowledge in their second language. However, professionals are probably more trained in the TfS task and accordingly more confident about their decisions, while students might look up words/phrases to make sure they translated them correctly. Hence, some lexical units are problematic for student translators, while professionals can make informed decisions on the translation choice according to their mental lexicon and their knowledge about register, text type/domain etc. On the other hand, there is no significant correlation between experience and MPE. This might have two reasons: First, both groups are not trained in this task and secondly MPE has less similarities to TfS than PE, because of the missing source text. While experienced translators might have some advantages in PE because they can apply their translation skills to some degree to the task, this experience probably does not help much for the monolingual task, or in other words, acquired problem solving behaviour and strategies cannot be adapted to the MPE task, while some can be adapted for the PE task.

Next, the focus will be on the questions of how many websites were or how often a website was consulted for one word/phrase. This means that it is also considered as two counts when one website was consulted twice for the same word/phrase, because this could imply that one difficult word/phrase was looked up, but the translation that was chosen first does not fit in the context or was not the perfect solution. It could also mean that the translator first had to deal with another translation unit and then had to come back to the lexical problem or that (s)he was not satisfied with his/her decision when revising the target text.

The diagrams in Figure 9.5 show that the search effort per word/phrase is almost the same for PE and TfS. It is a little higher for semi-professional transla-

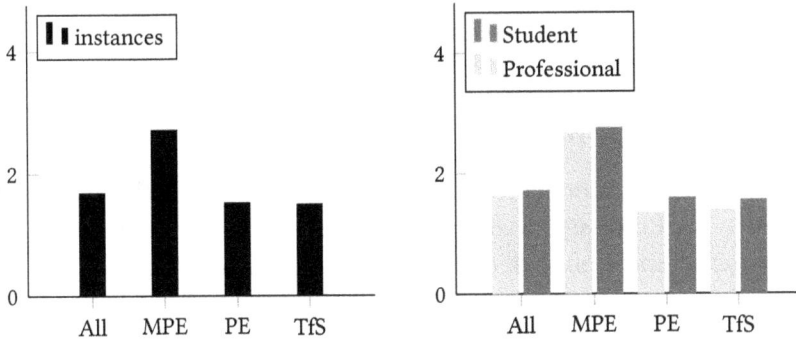

Figure 9.5: Websites per researched word (mean)

tors than for professional translators, but not very much and the difference is not significant when experience is correlated with the effort per word/phrase for all data ($r_\tau(0.19) = 0.02, p = 0.851$) – nor for the single tasks (TfS ($r_\tau(-1.41) = -0.18$, $p = 0.1577$), PE ($r_\tau(0.78) = 0.10, p = 0.4377$), MPE ($r_\tau(0.80) = 0.13, p = 0.4246$)). Further, the effort is much higher in MPE than in the other two tasks for both groups of translator. One reason for this higher rate could be a particular pattern: It was observed in the replays that translators often back translated the German MT output (single words/phrases or the whole text), then looked for a convenient hypothetical source word/phrase or considered the whole back translation of the text and finally use this as a basis to find a new target text solution. Hence, at least two steps are necessary.

The hypothesis H_2 that fewer words/phrases are looked up in PE than in TfS can be confirmed. Further, it is true that students research more than professionals in both tasks and that experience correlates with research behaviour: the more experienced a translator is, the less (s)he needs to research. This does not, however, apply to the amount of words/phrases looked up in PE and experience, where correlation did not prove significant, but could nonetheless have proved significant if the participant group had been larger. This finding is contradictory to Nord's (2002: 118–119) study in which no distinct relation between experience of her professional participants and amount of research was found, but is in line with De Almeida (2013: 180)[13]. She found in her PE study that her less experienced participants do more research than her more experienced participants. Finally, no significant differences could be found between status/experience and amount of research in MPE. This shows that translation experience might have

---

[13]Find detailed description of the study in §4.2

a positive influence on PE, but not on MPE – assuming that less research means less effort and more confidence in personal abilities.

9.2.4 Non-use of the Internet

H_3: The Internet is not consulted in some sessions at all. This happens more often in the PE session than in the TfS session; and experts do not consult the Internet more often in the entire session than students.

Consulting the Internet is a strategy that can be used for solving various translation problems like lexical, context, or grammatical problems (in this study most research was conducted to solve lexical problems though). However, it is not obligatory to use the Internet. Either no problem occurred in the respective session at all or the participant could draw on his/her internal resources to solve the problem (see PACTE (2005) as described at the beginning of this chapter). Accordingly, many participants did not need to consult the Internet at all during the experiments for one or more sessions in this study, because they did not feel the need to research a word or a phrase. It can be assumed that this is linked to experience and self-confidence in the respective task, as well.

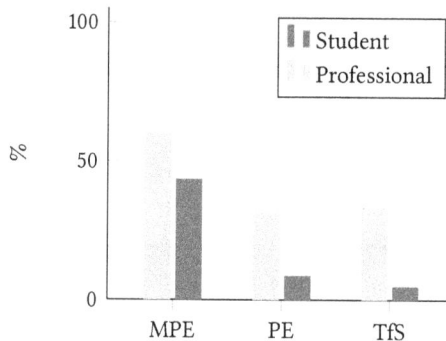

Figure 9.6: Percentage of texts which were translated/post-edited without Internet research

In Figure 9.6, the dark bars show the results for professional translators, the lighter ones the results for the semi-professionals. It is visible that the professional translators managed without consulting the Internet more often than the semi-professionals. However, the difference is not significant according to a chi-square test ($\chi^2(4, N = 38) = 6, p = 0.1991$); more sessions would probably be necessary to prove a statistically significant difference if the difference visible in Figure 9.6 did not emerge by accident. Further, the Internet was consulted less often for the MPE task than for the PE and TfS tasks. However, a difference between PE and TfS is hardly recognisable and due to the small numbers, a statistic test is not reasonable. The professional translators did not use the Internet slightly more often in the TfS than in the PE task, while the semi-professional translators did not use the Internet slightly more often for the PE task than in TfS. These differences are assumed to be accidental. If the status of the participant is disregarded, we have an equal percentage for PE and TfS: 19.1% of all participants did not use the Internet at all for PE or TfS. In Nord's (2002: 117) study, all participants used some research aids at some point; the sessions were, however, about two hours long. One participant, for example, used a translation aid only every 18.75 minutes, while some of the translation sessions did not last for over 18 minutes in the study at hand. Therefore, it is likely that the participants in this study might have consulted an online resource as well at some point if the texts had been longer. Further, the participants in Nord's study were concerned with their own translation jobs, which probably were in most (or all) cases more domain specific than the texts used in this study and might cause more problems and an increased need for research.

A Mann-Whitney-U-test showed that there is a significant experience difference between participants who decide to not use the Internet for research and participants who do use it ($W = 16129, p < 0.0001$) as opposed to the results we found when the test was only conducted according to groups. In detail, the mean experience coefficient of the participants who used Internet research is 9.88, while the mean experience of the no-research group is 20.66. Conclusively, the first part of hypothesis H_3 cannot be verified as there is no difference between PE and TfS. However, the second part proves to be right, namely that professionals do not need the Internet at all more often than students. There are only very few instances, where the students do not consult the Internet for help at all, while the professionals need no help in about 1/3 of the cases. Finally, there were a couple of participants who did hardly any research in all six sessions, e.g. P15 only investigated one word twice in one PE session. (S)he did not do any further research in the whole experiment; the same applies to P3, who only investigated one word in one TfS session. Hence, there seem to be individual preferences, whether or not to use the Internet for research. And this is not only dependent on the experience of a participant, e.g. P17, who has an experience coefficient of 19, did a lot of research in the MPE tasks as well as in one PE session (in one PE session no research was necessary at all) and the TfS tasks, while P3 has only an experience coefficient of two and did only research in one TfS session. Hence, the use/non-use of the Internet might also be an indicator of self-confidence.

9.2.5 Research effort in relation to the complexity level

H_4: The more complex a text, the more research is necessary.

In §7.6, the complexity levels of the different texts were introduced. The texts were ranked in the following order (least complex to most complex):

Text 1, Text 2, Text 5, Text 4, Text 6, Text 3.

Although the tests that were conducted only calculated the reading scores for the six texts, one could assume that lower reading scores also imply less research because the texts are easier. Further, in his complexity calculations for Text 1 to 3, Hvelplund (2011: 88–93) also included amongst others word frequency as a factor (see §7.6), making Text 1 the least complex and Text 3 the most, which is in line with the complexity calculations. Hence, it is expected that the less complex a text the less research is necessary to translate or (monolingually) post-edit the text: The less complex the texts the easier the texts should be to translate – for the human translator as well as for the MT system.

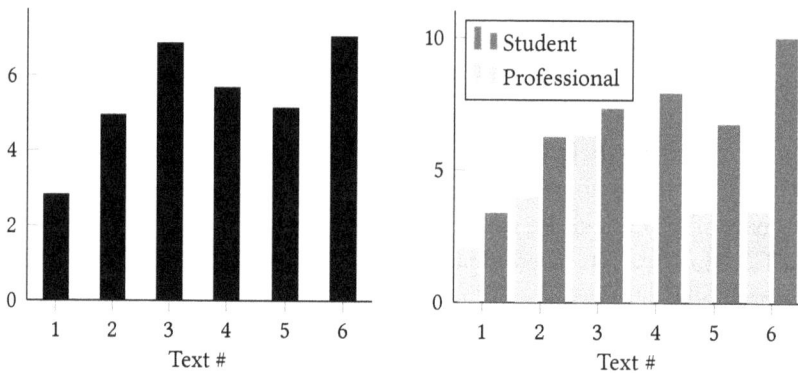

Figure 9.7: Research effort per text

When we simply look at the research effort (words looked up) per text, the text can be ranked as follows according to research effort taking all participants into account:

Text 1, Text 2, Text 5, Text 4, Text 3, Text 6.

This is almost the same ranking as for complexity level, except that Text 3 and 6 swap places – however, the difference between Text 3 and 6 is very small and values for complexity levels do not only represent lexical components, but also grammatical and syntactic components. Further, the different complexity scores that were taken into consideration did not agree in terms of which text is the most complex.

Interestingly, when the research effort is divided by group, the picture is quite different. The ranking for the professional group would be:

Text 1, Text 4, Text 5, Text 6, Text 2, Text 3;

while the ranking for the semi-professional group looks like this:

Text 1, Text 2, Text 5, Text 3, Text 4, Text 6.

The ranking for the semi-professional translators is closer to the automatically calculated complexity scores, except that Text 3 is in position four. In the professional group the ranking is a little more mixed. However, the only remarkable change in the ranking is that Text 2 is the second most research intensive for the group, although it was estimated to be the second least complex text. Further, it is interesting to see that the differences between the groups seem quite similar for texts one to three and that the increase of required research seems to grow equally linearly between both groups. The differences between the groups for Texts 4 to 6, however, do not show any similarities. Students looked up many more words than professionals and many more words than for Text 3 (except for Text 5, which had twelve words less than text three). However, the amount of research is lower for Texts 4 to 6 compared to texts two and three when professionals worked with the texts and the research amount is almost equal for all three texts.

The semi-professional group looked up words/phrases on the Internet more often than the professional group for every text. We have to keep in mind that the texts were randomised, which means that not every participant started with Text 1 and worked his/her way to Text 6, but the text order was different for every participant; although the texts were equally distributed across the tasks, they may not have been equally distributed to status of the participant.

Nord (2002: 119) observed in her study that the more domain-specific a text was, which also implies more domain-specific characteristics like terminology, the more research the participants conducted. Hence, it seemed promising that there is a connection between complexity level and research effort. However, the connection is too vague to draw this conclusion, when we take all participants into account, because when the participants are separated into the two groups (professional and semi-professional), research effort and text complexity do not seem connected. Hence, the hypothesis that complexity of a text and research effort are connected cannot be confirmed. One certain conclusion that can be drawn is that Text 1 is the least complex and the one that causes least research effort, although it was the longest in terms of the number of words. This might indicate that Text 1 is the least complex regarding lexical choices. Further, the differences between the professional and the student group – both in amount of research and in how many words required research – indicate that research habits develop and change with growing translation experience. Last but not least, the conducted comparison of text complexity and research behaviour was very simple and more fine-grained texts – including statistical tests – would be necessary to prove a causality.

9.2.6 Types of websites consulted

> H₅: In both PE and TfS, the bilingual dictionary is the source that is used the most often. However, bilingual dictionaries and other sources are distributed differently in both tasks. Students use bilingual dictionaries more often than professionals.

Similar as in Daems et al. (2016), the different websites that were accessed during the experiments were clustered into different groups. These clusters were created based on categories of traditional printed aids and will be introduced in the following.

Bilingual dictionaries, also referred to as dictionaries of equivalence, are one of the most important aids for translators, although they have a bad reputation in translation science, because they do not offer translations, but translation prepositions at most. Further, they do not offer any definitions and explications (cf. Albrecht 2013: 60-61). Translators, however, are supposedly trained to use bilingual dictionaries sensibly. This subgroup also includes websites that offer bilingual information and additional corpora information. *Monolingual dictionaries* can be used for the source and the target language and usually contain much more information for the single words than bilingual dictionaries. *Synonym dictionaries* list words that usually have very similar, but not necessarily the same meaning as the word in question. They are categorised as a sub-group of onomasiological dictionaries, because the word groups are content-oriented (ibid.: 69). The category *machine translation* refers to online MT systems. As these aids are based on electronic word processing, they do not have an equivalent printed aid. *Encyclopedias* can help with context research as they describe an issue in a broader context, but also with direct translation suggestions; the encyclopedia website used most often connects entries between languages. Therefore, the user can e.g. switch from the English entry to the German entry if available and if connected. *Search engines* can be used to find additional, more detailed information on the context. Furthermore, they are a great way to find words in the context they are used in and can verify or refute a translation for a word/phrase. Similar to encyclopedias, *news* websites can help to find out more about the context an event occurred in.

Other resources like websites that focus on grammar or pictorial dictionaries could not be identified and will therefore not be mentioned. Contrary to Daems et al. (2016), no distinction was made between concordancers and bilingual dictionaries, because only one website was used that could be characterised as a concordancer – though it was used quite frequently – and this website also presents regular lexicographic entries, before the bilingual corpus data are displayed. Hence, it would exceed the scope of this analysis, although possible in some cases through the eyetracking data, to reconstruct whether the decision for a particular translation was made on lexicographic data or corpus data (or if both influenced the problem solving process).

Bilingual dictionaries are the source that is used most often (511 of 685 instances – 74.6%), including all tasks and sessions as visualised in Figure 9.8. However, the other sources were consulted as well: monolingual dictionaries (15 instances – 2.2%), synonym dictionaries (7 instances – 1.0%), MT engines (18 instances – 2.6%), encyclopedia (44 instances – 6.4%), search engines (80 instances – 11.7%) and newspaper websites (10 instances – 1.5%). This relative website distribution changes according to the different tasks as can be seen in Figure 9.9.

This result concurs with Nord's (2002: 95–96) conclusion on the state of the art of translation aids research. The empirical studies showed that bilingual dictionaries are used most often, although critical dictionary research is very sceptical towards them. Although Daems et al. (2016: 116–117) did not differentiate between monolingual and bilingual dictionaries, the overall results on types of websites used seem to be comparable: The largest group of used aids is by far concordancers and dictionaries (which are represented in monolingual and bilingual dictionaries in this study). Search engines and encyclopedias were the two resources next in line of the aids used most often – although search engines seem to play a more important role for Daems et al.'s participants than for the participants of this study. News websites were used in both experiments and played a minor role. Interestingly, MT was used by Daems et al.'s participants as a research aid, although the study looked at TfS and PE, while MT was only used in MPE by the participants of this study and never for TfS or PE (see Figure 9.8).

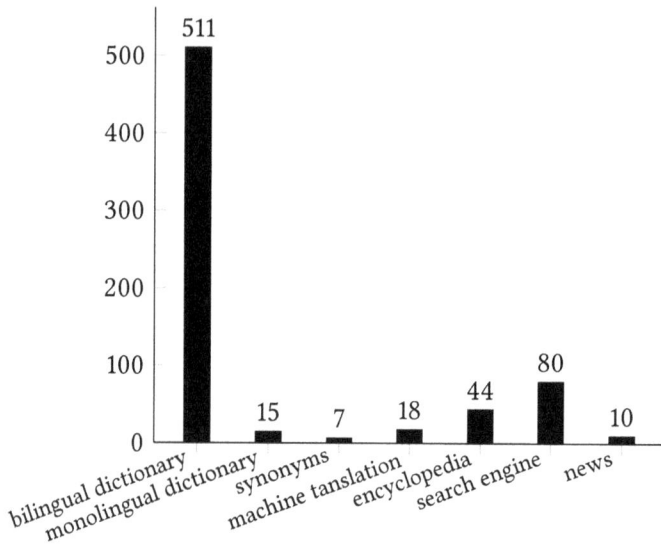

Figure 9.8: The use of online aids in all tasks

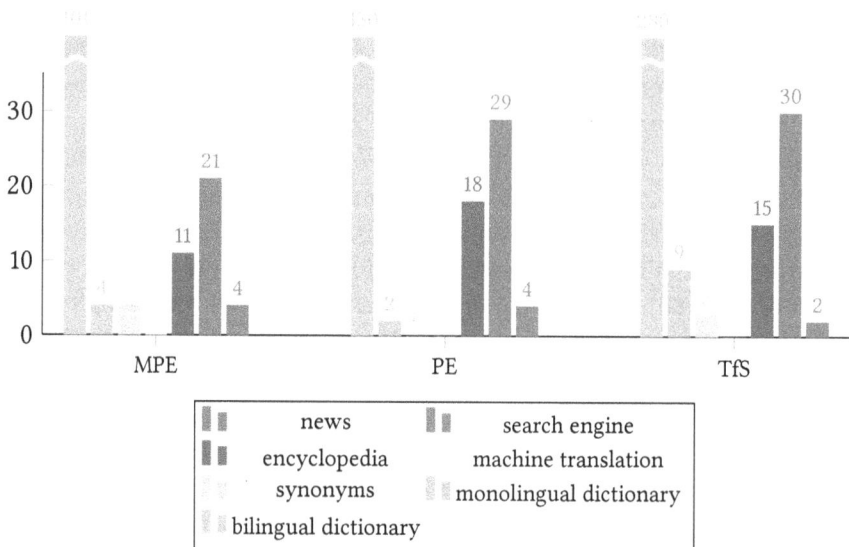

Figure 9.9: The use of online aids separated by tasks; left – monolingual post-editing; middle – post-editing; right – human translation

What becomes obvious at first glance is that bilingual dictionaries are used more often in TfS (82.6% of all TfS research) than in PE (71.0%) and finally in MPE (62.0%) in relation to other consulted resources. As mentioned before, it is very striking that MT engines were only used in the MPE task (11.0%). The reason is simple: The replays reveal that MT engines were consulted to recreate the source text so that the participants could use the back translation to make more sense of the raw MT output. It is inexplicable why the behaviour between the participants of this study and the study of Daems et al. (2016) differs so much concerning MT systems as an aid. Maybe the translation training of their participants was more focused on MT systems and hence they acknowledge MT systems as a valuable aid. Or MT systems have a better reputation for their participants than for the participants of this study. This, however, is mere speculation.

The data were tested for independence with Chi-Square Tests to find out if different patterns of the websites were used in the respective tasks. All tests turned out to be significant (all three tasks: $\chi^2(12, N = 1186) = 85.17, p < 0.0001$; TfS vs. PE: $\chi^2(5, N = 522) = 18.3, p < 0.003$; MPE vs. PE: $\chi^2(6, N = 346) = 28.22, p < 0.0001$; and TfS vs. MPE: $\chi^2(6, N = 502) = 51.68, p < 0.0001$). Hence, the behaviour of the participants varies significantly in the different tasks, although similar patterns can be recognised such the preference for bilingual dictionaries.

Next, the research behaviour between the two groups will be analysed according to the tasks. The use of bilingual dictionaries is the research choice number one, independent of task and status.

Figure 9.10 shows that the types of websites used for research differ visibly in MPE and in TfS according to status. Keeping in mind that translation students performed much more research than professionals (see also Table 9.8 for total numbers and proportion values), professionals use encyclopedias and search engines more often than students in these two tasks. This is a trend which cannot be detected in PE. The chi-square test confirms this impression – the differences between both groups turn out to be significant in MPE ($\chi^2(6, N = 163) = 25.61, p < 0.0003$) and in TfS ($\chi^2(5, N = 339) = 42.24, p < 0.0001$). Further, the test did not prove significant for the PE task ($\chi^2(4, N = 183) = 8.59, p = 0.0721$). Additionally, it is quite striking that students use bilingual dictionaries far more often as a research tool in TfS than they do in MPE and PE.

It is hard to explain, why the research patterns for MPE resemble the patterns of TfS more than the PE patterns concerning the kinds of websites used. Especially if we keep in mind that the analysis so far showed similar patterns for PE and TfS and deviating patterns for MPE.

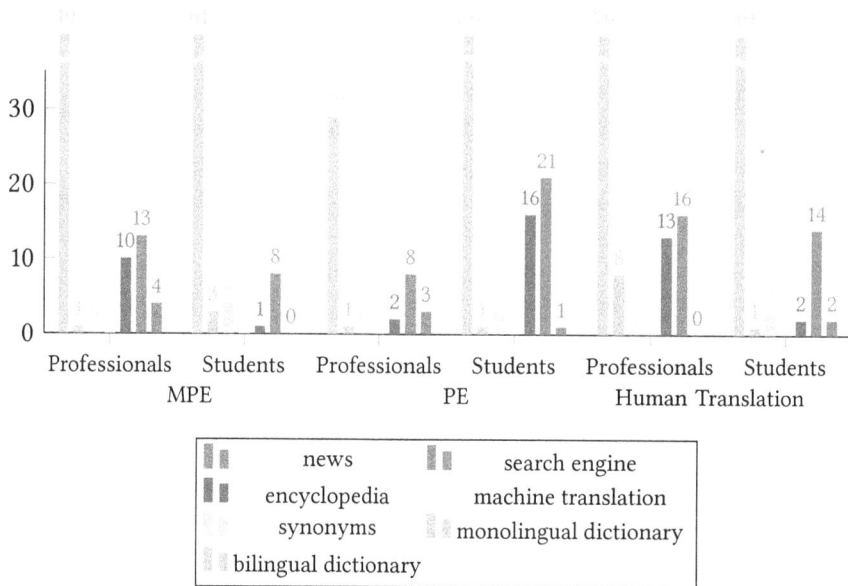

Figure 9.10: Different kinds of websites used for research according to the participant's status (green: professionals; purple: semi-professionals)

Table 9.7: Count of types of websites used for research according to task and status – Research Times

Website type	MPE		PE		HT	
	Prof.	Students	Prof.	Students	Prof.	Students
Bilingual dictionaries	40 (0.56)	61 (0.67)	29 (0.67)	101 (0.72)	79 (0.68)	201 (0.9)
Monolingual dictionaries	1 (0.01)	3 (0.03)	1 (0.02)	1 (0.01)	8 (0.07)	1 (0.00)
Synonym dictionaries	0 (0)	4 (0.04)	0 (0)	0 (0)	0 (0)	3 (0.01)
MT	4 (0.06)	14 (0.15)	0 (0)	0 (0)	0 (0)	0 (0)
Encyclopedia	10 (0.14)	1 (0.01)	2 (0.05)	16 (0.11)	13 (0.11)	2 (0.01)
Search engine	13 (0.18)	8 (0.09)	8 (0.19)	21 (0.15)	16 (0.14)	14 (0.06)
News	4 (0.06)	0 (0)	3 (0.07)	1 (0.01)	0 (0)	2 (0.01)

Moreover, it seems very peculiar that students use bilingual dictionaries by far the most for TfS and encyclopedias most often in PE. While professionals use bilingual dictionaries in the same relation in TfS and PE, the consistent use of bilingual dictionaries in TfS probably indicates a lower proficiency in the students English skills. Lexical problems arise in TfS, which are already partly solved by the MT output in the PE tasks. Students seem to consider bilingual dictionaries the most valid tool to overcome lexical problems, while they might encounter other kinds of problems in the PE tasks. The use of encyclopedias, however, indicates semantic research, which may have been useful in MPE, but no reason comes to mind why semantic research might be more important in PE than in TfS. Finally, the number of participants is very low. Hence, this tendency might only have occurred by chance.

9.2.7 Time spent on research

> $H_{6.1}$: Participants need more time on research per single word/phrase in PE than in TfS. Students need longer to find a translation than professionals if they research.

When we look at productivity and effort, we also have to consider the time translators spent on every research instance. I assume that – if research is conducted – research for one word/phrase takes longer in PE than in TfS, because the translator is primed by the MT output and has to overcome this first translation suggestion. At first glance, there appears to be no difference between the time needed for research in all three tasks (see Figure 9.11). The mean research times per research instance are very similar – MPE: 13.42 s, PE: 12.33 s, TfS: 13.04 s. Further, the standard deviation is very high for all three tasks (MPE: 13.89, PE:

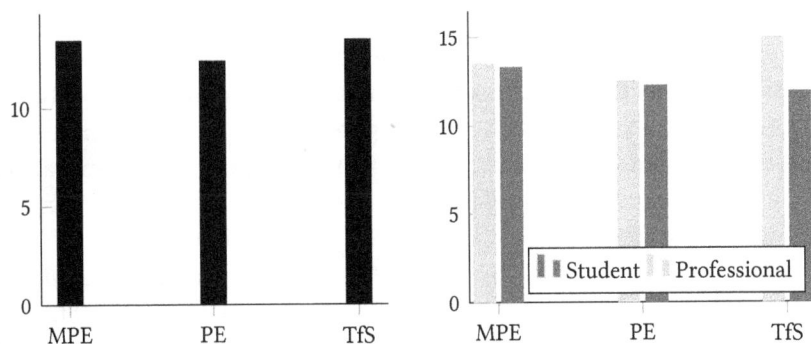

Figure 9.11: Mean time per research and task

8.74 s, TfS: 11.33 s), which shows that there is a lot of variety between the individual subjects, but also between the individual search instances.

When dividing the data by time, both groups need on average a similar amount of time for each research instance in MPE (professionals mean: 13.53 s, sd: 15.78 s; students mean: 13.32 s, sd: 12.12 s) and PE (professionals mean: 12.51 s, sd: 11.36 s, students mean: 12.27 s, sd: 7.62 s). However, the difference is noticeable in TfS (professionals – mean: 14.99 s, sd: 15.33 s, students – mean: 11.94 s, sd: 8.12 s). Also, there is no significant correlation between experience and research time neither for the whole data set, nor for the separate tasks (see Table 9.8).

Table 9.8: Correlation tests between task and experience for research time

	Total	MPE	PE	HT
r	r(741) =−0.0572	r(186) =−0.0622	r(153) =−0.0589	r(357) =−0.051
p	0.1194	0.3962	0.4132	0.3348

The research process takes equally long in all tasks and does not depend on experience. The participants read the website output and then decide whether it is useful or whether they have to consult another aid. However, with many more participants it might be possible to detect significant differences. Hence, the hypothesis could not be confirmed.

$H_{6.2}$: Participants spend more time on research in TfS than in PE in the overall session. Students spent more time on research than professionals.

Next, we want to have a look at how much time the participants spent on average for Internet research according to task, status, and experience. On average, the participants spent 9.03% (sd: 11.07%) in MPE, 7.95% (sd: 5.24%) in PE, and 10.49% (sd: 7.08%) in TfS of the total session duration on Internet research.

In total, the least time for research compared to the total session duration is spent during PE, followed by MPE, and most time is spent on human translation as can be seen in Figure 9.12. Professionals and students spent a similar amount of time on Internet research compared to the total session duration in the MPE task (professionals – mean: 8.34%, sd: 10.96%; students – mean: 7.65%, sd: 11.65%). However, professionals spent less time on the Internet relative to the total session duration for PE (mean: 4.43%, sd: 3.28%) and TfS (mean: 8.24%, sd: 6.66%) than the student group (PE – mean: 9.37%, sd: 5.63%; TfS – mean: 12.74%, sd: 6.76).

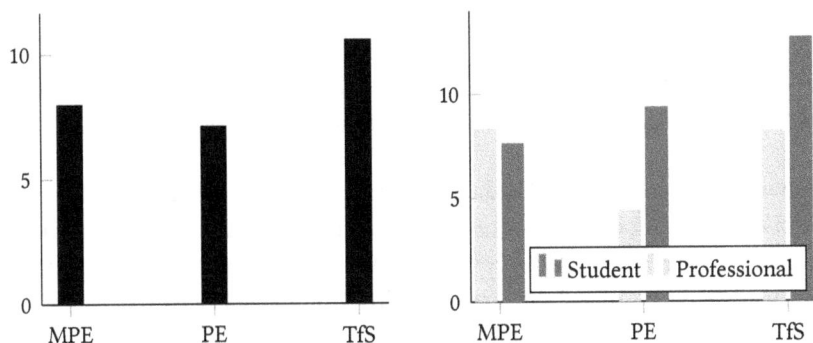

Figure 9.12: Mean Percentage of total session duration spent on Internet research

When we look at the correlation between experience and time related to total session length, there is no statistical significance for MPE ($r_\tau(-1.17) = -0.184$, $p = 0.243$) and PE ($r_\tau(-0.96) = -0.151$, $p = 0.3349$), but for TfS ($r_\tau(-2.47) = -0.367$, $p = 0.01357$). On the other hand, when the statistical test is performed by grouping the participants into students and professionals using a Mann-Whitney-U-test, the test turns out significant for PE ($W = 28.5$, $p = 0.0409$) and not significant in TfS ($W = 44$, $p = 0.122$). The test for MPE remains non-significant ($W = 64.5$, $p = 0.9499$).[14]

Here again, we can see that MPE seems to be equally unfamiliar for students and professionals as they spent an equal percentage of the total session duration on research. While students spent more time on research for PE and most for TfS, professionals spent less time for research in the TfS task and the least for PE. This, again, might have two reasons. First, the professionals may be more proficient in English than the student translator, because they have more work experience and second, they might be more confident about lexical choices, both for the choices they make from their own knowledge as well as for the choices from the research suggestions.

The first hypothesis of $H_{5.2}$ cannot be confirmed as the participants spent almost equally long on research instances, no matter which task. There seems to be a tendency that professionals need longer for research in general and especially in TfS than students. However, the correlation between experience and time did not become significant. So, the second part of the first hypothesis cannot be confirmed, either. The second hypothesis, on the other hand, can be confirmed. Participants spend more time on research in PE than in TfS and students spent more time on research than professionals.

---

[14]See discussion of the different statistical results in §9.4

9.2.8 Research according to phases in translation process

H_7: Translators research most in the drafting phase in TfS, while they conduct most research in the orientation and revision phase in PE.

In newer versions of the TPR database, three phases are indicated for keylogging and eyetracking data (Version 2.310 was used for this particular analysis) – an orientation, a drafting and a revision phase, which were probably appointed automatically, as well (see discussion below). Here, we assume a macro-level of phases, meaning there is only one orientation phase at the beginning, one drafting phase and a concluding revision phase. Therefore, the research instances were assigned to the single phases (see Table 9.9). Orientation and revision on micro-units that might be indicated by pauses as suggested by Jakobsen (2002) is not taken into consideration in this analysis. I suspect that the participants resort to Internet research on demand in TfS when they want to translate the problematic source text unit, because only few problems are recognised during the orientation phase. Further, research in the revision phase is only necessary to recheck their translation decision. In MPE/PE, on the other hand, research is much more distributed among the orientation and revision phase, because the MT output might produce translation suggestions that are not trustworthy, and which have to be approved before and after the drafting phase.

Table 9.9: Mean Research Instances per Translation Phase

	Orientation		Draft		Revision	
	Mean	SD	Mean	SD	Mean	SD
MPE	0.16	0.57	0.93	1.47	0.30	0.64
PE	0.12	0.33	2.45	2.36	0.38	0.73
TfS	0.20	0.46	3.88	3.83	1.51	2.17

As more research took place in TfS than in PE, and least in MPE, the numbers will be compared in total numbers and proportions:

- MPE: Orientation: 7 (0.12), Drafting: 40 (0.67), Revision: 13 (0.22)

- PE: Orientation: 5 (0.04), Drafting: 103 (0.83), Revision: 16 (0.13)

- TfS: Orientation: 8 (0.03), Drafting: 159 (0.69), Revision: 62 (0.27)

The most research was done in the drafting phase in all three tasks, followed by the revision phase, and the least research was done in the orientation phase. When we compare the phase distribution of the research instances with the experience of the participants, we find no significant difference for neither the orientation phase ($r_\tau(-1.92) = -0.145, p = 0.05437$) nor the revision phase ($r_\tau(-0.74) = -0.053, p = 0.4593$), but instead for the drafting phase ($r_\tau(-2.91) = -0.196, p < 0.004$). Similar results can be found when testing whether there is a significant difference between the groups (orientation phase $W = 1759.5, p = 0.06684$, drafting phase $W = 1320.5, p < 0.001$, revision phase $W = 1994.5, p = 0.9173$; see discussion in §9.4). This means that the research behaviour in the orientation and revision phase is very similar, independent of the experience, but the more experienced the translator, the less research (s)he does in the drafting phase. The correlation is very low though.

Unfortunately, we have to assume that the mapping of the phases in the data might have been defective in a few cases. For example, participant 22 translated Text 4 and the orientation phases was only defined as 0.59 minutes, the drafting phase lasted another 0.04 minutes and the rest of the session consisted of revision according to the tables. However, based on common knowledge, we can assume that the drafting phase in a translation session would take longer than two to three seconds. Accordingly, much of the research became part of the revision phase. Hence, the results would have been even clearer if the mapping had been 100% accurate. As, on the one hand, excluding the obvious mistakes would only have reinforced the result and not shifted it, and on the other hand knowing when to set the limit to exclude data or not would be difficult. Hence, no data points were dismissed.

Conclusively, H_7 cannot be confirmed, because most research is conducted in the drafting phase in all three tasks, although this is done to different degrees.

9.2.9 Research ending in no obvious result

H_8: Students re-check their translations more often than professionals.

There were a number of instances in which the research instance did not end in any immediate results, i. e. research took place, which did not effect the translation product directly, but is part of the translation process. Four categories of these instances, which did not lead directly to a translation result, were found in the data: The Internet was used for context research (CR), the word/phrase was not translated (no translation – NT), the participant read the MT of the machine translated target text (read back translation – RBT – only occurred in MPE), and the translator stuck with his/her former translation (SFT).

Table 9.10: Amount of research instances ending in no (obvious) results

Status	CR	NT	RBT	SFT	Total
Professional	10	6	0	30	46
Student	3	13	1	48	65
Total	13	19	1	78	111

All in all, there were 111 instances in which the participants did some research in the Internet without any direct results (see Table 9.10), which is 14.9% of all instances. Looking at simple counts, this occurred mostly in student research - professionals: 46, students: 64. However, if it is put in relation to the total instances during which each group conducted research, it occurred more often for professionals (17.2%, students: 13.4%). Further, the categories were differently distributed. Most of the times, the non-direct-result research ended in SFT (70.3%), then NT (17.1%), CR (11.7%), and finally RBT (0.01%). When the status of the participant is taken into consideration, the distribution changes a little. While SFT (professionals: 65.2%, students: 73.9%) occurs the most in both groups, NT is more often the result for students (20%, professionals: 13.0%) and professionals do more CR (21.7%, students: 4.6%). RBT only occurred once in a student translation (1.5%, professionals: 0%).

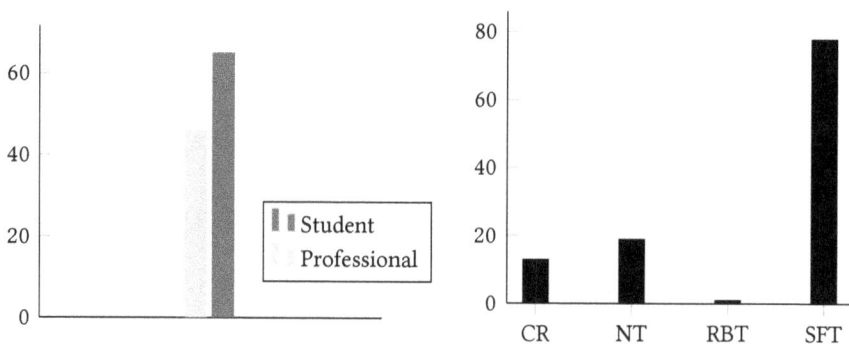

Figure 9.13: Distribution and amount of research instances ending in no (obvious) results according to status (left) and kind of non result (right)

Interestingly, over 70% of the research conducted without any obvious result was caused by the translators' deciding to stick with their former translation or the MT output which can be seen as an indicator of insecurity in their own translation or the MT output. A similar observation was already made by Krings (1986b: translated by J. N.) were he states that "the participants could improve the inferencing solution in 15 cases (39.5%) by using a dictionary, the solution was confirmed in 20 cases (52.6%), and in three cases (7.9%) the solution was impaired by using a dictionary."[15] Although Kring's group of participants (see §5.3) is not comparable to the participants of this study, it shows that insecurity with the translation first rendered is a common phenomenon. Similarly translators' insecurity was described by Prassl (2010: 59–60). She describes that emotions like intuition can make even very convincing possibilities for translation decisions seem unsuitable, which can lead to insecurity towards this possible translation choice. "In translation, we encounter situations in which the subject has already written down a piece of TT [=target text, J.N.] and suddenly stops to go on searching, very often wisely so." (ibid.: 60)

Further, a non-translation does not necessarily mean that content was omitted, but can also mean that redundancies were avoided, because the content was already delivered in another part of the sentence or another phrase. Finally, content research and reading the back translation can be seen as positive instances of research with no direct result, because the translator familiarises him/herself with the text or the context of the text. When both groups are separated we can see the different patterns the groups used (Figure 9.14).

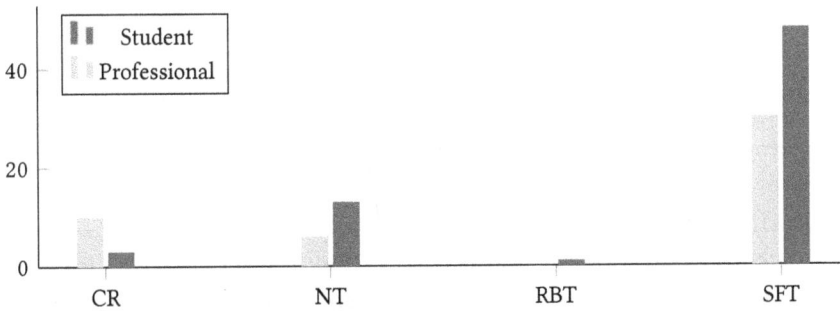

Figure 9.14: Types of no-research according to status of the participant

While both groups predominantly found no result after their research, because they opted for their translation, it happened much more often in the students group than in the group with professional translators. The same applies to non-

---

[15]"In 15 Fällen (39,5%) konnten die Versuchspersonen das Inferenzierungsergebnis durch die Wörterbuchbenutzung verbessern, in 20 Fällen (52,6%) wurde das Ergebnis bestätigt, in 3 Fällen (7,9%) wurde es durch die Wörterbuchbenutzung verschlechtert."

translations. However, the professionals found no results more often due to context research than students. More context research was done in the MPE task (7 instances), than in PE (5 instances) and only one context research instance could be found in TfS.

Table 9.11: Distribution of research instances ending in no (obvious) results according to task

Task	CR	NT	RBT	SFT	Total
MPE	7	7	1	16	31
PE	5	3	0	36	44
TfS	1	9	0	26	36
Total	13	19	1	78	111

Table 9.12: Distribution of research instances ending in no (obvious) results according to task and status

Task	CR		NT		RBT		SFT		Total
Status	S	P	S	P	S	P	S	P	
MPE	1	6	6	1	1	0	9	7	31
PE	1	4	3	0	0	0	29	7	44
TfS	1	0	4	5	0	0	10	16	36
Total	3	10	13	6	1	0	48	30	111

Table 9.11 shows the distribution of no-result research according to task, Table 9.12 according to task and status. Interestingly, students chose their initial translation much more often in the PE task than in the TfS task and much more often than professionals in general. This indicates that students are more insecure about the MT output than professionals. Further, professionals conducted more context research in MPE than students, while students left more words/phrases untranslated. However, there were too few research instances to call this a pattern.

9.2.10 Summary and conclusion – screen recording data

Three main reasons for consulting the Internet can be singled out from the previous analysis: The look up of lexical problems in bilingual and monolingual dictionaries, the search for more context information (two typical sources are the consultation of search engines and the websites of newspapers), and the generation of the source text with the help of MT. The latter is only used in the MPE task in the study at hand (in contrast to the research behaviour of the participants in Daems et al. 2016 study). There was no evidence in the data that the participants sought any help on syntactic or grammatical problems.

Participants do more research in TfS than in PE and professionals do less research than students both in TfS and PE, confirming H_1. This shows that fewer lexical problems occur in PE, because some are already solved by the MT output and some lexical mistranslations in the MT output can easily be corrected by consulting the target text. Interestingly, professionals research more in MPE than in PE, which indicates that the source text is often necessary to improve the MT output. While simple lexical errors can be remedied easily in PE due to the source text – making the improvement a task, not a problem if the source lexical item is known to the translators – lexical flaws in the MT output can become a problem in MPE. Further, I detected that professionals refer much more to their internal resources in human translation than students do, because they have long spans between two research instances, but not many words are processed. Similar to H_1, the most words per session are looked up in TfS, then PE, as well as MPE; and students look up more words per session than professionals confirming the first part of hypothesis H_2. Finally, more research instances are necessary per word in MPE than in PE and TfS, because of the missing source text. The difference between PE and TfS is very narrow, hence part two of H_2 was disproved. Experience does not influence how the look up behaviour is performed.

A whole session went by without the help of any online sources most often in MPE, then in PE, and least often in TfS. While professionals did not need the Internet in over 30% of the sessions in PE and TfS, students did not use it in less than ten percent. Surprisingly, there is no significant difference between PE and TfS, so that H_3 cannot be confirmed. Further, the complexity of a text measured by reading scores does not seem to influence research behaviour (so H_4 cannot be supported). Complexity does not only refer to reading scores and lexical complexity, but also syntactic complexity or length of sentence etc. Hence, further studies need to be carried out to investigate the topic properly.

As the study has shown, the most important research aid for all three tasks were bilingual dictionaries, both for student and professional translators. Further, students use bilingual dictionaries more often than professionals in all three tasks, confirming H_5. Hence, I consider it unreasonable to proclaim bilingual dictionaries to be useless for translators, as has been put forward so often in theoretical translation studies according to Nord (2002). Empirical analyses prove the discrepancy (see also Daems et al. 2016) – translators are trained to use bilingual dictionaries and trained to use them to combine their internal and external knowledge. The research behaviour is statistically different in TfS and MPE between the two groups concerning types of websites used for research, while their was no significant difference for PE.

The time a participant needs for each single research instance is almost the same in all three tasks and is not correlated with experience, although there are some indications that student translators are slightly faster in TfS. However, this did not prove significant. Hence $H_{6.1}$ cannot be confirmed. The participants spent most time of the total session on research in TfS, then in MPE, and least in PE. Separated by status, the picture is a little different: Professionals spent most time on research in relation to the total session duration in MPE, then in TfS, and least in PE. Student translators, however, spent the least time in MPE, then PE, and then TfS, confirming $H_{6.2}$ which did not include MPE. However, the relative time is approximately equal for both groups in MPE, which again shows that professionals are much more confident in PE and TfS as they do not do research as randomly as student translators.

Most research took place in the drafting phase in all three tasks, which disproves hypothesis H_7. Finally, there were instances when the participants researched a word/phrase, but did not transfer this new knowledge into a target text unit immediately. These instances can be grouped as context research, no translation of the source unit, reading the back translation of the MT output, and choosing the initial translation. Rechecking and opting for the own translation or MT output occurred most often, which indicates insecure behaviour (the risk of a mistranslation is averted). Accordingly, this occurred most often for student participants, which supports hypothesis H_8. Context research was conducted most often by professionals and no translation of the source unit occurs most in student translations.

Two of the arguments Nord (2002: 92) summarized from other empirical studies were analysed in the study at hand as well. First, that less experienced translators tend to use bilingual dictionaries, while professionals use other aids. It is true that in the study at hand professionals used bilingual dictionaries less often than students, and used monolingual dictionaries, encyclopaedias, and search engines more often in TfS, but this does not apply for PE. Professionals use less of all sources (except news items, which are hardly used anyway) in PE than students. The second argument that professionals do more research on one problem/source text unit cannot be confirmed. There was no statistically significant correlation between experience and research instances per word/problem.

The research patterns seem very similar for all participants in MPE, independent of their experience as translators. This shows that patterns between PE and TfS are different and also differ according to experience; translation experience influences the PE behaviour, while it has no influence on MPE behaviour. As was already mentioned in the analysis, it is assumed that MPE cannot be connected to the translation task, because strategies and behavioural patterns acquired in TfS cannot be transferred. Compared to the TfS task, the MT output solves problems in the PE task. If the MT output is not acceptable, a look at the source text unit helps the translator to either find an acceptable translation, which can be categorised as a task, or (s)he has to research to find a fitting target text item. However, it can be assumed that the translator would have needed to conduct research for this item in the TfS task, too. However, if the MT output is misleading in the MPE task, a new problem arises which may not have been a problem in the TfS task, because the translator cannot check the source text. Hence, misleading MT output creates new problems only in MPE, but not in PE.

9.3 Lexical problem solving: Eyetracking data on most researched words/phrases

This chapter analyses the eyetracking data of the most researched words/phrases in the six texts. The aim is to investigate whether there is a significant difference between certain eyetracking parameters when words/phrases were looked up in the Internet compared to when they were not. It is assumed that when a word/phrase needs investigation, the translator lacks some vital information on how to paraphrase the instance in the target language or, in other words, how to solve the translation problem. Therefore, more mental effort is needed and more gaze time is allocated.

The CRITT-TPR database (see §7.2) contains tables with keylogging and eyetracking data for each translator and task (Carl & Schaeffer 2013). To compare the data, three parameters were chosen, one concerned with production time (*Dur*) and two with gaze data (*GazeS* and *GazeT*):

Dur Duration of unit production time [...]

GazeS Total gaze time on source text unit [...]

GazeT Total gaze time on target text unit [...] (ibid.: 22)

Dur, GazeS, and *GazeT* include all instances in which the target word/phrase was produced or the source/target word/phrases was looked at. Therefore, these parameters can be used to compare technical effort (i.e. production time) and indications of mental effort (i.e. gaze time on source and target text) of the particular unit in the overall session. It is important to investigate the whole translation session because the word/phrase may not have been considered problematic in the first encounter. It is also not possible to imply that the word/phrase became unproblematic after the research instance or the (first) production of the target word/phrase. The following hypotheses are proposed for the keylogging and eye-tracking data:

- H_1: Longer production times and more gaze time can be found for a word/phrase when it has been researched in an online aid than when no research was conducted.

  H_{01}: Production time and gaze data are independent of conducted research.

- H_2: Longer production times and more gaze time is needed for TfS compared to PE.

  H_{02}: Production time and gaze data are independent of the task.

- H_3: Further, student translators need longer production times and more gaze than professional translators or, phrased differently, less experienced translators need longer production times and more gaze than more experienced translators.

  H_{03}: Production time and gaze data are independent of status/experience.

First, all words/phrases were filtered that had been looked up in the Internet at least four times to make sure that the word/phrase is considered problematic by at least some participants and, hence, worth investigating and that the number of instances is enough to conduct first tests for significance. In the second step, troublesome words/phrases were excluded from the list. The following reasons were taken into account:

- Words/phrases that concluded the heading or the text were excluded. When the eyetracking data were assigned, some gaze points were mapped incorrectly. This error occurs particularly often at the end of the headline, because all gaze that occurred in the rest of the empty line was mapped on the last word of the line; and the end of the text, because all gaze that occurred on the rest of the empty window was mapped on the last word of the text.

- Words/phrases that appear more than once in the source text were excluded, because it is impossible to narrow down the problematic instance or whether or not all appearances were equally problematic, etc.

- Some words/phrases were only used for content research, usually proper nouns. Therefore, the word/phrase itself was not problematic lexically, but was used to find more information on the topic. For example, participant P17 entered "Stephen Spielberg Olympic Beijing" into a search engine and read a news article about it afterwards.

After excluding the research instances that were not interesting for the following analysis, a total of 27 words/phrases can be analysed (see Table 9.13 and Appendix II Table B.1). These include six phrases, two two-item words (i.e. "below-inflation" and "pull out") and 19 words. All single words were content words, in particular nouns, adjectives, and verbs.

Table 9.13: Number of Analysed Words distributed per Text

	Text 1	Text 2	Text 3	Text 4	Text 5	Text 6
No. Words/Phrases	1	3	10	8	2	3

When phrases were looked up, the gaze data were collected for the whole phrase and not only for the words that were actually looked up. For example, in the dependent sub-clause *"which includes one minister charged with crimes against humanity by the International Criminal Court in The Hague"* some translators researched *Criminal Court, International Criminal Court, International Criminal Court in The Hague*, etc. Hence, the production time and gaze data of the whole phrase *the International Criminal Court in The Hague* was taken into consideration, even if only *Criminal Court* was looked up, so that the different research instances can be compared, no matter how the translator decided to gather information on the phrase.

This chapter summarizes and discusses the results and provides examples from the actual data. In Appendix B, all words/phrases used for analysis are listed as well as the corresponding mean and the standard variation (which is in most cases very high again; see the discussion in §9.3.1. Further, tests for statistical significance were conducted via non-directed t-tests for normal distribution or Mann-Whitney-U-tests for not normally distributed data, and correlations with experience coefficient were calculated (see §9.3.2). As the data points were so few and the main focus of the study at hand is on the difference between PE and TfS, not all analyses were performed for MPE as well. However, a more detailed discussion on the participants research behaviour in the MPE task can be found in Nitzke (2016b).

9.3.1 Mean values of eyetracking data

In most cases, the mean value for all three parameters (*Dur, GazeS, GazeT*) is higher for research instances than for no-research instances (find exact values in Appendix B, Table B.2). This was expected because researching a lexical item on the Internet indicates effort. However, the mean values were higher for the following words/phrases for one or more parameter when they were not looked up on the Internet:

- One parameter higher in no-research instances:

    - *Dur* – pull out, compromise, bureaucrats
    - *GazeS* – embarrass
    - *GazeT* – associate, bureaucrats, full-time leader, artisan

- Two or three parameters higher in no-research instances:

    - *Dur, GazeS* and *GazeT* – incentives

Altogether, 78 mean value pairs were compared (26 words ∗ 3 parameters) – in only 10 instances, the mean value was higher for no-research instances than for research instances (12.8%). The following paragraphs will discuss some possible explanations as to why the mean values may have been higher. However, as presented in the next chapter, none of these differences are significant. Therefore, it is possible that these instances occurred by chance and we also cannot eliminate the possibility of technical problems or defective gaze mapping.

Longer production times (*Dur*) in no-research instances may have been produced by a wide array of lexical choices that were activated in the participants' minds, while the Internet research may have accelerated the problem solving process. Instead of using the internal resources and pondering about which lexical item to choose, the problem was resolved quicker via Internet research. As a side note, if no Internet research was conducted, it does not necessarily mean that the translation unit was not problematic for the participant (if it was problematic, it would explain the high *Dur* time), but we do not have a distinct indicator. Two of the words mentioned above that required longer production times are verbs (*compromise* and *pull out*), which often present a lot of translation choices and need to be adapted to the grammatical and syntactic structures of the sentence. *Compromise* may require additional effort, because it can be both noun and verb. However, this should be a minor effect given the syntactic position in the sentence. The MT output can be considered partly acceptable for both verbs (in both cases parts of the full lexical or grammatical structure are missing), which may have caused longer production times as well. Further, *compromise* has a (more or less) false friend in German: *kompromittieren* - "damage one's or someone else's reputation through a statement or a manner; to compromise sb./sth."[16] (duden.de[17]). Although *kompromittieren* is one of the meanings of *compromise*, it is not appropriate in the context. Similarly, the word *bureaucrats* has a cognate – words with similar form but different meaning – in German, which may have caused higher production times, due to uncertain decision making (the MT system translated the word with the German cognate version).

The longer gaze time on the source text (GazeS) for *embarrass* might be explained by the syntactically highly complex sentence it is set in. In general, high gaze times on the source text could imply on a lexical level that the word/phrase is unknown to the translator, that the word/phrase can be categorised as low frequent, that the word/phrase is ambiguous, and/or that the word/phrase is used in an unusual context or in a context it is hardly used in.

Long gaze time on the target text (GazeT) might indicate insecurity with the (machine) translation of the source item. The MT output for the above mentioned words varies a lot: the MT output for *associate* is not acceptable, partly acceptable for *full-time leader*, and acceptable for *artisan*. Further, all three words are not embedded in informative context (*associate* is used to explain the Latin origin of another word; *full-time leader* and *artisan* are parts of a list), which may cause more insecurity with the MT output or the translation choice.

Incentives (a low frequency word) seemed to be a very problematic term as it required a lot of effort when it was not researched. All three parameters were on average higher when the word was not looked up on the Internet. The MT system did not translate the word so the MT output was of no help in the PE task. It could even be considered a burden – a hurdle between source and target text – because the untranslated word has to first be deleted in the target text.

All in all, the discussion of the mean values showed that no research does not mean that the participants did not struggle to come up with a good solution.

---

[16]"durch eine Äußerung oder ein Verhalten jemandes, dem eigenen Ansehen schaden; bloßstellen"

[17]http://www.duden.de/rechtschreibung/kompromittieren, last accessed 24th April 2015

However, the results strongly indicate that research causes more processing and production effort because the mean values are in most instances higher for research instances than for no-research instances. It would be interesting to test, whether there is a certain threshold at which the eyetracking data would indicate at which point translators fall back on their inner resources.

9.3.2 Statistical tests for eyetracking data

First, the data for all 27 words/phrases were compared as a whole data set. The first point of interest was whether there is a significant difference between research instances and no-research instances in those words. The tests turned out to be significant for all three parameters: Dur: $W = 21670.5$, $p < 0.0001$; $GazeS$: $W = 27137$, $p < 0.0001$; $GazeT$: $W = 32385$, $p = 0.001$. As the tests were not directed, the mean values were taken into consideration and they showed that all three parameters are higher for research instances than for no-research instances. In other words, the production time of researched words as well as the gaze duration on the source and target text is in general significantly higher when the participants research the word.

In a next step, we look at different sub-tests. First, it was tested whether there is still a significant difference between research and no-research, when only TfS and PE are taken into consideration together (Test 1) and for the each task individually (Test 2-4). Then, whether there is a significant difference between TfS and PE as well as between professionals and students independent of research behaviour (Test 5). The next tests investigated whether there is a difference in the research/no-research data for professionals and then for students combining the tasks (Test 6 and 7). The following three tests (Test 8, 9, and 10) considered whether there is a difference between the status of the participants in TfS, PE, and MPE. The last Mann-Whitney-U-tests focused on task and status (Test 11 and 12). In a final step, correlations were calculated for parameters and experience, experience and task, experience and research/no-research instance.

To summarise the results, nine of thirteen Mann-Whitney-U-tests (69.2%) became significant for the parameter Dur, and one of six (16.7%) correlations. 11 of 13 Mann-Whitney-U-tests (84.6%) became significant for total fixation duration on the source text ($GazeS$) and two of six (33.3%) correlations. The tests for $GazeT$ did not turn significant that often: three of thirteen Mann-Whitney-U-tests (23.1%) became significant and none of the correlation tests. Dur is not significant for status in general and, in particular, status considering the single tasks. This means that the production times of rather problematic words do not depend on the status of the participant. This is also mirrored in the correlation with experience. The production time and the experience coefficient only correlate when the words/phrases are produced without doing any research and the correlation is very weak, too. Gaze duration on the source text (*GazeS*) always became significant, except when only MPE was taken into consideration. The test for MPE needs to be excluded though, because there was only one window in the MPE task. Nonetheless, gaze was mapped on the source and the target text, which is a technical error. The correlations were only significant when experience was correlated with the overall *GazeS* and experience and PE. Both tests showed a (very) very small negative correlation. This means the more experienced a participant is the less (s)he looks at the source text item. However, the correlations are so small that the difference is hardly recognisable. *GazeT* only became significant when compared between TfS and PE, meaning that there is a significant difference between TfS and PE concerning gaze on the target text; and when the student data were compared for when they conducted research and when they did not.

The next chapter provides detailed insights on the single words/phrases. Five tests for significance were conducted for every word/phrase and for every parameter that was taken into consideration in the last chapter, which results in twelve tests for significance per word/phrase:

- First, it was tested whether there is a **significant difference between research instances and no-research instances**, independent of the tasks. First, all three tasks will be considered and then only PE and TfS in a second test.

- Then, a test was conducted on whether there is a **significant difference between PE and TfS**, independent of research behaviour.

- The last two tests calculated whether **the difference between research and no-research was significant in TfS and PE**, respectively.

Table 9.14 summarises how often the tests proved significance for all 28 analysed words and phrases. In these calculations, most tests for significance did not turn into a significant result. One explanation is the low number of instances (n) that can be analysed – especially in the last two tests – and therefore, the chances that the difference occurred by accident are too high. The data, for example, only presented one research instance for "halt" in the PE data which was than compared to six no-research instances. When testing significant differences between research and no-research for the single tasks, some tests could not be conducted, because the word/phrase was not researched in the task. However, some tests became significant and in the following, these significant differences will be discussed. As the tests were undirected, the mean values were used to identify which values were significantly higher/lower.

Table 9.14: Number of tests with $p < 0.05$

	Parameter		
	Dur	GazeS	GazeT
research yes/no (all)	10	5	4
research yes/no (PE and TfS)	6	2	3
different tasks (PE vs. TfS)	7	8	4
research yes/no for TfS	1	1	1
research yes/no for PE	0	0	0

As the tests were not directed, it was verified whether the parameters were significantly higher or lower when research was conducted compared to when no research was conducted or according to task. In all cases, the parameters turned out to be significantly higher when research was conducted. The test between TfS and PE, however, did not compare research/no research but the tasks. Interestingly, the parameters were significantly lower for PE in all cases.

The data suggest that more effort was necessary when the participants decided to research words/phrases compared to when they translated the same words/phrases without the help of any Internet resource, although only 52 of the 405[18] tests (12.5%) became significant, which might mainly be caused by the low n-values as mentioned above. This argument is strengthened by the fact that, when all data from all three tasks were used for testing significance, 19 tests turned out to be significant, while when the research instance in one single task was tested none (for PE) and three (for TfS) proved significant.

The tests that compared TfS and PE and were significant and in favour of PE, meaning that PE took less processing and production effort than TfS. In total, 19 of the 78[19] tests (24%) turned out to be significant. Here again, a bigger data collection might have led to more obvious results. Nonetheless, the results are in favour of MT as an aid on the lexical level for the PE process. Accordingly, the hurdle between source text and target text might sometimes be overcome by the

---

[18] 3 parameters * 5 tests (research yes/no; research yes/no in TfS only; research yes/no in PE only) * 28 words/phrases – 15 tests that could not be conducted due to missing data (e. g. when none of the participant researched the word/phrase in the post-editing task).
[19] 3 parameters * 26 words/phrases

MT output and sometimes not. However, the data do not suggest that MT creates new hurdle.

Again, the parameter *GazeT* was the least productive of the three parameters. However, the difference is not that obvious as it was when all words were compared. Twelve tests for *GazeT* became significant, while "only" 16 tests for *GazeS* became significant, which is only 33.3% more. Eleven tests became significant for *GazeS* in the overall data, while only three for *GazeT* became significant. Two reasons could explain these differences between single words/phrases and overall data. First, the lower n-value might cause far fewer tests for *GazeS* to turn significant. Second, there could be some words/phrases with very extreme data that influence the overall results rather than the single words/phrases. However, most tests for single words/phrases that became significant have p-values between 0.01 and 0.05, which does not implicate extreme values. Conclusively, this implies that problem solving is handled rather on a source text level than on a target text level.

9.3.3 Further analysis – Misleading machine translation

In contrast to what might have been expected, even if the participants had decided that the MT output was unacceptable for the target text, processing and production effort does not increase significantly in the PE task. Although some mean values of the parameters are higher in the PE task than in TfS (see §9.3.1), these few instances are more the exception than the rule. Hence, we will look at the influence of misleading MT. The purpose of post-editing MT output is to produce a target text more efficiently. Therefore, MT should reduce lexical problems and conclusively reduce research effort. However, practice shows that MT systems occasionally choose the wrong lexical entry for the context, which results in misleading or wrong translations in the MT output. These have to be corrected by the post-editor and hence a productivity gain cannot be detected.

Two of the most researched words/phrases were looked up more often in the PE task than in the TfS task (*compromise* and *incentives* – both were already discussed in §9.3.1 on mean values). The increased research effort might be caused by the PE task, which in a way restricts the participants. The translators have to use the MT output as a translation frame, which makes them work less freely. Hence, the target text representation might be primed by the MT output and cause less associations in the brain. However, this increased research effort is the exception not the rule – in our examples it only occurred in less than 8% of the analysed words. Usually more research is performed in TfS. Looking at it the other way around, this low figure rather speaks in favour of MT than against it.

Especially, when we look at the other words/phrases that were predominantly researched in TfS. *Insistence* and *flaring up again* were researched only in TfS and research was about equally distributed between TfS and PE in only a few examples like *associate* or *serve*. Hence, MT rather decreased the research necessity in the overall sessions, which supports the assumption mentioned earlier that MT helps to deconstruct hurdles rather than to erect new ones.

9.3.4 Comparing most researched words to least-/no-research words

In this chapter, we will compare words/phrases that were researched most often with comparable (or as comparable as possible) words/phrases that did not require research by most participants. Three words/phrases were picked for analysis from the 27 most researched, for which comparable words/phrases could be found in the relatively small text corpus provided by the six texts.

First, we will compare the phrase "the International Criminal Court in The Hague" (1) which was looked up eight times and "China's backing for Sudan's policy in Darfur"(2)[20], where parts of the phrases were looked up in six sessions, mostly for context research. In this respect, Phrase (2) was not considered a whole phrase by the participants but as single units, while Phrase (1) was considered one unit. Both phrases consist of seven words and a similar amount of characters (45 and 44, respectively, including spaces). Further, the MT output is not very error prone for both phrases, although the MT for Phrase (2) is missing one definite article[21]. Both phrases contain proper nouns, Phrase (1) an institutional name and a location name, and Phrase (2) three location names. There are German equivalents for the institutional and the location name of Phrase (1), whereas all location names in Phrase (2) can be retained. However, Phrase (2) is grammatically more complex. Another advantage of comparing these phrases is that they occurred in the same text. Hence, the participants translated the phrases within the same task and individual differences could be ruled out.

Next, the word *rattle* (looked up eleven times) will be compared to *adapt* (no research instances occurred) and *disliked* (looked up twice in the human translation tasks). *Adapt* and *disliked* were chosen for comparison, because they are both verbs, even though *disliked* is used in the simple past and is therefore grammatically more complex; they also have comparable frequencies. The TPR-DB indicates frequencies as the log10 probabilities according to the *British National Cor-*

---

[20]To avoid typing the entire phrases every time they need to be referred to, they will be referred to as Phrase (1) and Phrase (2) in the following.

[21](1) MT: „den Internationalen Strafgerichtshof in Den Haag" (2) MT: „Chinas Unterstützung für Sudan-Politik in Darfur"

pus (cf. Carl & Schaeffer 2013: 15), which are for *rattle* −5.5360, for *adapt* −5.0924, and for *dislike* −5.3152. *Dislike*, however, is a special case because it is followed by another verb (*working*) and hence is often realised as an adverb, like in the MT output 'nicht gern [...] arbeiten' ('not willingly [...] work'). Nonetheless, it was considered for comparison.

Finally, we will look at three adjectives with similar frequencies: *vulnerable* − looked up eight times, frequency: −4.7104; *extra* (as it occurred in text 2) − not researched, frequency: −4.1181; *extensive* − researched once, frequency: −4.4829.

I compared the parameter *Dur*, *GazeS*, and *GazeT* for research in TfS and PE, research in TfS, research in PE, according to task (TfS vs. PE), high research words/phrase against low research words/phrase (general, for TfS and PE, for TfS, for PE, for TfS and research, for TfS and no research, for PE and research, and for PE and no research).

In total, 19 of 108[22] tests (17.6%) turned out significant. The most promising test was comparing PE and TfS, which turned out significant in seven out of nine instances (77.8%). As the tests were undirected, the mean values were evaluated and it was always the PE sessions that showed less keylogging activity or eye movement. The parameter *Dur* is the most meaningful in the verbs chapter and turned out significant seven out of twelve times, while it was hardly significant for adjectives and phrases. Surprisingly, *Gaze S* and *GazeT* turned out significant equally often for all word/phrase-categories, namely five times (which is still not much), but no tendencies for one word/phrase-category can be detected.

In a final test series, a high frequency verb and a high frequency adjective were compared to the highly researched verb and adjective as the latter were low frequency words (*vulnerable* vs. *new* and *rattle* vs. *have*). The tests were conducted both with the original data and normalised to the number of characters. The most promising parameter was again *Dur*. Interestingly, the results of the tests were not as extreme as expected as only three of the 36 normalised tests turned significant for both verbs and adjectives.

9.3.5 Status and experience

In this chapter, we will analyse how experience (considering both the participants' status and experience vector) influences the parameter comparing highly researched words and low researched words as introduced in the previous chapter. Again, one aim of this analysis is to compare which measurement for experience might be more helpful for statistical analysis.

---

[22]3 word categories * 3 parameters *12 test conditions

When we compare professionals and students, statistically significant differences cannot be observed often. Differences only appear in *GazeS*, if at all, for all tasks or only for TfS or PE. *Dur* becomes significantly different in the verbs chapter for students and professionals considering research and no-research, no matter whether we compare low-frequency verbs or low- and high-frequency verbs. The students group shows a significant difference in *Dur* and *GazeS*, when we compare low- and high-frequency adjectives, which is not observable for professionals. When we look at the differences in tasks, all parameters are higher in TfS for students and professionals. Almost the same tests became significant for both groups, except for phrases regarding the gaze behaviour. In the latter case, professionals needed significantly longer to read source and target text units in the TfS task, while there was no difference for student translators. Finally, when we compare high-research and low-research words/phrases, the difference is significant much more often for students (six times) than for professionals (once). Interestingly, the only parameter that became significant for professionals – *Dur* for adjectives – became significantly higher for low-research words, while all significant instances for students were higher for high-research words.

The experience factor was a not very informative value in this analysis. Three of 18 tests (16.6%) became significant for the overall data. When we tested most researched words against low/no-research words, only one of 168 tests (0.6%) became significant. The test that became significant described the correlation between experience and gaze duration on the source text in the PE task when comparing high-research and low-research phrases. Again, we can only speculate that the number of data points is too small to turn out significant correlations or simply that no connection exists between experience and keylogging behaviour as well as eye movement.

In one final attempt to find statistical significant relations, a linear mixed model[23] was created for the most researched words. The individual participants and the different texts were set as random effects in the calculation. Task and research were included in the model. The data for MPE was excluded for the GazeS and GazeT models, because the mapping was arbitrary. There was an attempt to integrate status and/or experience into the model, but they did not influence the model significantly, and therefore were excluded. First, let us look at *Dur*. *Dur* is significantly different between TfS and MPE ($t = \pm 2.28$, $p = 0.0228$), but not between TfS and PE ($t = \pm 1.61$, $p = 0.107$) or PE and MPE ($t = \pm 0.77$, $p = 0.4426$). Further, it is significantly higher when research was conducted ($t = 4.61$, $p < 0.0001$). Total fixation duration on the source text (*GazeS*) is higher

---

[23]Using the packages "effects", "lmerTest" (Kuznetsova et al. 2015), and "lme4" (Bates et al. 2014).

for TfS (t = 4.82, p < 0.0001) and when research was conducted (t = 3.05, p = 0.0025). Finally the total fixation duration on the target text is higher for TfS as well (t = 1.98, p = 0.0486), but no significant difference can be found when research was conducted and when not (t = 1.60, p = 0.1108).

9.3.6 Summary and conclusion – Keylogging and eyetracking data

The most promising process parameter appears to be *Dur*, which seems quite reasonable, because the parameter describes production duration. Hence, the participants needed longer to produce these problematic words. This can either mean that many changes occurred during the session or that the participants literally needed more time to produce the word, because they might have thought about whether the translation decision is correct or suitable, or might have considered other options.

The eyetracking parameters were not as conclusive, but *GazeS* is more promising than *GazeT*. Higher *GazeS* times indicate problematic words/phrases. However, a problematic word/phrase does not necessarily trigger a higher reading time. The problem might not be caused by the source item itself as the translator knows what it means, but by transfer to the target text. Hence, this problematic situation might not be reflected in the reading time of the source text item itself, but in the whole surrounding text area, because the translator needs to grasp the context and transfer the problematic item to the context. On the other hand, it is reasonably safe to assume that reading time of the target text item does not reflect on problematic translation units, although we have to consider the lack of data points. Finally, a lot of the processing probably occurs during the research instance itself. The translator looks for examples for a solution in a bilingual dictionary. While (s)he does this, (s)he has the context in mind and integrates the research effort into the context. Hence, a reasonable solution might already be created during the research process, which is obviously not recognisable in the reading data of source and target text item.

Interestingly, the differences between PE and TfS were very often significant when similar words/phrases that caused different research behaviour were compared, except for *GazeT* in two cases. This indicates that the MT output is helpful for both words/phrases that were researched very often and that were not/hardly researched.

When comparing data for single tasks and/or only for research/no research instances, hardly any tests turned out significant. However, when the mean values are compared, a difference is often recognisable. The reason for the insignificant tests is either that there are no significant difference and/or that we do not have enough data points to compare the data. Some tests were not possible at all, because there were, for example, no research instances in the PE task. Conclusively, a larger data set would be necessary to perform meaningful calculations.

In summary, when we look at the overall data set, the hypothesis can be confirmed. Words/phrases that were researched often required longer production times and longer gazes on the source text unit. Research does not seem to have an influence on the gaze duration on the target text. Hence, more mental effort is necessary, when research is necessary. Further, there is a tendency that text units take longer to produce and are gazed at longer in the source text for TfS. Finally, student translators seem to need longer to produce the text unit and gaze longer at the source text, while no effect could be measured on the target text reading time. This, however, was not confirmed in the linear mixed model, in which no significant difference could be determined between students and professionals nor does the experience coefficient have a significant influence. Hence, problem solving behaviour seems to be indicated by text production time and the total gaze time on the source text, but not on the target text.

9.4 Overall conclusions and final remarks

The analyses of screen recording as well as eyetracking and keylogging show that sometimes different research patters can be observed both between PE and TfS as well as between students and professionals, while other results are equal between all participants and tasks. Participants did more research in the TfS task than in the PE task. Similarly, students researched more than professionals. Amount of research and experience correlate significantly for TfS and PE. Interestingly, participants decided not to use Internet research as often in PE as in TfS; professionals more often than students, although the test did not prove significant. The correlation of experience and not using Internet research, however, turned significant. When all participants are taken into consideration, the complexity levels of the texts seem to influence the amount of research, but this result might be accidental, because the distribution is different when the participants are separated into groups of professionals and students. Bilingual dictionaries are used most often for research by both groups and in all tasks. The research instances were about equally long, independent of status of the participant and task. The relation between research time and total session duration is almost equal between professionals and students in the MPE task, while it is higher for students than for professionals in PE and TfS. Testing for significance with a Mann-Whitney-U-test and correlations presented contradictory results (see discussion below).

Most research takes place in the drafting phase and, in most cases, translators choose their first translations if the research instance does not result in a direct target text decision. Students rechecked their translation choice or the MT output much more often than the professionals, which indicates insecurity.

In 87.2% of cases, the mean values of the eyetracking and keylogging parameters were higher for research instances than for no-research instances. When the parameters were tested for significance for the single words/phrases, they were not as productive, which is probably caused mainly by the low n-numbers. This argument is strengthened when we look at the overall data set. The tests for significance all resulted in p far below 0.05 when comparing research instances and no research instances, and also by the linear mixed model. When single words/phrases are examined, the most reliable parameter is *Dur*. Hence, long production times might indicate problematic words. The gaze parameters are not that productive. This might have two reasons: First, the problem might become visible in the reading times of the whole phrase around the problematic word/phrase, because the translator processes the context simultaneously; and second, a lot of processing might already occur during research, which is then not identifiable in the gaze data. When testing between two tasks, the tests that became significant were in favour of PE, meaning PE required less effort. Bad quality MT output usually does not increase the writing and reading effort, but it becomes equal to the effort of TfS instead. Hence, MT output solves some translation problems in PE, some are not solved, but no new problems are created either. In MPE, however, new problems are sometimes created because the translator cannot refer to the source text.

The analyses show that translation experience seems to have an influence on PE, because the patterns between students and professionals and the correlations between research behaviour and experience factor often suggest differences. However, this result could not be confirmed by the linear mixed model. A larger data set might be helpful to reinvestigate the issue. There were no implications that translation experience influences the MPE task. The task was probably new to all participants meaning they could not apply their usual strategies due to the missing source text.

A high standard deviation could be observed in screen-recording, keylogging and eyetracking data. This points to high individual differences in all data. There might be a tendency, towards what is perceived as a translation problem and therefore leads to higher production times and gaze data. Furthermore, less experienced participants might demonstrate different behavioural patterns than more experienced translators. Nonetheless, what is problematic for the individual varies a lot according to their internal knowledge – a parameter which could not be measured in this study.

In general, the experience vector was very helpful for the screen-recording observations as it often revealed significant differences. However, the parameter was less productive for keylogging and eyetracking data, which might be caused by the data sparseness. Another interesting aspect that was discussed in §9.2.6 is that statistical tests turned significant for different tasks, depending on whether they were grouped according to status (professional vs. students) or correlated with experience. The example in §9.2.6 considered the time spent on research in relation to the total session duration. The test turned out to be significant for PE when the required time was grouped according to status, but not when correlated with experience. Further, the opposite applies when TfS is tested: no significance when comparing groups, but a significant correlation between time and experience. That the tests turned out differently depending on the chosen test is more the exception than the rule. However, I assume that testing the correlation with the experience factor is a more valid test than testing with the groups, because the experience factor takes the individual differences into account more than grouping the participants according to status. As discussed in §8.1, both groups are very homogeneous and more details of personal experience would be desirable. However, as was shown in this chapter on research behaviour, it is still very useful to group the participants into professionals and students, on the one hand for visualisation reasons, and to arrive at a valid impression of the data distribution on the other. In another example, the results were comparable: In §9.2.8, we analysed the distribution of research instances on phases, which was analysed according to the experience of the participants. The results were for the orientation phase: $r_\tau(-1.92) = -0.145$, $p = 0.05437$, the drafting phase: $r_\tau(-2.91) = -0.196$, $p < 0.004$, and the revision phase: $r_\tau(-0.74) = -0.053$, $p = 0.4593$, while the results according to status for the orientation phase are: $W = 1759.5$, $p = 0.06684$, the drafting phase $W = 1320.5$, $p < 0.001$, and the revision phase $W = 1994.5$, $p = 0.9173$. These results are very similar and point in the same direction. In the following chapters, I will further investigate whether grouping according to status or experience coefficient is more informative.

10 Syntactic problem solving

After investigating conscious problem solving activity, the focus will now be on potentially subconscious problem solving in regard to syntax. In the next chapter, we will discuss the influence of the MT output on syntactic processing, which might lead to problem solving activities. Statistical MT systems seem to have difficulties with syntactic structure, because word order (especially verb positioning) follows different rules in English and German (e.g. Kolss et al. 2008: 178). Hence, syntax might be of particular interest in regard to problem solving in PE. On the one hand, it might be possible that syntactic structures are primed by the source text structure in all tasks and the MT output in PE and MPE (cf. Bangalore et al. 2016). On the other hand, syntactic error prone MT output might complicate the PE process. It is hypothesised that regular syntactic structures do not cause problems in the translation process for trained translators. However, as the MT system sometimes disarranges syntactic structures in the target language, syntax becomes a problem that the translator has to consciously solve in the PE task. Hence, syntactically unacceptable MT output should cause longer production and processing times.

- H_1: The production and processing data are significantly different according to the quality of the MT output regarding syntax.

  H_{01}: The quality of the MT output regarding syntax has no influence on the production and processing data.

- H_2: Syntax requires conscious problem solving in the PE task, while it is not considered a problematic feature in the TfS task. The processing data are statistically different between professionals and students (or between participants with different experience coefficients), as more experienced participants can handle syntactically less high quality MT output better than less experienced participants.

  H_{02}: Syntax cannot be categorised as problematic both in PE and TfS. The experience of the participants – independent of the quality of the MT output – has no influence on production and processing times.

First, the MT output at a sentence level was evaluated in terms of syntax for all six texts by three raters. The syntax in the MT sentence was categorised as either *acceptable*, *partly acceptable*, or *not acceptable*. This evaluation was done on a sentence basis, which might be subject to discussion, but as Krings (1986b: 197-198, translated J. N.) emphasises in his study on problem solving in translation:

> Apart from those two examples, the translators adhere to sentence bound-
> aries unconditionally. [...] This might be one of the most exciting results
> in respect to the translator's problem solving order [...]. Despite the strong
> textual relation between all sentences in both texts, the sentence is – simply
> characterised by ending with a dot – next to single translation problems the
> ultimate translation unit for the participants.[1]

The MT output was considered *acceptable* when syntactic structures did not include any mistakes, *partly acceptable* when some clauses were without errors, but some included errors, e.g. the main clause contained syntactic errors, but the subordinate clause did not, and *not acceptable* when most or all the clauses included errors. We have to keep in mind that the evaluation only considers syntax and no other aspect of the MT output. Hence, if a sentence was categorised as acceptable, it only means that the syntax of the sentence was acceptable, it may still include lexical or grammatical errors. Further, the PE instructions (see §7.2) did not specify any direct rules regarding how the participant should treat syntax. However, they were instructed to use "as much raw translation as possible" and change MT "only where absolutely necessary". However, whether adapting the target syntax is absolutely necessary is very subjective. An inter-rater agreement was calculated with Fleiss' kappa. A total of 41 sentences were assessed by 3 raters. The results were $\kappa = 0.52$, $z = 8.09$ and $p < 0.0001$, which can be interpreted as a moderate agreement.

All in all, the six texts comprise 41 sentences, of which 10 were categorised as *acceptable*, 20 as *partly acceptable*, and 11 as *not acceptable* (find the detailed evaluation in §C Table C.1). The MT system retained the sentence boundaries, meaning that there is a target sentence for every source sentence. This influenced the post-edited target text as well. While one source sentence was split into two

---

[1]Original text: „Abgesehen von diesen beiden Beispielen halten sich die Übersetzer un-
eingeschränkt an den Satzrahmen. [...] Dies ist vielleicht eines der erstaunlichsten Ergebnisse
im Zusammenhang mit der [...] diskutierten Reihenfolge in der Problembehandlung. Trotz der
starken textuellen Verflechtungen aller Sätze untereinander in den beiden ausgewählten Tex-
ten ist der Satz, und zwar rein interpunktorisch verstanden, für die Versuchspersonen neben
dem einzelnen Übersetzungsproblem die Übersetzungseinheit schlechthin."

target sentences in 18 instances in the TfS task, this only happened nine times in the PE task. Similarly, two source sentences were joined to one target sentences twelve times in the TfS task, but in only six instances in the PE task. In the following, we will discuss keylogging and eyetracking data for the difference in syntactic quality of the sentences.

10.1 Overview production and processing times

To analyse production and processing in the different tasks, the same parameters are used as in §10.3 on lexical analyses – *Dur, GazeS, GazeT*. Further, we will add two new parameters, namely *FixS* and *FixT*, because they will provide further insight into the processing of the sentences and different behaviour in the tasks. These two parameters are defined as the following:

"**FixS**: Number of fixations on source text unit […]

FixT: Number of fixations on target text unit […]." (Carl & Schaeffer 2013: 22)

When I dealt with lexical items, I usually considered one word or phrase (i.e. multi-word units). However, I will deal with sentences on the syntactic level, which leads to longer production and processing times, which are influenced by many additional factors other than only syntax. Hence, we will normalise the parameters on a character level for mean values, standard deviations, and first statistical tests. Further, eyetracking data on the source and target texts will be disregarded in the following chapters for the MPE, although they were accessible in the database. When the task was conducted, the participants only worked in one window in the editor. Hence, it is inexplicable why the eyetracking data were separated into source text and target text data and how this separation was conducted. However, the existing eyetracking data were combined to total fixation counts (*TFix*) and gaze durations (*TGaze*) on the whole text – introducing two additional new parameters to the analysis. When the fixation data are combined and normalized per character, the differences between the mean values are not extremely different between the tasks (see Table 10.1), however the differences are highly significant (see Table 10.2).

In the following, Table 10.1 provides an overview of the mean values of the parameters per character according to the tasks. It is hypothesised that the PE and MPE task should take less time to produce the target sentences than the TfS task. Further, as the source text becomes less important in the PE task, the gaze data on the source text (*GazeS* and *FixS*) should be smaller than in the TfS task. Finally, gaze on the target text (*GazeT* and *FixT*) should be about the same for both tasks or higher for PE as the MT output is the main source of information. The data for MPE should behave similarly to the PE data. The difference between MPE and PE data is expected to be low.

Table 10.1: Mean and SD of the Parameters per Task and per Character

Parameter	Mean			SD		
	MPE	PE	TfS	MPE	PE	TfS
Dur	693.33	739.22	1077.58	585.3	535.74	690.82
GazeS	–	303.17	506.56	–	792.83	907.77
GazeT	–	590.57	612.81	–	1018.37	792.64
FixS	–	1.75	2.74	–	4.59	4.82
FixT	–	3.59	3.17	–	7.03	4.76
TFix	2.21	2.75	2.95	5.06	5.80	4.61
TGaze	470.19	457.57	559.90	1760.07	1018.37	792.64

The mean values in Table 10.1 confirm that the parameters are highest for TfS, except for *FixT* which is on average higher in PE. Further, the data for MPE are always the lowest, except for *TGaze* which is slightly lower for PE. Interestingly, the total fixation count is higher in PE compared to MPE. This shows that single fixations take longer in MPE than in PE (and also as in TfS), which indicates that processing takes longer in MPE than in the other tasks. This seems reasonable as there is no source text to compare the MT output to, which is expected to be cognitively more demanding when the participants encounter problematic or error prone MT-output. The missing source text on the other hand also explains why there are less fixations in total, because there is less text that the participants need to process.

When longer processing results in longer fixation durations but smaller fixation counts, it also explains the high fixation counts and the low total fixation duration on the target text in PE compared to TfS, because TfS could be considered more cognitively demanding. Furthermore, the higher fixation counts and total fixation durations in the target text in TfS might indicate that the target text becomes more important in the revision task – the source text is only consulted when doubts about the translation arise – and hence is fixated more often and longer in the total session than the source text. Finally, the extraordinarily high standard deviations are very striking and might indicate great differences between individuals and/or segments.

Table 10.2: Mann-Whitney-U-Tests for the Parameters comparing the three tasks (statistically significant results are printed in bold)

Parameter	MPE vs. PE		MPE vs. TfS		PE vs. TfS	
	U	p	U	p	U	p
Dur	43374	0.088	29070	**<0.0001**	31479	**<0.0001**
GazeS	–	–	–	–	27342	**<0.0001**
GazeT	–	–	–	–	43180	0.143
FixS	–	–	–	–	28406.5	**<0.0001**
FixT	–	–	–	–	47453.5	0.6146
TFix	**34600.5**	**<0.0001**	**29100.5**	**<0.0001**	**39212**	**<0.001**
TGaze	**41241**	**0.0075**	**31270**	**<0.0001**	**35280**	**<0.0001**

The tests for significance confirm the impressions (Table 10.2). The data were not distributed normally. Therefore, a Mann-Whitney-U-test was conducted. The tests between PE and TfS turned out to be significant for *Dur*, *GazeS*, and *FixS* but not significant for *GazeT* and *FixT* as was expected. For the combined parameter *TFix* and *TGaze* the tests prove significant differences again. To put it in a nutshell, all parameters are significantly higher in TfS when comparing it to PE, except for the eyetracking data on the target text, where there is no significant difference. There is also a significant difference between MPE and TfS for the tested parameter, proving that the parameters are higher for TfS and hence TfS is (at least technically[2]) more demanding. The eyetracking data show significant differences between MPE and PE. The total fixation count is significantly lower for MPE (caused by the missing source text), while the total fixation duration is significantly lower for PE. This result supports the assumption that MPE requires more mental effort as was already discussed above.

The tests in Table 10.2 were also conducted on the parameter per character to rule out that the length of the sentences influences the results. However, as mentioned above, the values show high standard deviation values (Table 10.1). Next to individual differences, this might be caused by the different complexities of the sentences in the tasks and the quality of the MT output for the MPE/PE

---

[2]Krings (2001) differentiates between temporal, technical (meaning the text production effort) and cognitive effort in PE. This differentiation is also used in e.g. O'Brien (2006).

task. Therefore, the next chapter will analyse single sentences with regard to MT quality.

10.2 Analysis of the influence of syntactic MT quality

The aim of this chapter is to analyse the syntactic structures on a sentence level. The same parameters will be used for keylogging and eyetracking data that were used in the previous analysis (*Dur, GazeS, FixS, GazeT, FixT, TFix, TGaze*). Further, the syntactic quality of the MT output will be taken into consideration.

10.2.1 Analysis of production and processing data concerning the quality of the MT output

As mentioned in the introduction, the quality of the syntax of in MT output was rated as acceptable, partly acceptable, and not acceptable. Further, it was also shown that the keylogging and gaze data differ for PE and TfS. The hypothesis is that the quality of the MT output influences the data. While *Dur, GazeS, FixS, TGaze*, and *TFix* are still significantly lower for acceptable and partly acceptable MT output in the PE and MPE task in contrast to the TfS task, there is no significant difference when the MT output is considered not acceptable. This does probably not apply for *FixT* and *GazeT*, because there is no significant difference between the two tasks, even if the quality of the MT output is not considered. First, I will look at the mean values for the parameters according to the MT output quality for all three tasks combined in Table 10.3, excluding MPE for *GazeS, GazeT, FixS* and *FixT*, because only one text was available in the MPE task, and then the values will be separated per task.

As Table 10.3 shows, the mean values for production time (*Dur*) increase for partly acceptable and unacceptable quality of the MT output compared to acceptable MT output. However, the highest mean value is assigned to sentences with partly acceptable MT output. One reason could be that partly acceptable sentences are more complex than unacceptable ones. For the remainder of the data, the mean value was the lowest when the MT output was partly acceptable, which is contrary to the result of the production times. We have to keep in mind, though, that the MT output does not influence the TfS task and, therefore, this might (partially) explain why the values are lower for partly acceptable output. Including all three tasks, however, provides the advantage of enabling a general impression on sentence subset. Further, partly acceptable sentences tend to be long, because they often include two or more clauses (of which one is acceptable

Table 10.3: The Mean and SD values of the parameters according to syntactic quality per character (excluding MPE for GazeS, GazeT, FixS, FixT)

	Acceptable		Partly Acceptable		Not Acceptable	
	Mean	SD	Mean	SD	Mean	SD
Dur	628.01	658.35	939.04	648.16	831.53	514.43
GazeS	605.13	1263.54	331.21	712.23	364.37	598.04
GazeT	753.37	1209.84	535.59	796.9	591.11	787.83
FixS	3.34	6.63	1.87	4.15	1.97	3.41
FixT	4.13	8.24	3.1	5.37	3.25	4.58
TFix	3.51	6.58	2.27	4.62	2.51	4.64
TGaze	649.71	1133.48	419.11	799.68	499.08	907.1

in terms of syntactic MT output, while the other is not). Hence, the effect of this one syntactic error might be compensated by the length of the overall segment. Maybe sentences with no (syntactic) flaws are more suspicious to the participants than those with few errors and therefore are checked more often. However, why the gaze values are the highest for acceptable MT output is hardly explicable. One would assume that the sentences for which the MT system produces a syntactically acceptable output are less complex and therefore less difficult to process in TfS as well. Other factors such as lexical complexity and the position of the sentence in the text might, however, cause these high gaze values.

Another interesting observation is that the gaze duration and fixation count on the source text in relation to the target text is higher for acceptable quality than for partly/not acceptable quality. One way to explain this could be that more target text reading is necessary when the MT output is bad in PE. Hence, the focus shifts from the source text to the target text, while not especially much attention is necessary for good syntactic quality – neither on the source nor target text. Instead both texts are considered and checked whether they contain the correct information. If the MT output has flaws, however, the participants focus on the target text. Hence, the fixation count and fixation duration on the the source text decreases. Next, will we assess the mean values for the parameters according to the the tasks to see whether they shed more light on the unexpected result presented in Table 10.4.

First of all, Table 10.4 shows that all parameters are the highest for TfS when the MT output is syntactically acceptable, which shows that the participants ben-

Table 10.4: The Mean and SD values of the parameters per character
according to syntactic quality and task

	MPE		PE		TfS	
	Mean	SD	Mean	SD	Mean	SD
Acceptable						
Dur	373.80	483.52	468.21	515.70	1059.68	736.11
GazeS	–	–	458.99	1039.36	751.27	1446.36
GazeT	–	–	712.19	1203.41	794.56	1223.29
FixS	–	–	2.7	5.98	3.98	7.20
FixT	–	–	4.39	10.07	3.87	5.92
TFix	3.05	5.20	3.61	8.12	3.88	6.23
TGaze	589.79	1021.66	593.41	1116.35	770.09	1263.19
Partly Acceptable						
Dur	864.7	620.40	833.89	529.35	1114.55	741.42
GazeS	–	–	234.49	681.17	426.05	731.26
GazeT	–	–	506.6	930.97	564.02	640.66
FixS	–	–	1.37	4.08	2.36	4.17
FixT	–	–	3.11	6.10	3.09	4.57
TFix	1.77	4.49	2.29	5.03	2.74	4.30
TGaze	380.98	941.05	378.81	794.68	495.75	638.01
Not Acceptable						
Dur	679.91	472.88	802.83	488.98	1021.12	528.93
GazeS	–	–	292.81	722.83	439.61	421.55
GazeT	–	–	638.42	994.61	541.38	485.92
FixS	–	–	1.64	3.95	2.34	2.71
FixT	–	–	3.79	5.16	2.68	3.82
TFix	2.21	5.81	2.82	4.54	2.5	3.14
TGaze	521.06	1234.84	483.32	866.97	492.54	424.05

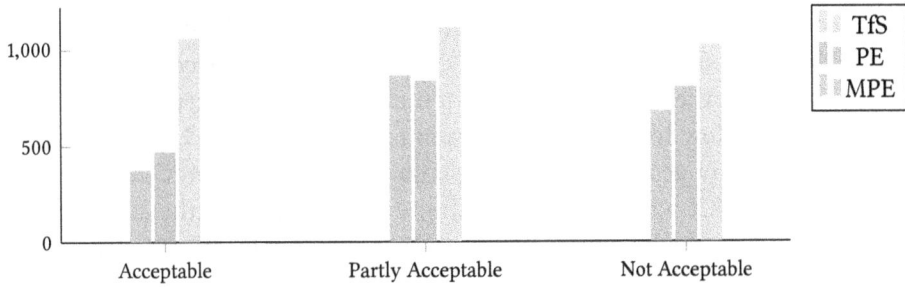

Figure 10.1: Visualisations of Table 10.4 according to production time Dur

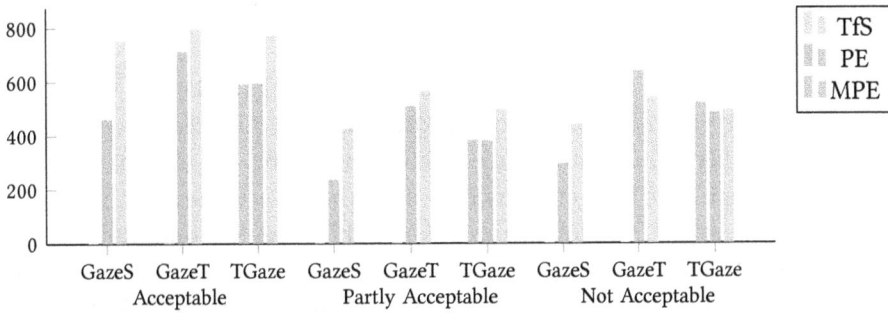

Figure 10.2: Visualisations of Table 10.4 according to total fixation duration on GazeS, GazeT, TGaze

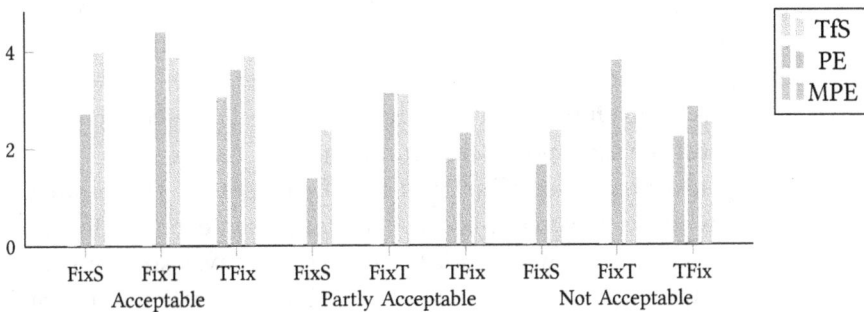

Figure 10.3: Visualisations of Table 10.4 according to total fixation count on GazeS, GazeT, TGaze

efit from the use of the MT system if it works properly. The only exception is fixation count on the target text (*FixT*), which is higher for PE. This again shows that
the focus in PE shifts to the target text. Many fixations are necessary to assess the
MT output, but the fixations are short if the MT output is acceptable, which leads
to a relatively low total fixation duration on the target text. However, when the
MT output is not acceptable, the gaze data on the target text (*GazeT*) are higher
in PE than in TfS, which is in line with previous results. Further, the production
times (*Dur*) are much lower in MPE and PE compared to TfS when the MT quality is acceptable. The production time remains the highest in TfS independent of
the MT output, which is understandable, because the complete target text has to
be produced in TfS but the time increases for PE and MPE and the differences
are no longer as obvious. There are no indications, yet that syntax needs to be
considered a problem in the translation process. However, the low production
times in PE and MPE show that the MT output accelerates the text production
task when it is syntactically acceptable.

What we can also observe in Table 10.4 is that the gaze data on the source text
as well as the gaze data on the total text decrease in all three tasks for partly acceptable quality (when data were collected) and increase again for unacceptable
quality, except for TfS. Note, however, that the gaze values on the source text
are the highest for the sentence in TfS, in which the MT output quality would
be acceptable in the PE and MPE task. This indicates that the processing data are
also influenced by the sentence itself and not only by the task. It might be reasonable, for example, to expect that the sentences with partly acceptable quality
are often considered less problematic or less complex than the ones with acceptable syntactic MT quality. The latter may include other issues that are not syntax
related. The sentences with low syntactic MT output quality might also be the
most problematic or most complex, which would also explain why the MT system struggles. On the other hand, the gaze data are even higher for acceptable
syntactic quality sentences than for low quality sentences in TfS, which indicates
that problems occur in the sentences that are not MT related – both categories
result in almost the same processing duration.

Although text production (*Dur*) was still the longest in TfS for unacceptable
MT output, which is reasonable because the target sentence had to be produced
completely from scratch, while in MPE and PE there was still some usable MT
output, *TFix* was highest for PE when the MT output was not acceptable and
almost equal in MPE and TfS. It was highest, however, in TfS when the MT output
was acceptable and partly acceptable and almost equal in PE and MPE, which
again indicates that more effort was necessary in MPE, because the participants

did not need to process the source text and still the value per character is as high as for PE. Further, *TGaze* was highest for MPE when the MT output was not acceptable, and almost equal for PE and TfS, which supports the argument that much effort was necessary in MPE, especially when the MT output was not acceptable. The total gaze duration was also almost equal for MPE and PE when the MT output was acceptable and partly acceptable. These results prove that the decreasing quality of the MT output had a negative influence on the gaze behaviour for the PE and MPE task. The high standard deviations of the gaze data in all three tasks also show that there were many individual differences and differences in the segments.

All data in Table 10.5 were not in a normal distribution. Therefore, a Mann-Whitney-U test was conducted. Further, the tests were not directed, but the mean

Table 10.5: Tests for significant differences between the tasks according to quality and parameter (statistically significant results are printed in bold)

	Quality of MT output					
	Acceptable		Partly Acceptable		Not Acceptable	
Parameter	U	p	U	p	U	p
PE vs. TfS						
Dur	**1289**	**<0.0001**	**8539**	**<0.0001**	**2359**	**0.0042**
GazeS	**1840**	**0.0027**	**6277**	**<0.0001**	**1791**	**<0.0001**
GazeT	2469	0.6245	10147	0.0547	3283	0.773
FixS	**1954.5**	**0.0109**	**6418.5**	**<0.0001**	**1866**	**<0.0001**
FixT	2622.5	0.9046	10742	0.2507	**3920**	**0.0138**
TFix	2299	0.2425	**8884.5**	**0.0004**	6183	0.9198
TGaze	**2096**	**0.0477**	**8233**	**<0.0001**	**2612**	**0.0456**
MPE vs. PE						
Dur	2381.5	0.1352	11419	0.9014	2792.5	0.0613
TFix	2600	0.5147	**7442.5**	**<0.0001**	**2186**	**0.0001**
TGaze	2910	0.6014	**8792**	**0.0008**	2903	0.1316
MPE vs. TfS						
Dur	**1077**	**<0.0001**	**8717**	**0.0002**	**1861**	**<0.0001**
TFix	2344	0.1044	**5721.5**	**<0.0001**	**1974.5**	**<0.0001**
TGaze	2398	0.156	**6094**	**<0.0001**	**2252**	**0.0012**

values can be verified in Tables Table 10.3 and Table 10.4. When comparing TfS and PE, the results of the tests all proved significance except for *GazeT,* and *FixT* for acceptable and partly acceptable MT output, which confirms the hypothesis for the difference between TfS and PE – except for gaze on the target text. The fixation count on the target text (*FixT*) is significantly higher in PE, which indicates that a lot of effort is required to process syntactically unacceptable MT output. *TFix* was only significantly different for partly acceptable MT output. The parameters were higher for TfS when there was a significant difference, except for *FixT* as mentioned. The MT output was helpful in the PE process and reduced both production time and processing effort. The gaze behaviour on the target text is not statistically different between the two tasks, which was expected, due to the previously discussed special role that the target text plays in the PE task. Surprisingly, *GaseS* and *FixS* are still significantly lower for unacceptable MT output. This could be interpreted again by the fact that the participants do not use the source text in PE to correct syntactic mistakes. They rather use the target text to rearrange the MT output into syntactically correct structures.

Although gaze data are available for source and target text in MPE, those data will not be used for the analysis because they were mapped incorrectly, as mentioned above. However, the parameter *Dur, TFix,* and *TGaze* will be compared for the remaining task. It is expected that no significant difference can be observed when comparing MPE and PE, because they originate from the same MT output, which is confirmed by the data, except for three parameters, namely *TFix* and *TGaze* for partly acceptable quality and *TFix* for not acceptable quality. These parameters are all higher in the PE task, which might be caused by the existing source text. When the syntactic quality is low(er), the participants might refer to the source text more often and hence more and longer fixations are generated.

Finally, we will compare MPE and TfS. It is expected that the difference is significant for acceptable and partly acceptable quality, but not for not acceptable quality. The assumptions is only partly confirmed by the data (see Table 10.5), because the difference in *TGaze* and *TFix* for acceptable MT output is not significant. The difference between *Dur* for MPE with unacceptable MT output and TfS is still significant (significantly higher for TfS). This might indicate that less changes are made in general in MPE and hence the difference is still significant. The fixation counts are still significantly higher for TfS even when the MT output is syntactically not acceptable. The total gaze duration, however, is significantly higher for the MPE task when the MT output is syntactically unacceptable. These two results show that more content needs to be processed in TfS as the target text still needs to be produced (hence, the fixation counts are higher), but the

low quality MT output needs longer to be processed reflected in the high *TGaze*
numbers. The total fixation durations (*TGaze*) and total fixation counts (*TFix*) on
source and target text are lower in MPE and PE than in TfS, when the syntactic
MT output is acceptable or partly acceptable. This implies that the mental effort
is lower in those tasks, when the syntactic MT output is at least partly acceptable. When the MT output, however, is not acceptable, it does not support the
translator, but makes the translation task more difficult.

Finally, a multiple linear regression was calculated to evaluate the influence
of different independent variables (task, status/experience, length of source and/
or target text, and acceptability of the MT output) on the parameters (*Dur, TFix,*
TGaze for all tasks and *FixS, GazeS, FixT,* and *GazeT* for PE and TfS). The different
participants were set as random effects in the models. As the length of the source
(TokS) or the target text (TokT) are included in the model as control variables, the
parameters do not have to be normalised.

First, we will consider the parameter *Dur.* The regression reported that neither
status nor experience have a significant influence on *Dur.* With the help of an
ANOVA, it was tested whether the regression model would be improved if the
variables were added, but both status ($\chi^2(1) = 0.65, p = 0.4191$) and experience
($\chi^2(1) = 1.36, p = 0.2443$) did not show significance. Hence, the model was calculated considering task and qualitative acceptability as fixed effects, length of
source and target text as control variables and participants as random effects.
Task has a significant influence on *Dur,* but this depends on the tasks that are
compared. When TfS is compared with PE ($t = \pm7.37^3, p < 0.0001$) and MPE
($t = \pm9.20, p < 0.0001$), the differences are significant. However, when MPE
and PE are compared, the tasks do not show a significant difference ($t = \pm1.83,$
$p = 0.0683$). The latter result, however, may have become significant if more
data points were available. Those results confirm what was expected from the
previous results: The production duration of the target text is significantly higher
for the TfS task, as the target text has to be produced completely from scratch.
The differences between the MPE and PE tasks are not significant as they start
with the same MT output. Acceptability also has a statistically significant influence. While the difference between acceptable and partly acceptable is significant ($t = \pm0.84, p < 0.0001$) as well as the difference between acceptable and

---

[3]When we have a parameter in a linear mixed model that is not numeric, the regression takes
one factor as a reference. When e.g. TfS is the reference in the parameter task, PE and MPE are
tested on TfS and the results are presented for comparing TfS and PE as well as TfS and MPE.
However, PE and MPE are not compared. Therefore, we can change the reference. When PE
is the reference task, it is compared to MPE, but also again to TfS. The latter yields the same
result as the first test, but with a different algebraic sign for t.

not acceptable sentences ($t = \pm3.69, p = 0.0002$), the difference between partly acceptable and not acceptable sentences is not significant ($t = \pm1.43, p = 0.1518$). This implicates on the one hand that a syntactically flawless MT output does impact the production time significantly. On the other hand, this shows that the production time for sentences with which the MT system had some syntactic problems is not statistically different to those for which the MT Output is not acceptable. Further, the control variables are both significant, too (*TokS* ($t = 2.09$, $p = 0.0371$) and *TokT* ($t = 5.28, p < 0.0001$)), which means that the text production of target text depends on the length of source text and the length of target text, which seems reasonable.

For the next four parameters, we will exclude the MPE task because of the missing source text and the previously mentioned mapping mistakes. First we will look at the gaze on the source text. The model for *FixS* is only influenced by the tasks of the MT output, while quality ($\chi^2(1) = 0.69, p = 0.7086$), status ($\chi^2(1) = 1.58, p = 0.2093$) and experience ($\chi^2(1) = 2.31, p = 0.1283$) do not have an impact. Further, the control variable *TokT* has no additional influence on the model ($\chi^2(1) = 0.85, p = 0.357$), when *TokS* is included, which is to be expected when analysing the fixation on the source text. Fixation counts on the source text are significantly different between PE and TfS ($t = \pm5.11, p < 0.0001$). The source text loses its essence in the PE task because of the target text outline provided by the MT output. The source text is only used as a reference and hence less fixations are necessary. For the same reason, the quality of the MT output has no statistical significant influence on the total fixation duration on the source text either. The control variable *TokS* has a statistical influence on the fixation count ($t = 3.67, p = 0.0003$), which is plausible because the longer the segment, the more fixations are expected.

The influence of status and experience of the participants on the model for *GazeS* is hard to judge. When both parameters are tested via the ANOVA, both seem to add to the model (as a single parameter, not both parameters in the model; status ($\chi^2(1) = 4.11, p = 0.0425$) and experience ($\chi^2(1) = 3.93, p = 0.0473$)), although the p-value is very close to 0.05. However, when they are both integrated into the model, they do not become significant (status ($t = \pm2.04$, $p = 0.0539$), experience ($t = \pm2.00, p = 0.0582$) – when the task is part of the model). It is not possible to finalise the observation whether or not the gaze duration on the source text is dependent on the status/experience of the participant. More participants or data may have produced a more obvious result and the assumption has to be re-tested in another experiment. However, the data point towards a potential statistically significant influence, which could not be observed for fixations on the source text. The difference between PE and TfS is again significant ($t = \pm5.98$, $p < 0.0001$). Similarly as for *FixS*, the model is not influenced by the syntactic quality ($\chi^2(1) = 1.74$, $p = 0.4183$), which indicates, as above, that improving the syntactic flaws has no impact on the gaze duration on the source text and that the source text is probably not required to repair syntax in the MT output. The control variable *TokS* is again statistically significant ($t = 5.65$, $p < 0.0001$) in the model for the same reasons as mentioned for *FixS*.

Finally, the gaze data on the target text will be analysed. Fixation counts on the target texts (*FixT*) are only influenced by the control variable *TokT* ($t = 5.87$, $p < 0.0001$), the other parameters do not add to the model (quality ($\chi^2(1) = 0.89$, $p = 0.6417$), task ($\chi^2(1) = 0.17$, $p = 0.4686$), status ($\chi^2(1) = 0.23$, $p = 0.6338$), and experience ($\chi^2(1) = 0.12$, $p = 0.7283$)). Interestingly, the task is not important for the model. However, this is in line with the former results we found for gaze data on the target text. There is no significant difference between TfS and PE as the MT output is more important than the source text in the PE task. Again, the quality of the MT output does not play a significant role. Finally, we will exclude *TokS* as a control variable, as we focus on fixation counts on the target text and *TokS* does not add to the model ($\chi^2(1) = 0.23$, $p = 0.6345$) when *TokT* is already included.

We find very similar results for *GazeT*: Only the control variable *TokT* influences ($t = 6.88$, $p < 0.0001$) the model (ANOVA results for the non-influencing data: task ($\chi^2(1) = 2.58$, $p = 0.1085$), quality ($\chi^2(1) = 3.15$, $p = 0.2074$), status ($\chi^2(1) = 1.13$, $p = 0.2888$), and experience ($\chi^2(1) = 1.33$, $p = 0.2494$)) and we exclude the length of the source text as this would not add to the model ($\chi^2(1) = 0.12$, $p = 0.726$) when *TokT* is already taken into consideration.

Starting with TFix, we will now analyse the influence of the variables on fixation counts and fixation duration on the whole text, for which MPE is again taken into consideration. Again, status and experience do not enhance the model (the models were tested again with an ANOVA with the following results: status ($\chi^2(1) = 0.00$, $p = 0.9732$) and experience ($\chi^2(1) = 0.32$, $p = 0.5702$)). The difference between the fixation count is significant when comparing all three tasks with each other (TfS vs. PE ($t = \pm2.04$, $p = 0.0418$), PE vs. MPE ($t = \pm2.73$, $p = 0.0065$) and TfS vs. MPE ($t = \pm4.76$, $p < 0.0001$)) with the highest mean value for TfS, followed by PE, and the lowest for MPE (see Table 10.1). This indicates that the most information needs to be processed in TfS in comparison to PE and MPE, which is again very plausible. The source text needs to be processed thoroughly in the TfS task, can be referenced in the PE task and is not available in the MPE task. The fixation counts are again not significantly influenced by the syntactic quality of the MT output ($\chi^2(1) = 0.50$, $p = 0.7807$). Intriguingly, the length of the source text or the target text significantly add to the model, but not when both factors are included in the model. Hence, it was decided to include TokT in the model as the length of the target text seems to be (slightly) more influential when added to the model ($t = 4.36^4$, $p < 0.0001$) and exclude TokS (value for adding TokS when TokT is already included: $\chi^2(1) = 0.03$, $p = 0.8524$).

The results for *TGaze* are very similar to those of *TFix*. The status of the participants does not add to the model ($\chi^2(1) = 1.69$, $p = 0.1934$), and neither does the experience coefficient according to the ANOVA test ($\chi^2(1) = 3.89$, $p = 0.0486$). The quality categorisation of the MT output of the sentences does not add to the model ($\chi^2(1) = 3.19$, $p = 0.2024$). The tasks differ significantly when comparing TfS and PE ($t = \pm3.68$, $p = 0.0002$) as well as TfS and MPE ($t = \pm4.46$, $p < 0.0001$). Between MPE and PE, however, there is no significant difference ($t = \pm0.77$, $p = 0.4446$). This result is not as obvious as it may seem at first glance: While a new text needs to be produced in TfS (which makes the total gaze data significantly higher), the MPE and PE texts rely on the same MT output. On the other hand, the source text is missing in the MPE task, which could lead to a significantly shorter gaze duration on the whole text. As was already mentioned above, the fixations are on average longer in the MPE task than in the PE task (see Table 10.1), which reflects the fact that there is less to process in MPE as there is only a target text. However the target text is harder to process, because of the missing source text, which prolongs the fixations. The control variable *TokT* will again be used to enhance the model ($t = 4.24$, $p < 0.0001$) as it is slightly more influential than *TokS*, but adding the latter to the model does not enhance it ($\chi^2(1) = 0.01$, $p = 0.9134$).

In summary, the syntactic quality of the MT output only has a significant impact on the production times of the sentences, but not on the eyetracking data. This might indicate that syntactic mistakes in the MT output do not cause an increased mental effort when participants are confronted with these mistakes. Hence, I conclude that the MT output does not create new problems. The correction of flaws in the syntax of the MT output can be considered a task rather than a problem. No hurdle between the source and target text is created. The participants may have to restructure the sentence, but as they can easily assess what the target syntax should look like, this is only a task. The different tasks, however, influence the models, except for gaze behaviour on the source text, which is not statistically different between PE and TfS. This emphasises the importance of the target text again. Although the MT output already created a target text template, this template needs to be processed thoroughly by the translator.

---

[4]For *TokS*, t would have been 5.04.

Interestingly, neither the status of the participant nor their experience coefficient had any significant influence on the parameters. This might have different reasons. Either the participants do not have enough experience in PE and MPE, or syntax is generally not a factor that is influenced by translation competence but rather by language competence and hence does not trigger higher processing data. Remember that not even the production time (*Dur*) was influenced by status/experience of the participants in the linear mixed models. Another reason might be that neither status nor the experience vector are diverse enough to reveal the differences between single participants with different translation competences. Finally, as was argued before, the text type and the contents are not very close to real life professional translations (the texts are not very domain specific) and hence might blur the differences between the participants.

As was mentioned before, not only the syntax of the MT output influences the quality of the MT output, but many other factors have an impact, too. Therefore, I will contrast two sentences in the next chapter, in which the syntactic quality is the most relevant factor in the MT output.

10.2.2 Syntactic analysis on the sentence level excluding non-syntactic factors

As was pointed out earlier, the keylogging and eyetracking parameters are potentially not only influenced by the quality of the syntax produced by the MT system, but also by other factors. Hence, we will compare single sentences that are syntactically correct or incorrect, but are flawless in all other aspects in this chapter. Therefore, we will compare the first sentence of Text 4 and Text 5 (both texts do not have a headline). The MT output of sentence one in Text 4 is syntactically not acceptable, but there are no additional problems in the sentence:

ST: Although developing countries are understandably reluctant to compromise their chances of achieving better standards of living for the poor, action on climate change need not threaten economic development.

MT output: Zwar sind die Entwicklungsländer sind verständlicherweise zurückhaltend, ihre Chancen auf Verbesserung des Lebensstandards für die Armen, Maßnahmen gegen den Klimawandel muss nicht bedrohen die wirtschaftlichen Entwicklung gefährden.

Back Translation: Although are the developing countries are understandably reluctant, their chances of improving the standards of living for the poor, actions against the climate change need not threaten the economic development endanger.

The main syntactic issue in this sentence is again verb positioning. The doubling of *sind* in the first part is not acceptable, and the positioning in the last two parts is incorrect as well. A possible correction of the MT output could look like the following, when as much of the MT output as possible is used:

Improved MT output: Zwar sind die Entwicklungsländer sind verständlicherweise zurückhaltend, ihre Chancen auf Verbesserung des Lebensstandards für die Armen *zu gefährden, jedoch müssen* Maßnahmen gegen den Klimawandel die wirtschaftliche Entwicklung *nicht bedrohen.*

Back Translation: Although are the developing countries understandably reluctant, their chances of improving the standards of living for the poor to endanger, but need actions against the climate change the economic development not threaten.

In comparison, the MT output of sentence one, Text 5 is syntactically unproblematic as well as in other aspects:

ST: Sociology is a relatively new academic discipline.

MT output: Die Soziologie ist eine relativ neue wissenschaftliche Disziplin.

As was already mentioned at the beginning of §10, the text corpus in this study only contains 41 sentences. Hence, the selection of MT output sentences that are syntactically correct or not correct and are additionally not influenced by any other factor is very small. Otherwise, two sentences would have been chosen that were more comparable in terms of length. However, the length of the source and target sentence are again included as control variables in the calculations. The parameters are again tested in a linear mixed models for all participants. An individual identifier called *SegU* was created for all texts and sentences. It is composed of the text number and the segment number based on the source text segmentation. Hence, sentence one of text four is SegU = 41 or sentence one of text five is SegU = 51. Consequently, the following analyses only deal with SegU = 41&51. As the sentences differ greatly in length, the length of the source and target text are again considered as control variables. The results shall help us understand whether syntactic quality of the MT output has an impact on the gaze behaviour after all, when all other mistakes in the MT output that could influence the PE effort are excluded. This would contradict the results of the previous chapter. Further, the effect on the production time (Dur) should be confirmed by the results.

Table 10.6: Results of ANOVA tests adding to the model excluding MPE for gaze data on source and target text (statistically significant results are printed in bold)

Parameter	SegU $\chi^2(1)$	p	Task $\chi^2(1)$	p	Status $\chi^2(1)$	p	Exp $\chi^2(1)$	p	TokS $\chi^2(1)$	p	TokT $\chi^2(1)$	p
Dur	44.61	<0.0001	13.51	0.0012	2.66	0.1032	0.67	0.4139	0	1	0.26	0.6128
FixS	1.02	0.3134	6.63	0.0100	0.05	0.8295	0.07	0.4029	1.02	0.3134	0.96	0.3283
GazeS	0.93	0.3341	7.57	0.0059	0.07	0.7863	0.95	0.3296	0.93	0.3341	0.86	0.3536
FixT	0.88	0.348	0.45	0.5031	0.03	0.8701	0.92	0.338	0	1	0.01	0.9105
GazeT	5.07	0.0243	3.42	0.0641	0.12	0.7315	0.92	0.338	0	1	0.13	0.7229
TFix	9.05	0.0026	11.13	0.0038	0	0.9908	0.82	0.3647	0	1	0.61	0.4333
TGaze	11.75	0.0006	11.47	0.0032	0.19	0.6634	0.66	0.4168	0	1	0.26	0.6113

Table 10.6 presents the results of the ANOVA tests that focus on the factors influencing the regression model significantly. As we can see in Table 10.6, none of the parameters are influenced by status or experience, which is in line with the previous results. However, neither the length of the source nor the length of the target text is determining for the two sentences. Further, *Dur*, *TFix*, and *TGaze* are the only parameters that are influenced by the segments and the task according to Table 10.6. *Dur* shows a significant difference between the segments ($t = -8.85$, $p < 0.0001$) and further varies significantly between PE and TfS ($t = \pm3.30$, $p = 0.0021$) as well as MPE and TfS ($t = \pm3.52$, $p = 0.0012$), but there is no significant difference between MPE and PE ($t = \pm0.17$, $p = 0.8681$). The mean values show that the production duration is much higher for TfS (mean: 150531.0s[5], sd: 153984.48s) than for PE (mean: 77874.33s, sd: 82589.05s) and MPE (mean: 63186.80s, sd: 77378.49s). Additionally, the mean values reveal the huge differences between the segments (low syntactic quality sentence from Text 4 – mean: 183225.78s, sd: 109143.16s; high syntactic quality sentence from Text 5 – mean: 13487.83s, sd: 21311.16s, which is of course also influenced by the length of the sentences, therefore the mean values are normalised in Table 10.6), which are even more obvious when Task and SegU are separated (see Table 10.7). While there is only very little production effort in MPE and PE in segment 51, the production effort for both tasks is much higher in segment 41. The differences between MPE and PE, however, are small in segment 41, which demonstrates that

---

[5]The mean and sd values are not normalised by character in this chapter if not explicitly mentioned as they only underpin the statistic tests and are not part of the analysis themselves.

the source text is not necessarily vital to correct syntactic errors in the MT out-put. Further, as the statistically significant differences between PE/MPE and TfS show in segment 41, even numerous syntactic mistranslations in the MT output do not prolong the overall production times, meaning that (monolingually) post-editing the MT output was still time saving compared to the TfS task.

Table 10.7: Dur per character on segment 41 and 51 separated by task

	MPE		PE		TfS	
SegU	Mean	SD	Mean	SD	Mean	SD
41	655.42	262.14	701.48	266.02	1294.66	691.70
51	18.18	21.95	50.55	104.02	713.14	464.91

Although the segment was predicted to influence the model for *GazeT*, the parameters did not become statistically significant, when the model was created ($t = \pm2.11$, $p = 0.0510$). Hence, we have a total of two parameters (*FixT* and *GazeT*) that are not influenced by any of the predictors and control variables, which means that they are, amongst other things, not statistically dependent on the quality of the MT output. Conclusively, the gaze behaviour on the target text is alike no matter what was the task, the syntactic quality of the MT output, the length of the target text, and the status/experience of the participants. Similarly, FixS ($t = \pm3.01$, $p = 0.0108$) and GazeS ($t = \pm3.29$, $p = 0.0055$) differ only significantly in the tasks[6], which can be explained by the fact that PE requires much less focus on the source text which influences the gaze behaviour, but they are not influenced by the quality of the MT output.

The total fixation count ($t = \pm19.91$, $p = 0.0054$) as well as the total gaze du-ration ($t = \pm19.88$, $p = 0.0015$) on both source and target text are influenced by the syntactic quality of the segments. Furthermore, both parameters are statisti-cally different when comparing TfS and PE (*TFix*: $t = \pm2.49$, $p = 0.0211$, *TGaze*: $t = \pm3.03$, $p = 0.0060$) and TfS and MPE (*TFix*: $t = \pm3.29$, $p = 0.0035$, *TGaze*: $t = \pm2.93$, $p = 0.0077$), but not when comparing PE and MPE (*TFixT*: $t = \pm0.54$, $p = 0.5972$, *TGaze*: $t = \pm0.28$, $p = 0.7841$), which could be expected on the one hand because of the similarity of the two tasks, but on the other hand the source text is missing in the MPE task.

All in all, the detachment of the two segments only proved that the syntactic quality of the MT output has an influence on production time and on the overall

---

[6]Difference between PE and TfS, MPE is excluded again.

eyetracking data considering both source and target text, but not on the eyetracking data divided by source and target text for PE and TfS. Therefore, the result of the analysis in §10.2.1 is confirmed regarding the production time (*Dur*), which is influenced by the syntactic quality, and regarding the gaze data on the source (*FixS* and *GazeS*) and target text (*FixT* and *GazeT*), which are not impacted by the syntactic MT quality. Counting and measuring gaze on both texts resulted in significant differences, which is unexpected. These differences could either indicate an influence of the syntactic quality or that the two sentences were not comparable enough and hence further studies are necessary.

10.3 Summary

This chapter analyses the influence of the syntactic quality of the MT output on production and processing data. The analysis was performed on a sentence level and the quality was categorised as acceptable, partly acceptable, and not acceptable. As was expected, the tasks have a significant influence on most production and processing parameters as was proven by the Mann-Whitney-U-tests and reinforced by the linear mixed models. The data are significantly higher for TfS than for PE, except for the gaze data on the target text. Similarly, the data are significantly higher for TfS than for MPE, except for the total gaze duration in sentences that produced syntactically unacceptable MT for which the opposite applies. The difference between PE and MPE is not significant concerning the production times and the total fixation duration, but is significant for *TFix*. Table 10.8 summarizes the results of the regression models, exploring which predictors influenced the model and which did not. For all models, the individual participants were used as random effects on the model and the length of the source and target text as control variables.

Surprisingly, the status and the experience of the participants had no influence on the linear regression models. Reasons might be (as mentioned in §10.2.1) that most participants are not experienced in the PE ad MPE task, that status and the experience vector are not diverse enough to represent the professionalism of the participants, that syntax is not a characteristic of a text that requires special translation skills or that the text types are potentially not realistic translation jobs.

As the analysis has shown, it is difficult to predict the influence of only the syntactic quality on gaze behaviour, because too many other MT defects can occur in a sentence that are not syntax related but influence the gaze data, too. The regression models for the overall data set do not yield an influence of the syntactic

Table 10.8: Summary of the influential predictors in the linear mixed models (✓: statistically significant, ✗: not statistically significant)

	Tasks			Quality				
	MPE vs. PE	MPE vs. TfS	PE vs. TfS	a vs. p	p vs. n	a vs. n	TokS	TokT
Dur	✗	✓	✓	✓	✗	✓	✓	✓
FixS	–	–	✓	✗	✗	✗	✓	✗
GazeS	–	–	✓	✗	✗	✗	✓	✗
FixT	–	–	✗	✗	✗	✗	✗	✓
GazeT	–	–	✗	✗	✗	✗	✗	✓
TFix	✓	✓	✓	✗	✗	✗	✗	✓
TGaze	✗	✓	✓	✗	✗	✗	✗	✓

MT output quality on the gaze values, which was affirmed by the direct comparison of one sentence with syntactically defective MT output and one flawless sentence in §10.2.2, which proved that the syntactic quality influences processing time but not gaze behaviour directly. The reason for this might be that error prone syntax in the MT output does not cause new problems for the translator when (s)he has to (monolingually) post-edit a text. Although these errors need correction and therefore increase the editing effort, which was shown by the increasing production times (*Dur*), they do not cause problems in the sense defined in Chapter 5, namely that no new hurdle is created between the source and the target text. Correcting the syntax of MT output can therefore be categorised as a task solving instead of a problem solving activity.

Curiously, the length of the target text as a control variable is often a better predictor than the length of the source text, except (obviously) when we look at the gaze data on the source text. For the two parameters that dealt with the gaze data on the whole text, *TokT* might be a better predictor because German translations tend to be longer than the English source texts and hence require longer production times and more processing. Further, both text lengths were only essential for *Dur*. When the single segments were compared in §10.2.2, neither the length of the source nor the target text influenced the parameter, which is on the one hand reasonable as there is not much overall variety; on the other hand, the two sentences vary drastically in length.

The first null hypothesis suggested at the beginning of this chapter cannot be rejected in most cases because the syntactic quality of the MT output only influences production times. Hence, the first hypothesis is only true for production times, which are influenced by the quality of the syntactic MT output, but not for gaze behaviour. However, as the status/experience of the participants does not have a significant impact on production and processing data, the second null hypothesis cannot be rejected. The second hypothesis could not be proved. In short, syntactic corrections in PE sessions are not categorised as problem solving but as part of a task, which is not dependent on the experience of the translator.

11 Hidden problem indicators

Chapter §9 and §10 presented examples of explicit problem indicators, i.e. research behaviour and the quality of the syntactic MT output. In this chapter, I want to explore further parameters that are included in the TPR-DB which can be used as indicators for problems, and which are not as obviously identifiable as problem indicators, such as research instances and the syntactic quality of the MT output. The aim is to find predictors for problems without consulting screen recording or using think-aloud protocols in the experiments, but to identify problems from mere keylogging data. First, I will look at additional parameters that might reveal problem solving activity. Or in other words, parameters that help identify problematic source text units taking into account the entire data set as well as single Part-of-Speech (PoS) classes as it can be assumed that the values for the parameters vary a lot between individual PoS classes. Then, those parameters will be matched to the production times and gaze behaviour of the participants. Finally, I will check how the results of those parameters behave for the most researched words. Version 2.310 of the database will be used as this newer version includes more parameters than the previous versions due to the fact that the range of available, automatically calculated parameters is sometimes expanded with updates to the database.

11.1 Discussion of problem identifying parameters

The TPR-DB offers many keylogging and eyetracking parameters that are automatically calculated from the raw keylogging and eyetracking data. I already used parameters concerning production times and gaze data, such as *Dur*, *GazeS* or *GazeT*, in previous chapters to analyse keylogging and eyetracking behaviour. In this chapter, I now want to focus on additional parameters that potentially help identify problematic source text units because they mirror the behaviour of the participants. These parameters are further analysed as to whether they are statistically influenced by the tasks, the status and the experience of the participants. The analysis will be conducted on a word level, referring to the source text word.

The first parameter that might be promising for problem identification is *Munit*, which states how many micro units were necessary to produce the source text unit, i.e. how often a participant worked on the unit (cf. Carl, Schaeffer & Bangalore 2016: 51). It provides no indication whatsoever of how many characters were changed/edited, or when the participant worked on the target text unit. A value of 1 would imply in TfS that the unit was produced and not changed in the remaining session; a value of 3 on the other hand represents that the unit was produced and changed twice during the session. A value of 0 is only possible in TfS if the source text unit was not produced in the target text. However, a value of 0 is common in PE and MPE, because this means that the MT output was accepted and left unedited. Hence, *Munit* is usually higher than 1 in TfS, but this is not necessarily always the case. This is also reflected in the high standard deviation of the values: TfS – mean: 1.12, sd: 0.68; PE – mean: 0.55, sd: 0.70; MPE – mean: 0.45, sd: 0.67. This shows that once the translation was produced, less changes were made to the translation draft than to the MT output in the PE and MPE tasks. An analysis for a linear mixed model (only including the tasks conducted as well as the status and experience of the participants) shows that *Munit* is influenced by the task and the difference is significant between all three tasks (TfS and PE: $t = \pm47.01$, $p < 0.0001$, TfS and MPE: $t = \pm55.28$, $p < 0.0001$, PE and MPE: $t = \pm7.87$, $p < 0.0001$). The status of the participant does not add to the model as was tested with an ANOVA ($\chi^2(1) = 0.57$, $p = 0.4508$) and neither does the experience ($\chi^2(1) = 1.74$, $p = 0.1865$). In this and the following analysis, the individual participants and the different texts are set as random effects in the calculation.

Next, I will concentrate on the parameter *InEff*, which "measures the ratio of the number of produced characters divided by the length of the final translation" (Carl, Schaeffer & Bangalore 2016: 26). A value of 1 is added to the token length of the final translation to cover the space that usually follows a word. However, sometimes a word is not followed by a space, e.g. at the end of a sentence or when the word is followed by a comma. Nonetheless, the extra value for the space is added automatically to the length of the final translation. Hence, the *InEff* value can become lower than 1 for a word (cf. ibid.). P05, e.g., edited the MT output *schwer* for the source word *hard* to *schwierig*. According to the recordings, (s)he did not delete any letters, but inserted the letter *i* and the syllable *ig*. Three letters were added, the final word has nine letters plus one space, which equals $\frac{3}{10} = 0.3$ for the *InEff* value. When a word was not edited in PE and MPE, it receives a value of 0. Usually, one would expect a value of at least around 1 for all words that were produced in TfS. However, some words also received an *InEff* value of 0 because they were not realised as single words in the target text. P06, e.g., realised the phrase *tend to have* with the German *tendenziell*; all final editing effort for this word was mapped on the source word *have*, which received an *InEff* value of 1.83, while *tend* and *to* received a value of 0. In contrast to *Munit*, *InEff* reflects how many characters were edited, but neither whether those edits were made during target text production or in the editing/reviewing phase nor how often the participant went back to the unit and changed/edited it. The mean values (0.76, sd: 2.67 for all tasks) of *InEff* are again higher for TfS (1.15, sd: 2.97) compared to PE (0.61, sd: 2.15) and MPE (0.50, sd: 2.78), because the target text first needs to be created in TfS. Again, the parameter is influenced by the task in a linear mixed model, but the differences are only significant between TfS and PE ($t = \pm11.65$, $p < 0.0001$) as well as TfS and MPE ($t = \pm7.19$, $p < 0.0001$), and between PE and MPE ($t = \pm13.95$, $p = 0.0277$). Again, the parameter neither statistically differs between students and professionals ($\chi^2(1) = 1.22$, $p = 0.2687$), nor does the experience vector have an influence ($\chi^2(1) = 0.15$, $p = 0.6993$).

Two more values that will be considered in the following analysis are *HTra* and *HCross*. Both parameters refer to the concept of *entropy* – a term coined by Claude E. Shannon for information entropy, which describes the uncertainty of the content of a message. The higher the value, the more uncertain is the information in a message. In translation, a high entropy value "represents a set of co-activated translation possibilities that are equally good choices for the translation of a source text item" (Bangalore et al. 2016: 213). The more variance between the individual translations, the higher the entropy value becomes. However, entropy not only represents the amount of different translation possibilities, but also weights them according to their frequency. "[I]t captures the distribution of probabilities for each translation option, so that more likely choices and less likely choices are weighted accordingly." (ibid.: 214; see also for more information on calculating entropy values) The first parameter (*HTra*) provided information about the word translation entropy of a source text unit (mean: 1.70, sd: 1.15). Entropy expresses how many different word translations were used within the data set considering how probable one translation choice is, i.e. it "is the sum over all observed word translation probabilities (i.e. expectations) of a given ST word [...] into TT words [...] multiplied with their information content." (ibid.: 31) The higher *HTra*, the higher the word entropy, and the more translation variety can be found in the data set for the particular source word. The second parameter (*HCross*) expresses the entropy of the word order (mean: 1.47, sd: 0.94). If it is 0, all participants chose the same word position for the word in the target text (cf. Carl, Aizawa, et al. 2016). As the two parameters are not calculated independently of the task and the participants – one value per word was calculated for the whole data set – they will not be analysed statistically themselves in a linear mixed model.

11.2 Problematic part-of-speech categories

In the following chapters, the parameters will be analysed according to PoS class to identify if certain PoS classes cause more effort than others. Punctuation marks were excluded from the analysis because they are not interesting for the research. In §11.3, the parameters and PoS classes will then be related to production times and eyetracking data.

11.2.1 Indications in *Munit*

This chapter will analyse the first indicators of problematic word classes according to their mean values of the parameters introduced in §11.1 (*Munit, InEff, HTra,* and *HCross*). An explanation of all part-of-speech abbreviations and an overview about all mean and sd values can be found in Appendix D, Tables D.1 and D.7.

First, I will consider *Munit*, which indicates how often a word was visited during one session. As can be seen in Figure 11.1 (the concrete numbers can be found in Table D.7 in Appendix D), the parameter is the highest in TfS for all PoS classes. This is expected because, in contrast to the PE tasks, the target text first has to be produced. Hence, *Munit* is usually higher than 1 and for this reason Figure 11.2 shows the same data but with *Munit* −1 for TfS to present the mere editing effort.

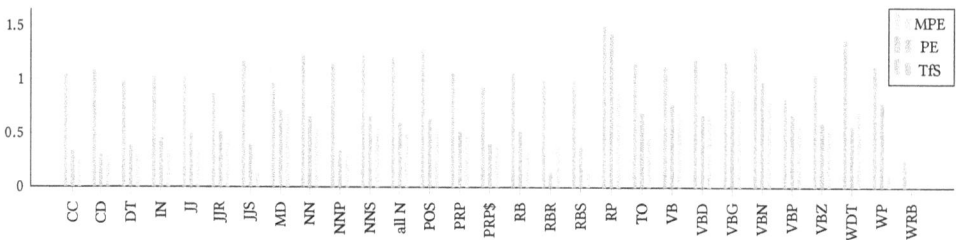

Figure 11.1: *Munit* according to PoS class and task

Figure 11.2 provides a very different impression than Figure 11.1. Here, *Munit* is the highest for PE in most cases, except for RBR and WDT, for which *Munit* is higher in MPE. However, as both word classes occured less than five times in all texts, this can be considered an exception[1]. The MT system translated the superlative *the most vulnerable (countries)* with *am meisten gefährdeten (Länder)* (literal translation: *the most endangered (countries)*), which can be considered a lexical mistranslation rather than a problematic translation of the grammatical form. In other words, the problem is not the PoS class itself, but the lexical item. Further, some PoS categories become negative for TfS when one is subtracted from the initial value, which indicates that some words or phrases were not realised as such in the target text, e.g. comparative adjectives (JJR). P03, for example, translated the phrase *[...] can support population densities 60 to 100 times greater than [...]* as *kann die 60- bis 100-fache Bevölkerungsdichte ermöglichen* (literal translation: *can the 60 to 100 times population density enable*). The comparison that needs the comparative adjective (JJR) in this sentence is paraphrased and hence a comparative adjective is not necessary in the target text any more.

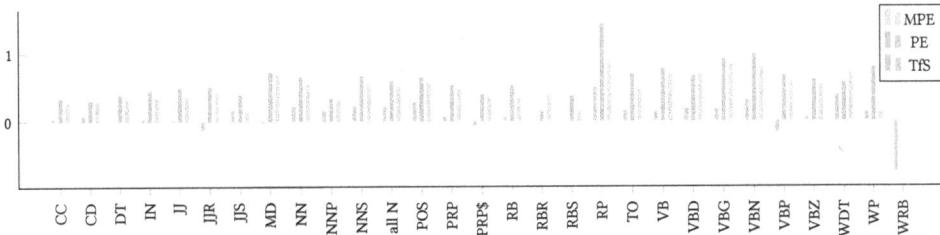

Figure 11.2: Munit −1 for TfS according to PoS class and task

Conclusively, I can see that more changes are made in the PE and MPE task when I compare Figure 11.1 and Figure 11.2. If I assume that the first translation can also be considered as the first draft that is improved in the revision phase, this first translation draft is much more reliable than the MT output, as far fewer changes are made in the TfS task. This is one additional argument why PE cannot simply be compared to reviewing or proof-reading tasks as it requires many more changes.

When I look at the results in Figure 11.2, *Munit* is the highest for particles (PR) in all three tasks. This PoS class, however, only occurred once in Text 2 and is furthermore a part of a verb construction (*to cough up*). Hence, I cannot conclude that this word class is especially hard to process without any further testing. The

---

[1]Table D.1 in Appendix D presents how often which PoS class occurred in the total data set (counting each participant) and how often they occurred in which source text. The categories JJR, JJS, POS, RBR, RBS, RP, WDT, WP, and WRB occurred less than five times. For this reason, some of them will be summarised or grouped with another category in the upcoming chapters.

Munit value is very similar for all other word categories in TfS ranging between −0.17 and 0.38, except for the *wh*-adverbs (WRB), which have a negative value of −0.75, but also only occurred once in Text 5. Another eye-catching result in the TfS data is the negative value for VBP (non-3. person singular present verbs). When looking into the data, the reason for this seems to be primarily that this PoS class was sometimes realised simultaneously with other classes and, therefore, the production and editing effort was mapped on the other involved PoS classes. In contrast to the TfS task, striking differences are visible between PE and MPE. These refer to modal words (MD), nouns (NN and NNS) with the exception of proper nouns (NNP), verbs (VB, VBG, VBN, VBP, VBZ), the preposition *to*, which is in most cases part of a verb construction, too, and finally *wh*-determiners and -pronouns. The latter two categories can be disregarded in this analysis as well because they occur only once in Text 2 and in Text 5. Therefore, a larger data set would be necessary to confirm those impressions.

It was tested whether the tasks influence the outcome of *Munit*. Further, it was tested whether status and/or experience of the participants contribute to the model, i.e. if they also statistically influence the parameter. The ANOVA test did not suggest that status and/or experience add to the model. If only status or experience add to the model, the values of the regression are indicated for the respective parameter. If both potentially add to the model, but only separately and not when they are both integrated in the model, the one that contributes the most is chosen. Finally, the individual participants and the single texts were set as random effects. The analysis was not possible for five PoS categories (RBR, RBS, RP, WDT, WRB) because there were not enough data points to be analysed. When the *Munit* value was chosen for which the production of the word is not included (*Munit–1*), *Munit* was always significantly higher for PE than for TfS, except for superlative adjectives (JJS). Similarly, the parameter was always higher for MPE than for TfS, except for superlative adjectives (JJS) and for possessive endings (POS). These exceptions might be caused by the few occurrences in the texts or by insufficient quality of the MT output. Further, the difference is significant between PE and MPE for prepositions and subordinate conjunctions (IN), adjectives (JJ), singular or mass nouns (NN), plural nouns (NNS), adverbs (RB), the preposition *to* (TO) and past participle verbs (VBN). These PoS classes were modified more often in PE than in MPE. The reasons can either be that the necessary changes were not detectable without the source text or that they were overedited in the PE task. It is hard to explain why the latter would happen in PE. One would expect this phenomenon in MPE as the participants might feel insecure about the meaning of the translation unit and hence edit it more often.

On the other hand, it is conceivable that the participants improve MT units that would not necessarily need editing because they know the source text and hence are not satisfied with an acceptable target text unit, but rather choose a better translation equivalent.

Conclusively, the PoS categories that show statistically different values for *Munit* might indicate problematic MT output that requires changes, but these changes may not be that clearly related to the individual PoS. For the categories IN (preposition / subordinate conjunction) and TO (*to*), it is also possible that they themselves are not that problematic, but that they introduce problematic text units and hence, must be changed as part of the overall translation unit. The status of the participants has a significant influence only on adjectives (JJ) and singular proper nouns (NNP),[2] the experience coefficient has no statistically significant impact.

The tests were also conducted for the initial *Munit* value, i.e. the parameter originally found in the table, where the production of the translation in TfS is still reflected in the value (remember that I subtracted a value of 1 from *Munit* to exclude the different approaches to the task) to verify that no patterns are missed. As was expected, the values were all statistically significant when comparing TfS and PE as well as TfS and MPE, even for superlative adjectives (JJS). The only exception is the value for *wh*-pronouns (WP), where there is no statistical significant difference between TfS and PE. The difference is that *Munit* is statistically higher for TfS in these analyses, while it was statistically smaller in the initial test. As the *Munit* values for PE and MPE are not changed, the results of the statistical tests obviously do not change, either. Further, the status of the participants again has a significant influence on adjectives (JJ) and singular proper nouns (NNP). It is not surprising that the status of the participant is such a negligible indicator in the linear regression models for the single PoS categories and that the experience vector has none at all. Especially when I consider that for the overall data, the experience vector had no significant influence as well as the status of the participant. This might point in the direction that not enough data have been gathered in this experiment to distinguish the influence of status or the experience of the participants. Another reason might be that this influence simply cannot be measured on a word class level.

In summary, the *Munit* value is influenced by the different tasks, but usually not by the characteristics of the participants' level of professionalism. While no particular PoS class of those I could analyse seems to increase the *Munit* value in the TfS task, the participants had to change the MT output more often for modal words, nouns and verbs than for other PoS classes.

---

[2]Plural proper nouns did not occur in the data set.

11.2.2 Indications in *InEff*

The parameter *InEff* is also influenced by the task because a target text has to first be produced in TfS, while there is already the MT output in PE and MPE. Therefore, similarly as for *Munit*, I will take the raw values for *InEff* into account (Figure 11.3) and will then again subtract the value 1 for TfS (Figure 11.4).

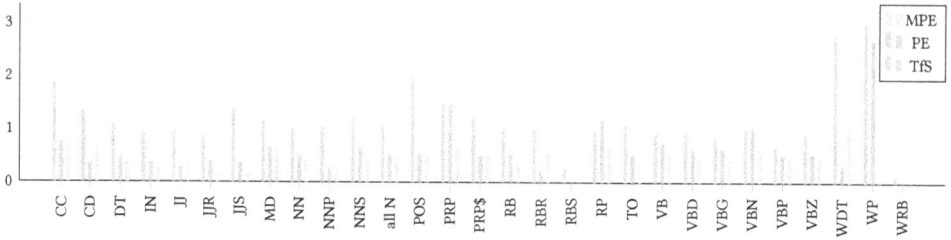

Figure 11.3: *InEff* for TfS according to PoS class and task

The values in Figure 11.3 are usually the highest for TfS, as was expected. However, the values are very similar between TfS and PE or even higher in PE for personal pronouns (PRP), particles (RP), some verb categories (VBG, VBN, and VBP), and *wh*-pronouns (WP). However, the occurrences of RPs and WPs is very low and can therefore be disregarded as more data would be necessary to make reasonable assumptions.

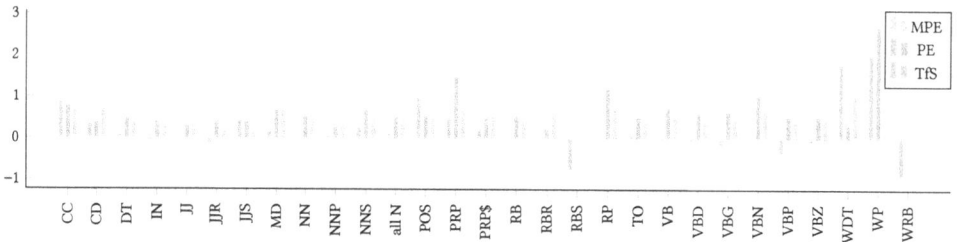

Figure 11.4: *InEff* −1 for TfS according to PoS class and task

As I can see in Figure 11.4, some *InEff* values drop below 0 when the initial production value of 1 is subtracted in TfS. This may indicate two things: First, it is possible that the PoS categories are sometimes not realised in the target text. Second, it indicates that for those PoS categories, most translators decided to retain their initial idea of the target word. If I assume that an *InEff* −1 value higher than 0.2^3 expresses high production effort, this applies to only nine PoS

---

[3] Assuming that this would represent a correction of one letter (one deletion activity and one extra insertion activity) in a ten-letter word: $\frac{12}{10} - 1 = 0.2$.

categories (CC, CD, JJS, NNS, POS, PRP, PRP$, WDT, WP). Further, the *InEff –1* value is still the highest for TfS in coordinating conjunctions (CC), superlative adjectives (JJS), possessive endings (POS), and *wh*-determiners (WDT).

The figures also show that the *InEff* values are usually very close between PE and MPE with some exceptions (CD, JJR, JJS, NNS, PRP, RBR, RP, VB, VBD, VBG, VBN, WDT, and WP), which are then usually higher for PE, except for CD, RBR, and WDT – the latter two, however, occur seldom in the data. When the values are higher for PE, however, this might indicate that the MT output contained mistakes that could not be corrected without the help of the source text.

In the following, I will again test whether the task as well as the status and/or experience of the participants has a significant influence on the parameter *InEff* with linear mixed models. As was done for *Munit*, the individual participants and the texts are taken as random effects. A dash "–" again marks when there was no significant result, or the ANOVA test did not suggest that status and/or experience add to the model. In this analysis, I will examine both result tables, one for the regular *InEff* value and one for *InEff –1* because Figure 11.3 and Figure 11.4 suggest that the the differences between TfS and PE/MPE are not that obviously influenced by the task as for *Munit*. With some exceptions, most data show statistically significant results when comparing TfS with PE and MPE. As can be seen in Table D.7 in Appendix D, no significant differences can be found at all for possessive markers (POS), personal pronouns (PRP), and non-3. person singular present verbs (VBP) for *InEff*. Furthermore, the difference is not significant for base form verbs (VB), past participle verbs (VBN), and *wh*-pronouns (WP) when comparing TfS and PE, nor for cardinal numbers (CD) when comparing TfS and MPE. When the differences are significant, they are significantly higher for TfS with the exception of particles (RP), which, as mentioned above, only occurred once in one text and hence no reasonable conclusions can be drawn from this. The difference between PE and MPE data is only significant for plural nouns (NNS), base form verbs (VB), and gerund verbs (VBG), which are all higher for PE.

The differences between PE and MPE obviously do not change when I subtract 1 from the *InEff* value for TfS. Although most differences are still significant, but then statistically higher in PE and/or MPE, some changes become visible when comparing TfS and PE/MPE. The tests show no significant difference at all for coordinating conjunctions (CC), cardinal numbers (CD), superlative adjectives (JJS), possessive endings (POS), possessive pronouns (PRP$), and *wh*-pronouns (WP). This shows that post-editing the MT output takes similar typing effort for those PoS classes as it does when translating the word from scratch. The differences are only significant for TfS and PE in personal pronouns (PRP) and comparative adjectives (JJR), but not between TfS and MPE.

Status and experience of the participants did not play a significant role in all tests. Hence, the efficiency (or inefficiency) on a word class level of the participants may not be dependent on their professional experience for the same reasons mentioned in §11.2.1 on the parameter *Munit*.

11.2.3 Indications in *HTra* and *HCross*

As was already mentioned in §11.1, *HTra* and *HCross* were calculated across the different tasks, including all tasks into the calculations. The values were calculated per source text item, including all sessions, independent of the tasks. Hence, I will first look at the mean values of the parameters (see Figure 11.5, Figure 11.6, and also Table D.7 in Appendix D).

I assume that higher *HTra* values might indicate longer production and processing times because the participant has more translation choices in his/her mental lexicon. Similarly, Schaeffer et al. (2016) hypothesise that the more literal units (identical word order, translation items correspond one-to-one, only one translation possible for the ST item) are translated, the easier they are to process and the stronger the priming effects. They therefore analyse whether *Cross* (the absolute numbers with which *HCross* is calculated) and *HTra* have an influence on early gaze behaviour, which would also support that reading for translation differs from reading for understanding. The results show that *Cross* and *HTra* have a positive significant influence on the first fixation duration, and *Cross* also on first pass gaze duration (ibid.). Accordingly, it seems plausible that higher *HTra* values might also indicate problem solving activity. On the other hand, a broad range of possible translations might also just be part of solving a task – deciding on one translation choice rather than solving a problem. In summary, I will include *HTra* in the analysis and will then decide whether it is an indicator for problem solving activity or not according to the results.

As I can see in Figure 11.5, the *HTra* values differ a lot regarding the PoS class. While I have only one word class with no entropy (comparative adverbs - RBR), superlative adverbs (RBS), gerund verbs (VBG), and past participle verbs (VBN) are on average higher than 2.5 and particles (RP) even have an average *HTra* value of more than 3. An obvious question arises: Why is there no entropy for comparative adverbs and a very high entropy for superlative adverbs? The only (and convincing) explanation is that both PoS classes only occurred once in the texts and hence no overall conclusions can be drawn. The same accounts for particles which only occur once in the texts, too. Most word classes range between

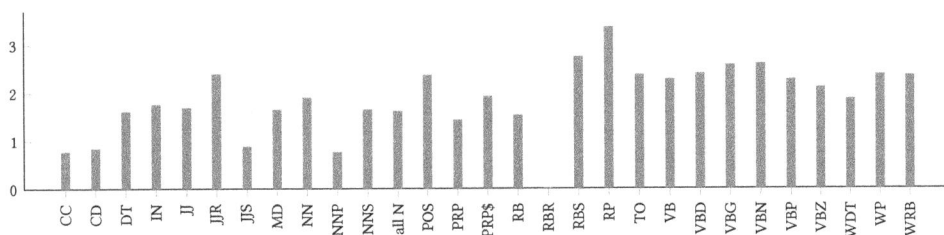

Figure 11.5: Mean values of *HTra* according to PoS class

1.5 and 2.5 (DT, IN, JJ, JJR, MD, NN, NNS, POS, PRP$, RB, TO, VB, VBD, VBN, VBP, VBZ, WDT, WP, WRB) and only coordinating conjunctions (CC), cardinal numbers (CD), superlative adjectives (JJS), proper nouns (NNP), and personal pronouns (PRP) are below 1.5. With the latter word classes, one might wonder how cardinal numbers (CD) and proper nouns (NNP) even received an entropy value above 1 at all. While the latter still seems plausible, because one can imagine that proper nouns might be translated in different ways as they have to be explicated or simplified, or have different grammatical properties in German, different translations for cardinal numbers cannot be explained easily. The data set was consulted to find examples. The phrase *Beijing Olympics* in text 3 - both words tagged as NNPs – was often translated as *Olympischen Spielen in Peking* (*Olympic Games in Beijing*; the phrase is grammatically adjusted to the sentence), where *Olympischen Spielen* was tagged on *Olympics* and *in Peking* on *Beijing*. One participant, however, decided to translate the unit as *Olympischen Sommerspielen in Peking* (Olympic Summer Games in Beijing), which is also a valid translation. When I look at the data for cardinal numbers, some variation appears as well. The phrase *four life sentences* (*four* being tagged as CD) in Text 1 cannot be translated literally into German, but was translated as *vierfach lebenslänglich, viermal lebenslänglich, vier Mal lebenslänglich* etc., which all basically express the same meaning. Finally, it is striking that the *HTra* values for verb categories in general seem higher than for other word classes, which might indicate that verbs naturally occur with many different translation choices (and therefore might be more difficult to translate).

In general, *HCross* values seem to be relatively high (see Figure 11.6), which indicates that translations from English into German require a lot of restructuring. On the other hand, repositioning one word in a sentence also affects the *Cross* value of the remaining words in the sentence. Except for JJS, NNP, RBR, and WDT the values for mean *HCross* are higher than 1. These exceptions, however, can again be explained by the low occurrences in the overall data set. The value is

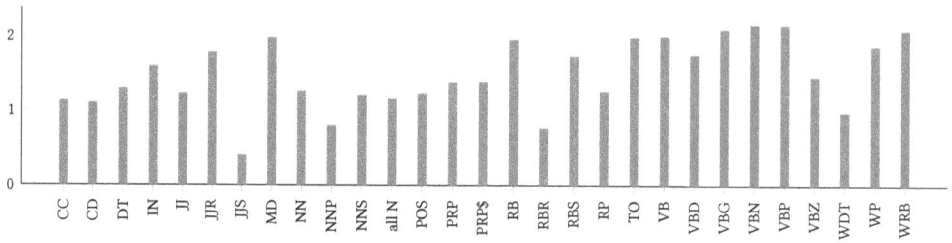

Figure 11.6: Mean values of *HCross* according to PoS class

more than 2 for four of the PoS classes. It is striking that of those four, three are verb categories, which reflects the different position of the verb in subordinate clauses in English and German and additionally often seems to be problematic for statistical MT. *HCross* will be integrated in the problem analysis because it is possible that it predicts problematic units. However, it also seems plausible that structural changes can only be categorised as part of the translation task rather than as a translation problem as was already indicated in §9.

11.3 Influence of problem indicators on keylogging and eyetracking data

In the following analysis, some PoS categories are condensed because they hardly appeared in the texts, as was mentioned in the preceding sections. Adjectives (JJ) now also include comparative adjectives (JJR) and superlative adjectives (JJS). The same applies for adverbs (RB), which now also comprise comparative (RBR) and superlative adverbs (RBS). Finally, *wh*-determiners (WDT), *wh*-pronouns (WP), and *wh*-adverbs (WRB) are summarised under the abbreviation WDT. Further, two additional categories are introduced that comprise all nouns (NN + NNP + NNS) and all verbs (VB + VBD + VBG + VBN + VBP + VBZ) to gain more insights into the overall results of these word classes. Linear mixed models were calculated to evaluate the influence of the parameters on the production and processing data, namely production duration, total fixation duration and total fixation count on the source and target text separately and combined. Two different approaches were tested in R to find the best fitting models, both including the individual participants and the individual texts as random effects. Finally, the models were created to include all significant parameters and exclude those that do not have a significant influence on the behavioural parameters, and following this formula (if all parameters were included; the example uses *Dur* as the parameter to be predicted):

(1) `summary(lmer(Dur ~ Task + Munit + InEff + HTra + HCross +`
     `(1|Part) + (1|Text), data = dataset))`

Colour patterns were created (Figure 11.7-Figure 11.11[4]) that visualise the statistic results. When a square is green, the predictor influences the behavioural parameter significantly, when a square is grey, no significant influence could be detected. When no test could be conducted because of the missing data for MPE, the squares are hatched. First, the results are discussed for the overall data set, independent of PoS classes (see pattern in Figure 11.7). *Dur* is influenced by all parameters, but there is no significant difference between MPE and PE. Gaze behaviour on the source text (*GazeS* and *FixS*) is influenced by the tasks and *HCross*. Fixation duration on the target text (*GazeT*) can be predicted by *Munit*, *InEff*, *HTra* and *HCross*, while fixation counts (*FixT*) on the target text are only influenced by *Munit* and *InEff*. It seems reasonable that the tasks do not influence the gaze behaviour on the target text because previous chapters have already shown that the eye movement behaviour on the source text is similar in TfS and PE. Finally, total fixation duration and fixation count on the whole text is influenced by the tasks, *Munit* and *HCross* – for *TGaze* the difference is only significant between both PE tasks and TfS, while for *TFix* it is only significant between MPE and TfS as well as between the PE tasks. Conclusively, *HCross*, *Munit*, and *Task* are the most promising indicators for cognitive effort. *HCross*, however, is negatively directed, meaning that the higher *HCross*, the shorter the production time becomes, which is surprising and contrary to what would be expected. Further, if the task plays an influential role, the production time becomes higher in TfS than in the PE tasks. In *TFix*, the production time is higher in PE than in MPE.

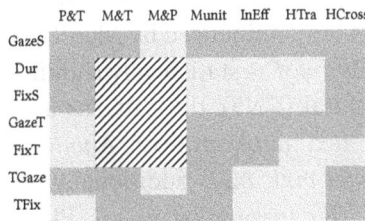

Figure 11.7: Pattern for statistical influence of predictors on parameters for all data

Coordinating conjunctions (CC) are only influenced by *Task* (all but eye movement on the target text), *Munit* (all but eye movement on the source text and total

---

[4]T = translation from scratch; P = (bilingual) post-editing; M = monolingual post-editing

fixation duration on the target text) and *InEff* (except on *GazeS*), while *HTra* and *HCross* do not predict production time or gaze behaviour (see patterns for CC, CD, DT, IN, JJ, and MD in Figure 11.8). Cardinal numbers (CD) are seldom influenced by the tasks (only in *FixS, TGaze,* and *TFix*) or by *Munit* (only in *Dur* and *FixT*). Further, *HCross* had to be excluded from the model, although it often also became significant because the correlation between *HTra* and *HCross* is too strong for this PoS category.[5] *InEff* – except for *FixS* – and *HTra* – except for *Dur* – are very predictive. The cognitive effort for determiners (DT) can hardly be predicted by the examined parameters. Only *Dur* is influenced by *Munit* and *HTra* and the gaze behaviour on the source text is influenced by *HCross* (with a negative direction). Production duration and gaze behaviour on both source and target text can be predicted by *Task, InEff* (except gaze on the source text and *FixT*), and *HTra* (except *Dur* and *FixS*) for prepositions and subordinate conjunctions (IN). *Munit* only played a role in *Dur*, and *HCross* only in *FixS* (though, *HCross* was the only foretelling parameter for *FixS*). Adjectives (JJ) hardly show a consistent pattern. They are influenced by the tasks, especially concerning the difference between PE and TfS, but not when considering the gaze data on the target text. *Dur, GazeT,* and *TFix* are influenced by *Munit, Dur* and *FixT* by *InEff*, gaze on the target text and on both texts combined is impacted by *HTra*, and, finally, *GazeS* is additionally influenced by *HCross*. The production time of modals (MD) is influenced by *Munit* and *InEff*, the gaze data on the source text by *Task, FixT* by *Munit*, and *GazeT, TGaze* and *TFix* by *InEff*.

When all noun categories are considered, the production time is influenced by *Munit, InEff,* and *HTra* and gaze data on the source text by *Task* and *HTra* (see patterns for all nouns and single noun categories in Figure 11.9). Total fixation duration on the target text can be predicted by *Munit* and *InEff*, while fixation count on the target text is only influenced by *Munit*. However, when combining source and target text, only *InEff* is statistically significant. When I divide nouns into singular (NN) and plural (NNS), the patterns are quite similar. *Task* influences gaze on the source text and both texts, *Munit* has an impact on *Dur* and eye movement in the target text, *InEff* additionally on gaze on both texts, and *HTra* on *Dur, GazeS* and *TFix* in singular nouns. Plural nouns are significantly impacted by *Task* (*Dur,* gaze on source text), Munit (gaze on target text and *TFix*), *InEff* (*GazeT, TGaze*), *HTra* (*Dur,* gaze on source and both texts), and *HCross* influences *TGaze*. However, proper nouns (NNP) induce different behaviour and only *Dur* is influenced by *Task* and *InEff*, while none of the parameters has a significant impact on the gaze behaviour.

---

[5]Which was tested for all significant parameters with the vif.mer() function, see https://github.com/aufrank/R-hacks/blob/master/mer-utils.R, last accessed 11 March 2017.

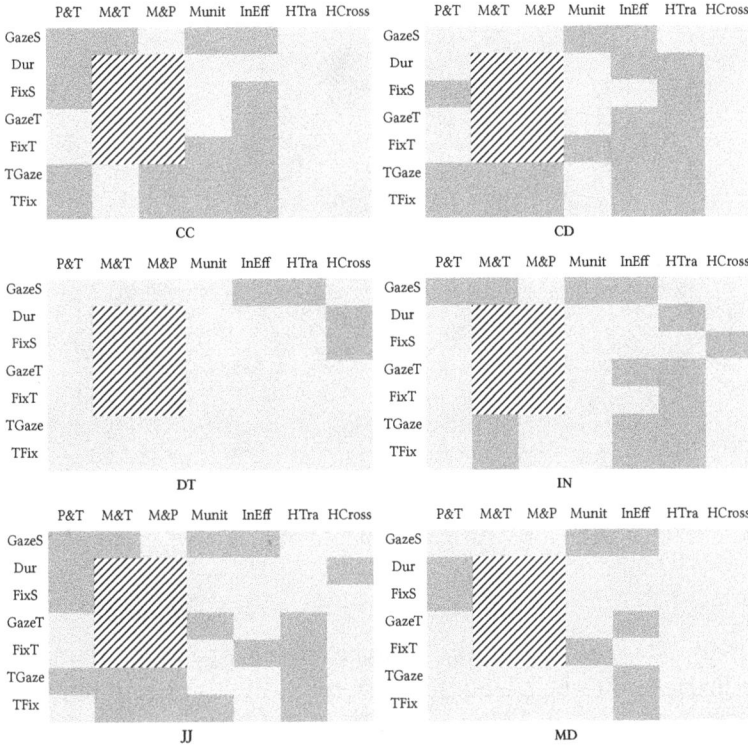

Figure 11.8: Patterns for statistical influence of predictors on parameters for CC, CD, DT, IN, JJ, MD

Possessive endings (POS) rarely occurred in the data set, but still show statistically significant results for *Task* (*GazeS, FixS, GazeT*), *Munit* (*Dur, FixT, TGaze, TFix*), and *InEff* (*Dur, GazeT, TGaze*). The production and processing effort of personal pronouns (PRP) is determined by *Task* and *HTra* when considering gaze on the source text, and usually by *Munit, InEff*, and/or *HTra* for the remaining variables. *TFix* is additionally influenced by *Task*, but only when comparing MPE and PE/TfS. *Task* (except for *Dur* and *GazeT*), *Munit* (gaze on target text & on both texts), *InEff* (*Dur, FixS*, gaze on the target text), and *HCross* (gaze on source text and *TGaze*) impact possessive pronouns (PRP$), while *HTra* is not important. The production times of adverbs (RB) can be predicted by *Munit, InEff*, and *HTra* values. Gaze on the source text is influenced by *Task* and *HTra*, while all parameters except *Task* have an impact on *GazeT*. *FixT* is influenced by none of the parameters. The gaze behaviour on both text parts is affected by *Task*, and *Munit* has an additional impact on the total fixation duration. Problem indicating parameters

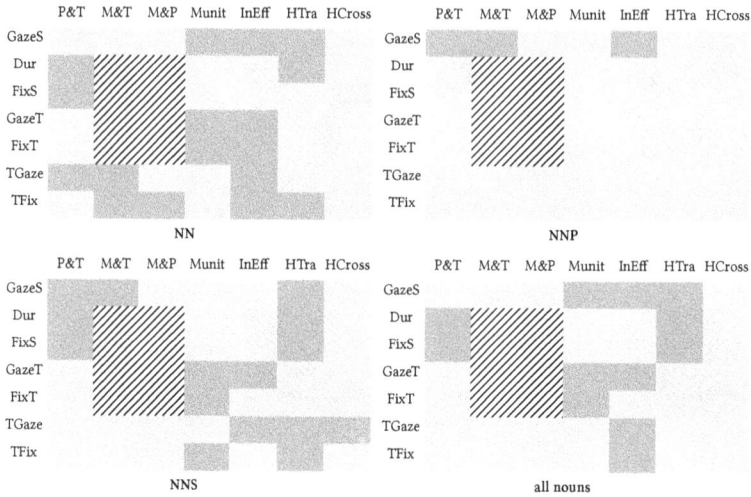

Figure 11.9: Patterns for statistical influence of predictors on parameters for all nouns

cannot be analysed for particles (RP), because only one particle occurred in the data set. The participant's behaviour for the word *to* in its different functions can be influenced by all parameters, but very differently: *Task* for all except *Dur* and *FixT*, *Munit* for all except gaze on the source text and *TFix*, *InEff* for *Dur* and *GazeS*, *HTra* for *FixT* and gaze behaviour on both text parts, and finally *HCross* for gaze on the source text and *GazeT* (see patterns for POS, PRP, PRP$, RB, RP, and TO in Figure 11.10).

When I look at all verb categories combined, most behaviour is influenced by *Munit* (except *FixS*). *Task* are also important except for *Dur*, which is quite surprising, and *FixT*. Production time and gaze on the source text are further influenced by *InEff* (also influential in *TGaze*) and *HTra* (also influential in *TFix*). Finally, *HCross* has an impact on *GazeT* and *TGaze* (see patterns for all verbs and single verb categories in Figure 11.11). Verb bases (VB) are influenced by *Task*, except for *Dur* and *FixT*, by *Munit*, except for gaze behaviour on the source text, and by *HTra*, except for *FixS* and gaze on the target text. *InEff* only has an impact on *Dur*, while *HCross* has an influence on the gaze behaviour on the target text. For past tense verbs (VBD), *Task* and *InEff* have an influence on production time and gaze data, excluding *FixT*. *Munit* plays a role for *TFix* and *HCross* for *TGaze* and *TFix*. Gerund verbs (VBG) were only influenced by *Task* (gaze on source text and both texts), *Munit* and *InEff* (gaze on target text and both texts, plus *Dur* for the latter). Past participle verbs (VBN) are influenced by *Task* in *Dur*,

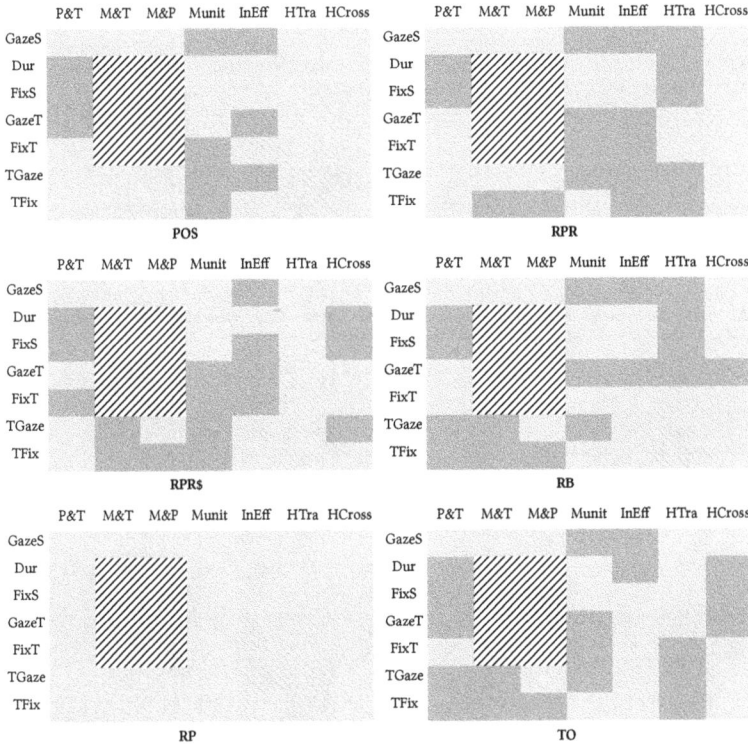

Figure 11.10: Patterns for statistical influence of predictors on parameters for POS, PRP, PRP$, RB, RP, and TO.

GazeS, TGaze, TFix, as well as *Munit* and *InEff* considering gaze on the target text and *TFix. TGaze* is also impacted by *InEff* and additionally by *HCross*. Non-3rd-person-singular present verbs (VBP) and 3rd-person-singular present verbs (VBZ) are influenced by *Task* when regarding gaze on the source text and on both texts. *Dur* for VBP is influenced by *InEff*, while it is in addition influenced by *Munit*, and *HTra. Wh*-words(WDT) can be predicted everywhere by *InEff*, except for gaze behaviour on the source text. Gaze behaviour on both texts is additionally influenced by *Task* and *FixT* by *Munit. FixS* is solely impacted by *HTra* (see Figure 11.12).

In the models that include *Task* as a significant parameter, the production and processing times become higher in TfS than in PE and MPE with three exceptions: Fixation counts on the target text in possessive pronouns and total fixation duration as well as total fixation count on the whole text in coordinating conjunctions. The differences in coordinating conjunctions became significant only for TfS and

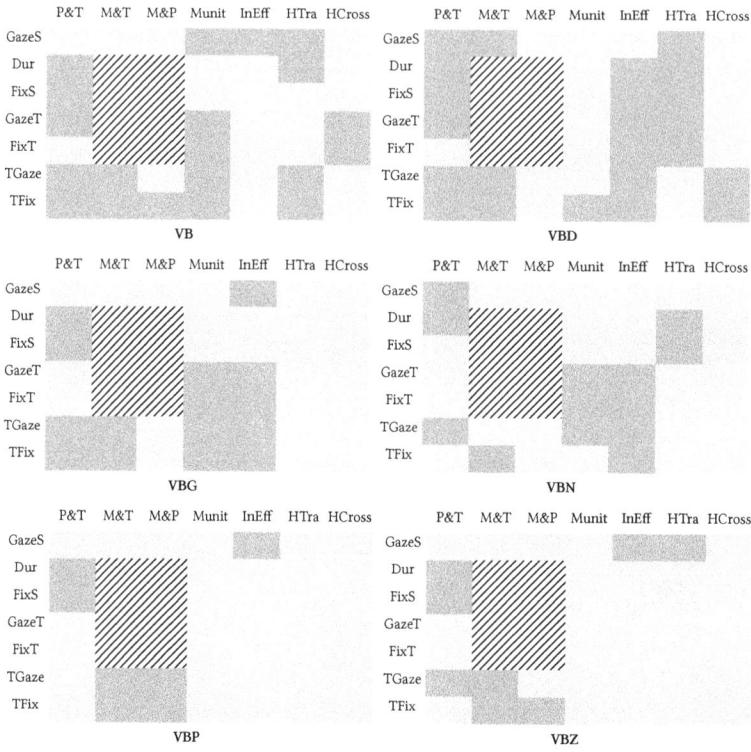

Figure 11.11: Patterns for statistical influence of predictors on parameters for verbs and WDT

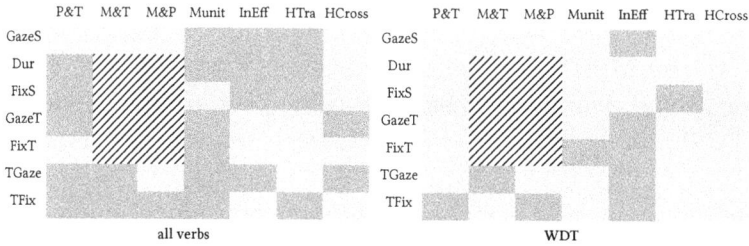

Figure 11.12: Patterns for statistical influence of predictors on parameters for verbs and WDT

PE, not TfS and MPE. Consequently, the times are never significantly higher for MPE than for TfS. The same applies to MPE and TfS. If the difference between the data is significant, it is always significantly higher for TfS than for MPE. The three mentioned exceptions may indicate that the MT output is especially error prone in these PoS classes.

The experience and/or status of the participant were added to the model if they were significant. Altogether, one of these characteristics was added to the model 16 times – 13 times the status of the participants had a significant influence, while the experience of the participants had only a significant impact in three cases. Both status and experience have a significant influence only in the production duration of cardinal numbers, and only if one of them is added to the model, not if they are both added, because they are closely related. In most cases, the results were as expected. Every time the status of the participants became influential, the students produced higher production and processing times. Also, the production duration of the cardinal numbers became lower, the more experienced the participants were. However, the total fixation duration and total fixation count on source and target text in *wh*-words became higher the more experienced the participants were. This might indicate that those words are especially delicate to translate and that an experienced translator perceives that they must be translated especially carefully.

In summary, some parameters predict production times and gaze behaviour more than others in the 175 models that were tested (see Table 11.1). *Task* (87 times) and *InEff* (81 times) are the most productive as they occurred in almost half of the models (49.7% and 46.3% respectively). *Munit* (65 times – 37.1%) and *HTra* (59 times – 33.7%) can be considered the second best parameters to predict production and processing times, because they occurred in around one third of the models. *HCross* is, in comparison, not very productive for determining typing and gaze data, because this predictor hardly became significant (25 times – 14.3%) and was often even directed negatively (10 times). The reason might be that reordering and restructuring is naturally necessary in English and German translations and hence cannot be considered a problem, but can rather be regarded a task. Furthermore, it hardly seems influential when single PoS classes are considered, but it had much influence when the whole data set was considered.

Table 11.1 presents how often which parameter became significant for which behaviour measurement. The different tasks have a huge influence on the source text gaze behaviour and on the gaze behaviour when combining source and target text as, in 68–76% of the models, *Task* plays a significant role. However, it hardly has an influence on the gaze behaviour on the target text with only one significant model for fixation count (4% of all models) and five for total fixation duration (25% of all models). This confirms earlier results that gaze on the source text is much less intensive in PE than in TfS. However, gaze on the target text is similar in both tasks and hence gaze behaviour on the target text is hardly influenced by the tasks. Accordingly, gaze behaviour on the target text cannot help in finding problems in the different tasks if I assume that longer production times indicate a problem in the translation of a unit. Finally, *Task* only influences production time in 32% of all models. One might have expected more influence of the tasks on the production times, but higher production times do not necessarily indicate that the unit was translated from scratch, nor do they help in indicating different problems in the different tasks.

The production time is often influenced by *Munit* (56% of the models), which was expected, because the total production time becomes longer if the word is changed after the first production (or if the MT must be edited). The values for *Munit* have (almost) no influence on gaze behaviour on the source text. One might have expected that the source unit is fixated more often and longer when the text is revised, but this is not the case. This indicates that revisions are often made only within the target text by considering the context and collocations of the translation rather than the source text unit. Another interpretation could be that the attention on the source text is equally distributed, but when problems arise more and longer fixations on the target text are necessary. Consequently, *Munit* has a more important role in target text gaze behaviour and becomes significant in over half of the models (52% for total fixation duration models and 64% for fixation counts). When both source and target text are considered, *Munit* has a significant impact in 44% and 40% of the models, respectively.

The values of *InEff* show a similar pattern as the values of *Munit*. However, *InEff* is a better problem indicator than *Munit*, although they are both keylogging values that show that the translation unit needed more work than simple production or that the MT output needed editing because *InEff* played more often a significant role in the models. The reason might be that *InEff* is more precise than *Munit*. In 84% of all models, the *InEff* value has a statistical impact on the production time. Similar to *Munit*, *InEff* has a very low influence on source text gaze behaviour (it became significant in 16% of the models for *TrtS* and *FixS*), while it played a bigger role for the models of the target text gaze behaviour (64% and 44%). *InEff* had a significant influence on 52% and 44% of the models combining source and target text.

HTra is not as influential as the previously analysed parameters. It has a considerable influence on production time and the gaze behaviour on the source text (it became significant in 44% of the models for each measure). However, it played a minor role for predicting gaze behaviour on the target text (24% and 20% of the models were influenced by *HTra*) and on the combination of source and target text (28% and 32%). This might show that the decision process for one translation is settled in the source rather than in the target text. As the word entropy represents how many different and equally reasonable translation choices existed, it seems that decision making already takes place when the participants consider the source text, which would also support Schaeffer et al.'s (2016) assumption that reading for translation influences the source text reading. Furthermore, this provides evidence that *HTra* indicates decision making behaviour rather than problem solving behaviour. Many choices might become a problem, but usually the translators can easily decide on one translation according to context and collocation.

HCross is not very productive as a problem indicator, because it only became significant in 4% of the models for *Dur* and *FixT*, 13% of the models for *TFix*, and 20% of the models for *TrtS*, *FixS*, *TrtT*, and *TGaze*.

Table 11.1: Number of significant results according to parameter per production time or gaze behaviour measure

Parameter	Dur	TrtS	FixS	TrtT	FixT	TGaze	TFix
Task	8	19	19	5	1	17	18
Munit	14	1	0	13	16	11	10
InEff	21	4	4	16	11	14	11
HTra	11	11	11	6	5	7	8
HCross	1	5	5	5	1	5	3

Conclusively, production time is best predicted by the *InEff* value. The gaze behaviour on the source text is highly influenced by the tasks, while the gaze behaviour on the target text is best predicted by *InEff* and *Munit*. The pattern is not that clear for source and target text combined. *Task* plays an important role again, but this might be further influenced by the MPE task, which was not included for gaze behaviour on the source and on the target text. Additionally, *Munit* and *InEff* might help to predict higher or lower fixation counts or shorter and longer fixation durations with *InEff* being a little more productive. The word entropy also has an important impact, but it is not as productive as *Munit* and *InEff*. Finally, a different position of a unit in the target than in the source text does not seem to be a very productive problem indicator (*HCross*) for single PoS classes, but when considering all data. Figures D.1–D.5 in Appendix D display visualisations for all predictors and separately for all parameters and all PoS classes. They are constructed in the same pattern in which Figures 11.8–11.12 were constructed.

11.4 Mapping the parameter with the results of the analysis of the research behaviour

Research was already identified as a primary problem solving indicator in Krings (1986b). Hence, the following section will compare the analysed parameters of the most-research words (see §9.3) according to the problem solving indicators introduced in the previous section.

For the analysis, I will look at the 18 single words that were researched most often (more than four times). Table D.8 in Appendix D lists the mean values of *Munit, InEff, HTra* and *HCross* for the most researched single words in comparison to the mean value of these parameters according to the word's PoS class. One has to bear in mind that all most researched single words are either nouns, verbs, or adjectives. This supports the assumption that content words require more research than function words, at least when translating into the L1. Furthermore, I also report whether the difference between mean value and mean value of the PoS class is significant (the results can be found in Table D.9 in Appendix D). Most mean values are significantly higher for the most researched words when comparing them to the average value of the PoS class. Eleven *Munit* values are significantly higher when the word was often researched. Only the *Munit* value of *bureaucrats* is significantly lower. Ten of the *InEff* values are significantly higher for the most researched words. The value for *HTra* is significantly higher in 14 cases, while it is also significantly lower in three cases. Remember that the *HTra* value is the same for the single words because it is calculated on the basis of all occurrences of the word and its translations. However, the *HTra* values for the PoS class vary and therefore a mean value has to be calculated. The same applies to *HCross*. The *HCross* values are significantly higher for the single words in eleven cases and significantly lower four times.

Of the 18 most researched words, 17 had at least one predictor that was significantly higher for the word than for the mean value. However, the word *bureaucrats* was researched often, but the mean values of all four predictors are lower than average for the PoS class (NNS), three of them even significantly. Hence, I can assume that the research was caused by a mere lexical problem – a problem which all 18 words have in common.[6] However, significantly high *HTra* and *HCross* values, like for the adjectives *reluctant* and *vulnerable*, might point to additional semantic or syntactic problems, respectively. High *Munit* and *InEff* values might indicate a general insecurity and/or indecisiveness of the participants about how to translate the source item in the context. If most or all values are significantly high, this might point to especially difficult words that may be lexically unknown and hard to integrate in the context.

---

[6]From my point of view, it should be open for discussion if the translation of a word can really be categorised as a translation problem and not only as a translation task when a word is simply unknown to the participant (at least in the context) and (s)he looks it up in a dictionary, finds a fitting translation, inserts it in the target text and is done with the translation process.

12 An approach to statistically modelling translation problems with the help of translation process data in R

In the final chapter, I want to introduce an approach with which to identify problematic units in translation process data according to mere keylogging and eye-tracking data as an alternative to think-aloud data. As we have learned, production times and eye movement data like fixation durations and fixation counts can be interesting variables to detect problems in process data. However, these data have the disadvantage that there is no guarantee that they indicate problems. Is the participant really thinking about this word, when (s)he looks at it longer? Maybe (s)he is already thinking about the upcoming phrase, or revising what was already translated or post-edited in his/her head. Or even unrelated thoughts and any action in the environment can distract the translator/post-editor. Hence, I want to propose a problem indicator model that relies on the more stable predictors introduced in the earlier analyses: *Task, Munit, InEff, HTra*, and *HCross*[1].

As we saw in §11.3, the overall data as well as the single PoS classes rely more or less strongly on different predictors. If we assume that one predictor has an impact on at least four of the behavioural parameters (production time and gaze data), it is included in the final formula to find the problem units. Before a first example is discussed, we have to determine a problem area. If we assume that every parameter is considerably high, when it exceeds its mean value plus one standard deviation, we could postulate the following problem area (PA) for each parameter (in R script) with "dataset" being representative for the data set a person wants to analyse:

(1)   `PAMunit <- mean(dataset\$Munit) + sd(dataset\$Munit)`
       `PAInEff <- mean(dataset\$InEff) + sd(dataset\$InEff)`

---

[1] Even if the participant types one translation, changes it, but then decides to go back to the initial translation, this insecurity might point to problematic units, too.

```
PAHTra <- mean(dataset\$HTra) + sd(dataset\$HTra)
PAHCross <- mean(dataset\$HCross) + sd(dataset\$HCross)
```

As the parameter *Task* is not numeric, a problem area cannot be calculated. The calculation of the PAs is based on calculations on the confidence intervals in normal distributions and outliers. Testing the data has shown that multiplying the standard deviation leads to the exclusion of too many data points. I tested different approaches to define the best fitting problem area with the specific formulas (the results can be found in Tables D.8 to D.15 in Appendix D). If the problem area is only defined as being higher than the mean of the particular predictors, too many words would be specified as problematic, which would lead to too many false positives. A total of 20.8% of all words would be considered problematic if the whole data set were approached, and for adjectives (46.4%), adverbs (53.7%), or verbs in the base form (48.3%) even approximately half of the occurrences would be considered problematic. However, if the problem areas are defined as mean plus $1.5 * sd$ (or higher), too many words would be excluded and hardly any problematic words could be defined, as indicated above. Accordingly, mean plus SD was established as the best fitting problem area. A selection of the most frequently occurring PoS classes was tested (see Table D.9 in Appendix D). The formula would predict a rate of 0.1–1.0% for function words which would need to be considered problematic[2] and 6–21% for content words[3]. Although 21% may be considered a bit too high, even for content words, the percentages seem to be plausible for most PoS classes.

Conclusively, we would arrive at the following basic command to filter out problematic units, considering *Munit, InEff, HTra*, and *HCross* are simultaneously significant influential (excluding *Task* for the moment), which they usually are not:

(2) `dataset[dataset\$Munit > PAMunit \& dataset\$InEff > PAInEff \&`
     `dataset\$HTra > PAHTra \& dataset\$HCross > PAHCross, ]`

This means that, if all four predictors are influential, every data point can be considered a problematic source text unit that has a *Munit* value that is in the PA, an *InEff* value that is in the PA, and a *HTra* value and a *HCross* value that is in the respective PA.

---

[2]Except for determiners, which, however, were calculated differently and will be discussed further below.

[3]The rate for combining all verbs, however, was very low (only 0.1%), which will be discussed further below.

In the next step, the predictor *Task* needs to be included. Let us, therefore, look at a first example: If we want to analyse the whole data set without focusing on a special PoS class, the predictors *Task, Munit,* and *HCross* need to be included, because they influenced at least four[4] of the behavioural parameters. Hence, we need to integrate those three predictors into the command. If the parameter *Task* is an influential part of the formula, the data set cannot be assessed as a whole, but TfS, PE and MPE have to be analysed separately as the tasks have an influential impact on the behavioural parameters. Accordingly, it has to be integrated both in the problem area of each parameter as well as in the final command. The problem areas for *Munit* and *HCross* can be specified as the following, already establishing that only TfS data are considered:

(3) `PAMunit <- mean(dataset[dataset\$Task == "TfS"]\$Munit) + sd(`
     `dataset[dataset\$Task == "TfS"]\$Munit))`

(4) `PAHCross <- mean(dataset[dataset\$Task == "TfS"]\$HCross) + sd(`
     `dataset[dataset\$Task == "TfS"]\$HCross))`

The final command is constructed of the three influencing predictors:

(5) `dataset[dataset\$Task == ""TfS \& dataset\$Munit > PAMunit \&`
     `dataset\$HCross > PAHCross, ]`

If the problematic source text units would be calculated for PE and MPE in the subsequent steps, the commands could remain the same, but `Task == "TfS"` would needed to be replaced by `Task == "PE"` (or `Task == "MPE"`). If an overview of all potential problematic units of all tasks is necessary, the problematic words have to be calculated separately per task and then combined because the problem areas have to be defined according to the tasks.

On the other hand, if *Task* is not an influential part in the formula, the research question, however, only requires inclusion of the problems in the PE task, *Task* can be integrated in the final formula, but does not need to be integrated in the problem area calculation. Prepositions and subordinate conjunctions (IN), for example, require *InEff* and *HTra* as predictors. Hence, the problem areas would be set as

(6) `PAInEff <- mean(dataset\$InEff) + sd(dataset\$InEff))`
     `PAHTra <- mean(dataset\$HTra) + sd(dataset\$HTra))`

---

[4]Why it has to be at least four, will be discussed in more detail later in this chapter.

and the final command could include the tasks, but would not have to, e.g.:

(7) (complete data set)
```
dataset[dataset\$InEff > PAInEff \& dataset\$HTra > PAHTra, ]
```

(8) (for problematic words only in the TfS task)
```
dataset[dataset\$Task == ""TfS \& dataset\$InEff > PAInEff \&
    dataset\$HTra > PAHTra, ]
```

Accordingly, the final command can include or exclude everything that is (not) necessary for the analysis, like *Text* or *Participant*. These additional distinctions on the data set might not only be included into the final command, but also into the problem area, depending on the research question. For example, if we want to investigate which of the problems in the whole data set belong to participant P04, we include the restriction only in the final command. However, if we want to detect which words were especially problematic for P04, we can also include the restriction into the function for the PAs.

If the researcher uses the CRITT TPR-DB or any other data collection method including numerous pieces of information, it might be convenient to include a restriction on the columns of the table that will be presented in the output. For the testing done in Tables D.8–D.15 in Appendix D, e.g., I only needed the information of columns two to eleven to determine which words are considered problematic and hence included this restriction in the command (dataset[..., 2:11]).

In the following, some issues will be discussed which were already addressed to some point or which may still need a solution. First, *Task* alone cannot be used to make any predictions. Although this did not occur in the PoS selection that was tested, Task would be the only predictor for VBPs (non 3rd-person-singular present verbs) and VBZs (3rd-person-singular present verbs). However, as it can be assumed that translators (trainees and professionals alike) do not have problems with the grammatical difference between VBPs and VBZs, it might be reasonable to synthesise those PoS classes (maybe also including verb bases) and recheck for this superordinate class if it has different predictors[5]. A closely linked issue emerges when Task and HTra are the only two predictors for a PoS class (as is the case for adjectives, adverbs, and verbs in their base forms), because the *HTra* value is calculated across the different tasks. Accordingly, the suggested

---

[5]Find a discussion on PoS classes with no predictors and a discussion why combining all verbs does not seem helpful to identify problematic words further below.

problematic words are the same for all three tasks. Therefore, it might be reasonable to include another – usually the next closest – predictor. Otherwise Task could also be excluded as a predictor, because it hardly influences the outcome of the calculation. This was tested for Adjectives (JJ) for which the next best predictor is *Munit*. Independent of the tasks, the adjectives predicted to be problematic decreased from 13.6% to 3.8%, which still seems plausible.

A second issue that needs to be discussed is what if only one predictor (except *Task*) falls under the given criterion introduced above for some PoS classes, which led to the question whether it is sufficient to specify problematic words. For example, the PoS group "all nouns" is only impacted by the *InEff* values. When only one PA is used for the prediction, it gives the impression that too many words might be identified as a problem. Hence, it was tested how many nouns would be considered problematic when only *InEff* is taken to define a PA. In a second test, the best three indicators for all nouns were taken into consideration (*Munit, InEff,* and *HTra*). When three predictors were included into the formula, only 0.1% of the nouns could be considered problematic, which is very few. However, if only *InEff* was included, 6% of the nouns would be considered problematic, which seems more realistic for content words (the detailed results can be found in Tables D.9–D.15 in Appendix D). Hence, I decided that only the predictors with a significant impact on at least four of the behavioural parameters should be included in the formula to prevent too many false negatives – except when the only predictor is *HTra/HCross* (and *HTra/HCross* combined with Task) as discussed above. Similarly, none of the predictors has a significant impact on determiners (DT) more than once. When a formula is established with those three predictors, which had an impact at all (*InEff, HTra,* and *HCross*), still 4.2% of the determiners could be considered problematic, which is a lot when three predictors are used, especially for function words. Therefore, we can assume that determiners cannot be predicted as problematic. The final basic model is presented in Figure 12.1.

Next, the focus should be on combining PoS classes. While it might be sensible to combine PoS classes in some cases, it might also cause misleading results. For example, if all verbs are combined, only 0.1% of the verbs can be considered problematic according to the formula. This would be a very small number, especially for verbs, as over 20% of all verbs in their base form (VB) would be considered problematic if the formula for VBs is applied to them. Hence, I suggest that word classes might only be combined if they obviously have the same root, like adjective, adverbs, nouns, verbs, etc., but only as long as the (grammatical) difference between the words can be considered easy to process. Accordingly, it

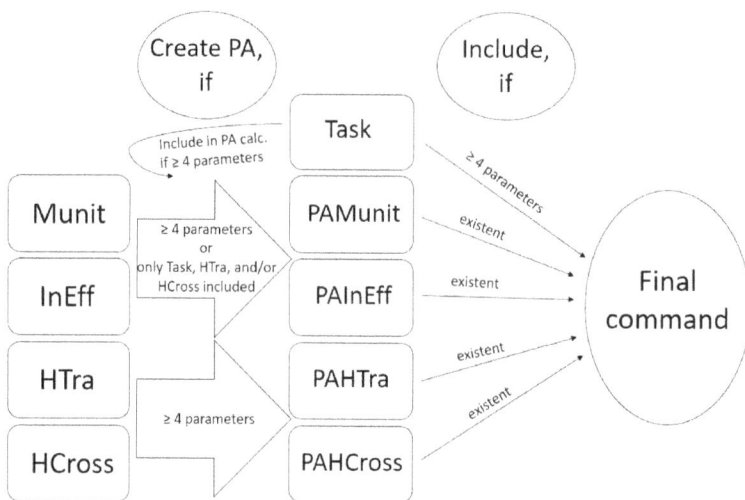

Figure 12.1: Overview of the final model

would be reasonable to combine singular and plural nouns, but maybe to exclude proper nouns as they are subject to special requirements in translation. Further, adjectives and adverbs, respectively, can be combined with their comparative and superlative forms because these grammatical differences most likely do not cause problems for the translators. Similarly, 3rd-person-singular and non-3rd-person-singular present verbs can presumably be combined, maybe even with verb base forms, but gerund verbs and verbs in the past tenses may be considered separately because the problem with these verbs might be translating the grammatical structure rather than any lexical or semantic problem, etc.

In the end, one has to bear in mind that this analysis is only on a word level, while many problems might instead occur on a phrase or sentence level or even higher. Hence, if one word is identified as problematic, it might not be the word itself but the phrase/context in which it is embedded. Accordingly, the interpretation of the identified problematic words must be performed very carefully.

13 Summary and discussion

This chapter summarises what we have learned in this study. The first three chapters after the introduction acknowledged MT and PE in general and how those topics are conceived in different fields of translation (theoretical translation studies, translation process research, translation practice, translation communities, and translation didactics), showing that MT and PE are nowadays integral parts of every aspect of translation.

§5 discussed the concept of problem solving in psychology and translation studies. We learned that translation studies do not necessarily differentiate between problem solving and decision making and the terms are not used consistently either. Therefore, the insights from both fields were combined and compared. I argued that translation is in general a task characterised by decisions that need to be made, in which problems occur that need to be solved more or less often. The difference between a translation problem and a translation task is that there is a hurdle between the source and the target text in a problem, which the translator has to overcome. In a task, there is no hurdle. The translator knows how to create the desired final text. Most translation problems are ill-defined because the steps required to solve the problem were not necessarily learned in advance, experience in different domains is required, personal opinions/judgements might be necessary. Further, different solutions and different solution paths are possible (and natural) in translation, which are all characteristics of ill-defined problems. Only very few translation problems could be categorised as well-defined, e.g. if a lexical item is unknown to the translator and the concept of the item is so concrete that when he/she looks it up in a dictionary, he/she will find only one possible solution. However, even in this scenario, different solution paths are imaginable (research in monolingual or bilingual dictionary, corpora, or encyclopedias, or asking a colleague or the client), which would characterise this lexical problem as an ill-defined problem again. While the decisions in a regular translation task can be made in a one step operation, it takes various steps to arrive at the solution to a problem. Increasing professionalism transforms what once was a translation problem into a standard translation task – problem solving operators and strategies become routinised and automatised

– and what once might have been an ill-defined problem becomes simple decision making task. Further, professionals tackle problems mostly through reasoning, they know translation rules and know how to explain their problem solving steps, while beginners often have a feeling for a (correct) solution or (correct) way to a solution, but do not know the reason or rules, respectively, for this feeling. However, even the most professional translator encounters translation problems. According to Funke (2006b) categorisation, translation problems do not qualify as complex problems in my perception. Although they can be categorised as complex and interconnected, and they can pursue multiple aims, they are on the other hand transparent and lack a certain dynamism. Finally, I combined the two problem solving models of Pretz et al. (2003) and Krings (1986a) to a translation problem solving cycle (see Figure 5.1) that includes eight steps. Of course, not all steps are necessary for every problems and some steps might occur unconsciously. Hence, not all, but many of these steps can be traced in the translation process recordings. In the following, the eight steps are complemented by the way they could possibly be traced in the translation process data: recognise and identify the problem (potentially visible in eye-tracking data), define and present the problems mentally (unconscious), organise the knowledge about the problem (potentially unconscious), develop solution strategies and/or choose operators (potentially unconscious), apply those strategies/operators (unconscious or visible in screen recording and/or eyetracking data), evaluate whether they solve the problem (potentially unconscious), solve the problem (eyetracking and keylogging data), evaluate the solution (unconscious or visible in keylogging and/or eyetracking data), and start the process again if necessary for the next or a new problem. In summary, translation requires problem solving abilities every time there is hurdle between source and target text. Finally, the translator engages not only in problem solving, (s)he also helps the reader of the translation to overcome the language hurdle and to solve problems, e.g. (s)he enables the reader to solve troubleshooting problems by providing a well written manual.

After the theoretical groundwork was laid, §6 introduced the research hypotheses that combine the thoughts on problem solving with the tasks of TfS and PE, which may require different problem solving behaviour, as the two tasks demand different approaches from the translator despite their similarities. Hence, I hypothesised that although the problematic source text units are the same for TfS and PE, different problem solving behaviour can be encountered in TfS and PE/MPE, because the MT output solves or adds problematic units, as well as between students and professionals because of their varying experience. Further, this study wanted to investigate problem solving indicators with the help of keylogging and eyetracking data and presented a model to detect the problems in translation process data so that the time-consuming analysis of screen recording and think aloud data lapse.

Before the data were analysed, the data set was introduced in §7. First, methods in translation process research were introduced in §7.1 with a special focus on the methods utilised in this study (questionnaires, keylogging, eyetracking). §7.2 described the data set concerning the texts, the participants, and the PE guidelines, the technical equipment, and the database from which the data originates. The research hypotheses and methods are placed in the field of translation process research in §7.3 and previous studies that were based on the data set were introduced in §7.4. Starting with §7.5, the first overall results from the study were presented, considering the time needed for the single tasks (TfS took more time than PE and MPE), the complexity of the texts (§7.6), which might be a reason why participants behave differently in different tasks, the participant's keystroke effort for modifications in the different tasks (§7.7), which was very heterogeneous, and a superficial error analysis of the target texts (§7.8), which provides indications about the target text quality. The chapter concluded with a critical assessment of what could have been improved in the setup of the experiments.

§8 showed the results of the pre- and post-experimental questionnaires. While, on the one hand, metadata were gathered, the questionnaires also asked for personal opinions on MT/PE and how satisfied the participants were with the PE task. Although the participants were quite satisfied with their performance in the PE and MPE task, the results outline a (very) negative attitude towards MT and PE which probably had an influence on other questions, too, such as "how often would you have preferred to translate from scratch rather than post-editing machine translation?" Nonetheless, more participants could imagine integrating MT into their professional work environment after the experiment than before the experiment. This contradictory behaviour might reflect an adverse attitude against MT and PE itself, even though they are not very familiar with the technology (see Figure 8.1) or the tasks (only 1/3 of all participants had post-edited before).

In the data analysis part, the focus was first on the Internet search instances in the analysis of the data (§9). According to Krings (1986b), research is a primary problem solving indicator and I generally agree. Most research was probably conducted when solving a lexical problem. In the majority of the instances, this external problem solving strategy is probably combined with internal knowledge. The participant does not know how to translate a lexical unit, because it is either unknown to him/her (in the given context) or (s)he cannot decide on a translation alternative (in the given context) – there is a hurdle between the source text and the target text and research is the chosen solving strategy. First, the screen recordings of all sessions were analysed and very often, a significant difference could be observed in the research behaviour in PE and TfS. Also, the experience of the translators seems to influence the research behaviour, which became visible when the participants were separated by status (professional vs. student) and/or when the experience coefficient introduced in §8.1 was taken into consideration. Less experienced translators do more research than more experienced translators. With growing experience lexical problems occur less often because of developing language skills in the L1 and L2 as well as increasing translation skills. Experienced translators may translate more freely and have a better feeling for the semantic meaning in the context. Further, the MT output in the PE task seems to solve lexical problems because less research was conducted than in the TfS task. However, no indications were found that the MT output creates new problems in the PE task because if the participants did not judge the MT output to be acceptable for the target text, they could refer to the source text and could either find a translation with the help of their internal knowledge (or as PACTE (2005) phrased it: their inner support), which can be categorised as a translation task, or they still have to solve the problem, which probably would have occurred in the TfS too, with the help of external support. This does not apply to MPE. When the MT output is not suitable for the target text context and no source text is available for the translator, a new problem may arise because the unit may not have been problematic in the TfS task, or the problem might be more difficult to solve because the translator does not know how to use the external resources to find a solution. Accordingly, we can summarise that translation strategies might be transferred to the PE task but not to the MPE task. This is supported by the fact that research behaviour does not seem to be influenced by experience (neither status nor experience coefficient) in MPE. In a next step, the parameters production time (*Dur*), gaze time on source text (*GazeS*), and gaze time on target text (*GazeT*) were analysed for the 27 most researched words to see whether they are influenced by the research task. When the individual words were analysed, not many statistical difference could be observed, which is probably caused by the few data points. However, if all words are analysed together, both the t-tests and the linear mixed models predict that the parameters are also impacted by the different tasks whether research was conducted or not – with the exception that the task does not influence gaze on the target text, which on the one hand could imply that problem solving eventuates in the source text and on the other hand that gaze on the target text is similar in TfS and PE. Conclusively, research as a problem solving activity is used in another intensity in the different tasks and in relation to the experience of the translator.

§10 analysed the influence of the syntactic quality of the MT output. I hypothesised that syntax is not problematic for the translator in the TfS task, but that the MT output might erect hurdles between the source and the target text, because syntax is often a problem for MT systems in the language pair English-German. To assess this question, I categorised the syntax of the MT output into acceptable, partly acceptable, and not acceptable and compared the production time and the eyetracking data to those of the TfS task. The analysis was expanded for the parameters fixation count on the source (*FixS*) and on the target text (*FixT*). Further, parameters that considered the total fixation duration (*TGaze*) and the fixation count (*TFix*) on both source and target text were created. If new hurdles were build by the MT output, when the syntactic MT output was not acceptable, the keylogging and eyetracking data should have been significantly higher in the PE task than in the TfS task. The analysis, however, showed that bad syntactic MT output does prolong the production time of the sentence, however no new problems are created because the gaze behaviour of the participant is not impacted by the syntactic MT quality. Hence, creating and correcting the structure of a MT sentences can be categorised as a task, but not as a problem.

As was mentioned above, some of the steps of the problem solving cycle might be visible in the translation process data. It is not necessary to label e.g. a very long fixation duration on one word as the step "identifying a problem" or "solving a problem" or "evaluating a solution", but this long fixation potentially shows us that there is a translation problem. Hence, §11 presented keylogging parameters (*Munit, InEff, HTra*, and *HCross*) that can be used to predict (hence called predictors) behavioural parameters of the eyetracking and keylogging data. The influence of these predictors can vary a lot according to the PoS class, though. Further, some predictors are more productive than others on these behavioural parameters. *Task* and *InEff* often have an influence, the influence of *Munit* and *HTra* is moderate, and *HCross* hardly has a significant influence. Interestingly, the status and/or the experience of the participants seldom had a statistical influence in the regression models that were created to analyse which predictor influences which parameter in which PoS class. The status of the participants was a little more productive than the experience coefficient. After testing the influence of the predictors on the single PoS classes, the values of the most researched words, as defined in §9.3, were checked against the mean values of the PoS class because we can safely assume that these are translation problems. The results show that many predictors are significantly above average for the most researched words and hence this proves that the predictors seem sensible to predict problems.

One major issue when talking about and analysing translation problems is to identify the problems in the process data. Think-aloud protocols can help with this issue, but the data are potentially incomplete and subjective, and the task is usually unfamiliar to the participants. Further, the assessment of think-aloud protocols is difficult and time-consuming. Hence, it is desirable to detect translation problems with the help of other translation process data. An approach to identifying problematic units in translation process data was introduced in §12, which is mainly based on the findings in §11. First, a problem area has to be defined for the influential predictors, i.e. *Munit, InEff, HTra,* and *HCross.* The problem area is calculated by the mean of the respective predictor plus one standard deviation. Then, all influential problem areas are combined in a command that also contains the predictor *Task* if required. The calculations can be done either for all words or for single PoS categories. According to the research question, additional characteristics can be included in the calculation like participant or text. When this formula is applied, R displays all words that were potentially problematic in the translation process, because they required above average keylogging effort (which were related to the eyetracking data in §11). The calculations, however, still need to be tested in real-life translation scenarios, in which ideally, the translators would still be available to verify whether the identified word was really problematic or not. I argued that keylogging data are more reliable than eyetracking data. However, it would still be interesting to expand these calculations with eyetracking parameters because many more steps in the problem solving cycle can potentially be identified with eyetracking data than with keylogging data.

The first main hypothesis was that some problems are already solved by the MT output, while some new problems (can) arise from the MT output. This hypothesis was only partly confirmed. The study at hand has shown that pre-translating the source text with an MT system does not create new problems for the translator. Sometimes the production process might be exceeded or a lexical item needs to be deleted and researched again (the lexical problem was not solved by the MT system), but these instances do not cause problems, they are only a task. Hence, the MT output might support the translator or might not support the translator, but it does not make the translation process more complicated. This, however, only applies to PE (bilingual post-editing) where the source text is available to the translator. As we have seen in the chapter on lexical items (§9), a mistranslation in the MT output can cause additional problems because it confuses the translator and (s)he has no source text to resolve the problem. In the end, I found different behaviour in TfS and PE. Very often the differences between the different tasks (also when MPE was included) turned out to be (statistically significantly) different in all aspects analysed in this study. Production times are often shorter in PE than in MPE. The source text is neglected much more in PE than in TfS. It is only consulted to check the MT output or when problematic units occur in the MT output in PE, while it is the main source of information in the TfS task. The target text, on the other hand, is consulted roughly equally as often in TfS as in PE. It is the main source of information in the PE task. Further, the tasks also have a vital impact on the research behaviour.

As a side note, this study has proven to me again that MPE is nothing that will be enforced in translation practice any time soon. The MT output is not reliable enough to support a monolingual editing process. Rather, trained translators should be assigned to bilingual post-editing task so they can transfer their translation knowledge and expertise to this new task. Additionally, I think, it is essential for translators to get training in the PE task, as well so that they can work efficiently and may enjoy the task rather than considering it a burden.

The second main hypothesis, namely that different problem solving patterns develop in relation to the expertise level of the participant, cannot really be confirmed or disproven. While many differences could be found between individual translators in the assessment of the screen recordings of the research behaviour in regard to their level of expertise, the statistical analysis of the keylogging and eyetracking data hardly proved any influence of the status of the participant nor the experience according to the experience coefficient. Disappointingly, the latter was even less often a significant influence than the status of the participants. However, in my opinion, we should not disregard experience as an influential factor in translation process research. I would rather claim that we have not found the right measure for competence yet. The status of the participants as well as the experience coefficient are (relatively) simple attempts to represent competence, which cannot depict all facets that may contribute. Therefore, it will be necessary in future research to find a way to measure competence in a more fine-grained way that is also applicable for empirical studies. Hence, a numeric value would be favourable.

It is also possible that the keylogging and eyetracking data do not reveal as many competency differences as the screen recording analysis because a certain translation item might be difficult for a more experienced translator as well. However, (s)he draws back on internal resources more extensively than the more inexperienced translator. Hence, especially the eyetracking data might not be as expressive. Bear in mind that this is only an hypothesis that needs to be tested in another study.

The calculations introduced in §12 to identify problematic words in a database could be applied to translation and post-editing courses quite easily, because they are only based on keylogging data. Keylogging data can be recorded much easier than eyetracking data because some keylogging solutions can be used for free or could be implemented into online applications, while recording eyetracking data requires expensive hard- and software. Further, keylogging programmes do not impact the natural translation situation. In a perfect scenario, the translation trainees would prepare their translation at home, using a software that tracks the keylogging data, and would hand in the finalised translation product together with the keylogging data. The translation trainer, on the other hand, could use the keylogging data to calculate in R according to the formulas presented in §12 which words in the translation assignment could be considered problematic and need discussion in the translation class. This procedure would also help verify, falsify, and assess the calculations presented in §12. Of course, these identified problematic words could only be used as an addition, because the calculations presented only consider the word level so far and problems may occur on a sentence or text level (or any other level), too. Also, problems concerning register, text type and domain conventions, etc. cannot exclusively be detected on a word level.

14 Final remarks and future research

As most studies do, this study raises more questions than it answers. Can similar patterns be found in larger data sets for lexical and syntactic problem solving? Further, it needs to be tested if the same predictors are influential for the single PoS classes in another and/or a larger data set. Also, it seems plausible that the results change and the predictors need to be adjusted for languages for special purposes. What are the patterns in other languages? Are some predictors universal to a PoS class independent of the language? The participants of this study had a rather negative attitude towards MT/PE and were dissatisfied with the PE/MPE tasks. However, does the negative attitude towards MT/PE influence the subconscious processes/the behaviour during the task? And is this attitude towards MT/PE changing at the moment? Are translators starting to accept that the occupational field for translators is changing and that recent developments concerning translation technologies can be seen as an opportunity rather than a threat?

As described in §7.9, the study design and execution had some flaws – some of them were inevitable, like the fact that the study was not conducted in the common working environment of the participants, and some of them could have been avoidable, like the suboptimal phrasing of some the questions in the questionnaire (see §8.3). These insights will be considered in the next study so that, on the one hand, mistakes are not repeated and, on the other hand, some issues will be weighted again, like ecological validity vs. feasibility.

The study at hand has shown a way to define translation problems, both theoretically and empirically. However, the analysis I conducted can only be considered a starting point for the interesting field of analysing and determining translation problems both in translation from scratch and in post-editing. The results and approaches of this study need to be verified and expanded and/or falsified and improved. The same applies for the analysis considering translation competence.

In conclusion, a lot of interesting research is still ahead of us and with the developing electronic aids for translators and other new advances, the whole field keeps in motion. This study had set the course to identifying translation problems (in contrast to translation decisions and other related behaviour) in process data, but there might be considerations to improve this identification methods. Further, I still strongly believe that problem perception between professionals and semi-professionals varies a lot, but we have not found the right measurement to identify translation competence yet. Mere education and experience do not seem to be enough to measure professionalism. Hence, the differences between the problem solving behaviour of individual translator might be easier to detect if we find an improved way to mirror professionalism.

Appendix A: Analysis of Research Instances

Table A.1: Words processed per Research Instances

Participant	HT1	HT2	PE1	PE2	ME1	ME2
P1	49.3	13.9	22	100	n.r.	28
P2	18.9	20	40.3	37.3	148	n.r.
P3	n.r.	56	n.r.	n.r.	n.r.	n.r.
P4	21.1	9.9	18.9	25	60.5	44
P5	18.9	33.3	30.3	56	148	139
P6	121	112	n.r.	n.r.	n.r.	n.r.
P7	n.r.	43	139	–	n.r.	n.r.
P8	22	30.3	50	112	n.r.	n.r.
P9	–	18.5	–	16	121	n.r.
P10	19.9	7.1	49.3	12	40.3	14
P11	12.5	11.2	43	30.3	n.r.	–
P12	–	–	74	30.3	132	n.r.
P13	29.6	7.3	139	60.5	50	56
P14	16.5	20.2	148	20	n.r.	56
P15	n.r.	n.r.	n.r.	112	n.r.	n.r.
P16	13.9	10	49.3	16	18.9	60.5
P17	16.7	–	n.r.	26.4	74	24.2
P18	23.2	28	12.5	24.2	n.r.	132
P19	14.7	n.r.	–	–	–	–
P20	46.3	12.1	n.r.	69.5	26.4	–
P21	n.r.	n.r.	n.r.	112	n.r.	n.r.
P22	20	–	–	–	27.8	–
P23	n.r.	28	139	33	50	n.r.
P24	19.9	–	100	24.2	n.r.	n.r.

Table A.2: Time between two research instances

Participant	HT1	HT2	PE1	PE2	ME1	ME2
P1	177.1	77.8	115.5	335.9	n.r.	173.1
P2	168.8	141.6	221.1	313.5	854.3	n.r.
P3	n.r.	367.3	n.r.	n.r.	n.r.	n.r.
P4	179.3	102.7	130.1	187.7	251.9	347.2
P5	221.0	431.1	212.3	452.5	784.8	1043.4
P6	1047	1007.5	n.r.	n.r.	n.r.	n.r.
P7	n.r.	359.4	807.5	–	n.r.	n.r.
P8	268.5	189.1	294.3	572.2	n.r.	n.r.
P9	–	114.7	–	149.4	557.2	n.r.
P10	128.2	80.0	232.7	108.9	231.6	136.6
P11	96.6	64.8	206.6	207.1	n.r.	–
P12	–	–	340.1	128.5	407.9	n.r.
P13	174.2	84.0	867.3	233.5	318.2	241.1
P14	86.9	116.8	437.1	100.7	n.r.	440.4
P15	n.r.	n.r.	n.r.	758.5	n.r.	n.r.
P16	97.0	73.8	283.7	146.7	113.2	245.5
P17	197.4	–	n.r.	172.1	386.3	185.3
P18	186.1	144.5	112.7	223.8	n.r.	588.9
P19	126.0	n.r.	–	–	–	–
P20	264.7	166.8	n.r.	301.7	214.9	–
P21	n.r.	n.r.	n.r.	334.2	n.r.	n.r.
P22	196.9	–	–	–	222.0	–
P23	n.r.	357.1	1019.6	247.3	306.4	n.r.
P24	98.1	–	508.5	129.4	n.r.	n.r.

Appendix B: Processing data for most researched words

Table B.1 lists all words and phrases taken into consideration for the analysis, to which text the word/phrase belongs, how often these were researched and a percentage showing the relation between how often the word/phrase was researched and how often the task was performed for the text. As mentioned in §9.2 researched words were excluded for several reasons.

The following table lists all words/phrases taken into account with the according means and standard deviations for all three parameters. Figures are marked in bold, when the mean value is higher for no-research instances than for research instances:

Table B.2: Mean and SD of Most Researched Words

Word/Phrase	Text	Research	Mean			Standard Deviation		
			Dur	GazeS	GazeT	Dur	GazeS	GazeT
serve	1	total	5531.5	9240.12	28161.5	6814.1	7625.0	25209.1
		yes	12962.6	13247	62284.6	7276.1	6711.0	22960.0
		no	3209.3	7988	18095.2	4663.6	7459.9	14297.6
below-inflation	2	total	5678.5	1741.9	8260.2	5102.9	2008.8	11362.5
		yes	7369.2	2474.6	**2671.6**	4771.9	1740.0	1595.3
		no	5114.9	1497.7	**10123**	5085.1	2032.8	12546.4
cut interest rates	2	total	3928.5	4833.9	6119.3	7328.4	4329.7	5734.8
		yes	8622.6	9158.4	7395.9	10402.9	4077.2	5212.1
		no	1400.8	2505.3	5431.9	2469.2	2096.9	5883.9
insistence	2	total	3474.3	3556.0	3271.6	2665.8	2860.2	3888.4
		yes	5199.4	4992.4	4099.4	3095.2	3041.7	3877.3
		no	2899.3	3077.1	2995.7	2227.0	2628.1	3852.8
embarrass	3	total	8419.5	1898.3	6231.8	16564.8	2245.5	9916.4
		yes	12424.9	**1791.4**	8599.6	18613.0	1401.9	12059.0
		no	6416.9	**1951.8**	5047.9	15788.8	2615.5	8924.1
rattle	3	total	6922.5	2080.0	9992.9	8063.4	1742.9	16374.1

B Processing data for most researched words

Word/ Phrase	Text Research		Mean			Standard Deviation		
			Dur	GazeS	GazeT	Dur	GazeS	GazeT
		yes	10796.5	2350.7	14353.5	9520.7	1896.5	20055.9
		no	2817.7	1663.9	4764.1	2235.3	1569.6	9597.4
atrocities	3	total	1677.3	962.0	2646.2	2636.2	1569.7	2817.0
		yes	2859	1851.1	3159.6	1764.8	2229.4	4286.0
		no	1086.4	517.5	2389.5	2850.7	926.4	1875.4
fallout	3	total	3571.4	2182	4149.4	6088.4	2492.6	3193.9
		yes	6065.4	3136.4	4223.8	5573.3	3206.8	2966.8
		no	2036.7	1594.7	4103.7	6079.7	1837.2	3444.0
flaring up again	3	total	3169.0	2930.9	7807.8	5371.2	3719.5	10723.3
		yes	9726.3	8207.3	22148	10293.2	2627.7	15418.0
		no	1626.1	1689.4	4433.6	1708.2	2738.2	5971.3
halt	3	total	3198.1	1499.2	3282.3	9175.2	1894.1	5654.3
		yes	10421.2	1865.4	7217.6	18464.8	1046.2	10212.5
		no	940.9	1384.8	2052.5	980.3	2105.5	2835.7
International Criminal Court in The Hague	3	total	9447.9	6900.4	11216.5	15806.5	8834.1	9825.4
		yes	20097	13463.1	18026.8	19712.5	10689.1	11107.9
		no	2894.5	2861.8	7025.6	8222.4	4114.1	6243.1
Khartoum	3	total	6285.5	2358.0	1617.4	12781.9	2427.6	2873.7
		yes	13478.8	4211.8	2330.5	14845.8	2815.3	1884.4
		no	3330.8	1615.2	1329.6	10746.7	1814.2	3089.1
pull out	3	total	3578.8	5289.4	4944.0	10137.3	5200.9	6127.4
		yes	2712.3	9224.8	5594	1022.5	5563.1	2439.2
		no	3782.7	4363.5	4791	11315.0	4819.4	6759.0
bear the brunt	4	total	3655.8	3539.4	4632.3	3542.2	3506.7	4545.1
		yes	5576.3	5392.5	8806	4850.5	4357.7	5610.1
		no	3091.5	3279	3254.8	2761.7	3412.4	2982.3
compromise	4	total	5373.1	5324.8	4301.8	10585.9	4271.1	10375.8
		yes	4342	6366.2	8987	4344.1	6142.7	19217.9
		no	6192.6	5548	5219.3	11992.5	4242.0	1168.7
deforestation	4	total	4028.6	2397.1	2636.4	3800.9	3311.7	4864.6
		yes	5781	3297.1	6528.7	2780.7	4314.5	7101.1
		no	3210.9	1977.1	820	4013.1	2806.9	1665.9
go the extra green mile	4	total	15702.0	4740.3	6066.1	19447.4	6594.8	6068.9
		yes	23413.4	8237.4	8391.1	20800.8	9597.3	6051.7

Word/ Phrase	Text Research		Mean			Standard Deviation		
			Dur	GazeS	GazeT	Dur	GazeS	GazeT
		no	11295.6	2741.9	4737.6	17901.4	2971.9	5877.9
incentives	4	total	4368.8	2205.4	3522.7	4666.0	2439.3	5882.4
		yes	2756.8	2122.4	2484	1827.5	2584.8	3671.0
		no	5712.2	2274.6	4388.3	5873.6	2425.2	7296.2
mitigation effort	4	total	10591.6	4221.8	14042.0	19846.0	4414.8	13990.8
		yes	21282.3	6372.9	15059.4	28131.8	5449.6	18994.1
		no	3190.4	2732.6	13337.5	4074.5	2904.5	10035.9
reluctant	4	total	769.9	4306.6	6525.7	1132.8	4247.1	6778.4
		yes	1568.4	7009.2	10859.8	915.9	7176.9	10375.1
		no	535.1	3511.8	5250.9	1103.1	2800.8	5079.1
vulnerable	4	total	1637.6	1754.8	3369.1	2492.3	2073.9	3830.8
		yes	2716.3	3272.9	3149.1	2546.3	2294.7	2361.8
		no	1021.3	887.3	3494.9	2327.7	1372.6	4544.8
associate	5	total	1242.3	2074.5	1933.4	1258.3	2583.3	1543.7
		yes	1753.5	3047.5	1578.1	1233.5	3499.5	1762.5
		no	777.6	1190	2256.5	1139.4	719.6	1315.1
warrant	5	total	2965.0	3375.0	2071.0	2513.3	3596.9	2786.2
		yes	3262	2766.1	2239.3	2090.3	2689.7	2864.7
		no	2782.3	3749.6	1967.4	2807.9	4116.2	2849.7
bureaucrats	6	total	1228.7	72317	7721.8	1785.4	3270.4	11418.3
		yes	1015.7	4326.7	11018.7	1685.7	3587.4	16514.0
		no	1281.6	2592.4	5249.2	1972.8	2947.5	4811.5
full-time leader	6	total	10303.1	9296.7	6746.9	21738.9	10400.7	6886.4
		yes	20733.8	12875.4	6062.9	33184.6	9113.2	5540.8
		no	3884.3	7094.5	7167.8	5299.9	10865.3	7786.2
artisans	6	total	1559.2	1330.7	13044.3	1859.8	1518.2	13045.8
		yes	3403.2	1437.8	10178	2130.1	1807.4	9550.2
		no	1233.4	1287.9	14190.9	1677.3	1455.7	14339.8

Table B.1: Occurrence count and percentage of most researched words/phrases

Word	Text #	Count			Percentage		
		HT	PE	MED	HT	PE	MED
	1	7	7	7			
serve	1	2	2	1	28.6	28.6	14.3
	2	8	5	7			
below-inflation	2	3	1	1	37.5	20	14.3
cut interest rates	2	5	0	2	62.5	0	28.6
insistence	2	5	0	0	62.5	0	0
	3	7	7	7			
embarrass	3	4	3	0	57.1	42.9	0
rattle	3	5	4	2	71.4	57.1	28.6
atrocities	3	5	2	0	71.4	28.6	0
fallout	3	5	3	0	71.4	42.9	0
flaring up again	3	4	0	0	57.1	0	0
halt	3	3	1	1	42.9	14.3	14.3
International Criminal Court in The Hague	3	6	2	0	85.7	28.6	0
Khartoum	3	4	1	1	57.1	14.3	14.3
pull out	3	3	0	1	42.9	0	14.3
	4	8	7	7			
bear the burnt	4	3	1	0	37.5	14.3	0
compromise	4	2	3	0	25	42.9	0
deforestation	4	5	2	0	62.5	28.6	0
go the extra green mile	4	3	1	0	37.5	14.3	0
incentives	4	3	5	2	37.5	71.4	28.6
mitigation effort	4	7	2	0	87.5	28.6	0
reluctant	4	4	1	0	50	14.3	0
vulnerable	4	5	3	0	62.5	42.9	0
	5	6	7	8			
associate	5	4	4	2	66.7	57.1	25
warrant	5	3	4	1	50	57.1	12.5
	6	6	8	7			
bureaucrats	6	3	2	4	50	25	57.1
full-time leader	6	3	3	2	50	37.5	28.6
artisans	6	4	2	0	66.6	25	0

Appendix C: Analysis of machine translation output

In the following, the machine translation output will be evaluated for syntactic acceptability for all six texts.

Table C.1: Rating of Syntactic MT Output. a: acceptable; pa: partly acceptable; na: not acceptable.

Word/Sentence	Rater 1	Rater 2	Rater 3	Final rate	Comment
			Text 1		
SS1 → TS1	na	na	na	na	headline; MT contains two main verbs
SS2 → TS2	pa	na	pa	pa	main verb in the middle of the sentence
SS3 → TS3	pa	pa	pa	pa	misses verb in subordinate clause
SS4 → TS4	pa	pa	pa	pa	main verb in the middle of the sentence
SS5 → TS5	na	na	na	na	verb positioning
SS6 → TS6	pa	pa	na	pa	verb positioning
SS7 → TS7	pa	pa	pa	pa	main verb in the middle of the sentence in subordinate clause
SS8 → TS8	na	na	na	na	accusative object wrong position; misses auxiliary verb
SS9 → TS9	a	a	a	a	
SS10 → TS10	a	a	a	a	
SS11 → TS11	pa	na	na	na	misses main verb
			Text 2		
SS1 → TS1	a	na	na	pa	headline
SS2 → TS2	pa	na	na	na	main verb in the middle of main clause
SS3 → TS3	a	a	a	a	
SS4 → TS4	pa	pa	pa	pa	one verb misses
SS5 → TS5	pa	na	na	na	verb order
SS6 → TS6	pa	na	na	na	misses main verb
SS7 → TS7	a	a	a	a	

C Analysis of machine translation output

Word/Sentence	Rater 1	Rater 2	Rater 3	Final rate	Comment
			Text 3		
SS1 → TS1	pa	pa	a	pa	headline; dative object at the wrong position
SS2 → TS2	a	pa	pa	pa	
SS3 → TS3	pa	pa	pa	pa	verb positioning in second main clause incorrect
SS4 → TS4	pa	pa	pa	pa	verb positioning in first subordinate clause incorrect
SS5 → TS5	pa	pa	na	pa	verb positioning in first & second subordinate clause incorrect
			Text 4		
SS1 → TS1	na	na	na	na	verb positioning
SS2 → TS2	pa	pa	na	pa	misses one auxiliary verb and one main verb
SS3 → TS3	pa	na	na	na	misses one auxiliary verb and one main verb
SS4 → TS4	pa	na	pa	pa	word order
SS5 → TS5	a	a	a	a	
			Text 5		
SS1 → TS1	a	a	a	a	
SS2 → TS2	a	a	a	a	
SS3 → TS3	pa	pa	pa	pa	subordinate clause integrated in main clause
SS4 → TS4	(partly) a	pa	pa	pa	one main verb should have been split up
SS5 → TS5	a	pa	pa	pa	
SS6 → TS6	a	a	a	a	
			Text 6		
SS1 → TS1	a	a	a	a	
SS2 → TS2	a	pa	na	pa	
SS3 → TS3	a	pa	pa	pa	
SS4 → TS4	na	na	na	na	verb positioning in main clause, no verb in subordinate clause
SS5 → TS5	pa	na	na	na	no verb in last subordinate clause
SS6 → TS6	pa	pa	na	pa	wrong verb order in first subordinate clause and main clause
SS7 → TS7	a	a	a	a	

Appendix D: Part-of-speech categories, and their relation to different parameters

Part-of-Speech abbreviations, their explanation Marcus et al. (1993: 5) and their occurrences in the whole data set and in the individual texts:

Table D.1: Explaining the Part-of-Speech Categories, and their mean and SD values

Abbr.	Explanation	data set	Text 1 (n=22)	Text 2 (n=23)	Text 3 (n=23)	Text 4 (n=23)	Text 5 (n=23)	Text 6 (n=24)
CC	Coordinating conjunction	437	1	4	2	4	7	1
CD	Cardinal number	500	9	4	1	0	5	3
DT	Determiner	1672	15	11	15	9	15	8
IN	Preposition/subordinate conjunction	2473	23	23	22	12	16	12
JJ	Adjective	1033	10	5	5	7	10	8
JJR	Adjective, comparative	94	0	1	0	1	0	2
JJS	Adjective, superlative	68	1	1	0	1	0	0
MD	Modal	207	2	1	1	3	0	2
NN	Noun, singular or mass	3063	21	27	20	17	23	25
NNP	proper noun, singular	1096	11	2	26	0	6	3
NNS	Noun, plural	1817	15	19	6	11	13	15
POS	Possessive ending	92	0	2	2	0	0	0
PRP	Personal pronoun	272	6	2	0	1	1	2
PRP$	Possessive pronoun	183	2	2	1	1	1	1
RB	Adverb	559	2	5	2	3	3	9
RBR	Adverb, comparative	23	0	1	0	0	0	0
RBS	Adverb, superlative	23	0	0	0	1	0	0
RP	Particle	23	0	1	0	0	0	0
TO	to	761	4	6	6	6	5	6
VB	Verb, base form	764	3	7	5	9	1	8
VBD	Verb, past tense	474	10	1	3	0	6	1
VBG	Verb, gerund	548	5	5	3	6	4	1
VBN	Verb, past participle	527	6	4	2	3	4	4
VBP	Verb, non-3rd person singular present	487	2	8	0	5	0	6
VBZ	Verb, 3rd person singular present	324	0	1	8	0	3	2
WDT	wh-determiner	69	0	0	3	0	0	0
WP	wh-pronoun	46	0	1	0	0	1	0
WRB	wh-adverb	23	0	0	0	0	1	0

Table D.2: Mean and standard deviations for the parameters *Munit*, *In-Eff*, *HTra*, and *HCross* for CC, CD, DT, IN, and JJ.

		CC		CD		DT		IN		JJ	
		Mean	SD	Mean	SD	Mean	SD	Mean	SD	Mean	SD
Munit	TfS	1.046	0.389	1.084	0.531	0.989	0.541	1.027	0.675	1.023	0.566
	PE	0.338	0.519	0.307	0.512	0.389	0.581	0.451	0.630	0.494	0.631
	MPE	0.279	0.594	0.293	0.541	0.330	0.570	0.338	0.589	0.364	0.586
InEff	TfS	1.869	6.146	1.334	1.763	1.071	1.874	0.931	2.147	0.966	0.852
	PE	0.750	1.450	0.363	1.201	0.453	1.047	0.365	0.999	0.285	0.546
	MPE	0.677	2.036	0.687	5.357	0.388	1.352	0.254	0.662	0.395	2.472
HTra		0.773	0.633	0.839	0.805	1.614	1.005	1.759	1.002	1.689	0.913
HCross		1.136	0.690	1.106	0.956	1.294	0.928	1.600	0.919	1.233	0.802

Table D.3: Mean and standard deviations for the parameters *Munit*, *In-Eff*, *HTra*, and *HCross* for JJR, JJS, MD, NN, and NNP.

		JJR		JJS		MD		NN		NNP	
		Mean	SD	Mean	SD	Mean	SD	Mean	SD	Mean	SD
Munit	TfS	0.875	0.609	1.174	0.388	0.971	0.564	1.229	0.704	1.153	0.535
	PE	0.516	0.677	0.391	0.583	0.714	0.486	0.657	0.773	0.34	0.583
	MPE	0.419	0.765	0.136	0.351	0.687	0.722	0.553	0.734	0.316	0.574
InEff	TfS	0.864	0.520	1.403	1.017	1.143	1.302	1.037	1.578	1.059	0.976
	PE	0.392	0.919	0.376	0.579	0.655	0.763	0.505	1.085	0.252	0.686
	MPE	0.151	0.347	0.120	0.355	0.661	0.968	0.458	1.384	0.297	1.028
HTra		2.402	0.672	0.877	0.550	1.643	0.838	1.902	1.124	0.764	0.769
HCross		1.786	0.615	0.403	0.198	1.986	0.738	1.262	0.865	0.799	0.785

Table D.4: Mean and standard deviations for the parameters *Munit, InEff, HTra*, and *HCross* for NNS, POS, PRP, PRP$, and RP.

		NNS		POS		PRP		PRP$		RB	
		Mean	SD	Mean	SD	Mean	SD	Mean	SD	Mean	SD
Munit	TfS	1.230	0.681	1.281	0.683	1.067	0.596	0.935	0.624	1.063	0.710
	PE	0.665	0.766	0.643	0.559	0.527	0.601	0.4	0.558	0.527	0.654
	MPE	0.553	0.713	0.563	0.564	0.472	0.605	0.377	0.582	0.337	0.538
InEff	TfS	1.247	1.469	1.969	5.453	1.486	2.946	1.209	2.471	1.032	0.909
	PE	0.665	1.392	0.526	0.727	1.481	3.501	0.487	1.384	0.527	1.150
	MPE	0.421	0.730	0.479	0.964	0.654	1.274	0.53	1.038	0.397	0.827
HTra		1.649	0.958	2.377	0.990	1.431	1.113	1.926	1.224	1.534	0.930
HCross		1.207	0.763	1.229	0.728	1.380	0.669	1.384	1.018	1.959	0.840

Table D.5: Mean and standard deviations for the parameters *Munit, InEff, HTra*, and *HCross* for RBR, RBS, RP, TO, and VB.

		RBR		RBS		RP		TO		VB	
		Mean	SD	Mean	SD	Mean	SD	Mean	SD	Mean	SD
Munit	TfS	1	0	1	0.535	1.5	1.069	1.154	0.824	1.130	0.733
	PE	0.143	0.378	0.375	0.518	1.429	1.134	0.696	0.842	0.773	0.732
	MPE	0.375	0.518	0.143	0.378	0.875	0.641	0.461	0.692	0.690	0.778
InEff	TfS	1	0	0.25	0.463	0.966	0.129	1.074	2.676	0.944	1.484
	PE	0.229	0.605	0	0	1.176	0.577	0.522	1.055	0.733	1.542
	MPE	0.55	1.125	0	0	0.675	0.427	0.375	0.967	0.486	0.759
HTra		0	0	2.757	0	3.376	0	2.386	1.259	2.292	1.113
HCross		0.765	0	1.739	0	1.260	0	1.994	0.984	2.004	0.936

Table D.6: Mean and standard deviations for the parameters *Munit, In-Eff, HTra,* and *HCross* for VBD, VBG, VBN, VBP, and VBZ.

		VBD		VBG		VBN		VBP		VBZ	
		Mean	SD	Mean	SD	Mean	SD	Mean	SD	Mean	SD
Munit	TfS	1.184	0.756	1.176	0.692	1.309	0.774	0.831	0.639	1.054	0.655
	PE	0.671	0.718	0.911	0.711	0.983	0.815	0.675	0.630	0.6	0.725
	MPE	0.677	0.883	0.823	0.775	0.794	0.753	0.578	0.607	0.527	0.697
InEff	TfS	0.947	1.611	0.852	0.923	1.019	0.942	0.661	1.179	0.924	0.898
	PE	0.616	1.631	0.635	1.143	1.031	1.828	0.514	1.065	0.532	0.630
	MPE	0.448	0.830	0.443	0.785	0.709	1.274	0.470	0.873	0.467	0.660
HTra		2.404	1.337	2.583	0.940	2.611	0.924	2.282	1.324	2.105	1.309
HCross		1.762	0.907	2.100	0.830	2.165	0.782	2.159	0.930	1.461	0.912

Table D.7: Mean and standard deviations for the parameters *Munit, In-Eff, HTra,* and *HCross* for WDT, WP, and WRB.

		WDT		WP		WRB	
		Mean	SD	Mean	SD	Mean	SD
Munit	TfS	1.375	0.875	1.125	0.5	0.25	0.707
	PE	0.571	0.811	0.786	1.188	0	0
	MPE	0.708	0.908	0.125	0.342	0	0
InEff	TfS	2.798	5.938	3.037	5.878	0.125	0.354
	PE	0.318	0.810	2.691	5.690	0	0
	MPE	1.042	2.554	0.072	0.250	0	0
HTra		1.865	1.154	2.380	0.919	2.364	0
HCross		0.986	0.340	1.876	0.711	2.086	0

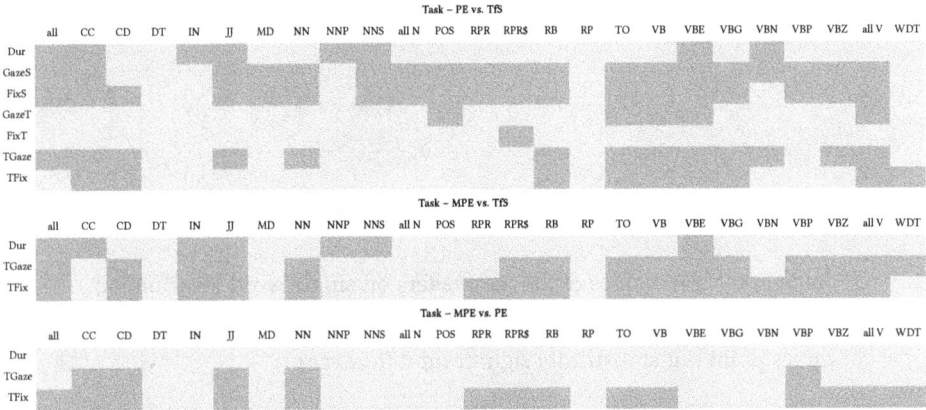

Figure D.1: Pattern according to predictor – *Task*

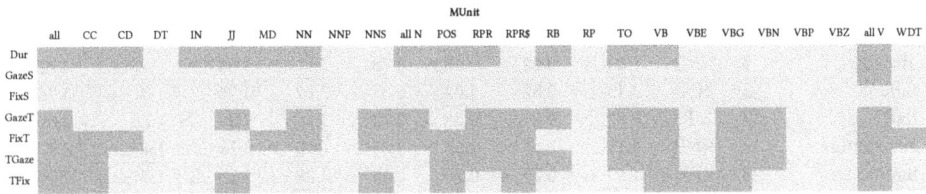

Figure D.2: Pattern according to predictor – *Munit*

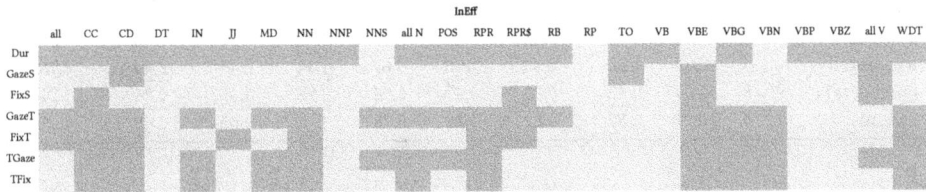

Figure D.3: Pattern according to predictor – *InEff*

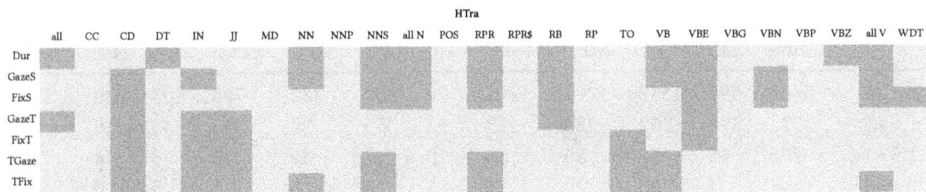

Figure D.4: Pattern according to predictor – *HTra*

281

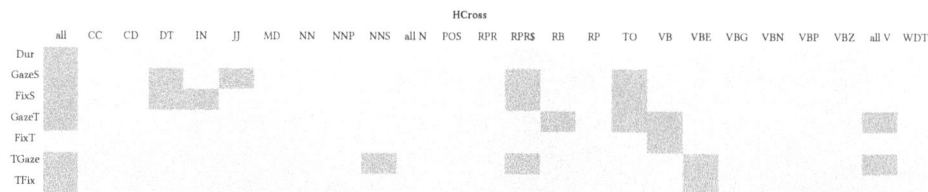

Figure D.5: Pattern according to predictor - *HCross*

Table D.8: Mean values of the parameters on single word level and on PoS-level (TMunit, TInEff, THTra, THCross); Mean single word values in bold are higher than the average of the PoS class and underlined values point out statistically significant differences

Word	Text	PoS	Munit	TMunit	InEff	TInEff	HTra	THTra	HCross	THCross
serve	1	VB	**1.09**	0.87	**1.15**	0.72	2.77	2.29	**2.68**	2.00
insistence	2	NN	**1.13**	0.82	**1.04**	0.67	**3.85**	1.90	**2.47**	1.26
embarrass	3	NN	**1.26**	0.82	**1.13**	0.67	2.28	1.90	**2.90**	1.26
rattle	3	VB	**1.17**	0.87	**1.39**	0.72	**4.23**	2.29	**2.87**	2.00
atrocities	3	NNS	**1.04**	0.82	0.45	0.78	1.17	1.65	0.51	1.21
fallout	3	NN	**1.13**	0.82	**1.02**	0.67	2.67	1.90	1.01	1.26
halt	3	VB	0.87	0.87	**0.83**	0.72	**3.76**	2.29	1.26	2.00
Khartoum	3	NNP	**1.13**	0.61	**1.65**	0.54	**1.00**	0.76	**1.42**	0.80
maintains	3	VBZ	**1.07**	0.73	**0.76**	0.65	**2.88**	2.11	**1.64**	1.46
compromise	4	VB	**1.35**	0.87	**1.19**	0.72	**4.09**	2.29	**3.26**	2.00
deforestation	4	NN	**1.09**	0.82	**0.83**	0.67	**2.76**	1.90	**2.44**	1.26
Incentives	4	NNS	**1.61**	0.82	**1.74**	0.78	**2.99**	1.65	**2.96**	1.21
reluctant	4	JJ	0.70	0.63	0.37	0.55	**2.57**	1.70	**1.77**	1.23
vulnerable	4	JJ	0.57	0.63	0.52	0.55	**2.70**	1.70	**1.63**	1.23
associate	5	NN	0.96	0.82	**0.94**	0.67	**2.32**	1.90	0.56	1.26
warranted	5	VBD	**1.30**	0.84	**1.90**	0.67	**4.14**	2.40	**2.43**	1.76
bureaucrats	6	NNS	0.42	0.82	0.47	0.78	0.98	1.65	0.74	1.21
artisans	6	NNS	**0.88**	0.82	1.76	0.78	0.9	1.65	0.49	1.21

Table D.9: Problematic words per formula, depending on $n * sd$, for all texts, Text 1 and Text 2

	All Texts				Text 1				Text 2			
	Total	TfS	PE	MPE	Total	TfS	PE	MPE	Total	TfS	PE	MPE
no sd	3669	597	1582	1290	601	90	289	222	725	108	310	307
1 * sd	723	338	202	183	123	53	36	34	112	48	30	34
1.5 * sd	205	43	82	80	46	10	17	19	15	3	4	8
2 * sd	41	11	10	20	14	5	3	6	1	0	0	1
2.5 * sd	0	0	0	0	0	0	0	0	0	0	0	0

Table D.10: Problematic words per formula, depending on $n * $ sd, for Text 3 to Text 6

	Text 3				Text 4				Text 5				Text 6			
	Total	TfS	PE	MPE	Total	TfS	PE	MPE	Total	TfS	PE	MPE	Total	TfS	PE	MPE
no sd	706	112	269	225	527	100	230	197	373	74	165	134	615	105	302	208
1 * sd	131	67	26	36	85	42	24	19	199	40	89	70	111	52	34	25
1.5 * sd	69	16	23	30	14	2	3	9	65	33	18	14	53	17	21	15
2 * sd	12	3	4	5	0	0	0	0	27	3	16	8	4	2	0	2
2.5 * sd	0	0	0	0	0	0	0	0	5	0	4	1	0	0	0	0

Table D.11: Problematic Words per formula and according to PoS class (CC, CD, IN), depending on $n * $ sd

	CC – Task, Munit, InEff				CD – Task, InEff, HTra				IN – InEff, HTra			
	Total	TfS	PE	MPE	Total	TfS	PE	MPE	Total	TfS	PE	MPE
no sd	28	1	15	12	76	46	14	16	363	166	111	86
1 * sd	3	0	2	1	3	2	1	0	9	3	2	4
1.5 * sd	0	0	0	0	0	0	0	0	0	0	0	0

Table D.12: Problematic Words per formula and according to PoS class (JJ 1, JJ 2, NN), depending on $n * $ sd

	JJ 1 – Task, HTra				JJ 2 – Task, Munit, HTra				NN – Task, InEff			
	Total	TfS	PE	MPE	Total	TfS	PE	MPE	Total	TfS	PE	MPE
no sd	555	189	183	183	208	26	104	78	776	242	286	253
1 * sd	162	56	53	53	46	8	12	26	180	42	83	55
1.5 * sd	116	40	38	38	24	6	10	8	129	32	59	38

Table D.13: Problematic Words per formula and according to PoS class (RB, VB, all verbs), depending on $n * $ sd

	RB – Task, HTra				VB – Task, HTra				all verbs – Task, Munit, InEff, HTra			
	Total	TfS	PE	MPE	Total	TfS	PE	MPE	Total	TfS	PE	MPE
no sd	325	111	105	109	369	125	123	121	586	103	257	226
1 * sd	69	24	22	23	162	56	54	52	30	5	8	17
1.5 * sd	23	8	7	8	46	16	15	15	7	2	1	4

Table D.14: Problematic Words per formula and according to PoS class
(all nouns 1, all nouns 2, DT), depending on $n * sd$

	all nouns 1 – InEff				all nouns 2 – Munit, InEff & HTra				DT – InEff, HTra, HCross			
	Total	TfS	PE	MPE	Total	TfS	PE	MPE	Total	TfS	PE	MPE
no sd	2604	1638	523	443	1241	640	332	269	125	55	37	33
1 * sd	361	150	121	90	49	16	22	11	70	28	22	20
1.5 * sd	217	84	79	54	12	3	5	4	59	25	19	15

Table D.15: Problematic Words per Formula and PoS class in Percent,
Depending on $n * sd$

	all words	CC	CD	DT	IN	JJ 1	JJ 2	NN	all nouns 1	all nouns 2	RB	VB	all verbs
% (no sd)	20.8	6.4	15.2	7.5	14.7	46.4	17.4	25.3	43.6	20.8	53.7	48.3	18.8
% (1 * sd)	4.1	0.7	0.1	4.2	0.4	13.6	3.8	5.9	6.0	0.1	11.4	21.2	0.1
% (1.5 * sd)	1.2	0	0	3.5	0	9.7	2.0	4.2	3.6	0.0	3.8	6.0	0.0

References

ACCEPT. 2012. *Definition of pre-editing rules for English and French.* European Community's Seventh Framework Programme (FP7/2007 - 2013) under grant agreement n° 288769. http://cordis.europa.eu/docs/projects/cnect/9/288769/ 080 / deliverables / 001 - D21DefinitionofpreeditingrulesforEnglishandFrench . pdf, accessed 2016-11-4.

Aghamohammadi, Asghar & Nima Rezaei. 2012. *Clinical cases in primary immunodeficiency diseases: A problem-solving approach.* Berlin & Heidelberg: Springer.

Ahrens, Barbara, Eliza Kalderon, Christoph M Krick & Wolfgang Reith. 2010. fMRI for exploring simultaneous interpreting. In Daniel Gile, Gyde Hansen & Nike Pokorn (eds.), *Why translation studies matters*, vol. 88, 237–249. Amsterdam & Philadelphia: John Benjamins Publishing Company.

Albrecht, Jörn. 2013. *Übersetzung und Linguistik.* 2nd edn. (Grundlagen der Übersetzungsforschung Bd. 2). Tübingen: Narr. 312 pp.

Allen, Jeffrey. 2003. Post-editing. In Harold Somers (ed.), *Computers and translation: A translator's guide*, vol. 35, 297–318. Amsterdam & Philadelphia: John Benjamins Translation Library.

Alves, Fabio. 2003. *Triangulating translation: Perspectives in process oriented research.* Vol. 45. Amsterdam & Philadelphia: John Benjamins Publishing.

Alves, Fabio & Tania Liparini Campos. 2009. Translation technology in time: Investigating the impact of translation memory systems and time pressure on types of internal and external support. In Susanne Göpferich, Arnt Lykke Jakobsen & Inger M. Mees (eds.), *Behind the mind: Methods, models and results in translation process research*, vol. 37, 191–218. Copenhagen: Copenhagen Studies in Language.

Angelone, Erik. 2010. Uncertainty, uncertainty management and metacognitive problem solving in the translation task. In Gregory M. Shreve & Erik Angelone (eds.), *Translation and cognition* (American Translators Association Scholarly Monograph Series 15), 17–40. Amsterdam & Philadelphia: John Benjamins Publishing Company.

Arenas, Ana Guerberof. 2008. Productivity and quality in the post-editing of outputs from translation memories and machine translation. *The International Journal of Localisation* 7(1). 11–21.

Aymerich, Julia. 2004. Using machine translation for fast, inexpensive, and accurate health information assimilation and dissemination: Experiences at the Pan American Health Organization. In *ATMA 2004: Sixth biennal conference of the Association for Machine Translation in the Americas*, 1–9. Waschington.

Aymerich, Julia. 2005. Using machine translation for fast, inexpensive, and accurate health information assimilation and dissemination: Experiences at the Pan American Health Organization. In *9th World Congress on Health Information and Libraries*. Salvador.

Baaijen, Veerle M., David Galbraith & Kees de Glopper. 2012. Keystroke analysis: Reflections on procedures and measures. *Written Communication* 29(3). 246–277.

Bahdanau, Dzmitry, Kyunghyun Cho & Yoshua Bengio. 2014. Neural machine translation by jointly learning to align and translate. In *ICLR 2015*.

Baker, Mona. 1996. Corpus-based translation studies: The challenges that lie ahead. In Harold Somers (ed.), *Terminology, LSP, and translation: Studies in language engineering in honour of Juan C. Sager*, vol. 18, 175–186. Amsterdam & Philadelphia: John Benjamins Publishing Company.

Bangalore, Srinivas, Bergljot Behrens, Michael Carl, Maheshwar Ghankot, Arndt Heilmann, Jean Nitzke, Moritz Schaeffer & Annegret Sturm. 2016. Syntactic variance and priming effects in translation. In Michael Carl, Srinivas Bangalore & Moritz Schaeffer (eds.), *New directions in empirical translation process research*, 211–238. Heidelberg; New York; Dordrecht; London: Springer.

Bates, Douglas, Martin Maechler, Ben Bolker, Steven Walker, R. H. B. Christensen & H. Singmann. 2014. Lme4: Linear mixed-effects models using Eigen and S4. *R package version* 1(7). 1–23.

Baur, W., S. Kalina, F. Mayer & J. Witzel (eds.). 2009. *Übersetzen in die Zukunft: Herausforderungen der Globalisierung für Übersetzer und Dolmetscher* (Schriften des BDÜ 32). BDÜ.

BDÜ. 2012. *Mensch ./. Maschine - Ergebnisse der BDÜ-Untersuchung zur Qualität der Übersetzungen durch Google Translate*. Pressedossier. Berlin: BDÜ. 44. http://www.bdue.de/uploads/media/2796_BDUe__Pressedossier_MenschMaschine_10.2012.pdf.

Belam, Judith. 2003. Buying up to falling down: A deductive approach to teaching post-editing. In *MT Summit IX Workshop on Teaching Translation Technologies and Tools (T4 Third Workshop on Teaching Machine Translation)*, 1–10. Citeseer.

Biello, David. 2006. Fact or fiction?: Archimedes coined the term 'Eureka!' in the bath. *Scientific American* 8. https://www.scientificamerican.com/article/fact-or-fiction-archimede/.

Binder, Jeffrey R. 2006. fMRI of language systems: Methods and applications. In Scott H Faro, Feroze B Mohamed, Meng Law & John T. Ulmer (eds.), *Functional neuroradiology*, 245–277. New York: Springer.

Bonet, Josep. 2013. No rage against the machine. *Languages and Translation* 6. 4–5.

Busemann, S., O. Bojar, C. Callison-Burch, M. Cettolo, M. Federico, R. Garabik, J. van Genabith, P. Koehn, D. Matuska, H. Schwenk, K. Simov, H. Uszkoreit & P. Wolf. 2012. *EuroMatrixPlus - final report*. http://www.euromatrixplus.org/resources/86, accessed 2017-3-16.

Carl, Michael. 2012. Translog-II: A program for recording user activity data for empirical reading and writing research. In *LREC*, 4108–4112.

Carl, Michael, Akiko Aizawa & Masaru Yamada. 2016. English-to-Japanese translation vs. dictation vs. post-editing. In *LREC 2016 Proceedings: Tenth International Conference on Language Resources and Evaluation*, 4024–4031. ELRA.

Carl, Michael, Barbara Dragsted, Jacob Elming, Daniel Hardt & Arnt Lykke Jakobsen. 2011. The process of post-editing: A pilot study. *Copenhagen Studies in Language* 41. 131–142.

Carl, Michael, Silke Gutermuth & Silvia Hansen-Schirra. 2014. Post-editing machine translation–a usability test for professional translation settings. In Aline Ferreira & John W. Schwieter (eds.), *Psycholinguistic and cognitive inquiries in translation and interpretation studies*, 145–174. Newcastle upon Tyne: Cambridge Scholars Publishing.

Carl, Michael & Silvia Hansen. 1999. Linking translation memories with example-based machine translation. In *Machine Translation Summit VII*, 617–624.

Carl, Michael & Moritz Schaeffer. 2013. *The CRITT translation process research database v1.4*. http://bridge.cbs.dk/resources/tpr-db/TPR-DB1.4.pdf, accessed 2014-6-10.

Carl, Michael, Moritz Schaeffer & Srinivas Bangalore. 2016. The CRITT translation process research database. In Michael Carl, Srinivas Bangalore & Moritz Schaeffer (eds.), *New directions in empirical translation process research*, 13–54. Heidelberg; New York: Springer.

Cassemiro, William. 2015. PEMT yourself! *The ATA Chronicle* 9. 13–15. http://www.atanet.org/chronicle-online/wp-content/uploads/ATA-Chronicle-ND2015.pdf, accessed 2017-3-18.

Chesterman, Andrew. 2011. Reflections on the literal translation hypothesis. In Cecilia Alvstad, Adelina Hild & Tiselius (eds.), *Methods and strategies of process research: Integrative approaches in translation studies*, vol. 94, 23–35. Amsterdam, Philadelphia: John Benjamins Publishing Company.

Chesterman, Andrew. 2016. *Memes of translation: The spread of ideas in translation theory*. Revised Edition (Benjamins translation library v. 123). Amsterdam; Philadelphia: John Benjamins Publishing Company.

Colman, Andrew M. 2009. *A dictionary of psychology*. 3rd ed (Oxford paperback reference). Oxford; New York: Oxford University Press. 882 pp.

Corsini, Raymond J. 2002. *The dictionary of psychology*. New York: Brunner-Routledge. 1156 pp.

Cronin, Michael. 2003. *Translation and globalization*. London; New York: Routledge.

Čulo, Oliver. 2014. From translation machine theory to machine translation theory: Some initial considerations. In *The future of information science*, 31–38.

Čulo, Oliver, Silke Gutermuth, Silvia Hansen-Schirra & Jean Nitzke. 2014. The influence of post-editing on translation strategies. In Laura Winther Balling & Michael Carl (eds.), *Post-editing of machine translation: Processes and applications*, 200–218. Newcastle upon Tyne: Cambridge Scholars Publishing.

Čulo, Oliver & Jean Nitzke. 2016. Patterns of terminological variation in post-editing and of cognate use in machine translation in contrast to human translation. *Baltic Journal of Modern Computing* 4(2). 106–114.

Daems, Joke, Michael Carl, Sonia Vandepitte, Robert Hartsuiker & Lieve Macken. 2016. The effectiveness of consulting external resources during translation and post-editing of general text types. In Michael Carl, Srinivas Bangalore & Moritz Schaeffer (eds.), *New directions in empirical translation process research*, 111–133. Heidelberg; New York: Springer.

DARPA. 2008. Translation technology: Breaking the language barrier. In *DARPA: 50 Years of bridging the gap*, 98–101.

Davarpanah Jazi, Mohammad, Ana-Maria Ciobotaru, Elaheh Barati & Mehdi Dadkhah. 2014. An introduction to undetectable keyloggers with experimental testing. *International Journal of Computer Communications and Networks (IJCCN)* 4(3). 1–5.

De Almeida, Giselle. 2013. *Translating the post-editor: An investigation of post-editing changes and correlations with professional experience across two Romance languages*. Dublin City University dissertation. http://doras.dcu.ie/17732/1/THESIS_G_de_Almeida.pdf.

Depraetere, Ilse. 2010. What counts as useful advice in a university post-editing training context? Report on a case study. In *EAMT 2010: Proceedings of the 14th annual conference of the European association for machine translation*. Saint-Raphaël, France.

Doherty, Stephen & Dorothy Kenny. 2014. The design and evaluation of a statistical machine translation syllabus for translation students. *The Interpreter and Translator Trainer* 8(2). 295–315.

Döring, Nicola & Jürgen Bortz. 2014. *Forschungsmethoden und Evaluation*. 5th edn. Berlin / Heidelberg: Springer.

Dörner, Dietrich. 1987. *Problemlösen als Informationsverarbeitung*. 3. Aufl (Kohlhammer-Standards Psychologie Basisbücher und Studientexte). Stuttgart: Kohlhammer. 151 pp.

Dörner, Dietrich. 2006. Sprache und Denken. In Joachim Funke (ed.), *Denken und Problemlösen*, vol. Enzyklopädie der Psychologie Themenbereich C Theorie und Forschung Ser. 2 Kognition, 617–643. Göttingen: Hogrefe.

Duchowski, Andrew T. 2003. *Eye tracking methodology: Theory and practice.* New York: Springer. 251 pp.

Ebling, Sarah. 2016. Hier liegt maschinelle Übersetzung auf der Hand. *MDÜ* 2016(1). 28–31.

Eisele, Andreas. 2007. Hybrid machine translation: Combining rule-based and statistical MT systems. Edinburgh. http://mt-archive.info/MTMarathon-2007-Eisele.pdf, accessed 2013-4-15. First Machine Translation Marathon.

Elmer, Stefan, Martin Meyer & Lutz Jancke. 2010. Simultaneous interpreters as a model for neuronal adaptation in the domain of language processing. *Brain Research* 1317. 147–156.

Elsen, Harald. 2012. Postediting - Schreckgespenst oder Perspektive. *MDÜ* 58(4). 16–21.

Engel, Arthur. 1998. *Problem-solving strategies.* New York: Springer.

Ericsson, A. 2003. The acquisition of expert performance as problem solving. In Janet E Davidson & Robert J. Sternberg (eds.), *The psychology of problem solving*, 31–83. Cambridge: Cambridge University Press.

Eysenck, Michael W. 2004. *Psychology: An international perspective.* Hove & New York: Taylor & Francis.

Faro, Scott H & Feroze B. Mohamed. 2006. *Functional MRI: Basic principles and clinical applications.* New York: Springer Science & Business Media.

Ferlein, Jörg & Nicole Hartge. 2008. *Technische Dokumentation für internationale Märkte: Haftungsrechtliche Grundlagen - Sprache - Gestaltung - Redaktion und Übersetzung.* Renningen: Expert.

Fiederer, Rebecca & Sharon O'Brien. 2009. Quality and machine translation: A realistic objective. *Journal of Specialised Translation* 11. 52–74.

Flanagan, Marian & Tina Paulsen Christensen. 2014. Testing post-editing guidelines: How translation trainees interpret them and how to tailor them for translator training purposes. *The Interpreter and Translator Trainer* 8(2). 257–275.

FORD. 2016. *Ford motor company 2015 annual report*. Ford Motor Company. http://corporate.ford.com/content/dam/corporate/en/investors/reports-and-filings/Annual%20Reports/2015-Annual-Report.pdf.

Franceschini, Rita, Daniela Zappatore & Cordula Nitsch. 2003. Lexicon in the brain: What neurobiology has to say about languages. In Jasone Cenoz, Britta Hufeisen & Ulrike Jessner (eds.), *The multilingual lexicon*, 153–166. New York: Kluwer Academic Publishers.

Franzen, Axel. 2014. Antwortskalen in standardisierten Befragungen. In Nina Baur & Jörg Blasius (eds.), *Handbuch Methoden der empirischen Sozialforschung*, 701–711. Wiesbaden: Springer.

Freeman, Walter & Rodrigo Quian Quiroga. 2012. *Imaging brain function with EEG: Advanced temporal and spatial analysis of electroencephalographic signals*. New York: Springer Science & Business Media.

Funke, Joachim. 2006a. Denken und Problemlösen: Vorwort und Einleitung. In Joachim Funke (ed.), *Denken und Problemlösen*, vol. Ser. 2 Kognition (Enzyklopädie der Psychologie Themenbereich C Theorie und Forschung), XVII–XXVIII. Göttingen: Hogrefe.

Funke, Joachim. 2006b. Komplexes Problemlösen. In Joachim Funke (ed.), *Denken und Problemlösen* (Enzyklopädie der Psychologie Themenbereich C Theorie und Forschung Ser. 2 Kognition), 373–443. Göttingen: Hogrefe.

Garcia, Ignacio. 2009. Beyond translation memory: Computers and the professional translator. *The Journal of Specialised Translation* 12(12). 199–214. http://www.jostrans.org/issue12/art_garcia.php.

Gaspari, Federico, Hala Almaghout & Stephen Doherty. 2015. A survey of machine translation competences: Insights for translation technology educators and practitioners. *Perspectives* 23(3). 333–358.

Gaspari, Federico & W. John Hutchins. 2007. Online and free! Ten Years of online machine translation: Origins, developments, current use and future prospects. In *Proceedings of MT summit XI*, 199–206. Copenhagen.

Gómez-Pérez, José Manuel. 2010. *Acquisition and understanding of process knowledge using problem solving methods*. [Amsterdam]; Heidelberg, Germany: IOS.

Göpferich, Susanne. 2008. *Translationsprozessforschung: Stand, Methoden, Perspektiven* (Translationswissenschaft 4). Tübingen: G. Narr. 313 pp.

Göpferich, Susanne, Gerrit Bayer-Hohenwarter & Hubert Stigler. 2008. *TransComp—the development of translation competence. Corpus and asset-management-system for the longitudinal study TransComp*. Graz: University of Graz. http://gams.uni-graz.at/container:tc, accessed 2009-8-31.

Goutte, Cyril, Nicola Cancedda, Marc Dymetman & George Foster (eds.). 2009. *Learning machine translation* (Neural information processing series). Cambridge, Mass: MIT Press. 316 pp.

Grabner, Roland H, Clemens Brunner, Robert Leeb, Christa Neuper & Gert Pfurtscheller. 2007. Event-related EEG theta and alpha band oscillatory responses during language translation. *Brain Research Bulletin* 72(1). 57–65.

Green, Spence. 2015. Beyond post-editing: Advances in interactive translation environments. *The ATA Chronicle* 9. 19–22. http://www.atanet.org/chronicle-online/wp-content/uploads/ATA-Chronicle-ND2015.pdf, accessed 2017-3-18.

Hanly, Jeri R., Elliot B. Koffman & Mohit P. Tahiliani. 2013. *Problem solving and program design in C*. Harlow: Pearson Education.

Hansen-Schirra, Silvia. 2017. EEG and universal language processing in translation. In John W. Schwieter & Aline Ferreira (eds.), *The handbook of translation and cognition*, 232–247. Malden, MA/Oxford, England: Wiley-Blackwell.

Hearne, Mary & Andy Way. 2011. Statistical machine translation: A guide for linguists and translators. *Language and Linguistics Compass* 5(5). 205–226.

Heller, Lavinia. 2012. *Translationswissenschaftliche Begriffsbildung und das Problem der performativen Unauffälligkeit von Translation*. Vol. 51. Berlin: Frank & Timme GmbH.

Holmqvist, Kenneth, Marcus Nyström, Richard Andersson, Richard Dewhurst, Halszka Jarodzka & Joost van de Weijer. 2011. *Eye tracking: A comprehensive guide to methods and measures*. Oxford; New York: Oxford University Press. 537 pp.

Hommerich, Christoph & Nicole Reiß. 2011. *Ergebnisse der BDÜ-Mitgliederbefragung*.

Hönig, Hans G. 1997. Positions, power and practice: Functionalist approaches and translation quality assessment. *Current Issues in Language & Society* 4(1). 6–34.

Horn-Helf, Brigitte. 1999. *Technisches Übersetzen in Theorie und Praxis*. Tübingen, Basel: Francke.

Horn-Helf, Brigitte. 2007. *Kulturdifferenz in Fachtextsortenkonventionen: Analyse und Translation: Ein Lehr-und Arbeitsbuch* (Leipziger Studien zur angewandten Linguistik und Translatologie 4). Frankfurt a.M.: Peter Lang.

House, Juliane. 1997. *Translation quality assessment: A model revisited*. Vol. 410. Tübingen: Gunter Narr Verlag.

Hutchins, W. John. 1995. Machine translation: A brief history. In E. F. K. Koerner & R. E. Asher (eds.), *Concise history of the language sciences: From the Sumerians to the cognitivists*, 431–445. Cambridge: Cambrige University Press.

Hutchins, W. John. 2004. Two precursors of machine translation: Artsrouni and Trojanskij. *International Journal of Translation* 16(1). 11–31.

Hutchins, W. John & Harold Somers. 1992. *An introduction to machine translation*. London: Academic Press Inc. 320 pp. http://www.hutchinsweb.me.uk/IntroMT-TOC.htm.

Hvelplund, Kristian Tangsgaard. 2011. *Allocation of cognitive resources in translation: An eye-tracking and key-logging study*. Copenhagen, Denmark: Copenhagen Business School - PhD Series.

Jääskeläinen, Riitta. 2010. Think-aloud protocol. In Yves Gambier & Luc van Doorslaer (eds.), *Handbook of translation studies*, vol. 1, 371–374. Amsterdam; Philadelphia: John Benjamins Publishing Company.

Jääskeläinen, Riitta & Sonja Tirkkonen-Condit. 1991. Automatised processes in professional vs. non-professional translation: A think-aloud protocol study. In Sonja Tirkkonen-Condit (ed.), *Empirical research in translation and intercultural studies*, 89–109. Tübingen: Gunter Narr.

Jakobsen, Arnt Lykke. 2002. Translation drafting by professional translators and by translation students. In Gyde Hansen (ed.), *Empirical translation studies: Process and product* (Copenhagen Studies in Language 27), 191–204. Copenhagen: Samfundslitteratur.

Jakobsen, Arnt Lykke. 2003. Effects of think aloud on translation speed, revision and segmentation. In Fabio Alves (ed.), *Triangulating translation: Perspectives in process oriented research*, 69–95. Amsterdam; Philadelphia: John Benjamins.

Jakobsen, Arnt Lykke. 2005. Investigating expert translators' processing knowledge. In Helle V. Dam, Jan Engberg & Heidrun Gerzymisch-Arbogast (eds.), *Knowledge systems and translation* (Text, Translation, Computational Processing [TTCP] 7), 173–189. Berlin, New York: Mouton de Gruyter.

Jakobsen, Arnt Lykke. 2011. Tracking translators' keystrokes and eye movements with Translog. In Cecilia Alvstad, Adelina Hild & Elisabet Tiselius (eds.), *Methods and strategies of process research*, 37–55. Amsterdam, Philadelphia: John Benjamins Publishing Company.

Jonassen, David H. 2000. Toward a design theory of problem solving. *Educational technology research and development* 48(4). 63–85.

Jungermann, Helmut, Hans-Rüdiger Pfister & K. Fischer. 2005. *Die Psychologie der Entscheidung: Eine Einführung*. 2. Heidelberg: Spektrum Akademischer Verlag.

Jungermann, Helmut, Hans-Rüdiger Pfister & Katrin Fischer. 2010. *Die Psychologie der Entscheidung: Eine Einführung*. 3rd edn. Heidelberg: Spektrum, Akad. Verl. 481 pp.

Just, Marcel A. & Patricia A. Carpenter. 1980. A theory of reading: From eye fixations to comprehension. *Psychological Review* 87(4). 329.

Kaiser-Cooke, Michèle. 1993. *Machine translation and the human factor: Knowledge and decision-making in the translation process*. University of Vienna dissertation.

Kaiser-Cooke, Michèle. 1994. Translatorial expertise: A cross-cultural phenomenon from an interdisciplinary perspective. In Mary Snell-Hornby, Franz Pöchhacker & Klaus Kaindl (eds.), *Translation studies. An interdiscipline*, 135–139. Amsterdam, Philadelphia: John Benjamins Publishing Company.

Kamal, Ahmad A. 2010. *1000 solved problems in modern physics*. Heidelberg; New York: Springer.

Keller, Nicole, Petra Dutz & Nadria Hofmann. 2016. Drei Modelle im Fokus. *MDÜ* 2016(1). 10–14.

Kenny, Dorothy & Stephen Doherty. 2014. Statistical machine translation in the translation curriculum: Overcoming obstacles and empowering translators. *The Interpreter and Translator Trainer* 8(2). 276–294.

Kim, Seong-Gi & Peter A. Bandettini. 2006. Principles of functional MRI. In Scott H. Faro & Feroze B. Mohamed (eds.), *Functional MRI: Basic principles and clinical applications*, 3–22. New York: Springer.

Kiraly, Donald C. 1995. *Pathways to translation: Pedagogy and process* (Translation studies 3). Kent, Ohio: Kent State University Press. 175 pp.

Klöckner, Jennifer & Jürgen Friedrichs. 2014. Gesamtgestaltung des Fragebogens. In Nina Baur & Jörg Blasius (eds.), *Handbuch Methoden der empirischen Sozialforschung*, 675–685. Wiesbaden: Springer.

Knoblich, Günther & Michael Öllinger. 2006. Einsicht und Umstrukturierung beim Problemlösen. In Joachim Funke (ed.), *Denken und Problemlösen* (Enzyklopädie der Psychologie Themenbereich C Theorie und Forschung Ser. 2 Kognition), 1–83. Göttingen: Hogrefe.

Koby, Geoffrey S. 2001. Editor's introduction: Post-editing of machine translation output: Who, what, why, and how (much). In Hans P. Krings (ed.), *Repairing texts: Empirical investigations of machine translation post-editing processes*, 1–23. Kent, Ohio: Kent State University Press.

Koehn, Philipp. 2005. Europarl: A parallel corpus for statistical machine translation. In *MT summit*, vol. 5, 79–86.

Koehn, Philipp. 2010. *Statistical machine translation*. Cambridge; New York: Cambridge University Press. 433 pp.

Koehn, Philipp. 2017. Chapter 13 - neural machine translation - draft. In *Statistical machine translation*. https : / / pdfs . semanticscholar . org / 2473 / 28a082d86199ed5a98e1d726aa205c1da9df.pdf.

Kolss, Muntsin, Matthias Wölfel, Florian Kraft, Jan Niehues, Matthias Paulik & Alex Waibel. 2008. Simultaneous German-English lecture translation. In *Proceedings of IWSLT*, 174–181. Hawaii.

Koppenjan, Johannes Franciscus Maria & Erik-Hans Klijn. 2004. *Managing uncertainties in networks: A network approach to problem solving and decision making*. London; New York: Routledge. 289 pp.

Krings, Hans P. 1986a. Translation problems and translation strategies of advanced German learners of French (L2). In Juliane House & Shoshana Blum-Kulka (eds.), *Interlingual and intercultural communication*, 263–276. Tübingen: Gunter Narr Verlag.

Krings, Hans P. 1986b. *Was in den Köpfen von Übersetzern vorgeht: Eine empirische Untersuchung zur Struktur des Übersetzungsprozesses an fortgeschrittenen Französischlernern*. Vol. 291. Tübingen: Gunter Narr Verlag.

Krings, Hans P. 2001. *Repairing texts: Empirical investigations of machine translation post-editing processes*. Geoffrey S. Koby (ed.). Kent, Ohio: Kent State University Press. 635 pp.

Krings, Hans P. 2005. Wege ins Labyrinth–Fragestellungen und Methoden der Übersetzungsprozessforschung im Überblick. *Meta: Journal des traducteurs / Meta: Translators' Journal* 50(2). 342–358.

Kubiak, Paweł. 2009. *Übersetzer als Problemlöser. Eine qualitative Studie zum Problemlöseverhalten von semiprofessionellen Übersetzern*. Wydawnictwo Naukowe UAM dissertation.

Kußmaul, Paul. 1986. Übersetzen als Entscheidungsprozeß. Die Rolle der Fehleranalyse in der Übersetzungsdidaktik. In Mary Snell-Hornby (ed.), *Übersetzungswissenschaft: Eine Neuorientierung*, 206–229. Tübingen; Basel: Francke.

Kutas, Marta & Kara D. Federmeier. 2011. Thirty years and counting: Finding meaning in the N400 component of the event related brain potential (ERP). *Annual Review of Psychology* 62. 621–643.

Kuznetsova, Alexandra, Per Bruun Brockhoff & Rune Haubo Bojesen Christensen. 2015. *Package 'lmerTest'*. R package version 2.0.

Lacruz, Isabel, Michael Denkowski & Alon Lavie. 2014. Cognitive demand and cognitive effort in post-editing. In *Proceedings of the Third Workshop on Post-Editing Technology and Practice*, 73–84. AMTA.

Läubli, Samuel, Mark Fishel, Gary Massey, Maureen Ehrensberger-Dow & Martin Volk. 2013. Assessing post-editing efficiency in a realistic translation environment. In *Proceedings of MT Summit XIV Workshop on Post-editing Technology and Practice*, 83–91.

Laurian, Anne-Marie. 1984. Machine translation: what type of post-editing on what type of documents for what type of users. In *Proceedings of the 10th international conference on computational linguistics and 22nd annual meeting on association for computational linguistics*, 236–238.

Lavie, Alon & Michael J. Denkowski. 2009. The METEOR metric for automatic evaluation of machine translation. *Machine Translation* 23(2). 105–115.

Lehrndorfer, Anne. 1996. Kontrollierte Sprache für Technische Dokumentation – Ein Ansatz für das Deutsche. In Hans P. Krings (ed.), *Wissenschaftliche Grundlagen der technischen Kommunikation*, 339–368. Tübingen: G. Narr.

Leijten, Mariëlle & Luuk Van Waes. 2013. Keystroke logging in writing research using inputlog to analyze and visualize writing processes. *Written Communication* 30(3). 358–392.

Levỳ, Jiří. 1968. Translation as a decision process. In Lawrence Venuti (ed.), *The translation studies reader*, 148–159. London; New York: Routledge.

Lommel, Arle, Hans Uszkoreit & Aljoscha Burchardt. 2014. Multidimensional quality metrics (MQM). *Tradumàtica* 12. 455–463.

Lörscher, Wolfgang. 1986. Linguistic aspects of translation processes: Towards an analysis of translation performance. In Juliane House & Shoshana Blum-Kulka (eds.), *Interlingual and intercultural communication*, 277–292. Tübingen: Gunter Narr Verlag.

Lubart, Todd I. & Christophe Mouchiroud. 2003. Creativity: A source of difficulty in problem solving. In Janet E. Davidson & Robert J. Sternberg (eds.), *The psychology of problem solving*, 127–148. Cambridge: Cambridge University Press.

Marcus, Mitchell P, Mary Ann Marcinkiewicz & Beatrice Santorini. 1993. Building a large annotated corpus of English: The penn treebank. *Computational Linguistics* 19(2). 313–330.

Martínez-Gómez, Pascual, Akshay Minocha, Jin Huang, Michael Carl, Srinivas Bangalore & Akiko Aizawa. 2014. Recognition of translator expertise using sequences of fixations and keystrokes. In *Proceedings of the Symposium on Eye Tracking Research and Applications*, 299–302. ACM.

Massardo, Isabella, Jaap van der Meer, Sharon O'Brien, Fred Hollowood, Nora Aranberri & Katrin Drescher. 2016. *TAUS MT post-editing guidelines*. Amsterdam. https://www.taus.net/think-tank/articles/postedit-articles/taus-post-editing-guidelines, accessed 2017-3-16.

Mehlhorn, Heinz. 2011. *Nature helps: How plants and other organisms contribute to solve health problems.* Heidelberg; New York: Springer. http://public.eblib.com/EBLPublic/PublicView.do?ptiID=763732, accessed 2014-1-21.

Mertin, Elvira. 2006. *Prozessorientiertes Qualitätsmanagement im Dienstleistungsbereich Übersetzen.* Leipzig: Lang.

Moorkens, Joss & Sharon O'Brien. 2015. Post-editing evaluations: Trade-offs between novice and professional participants. In *Proceedings of European Association for Machine Translation (EAMT)*, 75–81.

Moorkens, Joss, Sharon O'Brien, Igor AL da Silva, Norma B de Lima Fonseca & Fabio Alves. 2015. Correlations of perceived post-editing effort with measurements of actual effort. *Machine Translation* 29(3). 267–284.

Muegge, Uwe. 2016. Do-it-yourself-MÜ. *MDÜ* 2016(1). 19–23.

Müller-Spitzer, Carolin, Sascha Wolfer & Alexander Koplenig. 2015. Observing online dictionary users: Studies using wiktionary log files. *International Journal of Lexicography* 28(1). 1–26.

Mylonakis, Markos. 2012. *Learning the latent structure of translation.* Amsterdam; Amsterdam: ILLC; Universiteit van Amsterdam [Host]. http://staff.science.uva.nl/~mmylonak/publications/thesis/mylonakis_thesis.

Newell, Allen & Herbert Alexander Simon. 1972. *Human problem solving.* Vol. 104. Englewood Cliffs, NJ: Prentice-Hall.

Nitzke, Jean. 2016a. Auch nur Korrekturlesen? – Post-Editing. *MDÜ* 2016(1). 24–27.

Nitzke, Jean. 2016b. Monolingual post-editing: An exploratory study on research behaviour and target text quality. In Silvia Hansen-Schirra & Sambor Gruzca (eds.), *Eyetracking and Applied Linguistics*, 83–108. Berlin: Language Science Press.

Nord, Britta. 2002. *Hilfsmittel beim Übersetzen: Eine empirische Studie zum Rechercheverhalten professioneller Übersetzer* (FASK, Publikationen des Fachbereichs Angewandte Sprach- und Kulturwissenschaft der Johannes Gutenberg-Universität Mainz in Germersheim Bd. 32). Frankfurt am Main; New York: Lang. 286 pp.

Nord, Christiane. 1987. Übersetzungsprobleme- Übersetzungsschwierigkeiten. Was in den Köpfen von Übersetzern vorgehen sollte. *Mitteilungsblatt für Dolmetscher und Übersetzer* 2(1987). 5–8.

O'Brien, Sharon. 2002. Teaching post-editing: A proposal for course content. In *6th EAMT Workshop Teaching Machine Translation*, 99–106.

O'Brien, Sharon. 2006. *Machine-translatability and post-editing effort: An empirical study using translog and choice network analysis*. Dublin City University dissertation.

O'Brien, Sharon. 2009. Eye tracking in translation process research: Methodological challenges and solutions. In Inger M. Mees, Fabio Alves & Susanne Göpferich (eds.), *Methodology, technology and innovation in translation process research: A tribute to Arnt Lykke Jakobsen*, vol. 38 (Copenhagen studies in language), 251–266. Copenhagen: Samfundslitteratur.

O'Brien, Sharon. 2011. Towards predicting post-editing productivity. *Machine Translation* 25(3). 197–215. http://www.springerlink.com/index/10.1007/s10590-011-9096-7, accessed 2013-2-28.

Al-Onaizan, Yaser, Jan Curin, Michael Jahr, Kevin Knight, John Lafferty, Dan Melamed, Franz-Josef Och, David Purdy, Noah A Smith & David Yarowsky. 1999. Statistical machine translation. In *Final Report, JHU Summer Workshop*, vol. 30.

Orlando, Marc. 2016. *Training 21st century translators and interpreters: At the crossroads of practice, research and pedagogy*. Vol. 21. Berlin: Frank & Timme GmbH.

Ottmann, Angelika. 2017. *Best Practices - Übersetzen und Dolmetschen: Ein Nachschlagewerk aus der Praxis für Sprachmittler und Auftraggeber*. Berlin: BDÜ Fachverlag.

PACTE, Group. 2005. Investigating translation competence. *Meta: journal des traducteurs* 50(2). 609–619.

Papineni, Kishore, Salim Roukos, Todd Ward & Wei-Jing Zhu. 2002. BLEU: A method for automatic evaluation of machine translation. In *Proceedings of the 40th annual meeting on association for computational linguistics*, 311–318. Association for Computational Linguistics.

Pavlović, Nataša & Kristian Jensen. 2009. Eye tracking translation directionality. In Anthony Pym & Alexander Perekrestenko (eds.), *Translation research projects 2*, 93–109. Tarragona: Intercultural Studies Group,

Poole, Alex & Linden J. Ball. 2005. Eye tracking in human-computer interaction and usability research. In Claud Ghaoui (ed.), *The encyclopedia of human computer interaction*, 211–219. Hershey PA, London: Information Science Pub.

Porsiel, Jörg. 2017. *Machine Translation - What Language Professionals Need to Know*. Berlin: BDÜ Fachverlag.

Porst, Rolf. 2014. Frageformulierung. In Nina Baur & Jörg Blasius (eds.), *Handbuch Methoden der empirischen Sozialforschung*, 687–699. Wiesbaden: Springer.

Prassl, Friederike. 2010. Translators' decision-making processes in research and knowledge integration. In *New approaches in translation process research*

(Copenhagen Studies in Language 39), 57–82. Frederiksberg: Samfundslitteratur.

Pretz, Jean E., Adam J. Naples & Robert J. Sternberg. 2003. Recognizing, defining, and representing problems. In Janet E. Davidson & Robert J. Sternberg (eds.), *The psychology of problem solving*, vol. 30, 3–30. Cambridge: Cambridge Scholars Publishing.

Pym, Anthony. 2013. Translation skill-sets in a machine-translation age. *Meta: Journal des traducteurs/ Meta: Translators' Journal* 58(3). 487–503.

Quirk, Thomas Joseph, Meghan Quirk & Howard Horton. 2013. *Excel 2010 for physical sciences statistics a guide to solving practical problems*. Cham; New York: Springer.

R Core Team. 2013. R: A language and environment for statistical computing.

Reason, J. T. 1990. *Human error*. Cambridge: Cambridge University Press. 302 pp.

Reinecke, Jost. 2014. Grundlagen der standardisierten Befragung. In Nina Baur & Jörg Blasius (eds.), *Handbuch Methoden der empirischen Sozialforschung*, 601–617. Berlin: Springer.

Reinke, Uwe & Uta Seewald-Heeg. 2012. Den tiger reiten. *MDÜ* 58(4). 10–14.

Reiss, Katharina. 1981. Type, kind and individuality of text: Decision making in translation. *Poetics Today* 2(4). 121–131.

Reiss, Katharina. 2014. *Translation criticism-potentials and limitations: Categories and criteria for translation quality assessment*. London & New York: Routledge.

Risku, Hanna. 1998. *Translatorische Kompetenz*. Tübingen: Stauffenburg.

Rösener, Christoph. 2016. Eye tracking and beyond: The dos and don'ts of creating a contemporary usability lab. In Silvia Hansen-Schirra & Sambor Gruzca (eds.), *Eyetracking and Applied Linguistics*, 143–162. Berlin: Language Science Press.

Rozmyslowicz, Tomasz. 2014. Machine translation: A problem for translation theory. *New Voices in Translation Studies* 11. 145–163.

Rüth, Lisa, Annette Hunger & Manfred Altmann. 2016. Erfahrungsberichte. *MDÜ* 2016(1). 24–27.

Rychtyckyj, Nestor. 2006. Standard language at Ford Motors: A case study in controlled language development and deployment. In *CLAW 2006: 5th International Workshop on Controlled Language Applications*. Cambridge, MA, USA.

Rychtyckyj, Nestor. 2007. Machine translation for manufacturing: A case study at Ford Motor Company. *AI Magazine* 28(3). 1728–1735.

Savitch, Walter J. & Frank M. Carrano. 2012. *Java: An introduction to problem solving & programming*. London: Pearson.

Schaeffer, Moritz & Michael Carl. 2014. Measuring the cognitive effort of literal translation processes. *EACL 2014*. 29–37.

Schaeffer, Moritz, Barbara Dragsted, Kristian Tangsgaard Hvelplund, Laura Winther Balling & Michael Carl. 2016. Word translation entropy: Evidence of early target language activation during reading for translation. In Michael Carl, Srinivas Bangalore & Moritz Schaeffer (eds.), *New directions in empirical translation process research*, 183–210. Berlin: Springer.

Schäfer, Falko. 2003. MT post-editing: How to shed light on the "unknown task". Experiences at SAP. In *Controlled language translation*, 133–140. Dublin, Ireland.

Schmitt, Peter A. 2003a. Berufsbild. In Mary Snell-Hornby, Hans G. Hönig, Paul Kußmaul & Peter A. Schmitt (eds.), *Handbuch Translation*, 2nd edn., 1–5. Tübingen: Stauffenburg.

Schmitt, Peter A. 2003b. Marktsituation der Übersetzer. In Mary Snell-Hornby, Hans G. Hönig, Paul Kußmaul & Peter A. Schmitt (eds.), *Handbuch Translation*, 2nd edn., 5–13. Tübingen: Stauffenburg.

Schmitt, Peter A., Lina Gerstmeyer & Sarah Müller. 2016. *Übersetzer und Dolmetscher: Eine internationale Umfrage zur Berufspraxis*. Berlin: BDÜ Fachverlag.

Senez, Dorothy. 1998. Post-editing service for machine translation users at the European Commission. In *Translating and the Computer 20. Proceedings from Aslib conference*, 1–6. London.

Silva, Roberto. 2014. Integrating post-editing MT in a professional translation workflow. In Sharon O'Brien, Laura Winther Balling, Michael Carl, Michel Simard & Lucia Specia (eds.), *Post-editing of machine translation*, 24–51. Cambridge: Cambridge Scholars Publishing.

Singla, Karan, David Orrego-Carmona, Ashleigh Rhea Gonzales, Michael Carl & Srinivas Bangalore. 2013. Predicting post-editor profiles from the translation process. In *Proceedings of the Workshop on Interactive and Adaptive Machine Translation, AMTA Workshop*, 51–60.

Snell, Richard S. & Michael A. Lemp. 2013. *Clinical anatomy of the eye*. Oxford: Blackwell Science.

Strohschneider, Stefan. 2006. Kulturelle Unterschiede beim Problemlösen. In Joachim Funke (ed.), *Denken und Problemlösen*, vol. Enzyklopädie der Psychologie Themenbereich C Theorie und Forschung Ser. 2 Kognition, 547–615. Göttingen: Hogrefe.

Thurmond, Veronica A. 2001. The point of triangulation. *Journal of nursing scholarship* 33(3). 253–258.

tobii. 2016. *Tobii TX300 Eye Tracker - For research of oculomotor functions and natural human behavior.* http://www.tobiipro.com/siteassets/tobii-pro/brochures/tobii-pro-tx300-brochure.pdf, accessed 2016-11-20.

Vermeer, Hans J. 1978. Ein Rahmen für eine allgemeine Translationstheorie. *Lebende Sprachen* 23(3). 99–102.

Waibel, Alexander. 2015. Sprachbarrieren durchbrechen: Traum oder Wirklichkeit? *Nova Acta Leopoldina NF* 122(410). 101–123.

Warwick, K. 2012. *Artificial intelligence: The basics.* New York: Routledge. 183 pp.

Weaver, Warren. 1955. Translation. *Machine translation of languages* 14. 15–23.

Wenke, Dorit & Peter A. Frensch. 2003. Is success or failure at solving complex problems related to intellectual ability. In Janet E Davidson & Robert J. Sternberg (eds.), *The psychology of problem solving*, 87–126. Cambridge: Cambridge University Press.

Whitten, Shannon & Arthur C. Graesser. 2003. Comprehension of text in problem solving. In Janet E. Davidson & Robert J. Sternberg (eds.), *The psychology of problem solving*, 207–229. Cambridge: Cambridge University Press.

Wilks, Yorick. 2008. *Machine translation: Its scope and limits.* New York: Springer.

Wilss, Wolfram. 1981. Handlungstheoretische Aspekte des Übersetzungsprozesses. *Europäische Mehrsprachigkeit. Festschrift zum* 70. 455–468.

Wilss, Wolfram. 1994. A framework for decision-making in translation. *Target* 6(2). 131–150.

Wilss, Wolfram. 1996. *Knowledge and skills in translator behavior.* Amsterdam: Benjamins.

Winther Balling, Laura & Michael Carl. 2014. Production time across languages and tasks: A large-scale analysis using the CRITT translation process database. In Aline Ferreira & John W. Schwieter (eds.), *The development of translation competence: Theories and methodologies from psycholinguistics and cognitive science*, 239–268. Newcastle upon Tyne: Cambridge Scholars Publishing.

Zhang, Zili & Chengqi Zhang. 2004. *Agent-based hybrid intelligent systems: An agent-based framework for complex problem solving.* Berlin; New York: Springer.

Name index

Language index

Subject index

www.ingramcontent.com/pod-product-compliance
Lightning Source LLC
Chambersburg PA
CBHW080916100426
42812CB00007B/2298